BEITRÄGE ZUR HISTORISCHEN THEOLOGIE

Herausgegeben von Johannes Wallmann

78

Jean Gerson and
De Consolatione Theologiae
(1418)

The Consolation of a Biblical and
Reforming Theology for a Disordered Age

by

Mark Stephen Burrows

J.C.B. Mohr (Paul Siebeck) Tübingen

BT
70
. G47
B87
1991

CIP-Titelaufnahme der Deutschen Bibliothek

Burrows, Mark Stephen:
Jean Gerson and De consolatione theologiae (1418) : the consolation
of a biblical and reforming theology for a disordered age /
by Mark Stephen Burrows. — Tübingen : Mohr, 1991
  (Beiträge zur historischen Theologie ; 78)
  ISBN 3-16-145600-9
  ISSN 0340-6741

NE: GT

© 1991 by J.C.B. Mohr (Paul Siebeck), P.O. Box 20 40, D-7400 Tübingen.

The book was typeset by Computersatz Staiger in Pfäffingen using Bembo typeface,
printed by Gulde-Druck in Tübingen on non-aging paper from Papierfabrik Buhl in
Ettlingen and bound by Heinr. Koch in Tübingen.

Printed in Germany.

For Liz, Emma Clare, and one yet unnamed

"We shall not cease from exploration
And the end of all our exploring
Will be to arrive where we started
And know the place for the first time."

T. S. Eliot, from "Little Gidding"

Preface

In a general study of medieval philosophy Etienne Gilson observed that »Gerson did not propose a system but a remedy for the evil which the clash of systems was for the Church. This remedy, he believed he would find not in any philosophy whatever, but in a certain notion of theology.«[1] This attempt to conceive of theology as a »remedy« to address the ills of society is an apt description of Gerson's diverse writings, early and late: whether as chancellor of the University of Paris or as teacher of children at the Celestine priory in Lyon, in his academic sermons and lectures as in his occasional letters, Jean Gerson (1363–1429) addressed himself consistently to the concrete problems — ecclesiastical, theological, pastoral, pedagogical — facing the individual within the social matrices of church and society. He was, to borrow the descriptive expression of recent vintage, a »contextual« theologian, one concerned not only with the precise arguments of scholastic theology but with the practice of professional ministry and the exercise of the Christian life among those he referred to without disparagement as »the simple.«

As a consequence of this conviction, his vision of reform — both of the human person, or *viator,* and of society — had little to do with perfected systems of scholastic theology. Rather, he focused upon the »edifying« tasks of theology, and later in his life devoted increasing attention to what he called the »consolation of theology,« the »remedy« needed in the face of the despair and disorder of the age. This was, after all, the period of rising civil strife in France, the lingering unrest and conflict of the Hundred Years' War, the confusion of papal schism and the emergence of reform councils, the looming threat of the Wyclifite heresy in its migration to Bohemia, and vexing frustrations resulting from the school debates at Paris. This sense of confusion and frustration dominates the opening elegy (I m. 1) of his *De consolatione theologiae* (1418), written at the close of the Council of Constance, in which he surveys the political affairs of the day:

> Often had I been sent to foreign shores;
> Returning now, I see my homeland's walls.
> Hail, sweet land of my birth, O favored France!

---

[1] Etienne Gilson, *History of Christian Philosophy in the Middle Ages* (New York, 1955), p. 529.

Famed Paris, noble guardian of our land.
Alas! What is this that I see? A goddess, raging
In cruel civil strife, filling all with gore.
In their midst a spirit of upheaval roams;
They slay themselves in turn with their own swords. . . .
Cleric, soldier, citizen alike: jailed without law;
All are strangled, like sheep by a maddened mob. . . .
Lucky stranger, you [who] sojourn elsewhere;
Such great evils are not now before your eyes. . . .[2]

In such an unstable climate Gerson interpreted the theological »remedy« not solely as an intellectual matter, but as the motor for a re-forming of the social order. Against the force of such public turmoil, Gerson worked as a conservative reformer to restore the church to the dignity which had been obscured or disfigured in his day. Thus it is that Gerson closes his *De consolatione theologiae* with a fervent cry for God's peace, praying that the *pax Dei* which »passes all understanding«[3] might keep »our hearts and minds in the love of God and in the patience of Christ [*corda et intelligentias nostras custodiat‹ in charitate Dei et patientia Christi*]. «[4] Beginning this text with a mournful admission of the chaos which had disrupted public life, Gerson closes it with this fervent prayer for peace. The gloss he adds to this Pauline text to emphasize the *patientia Christi* illustrates, as if in direct opposition to the »apocalyptic patience« advocated by John Hus,[5] the conservatism which dominates his later writings.

Indeed, it is this conservatism which might well characterize the »certain notion of [Gerson's] theology,« to recall Gilson's phrase, establishing the foundation from which he addresses himself as theologian-cum-pastor to the various issues and problems facing the church. His unswerving commitment to the *virtus patientiae* establishes the fundamental logic governing the exercise of his pastoral office: his formal treatises, poems, letters, and sermons of the early

---

[2] See Jean Gerson, *Œuvres complètes*, Vol. 4, *L'œuvre poétique*, ed. P. Glorieux (Paris, 1962), p. 135.

[3] The biblical reference is to Phil. 4.7: »Fiat ita precor, et pax Dei, quae exuperat omnem sensum, corda et intelligentias nostras custodiat. . . .«; see *De consolatione theologiae*, in *Œuvres complètes*, Vol. 9: *L'œuvre doctrinale*, ed. P. Glorieux (Paris, 1973), p. 245.

[4] Gerson introduces this discussion of »the patience of Christ« through an intriguing cross reference to Rom. 15.4, with which he had also opened this treatise: »Quaecumque enim scripta sunt ad nostram doctrinam scripta sunt; ut *per patientam* et consolationem scripturarum, spem habeamus.« He also speaks of God as the »father of mercy and all consolation,« the one from whom we receive *virtus patientiae,* the »virtue of patience.« On Gerson's use of Rom. 15.4, and the textual precedent for this in a treatise of identical name written by Johannes of Dambach, see below, p. 41, and nn. 26, 27.

[5] The letters which Hus wrote during the final month of his imprisonment often speak of patience, the patience which those assaulted by »Antichrist and his ministers« must manifest in response to their suffering; on this point, see Hus, »Letters,« in *John Hus at the Council of Constance,* trans. and intro. Matthew Spinka (New York, 1965), pp. 271, 273, 279.

conciliar period (ca. 1409–1418) demonstrate his patient and moderating efforts on behalf of *reformatio in capite et membris*.[6] It is as »patient reformer« and conservative churchman that we confront in the mature Gerson the man later known not only as *doctor consolatorius* but as *doctor christianissimus*. It is in the *De consolatione theologiae* that we see the distinctive form, when compared with his earlier writings, which his theology took at this late juncture of his career.

The initial impetus for this study grew out of my reading of Gerson's later, post-Parisian writings (i.e., 1415–1429). It was with surprise that I discovered that recent Gerson studies devote relatively little attention to this period of his career. My surprise grew in realizing that most of these studies, despite Gerson's legacy as *doctor consolatorius,* ignore the treatise in which he addressed himself to this theme in sustained fashion. This literature also tends to focus upon the narrowly academic, mystical, or controversial writings, in general, and those emerging from his earlier university career, more specifically, and thus overlooks treatises such as this which fit none of these neat categories. Such a restricted focus has allowed for interpretations of his works as a consistent theological »system,« an irony not lost on those familiar with Gerson's vigorous criticism of rigid loyalties among academic theologians to schools or systems. As a consequence, Gerson's œuvre has often been read without an attentiveness to the specific maladies of the day which shaped and re-shaped the varying remedies he offered, to carry forth Gilson's apt description. In a word, the development in Gerson's thought has been largely ignored in this literature.

My greatest surprise, however, came in realizing that the various remedies which Gerson offers in *De consolatione theologiae* articulate theological and pastoral themes either altogether absent or not yet fully developed in his earlier writings, an observation which eventually led me to recognize a distinctive theological shift in his thought during the period of his sojourn in Constance (1415–1418). Themes in this treatise depart in significant ways from the earlier university writings, including, for example, a defense of the cloistered life as the most effective means of church reform; the suggestion that a pious lay person embodied the »spirit of catholic judgment« more faithfully than an erudite but immoral academic theologian; and the avoidance of the soteriological language of *facientibus quod in se est* in favor of a mystical doctrine of justification based upon Heb. 11.6b. These departures from earlier theological positions were more than incidental, suggesting that the shape of Gerson's later theology had developed in decisive directions. And, as I came to realize in working with materials emerging from the ecclesiastical controversies of the Constance period, the »evil« confronting Gerson was not so

---

[6] This phrase is from the reform decree »Sacrosancta« which emerged at the Council of Constance, dated March 30, 1415; see Giovanni Domenico Mansi, *Sacrorum Conciliorum nova et amplissima collectio* (Paris, 1900), 27: 585.

much a matter of school debate, a clash in the academic arena of competing
theological systems, but the conflicts emerging from the Hussite controversy
— many of which were anchored at their deepest stratum in exegetical disputes.
With this realization in mind I undertook the present study of the later Gerson,
focused as a close and critical reading of the treatise he apparently presumed in
Boethian style to be his final literary effort: viz., *De consolatione theologiae*.

The original form of this study was the result of my doctoral studies at
Princeton Theological Seminary, appearing first as a dissertation bearing the
same title.[7] I am glad to recognize here the tangible support I received in the
midst of this research which allowed me to devote my full energies to this
project: first, my selection as recipient of a National Graduate Fellowship,
subsequently renamed the Jacob Javits Graduate Fellowship (1986–1988); and,
second, a leave of absence from Wesley Theological Seminary during my first
year as a member of its faculty to complete this dissertation. In addition to such
institutional support, thanks are due above all to the readers of that early draft
who comprised my dissertation committee: E. Jane Dempsey Douglass,
Edward A. Dowey, Jr., and Karlfried Froehlich. Each of these readers perused
the manuscript with care and offered numerous critical suggestions which have
undoubtedly strengthened this study in its now significantly revised form. To
all of these generous and critical readers I remain grateful.

Other historians have offered encouragement and assistance of various sorts
as this study progressed. Clyde Lee Miller (SUNY, Stony Brook) took an early
interest in my project, as we found ourselves both working on the same text.
Prof. Miller generously shared with me his own work as translator of an
edition of this treatise which is still in progress. Conversations with him during
the past several years as I advanced with my own work on this text and the
wider Gerson œuvre have clarified my own reading of Gerson at several points,
both textual and thematic. My own translations of the poetic material in
particular rely upon his more seasoned linguistic instincts. What began as a
collaboration on this treatise blossomed into a friendship of professional as well
as personal dimensions, for which I am appreciative. I have also benefitted from
the interest which Louis Pascoe, SJ (Fordham University) and Christoph
Burger (Eberhard-Karls-Universität Tübingen) have expressed in this project.
I would also like to thank all those who listened with patience and responded to
portions of this research delivered in papers at various conferences: the
American Society of Church History meeting (Cincinnati, OH; December,
1988), the Villanova Patristic, Mediaeval, and Renaissance Studies Conference
(Philadelphia, PA; September, 1989), and the Symposium on the History of
Biblical Interpretation (Princeton, NJ; May, 1990). Finally, I am grateful to the

---

[7] See *Jean Gerson and ›De Consolatione Theologiae‹: The Consolation of a Biblical and
Reforming Theology for a Disordered Age* (Princeton Theological Seminary dissertation, 1988;
Ann Arbor, MI: University Microfilms Incorporated, 1988, no. 8818496).

Committee on Research of the American Society of Church History for recently awarding an essay presenting the broad conclusions of this research the »Sidney E. Mead Prize.«[8]

It is a great pleasure, both professionally and personally, to acknowledge here my profound appreciation for my Doktorvater and colleague, Karlfried Froehlich. He it is who encouraged my early interest in Gerson, who introduced me to the complexities of historical research generally and medieval studies more specifically, and who has always provided the rare combination of intellectual insight and scholarly precision by which I shall always measure – with humility and respect – my own efforts. Beyond such formalities, he has shared with me a generous measure of his restless curiosity and contagious joy in engaging in the tasks of historical research. As scholar and teacher he has embodied Gerson's characterization of the *theologus* as »a good man, learned in sacred scripture.« Yes, this, and much more!

Beyond these notes of thanks for those whose encouragement and advice have helped to shape this study in its present form, I am pleased to express my thanks to Prof. Johannes Wallmann who accepted this study for inclusion in the series, »Beiträge zur historischen Theologie.« Several persons have assisted in differing capacities with the technicalities always involved in such projects: Mr. Ulrich Gaebler and Ms. Ilse König of J.C.B. Mohr (Paul Siebeck), who coordinated the technical handling of the manuscript; my father, Dr. Robert Burrows, who read the manuscript in an early draft and suggested numerous stylistic improvements; Dr. Charles Tidball (George Washington University, Washington, DC), whose insight into the mysteries of electronic technologies helped to translate a file generated by an American computer into a format legible by its European sibling; and, finally, Mr. Jeff Noyes Aamot, who provided diligent and careful assistance in proofreading the manuscript and in preparing the indices for this volume.

One final word of gratitude must be made for the one whose presence has been real if not also substantial throughout the germination and growth of this study, my wife Liz. During the decade in which we have shared common life and labors, she has created the atmosphere in which scholarly work has been not only sustainable but enjoyable. The *virtus patientiae* of which Gerson speaks at the close of *De consolatione theologiae* and which she embodies is, after all, a divine gift of domestic proportions! And, as the first chapters of this research took shape and form, her own labor brought Emma Clare, our first daughter, into the world to share our life and win her father's affection. For all of this, and with sentiments exceeding words, I reserve my deepest gratitude for her.

All Saints' Day, 1990   Washington, DC   Mark S. Burrows

---

[8] See »Jean Gerson after Constance: *Via media et regia* as a Revision of the Ockhamist Covenant,« *Church History* 59/4 (December, 1990); pp. 467–81.

Table of Contents

Abbreviations

CCSL   Corpus Christianorum. Series Latina. Turnhold: Brepols, 1954 ff.

CUP   Chartularium Universitatis Parisiensis. Edited by E. Chatelain and H. Denifle. 4 vols. Paris: Delalain, 1889–1897.

DSAM   Dictionnaire de spiritualité, ascétique et mystique. Edited by M. Viller, F. Cavaller, J. de Guibert, et al. Paris: Beauchesne, 1932 ff.

Du Pin   Joannis Gersonii. Opera omnia. Edited by Louis Ellies du Pin. 4 vols. Antwerp: Petrus de Hondt, 1706.

G   Jean Gerson. Œuvres complètes. Edited by Palémon Glorieux. 10 vols. Paris: Desclée et Cie, 1960–1973.

PG   Patrologiae cursus completus. Series Graeca. Edited by J.-P. Migne. 161 vols. Paris: Garnier Fratres, 1866–1886.

PL   Patrologiae cursus completus. Series Latina. Edited by J.-P. Migne. 221 vols. Paris: Garnier Fratres, 1844–1890.

RGG   Die Religion in Geschichte und Gegenwart. Handwörterbuch für Theologie und Religionswissenschaft. 3rd edition. Edited by Kurt Galling, with Hans Frhr. v. Campenhausen, Erich Dinkler, Gerhard Gloege, and Knud Løgstrup. Tübingen: J.C.B. Mohr (Paul Siebeck), 1957.

WA   D. Martin Luthers Werke, Kritische Gesamtausgabe. 72 vols. Weimar: Hermann Böhlau und Hermann Böhlaus Nachfolger (Weimar edition), 1883 ff.

Chapter I

Introduction

Few historical periods have provoked as much debate and elicited such divergence of interpretation as the later Middle Ages. These centuries have acquired in the hands of historians a largely derivative character, having been frequently and persistently studied in terms of what they either succeeded or anticipated: the vantage point of an earlier tradition of Roman Catholic historiography has portrayed this era as a decline from the crest of the high Middle Ages, a decadent interlude between the height of papal influence during the thirteenth century and the reclaiming of that power in the Catholic reform of the sixteenth, while older Protestant histories have often viewed it with either benign neglect or more aggressive contempt as little more than the prelude if not indeed the cause itself of the true apogee in the church's history. In both cases confessional interests, bolstered by the too facile approach of historical retrospect, have rendered this an interim period, either criticizing or dismissing it for what it was not, rather than understanding it for what it was. These days of rancor and parochialism are, fortunately, largely a memory now that a more ecumenically sensitive spirit seems to prevail among ecclesiastical historians, but the easing of the pressure exerted by confessionally inspired histories in general has not yet ushered in a consensus of interpretation with regard to the turbulent though highly creative period of the later Middle Ages. Thus, in a recent study of this period one historian has observed that »in the historiography of the later medieval church complexity now reigns as king.«[1] This conclusion betrays his generosity of perspective. A less involved bystander to the recent terminological debates among historians of this period might no longer detect in this interpretive »complexity« the vitriol of a former age, but confusion and disagreement still dominate the scene. Indeed, one witness to this spectacle has designated one of the crucial intellectual developments of this period, the still widely disputed and complex phenomenon of nominalism, as »evanescent« because of the surging controversy it has provoked among recent interpreters,[2] while another characterizes »the so-called

---

[1] Francis Oakley, *The Western Church in the Later Middle Ages* (Ithaca, NY, and London, 1979), p. 17.
[2] Charles Trinkaus, *In Our Image and Likeness. Humanity and Divinity in Italian Humanist Thought*, 2 vols. (London, 1970), I: 59.

nominalistic movement« less cautiously as »a tangled and embattled subject. «[3]

It is within the horizon of this »tangled and embattled subject« — viz. the
broad trajectory of late-medieval nominalist theology — that the present study
of Jean Gerson is to be situated. Of course to say this is to immerse this work at
the outset into an arena of unsettled and perhaps irresolvable controversy; for
this reason an explanatory word on terminology and the approach here
embraced toward nominalism is in order. During the past several decades the
study of nominalism has devoted increased attention to the theological
concerns of scholars associated with the *via moderna*; this has been a
development led earlier in this century by Paul Vignaux and, more recently,
Heiko Oberman and his students. According to this approach, nominalism has
been identified quite closely with the theological contribution of the Venerable
Inceptor, William of Ockham, and later heirs to his thought. Following this
lead, nominalism and »Ockhamism« come to be used interchangeably, such
that a reference to the former points to the trajectory of scholars loyal to certain
fundamental tenets of Ockham's »modern« theology; one might speak more
accurately in this regard of an »Ockhamist nominalism« or simply
»Ockhamism,« principally because this perspective represents a coherent
intellectual tradition — albeit one which has been characterized as »the inner
core« or »the main stream« of nominalism more generally[4] — among
theologians of the *via moderna*. Our study of Gerson utilizes this approach as a
working definition, at least as a starting point since Gerson has been
persistently and persuasively identified in the recent literature as belonging to
this »moderate nominalist« school.[5] Yet a closer examination of the later

---

[3] Charles T. Davis, »Ockham and the Zeitgeist,« *The Pursuit of Holiness in Late Medieval
and Renaissance Religion*, ed. Charles Trinkaus, Heiko Oberman (Leiden, 1974), p. 59; my
emphasis, though this admission already recognizes the complex discussion surrounding
this terminology.

[4] See here Heiko Oberman, »Some Notes on the Theology of Nominalism with
Attention to its Relation to the Renaissance,« *Harvard Theological Review* 53 (1960), pp. 49,
55, 56. On the question of terminology and the larger matter of recent historiography on
nominalism, see also William Courtenay, »Nominalism and Late Medieval Religion,« in
The Pursuit of Holiness in Late Medieval and Renaissance Religion, pp. 32—35. In the same
study Courtenay concludes that »Ockhamism« is »the least undesirable term« to describe
the theological trajectory from Ockham through Biel; see *ibid.*, p. 53.

[5] This is above all due to the influence of Oberman's work; see his early essay, »Some
Notes on the Theology of Nominalism« in which he articulates a model of four basic
»threads of tradition« or »schools« of nominalism, a thesis later expanded in his *The Harvest
of Medieval Theology. Gabriel Biel and Late Medieval Nominalism* (Cambridge, MA, 1963).
Courtenay surveys the recent historiography of nominalism in his »Nominalism and Late
Medieval Thought: A Bibliographical Essay,« *Theological Studies* 33 (1972), pp. 716—34,
and his later essay, »Nominalism and Late Medieval Religion,« as well as a subsequent
updated study, »Late Medieval Nominalism Revisited: 1972—1982,« *Journal of the History of
Ideas* 44 (1983), pp. 159—64. More recently, Michael Shank has abandoned the use of the

writings of the Parisian chancellor now calls for a revision of this view: we now see that the mature Gerson moved away from this »school« — perhaps better described as a late-scholastic theological tradition — abandoning after the Council of Constance this moderate (i. e., Ockhamist) nominalism in favor of themes associated with Scotist theology.[6] This study hence does not diminish but actually magnifies the problem of terminology by identifying in Gerson's post-conciliar thought a distinct and fundamental shift of theological perspective. Thus, rather than abandoning »nominalism« as a term appropriately descriptive for this late-scholastic theological tradition, this study offers a revisionist perspective to earlier work on one of the key figures occupying the mid-point of the supposed trajectory of Ockhamist theologians. That is, we find in the later Gerson a decisive reshaping of the covenantal basis of this scholastic tradition, a shift which accentuates the complex and fluid spectrum of »nominalist« theological traditions, particularly that ascribed to the self-designated heirs to the Venerable Inceptor (Ockhamists) among whom Gerson has often been portrayed. It is within the scope of this »embattled« subject, then, that this study must be placed, and our thesis regarding Gerson's theological development will inevitably further complicate the existing »tangle.«

One further word regarding late-medieval historiography — that subject in which complexity still reigns — is in order. The period of Gerson's life, the late fourteenth and early fifteenth centuries, was an era marked by intense theological debate, new and variegated expressions of public and private piety, and attendant forms of social, political, and ecclesiastical unrest. It is a period which has been described by one school of historians as a time of decline, a »waning« or »dissolution« of a supposed synthesis or highpoint of medieval

---

term »nominalism« altogether, arguing that »given the inevitable ambiguities of these terms in current historiography, it has seemed preferable to describe the positions of individual thinkers rather than to give them labels that only spread confusion«; see his »*Unless You Believe, You Shall Not Understand*«: *Logic, University, and Society in Late Medieval Vienna* (Princeton, 1988), p. xiii.

[6] In his early study »Some Notes on the Theology of Nominalism, « Oberman identifies as one of the nominalist »schools« what he called the »Parisian syncretistic school« of John of Ripa and Peter of Candia; see *ibid.*, pp. 54–55. It is worth noting that Oberman here disavows Gerson's association with this »school« — i. e., John of Ripa and Peter of Candia — citing his criticism of the Scotists as *formalizantes* who occupied themselves in »idle curiosity« with questions surpassing the use of reason. This point certainly holds true for the early Gerson, including his strident university lectures *Contra curiositatem studentium* (see Vol. 3 *L'œuvre magistrale* (Paris, 1962), pp. 224–49; all further references to Gerson's works, unless otherwise noted, are cited from this edition (*Œuvres complètes*, edited by Palémon Glorieux [Paris, 1960–1973]) as »G« followed by volume and page numbers). But our research on the later Gerson would suggest that Gerson's theological perspective after Constance had embraced central aspects of Scotism; see below, Ch. 5.

thought, characterized by »extreme doctrinal confusion.«[7] To conclude this, however, is to misread the intellectual creativity and pastoral sensitivity of university masters such as Gerson, deliberately eclectic theologians in whose works we find a contribution aptly described as a »harvest« of earlier theological themes, to borrow Oberman's revisionist metaphor.[8] Yet the »harvest« we find in the later Gerson, and this against the grain of historians who have concentrated on the earlier university writings, reverses the emphases which historians have traditionally identified in his earlier »university« writings: thus, for example, we find the later Gerson underscoring the »sufficiency« of scripture as the norm for doctrine and life, and advocating a decidedly anti-Pelagian understanding of justification in the Scotist tradition. More will be said about this reversal in subsequent chapters. Let it suffice at the outset to suggest that this development raises one of two questions: either we must now reconsider the question of the »catholicity« of nominalism which Oberman advanced at the close of *The Harvest of Medieval Theology,* or we must

---

[7] See Johan Huizinga, *The Waning of the Middle Ages. A Study of the Forms of Life, Thought, and Art in France and the Netherlands in the XIVth and XVth Centuries* (Garden City, NY, 1954), and Gordon Leff, *The Dissolution of the Medieval Outlook. An Essay on Intellectual and Spiritual Change in the Fourteenth Century* (New York, 1976). Huizinga concludes his study by observing that »the soul of Western Christendom itself was outgrowing medieval forms and modes of thought that had become shackles. The Middle Ages had always lived in the shadow of Antiquity, always handled its treasures, or what they had of them, interpreting it according to truly medieval principles: scholastic theology and chivalry, asceticism and courtesy. Now, by an inward ripening, the mind, after having been so long conversant with the forms of Antiquity, began to grasp its spirit.... Europe, after having lived in the shadow of Antiquity, lived in its sunshine once more.« *Waning,* p. 335. Leff takes a decidedly different approach, focusing not on the recovery of pagan antiquity but on a renewed vision of the primitive church: »What all these [late-medieval] thinkers, and, in an indirect way, the popular movements that echo many of their emphases, have in common is a reinterpretation of the source and the nature of spiritual power away from its institutional forms to conformity with Christ's life and teachings. In almost every case it meant the exclusion of the hierarchy from the dialogue between the individual believer and Christ, with his word, not the sacramental power of the church, as mediator. It made for a new spirituality which, whether it took an apocalyptic or a directly antisacerdotal form, was impelled by the same ideal of a return to an archetypal church.« *Dissolution,* p. 144. Finally, Etienne Gilson concludes his *History of Christian Philosophy in the Middle Ages* (New York, 1955) with a chapter entitled »Journey's End,« in which he laments the »tired« and »sceptical disintegration« of theological thought, a period of increasing decadence in which »the doctrines accumulated by the successive masters [and particularly those of the thirteenth century], backed by their Orders, exploited by their schools and continually distorted in the heat of endless controversies, finally created what cannot be described otherwise than an extreme doctrinal confusion.« *Ibid.,* p. 528.

[8] Cf. Oberman, *Harvest.* In stark contrast to Gilson's evaluation, Oberman sees in this »harvest« »not the barren wastelands of sterile debates that we had been led to expect by traditional late medieval scholarship, but a richness of deep pastoral and searching theological concern,« a conclusion which leads him to deny speaking of nominalism as a »disintegration of late medieval thought.« See *ibid.,* pp. 5, 423 ff.

extricate Gerson from the supposed »nominalist« trajectory leading from Ockham to Biel. Embracing the former will raise afresh the complex question of how the fifteenth century must be seen as anticipating the later age of Reformation, while endorsing the latter will cause us to look again at the question of Gerson's influence and legacy – and first of all during the *fifteenth* century. In either event this study will add another clarifying voice to our grasp of the later Middle Ages, the period of uncertainty and innovation which seems to us to stand so clearly »zwischen den Zeiten« but which viewed itself as the »modern« age facing overwhelming ecclesiastical and political obstacles. It is at the midpoint of this turbulent period – marked at its beginning by the Avignon »captivity« of the papacy, at its median by the »Great Schism« of the papacy, and in its final stages by the extravagancies of the Renaissance popes – that we must situate this study of Jean Gerson, who as *doctor christianissimus* dominated the period which has been called »le siècle de Gerson.«[9]

Not surprisingly, the complexity which characterizes late-medieval historiography has not left Gerson research unaffected. This is perhaps even inevitable given his authoritative role at the very heart of the controversies that divided the church during his lifetime. Gerson was anything but a spectator. Indeed, his efforts as reform-minded university chancellor and conciliarist during this turbulent period kept him in the mainstream of European affairs, civil and ecclesiastical, prompting modern commentators of this era to characterize him variously as »a mirror of his times« or a »reservoir« of late-medieval thought.[10] But what can this mean given the volatile tenor of his age? What does one finally perceive within a »mirror« which must reflect such shifting images, and how does his thought gather together the complex legacy – in »waning« or in »harvest«? – of the ages he inherited? In a word, what exactly was Gerson's reform, theological and ecclesiastical? Complexity reigns here, too, upon the throne, not only in terms of the unsettled historiography but in the equally unsettled history itself. How, then, are we to make sense of this pivotal figure who sought to »re-form« the fragmented church of his day? In approaching this task historians have reached no consensus, as we might well expect, assessing the character of his work as churchman and reformer from divergent perspectives. Yet here complexity appears to be the consequence in large measure of Gerson's own ambivalence, and of the shifting contours of his admittedly widely eclectic thought. On the

---

[9] See E. Delaruelle *et al.*, *L'Eglise au temps du Grand Schisme et de la crise conciliaire*, Vol. XIV/2, *Histoire de l'église depuis les origines jusqu'à nos jours*, ed. A. Fliche, V. Martin (Paris, 1964), pp. 837 ff.
[10] Delaruelle, *L'Eglise*, p. 837 and Johann Stelzenberger, *Die Mystik des Johannes Gerson* (Breslau, 1928), p. 102, respectively.

one hand, it is easy enough to point to his »conservatism«[11] as the organizing principle of a vigorous reactionary, a counter-measure not only against abusive »novelties« within the theological faculty at Paris but against what he considered the arrogant and ultimately destructive reform of the Hussite circle; in this sense reform could mean little more than defense of the threatened status quo. But this would be to underestimate the constructive depth of Gerson's program of reform, and finally to distort the theologically nuanced if also eclectic foundation he laid in this effort. Thus we must also, on the other hand, account for the progressive dimensions of Gerson's thought, weighing these finally on the other side of the interpretive balance: Gerson advanced his notion of reform not in order to ossify the church in the present or return it to some golden age of a sentimentalized past, but in order to lead it forward toward its goal *in Deum*. In this sense a striking progressivism emerges in his vision of reform, a characteristic attributable above all to the Dionysian influence upon his theology and ecclesiology as we shall see.[12] His conservatism, in other words, meant to preserve the outward form of the church's integrity in the midst of its progress toward reform, and in this we discern the constructive effects of his convictions as a churchman and indeed as a »pastoral theologian.«[13] His reform in the first instance was a matter not of control, as we

---

[11] On this point see Wolfgang Hübener, »Der theologisch-philosophische Konservativismus des Jean Gerson,« *Antiqui und Moderni. Traditionsbewußtsein und Fortschrittsbewußtsein im späten Mittelalter*, ed. A. Zimmerman, G. Vuillemin-Diem (Berlin, 1974), pp. 171–200. Hübener interprets the censure by the Paris theological faculty of Johannes de Montesono (July, 1387), in which Gerson as a young *cursor biblicus* participated *motu proprio* and later described (1400) in a letter as *rationalibiliter et catholice facta*, as the »Schlüsselerlebnis« by which we might understand his lifelong conservatism. Furthermore, he rightly emphasizes the importance of Gerson's reliance upon Augustine's claim, in *De civitate dei* (X.23), that »liberis enim verbis loquuntur philosophi, nec in rebus ad intelligendum difficillimis offensionem religiosarum aurium pertimescunt. Nobis autem ad certam regulam loqui fas est... .« *CCSL* 47:297. What he does not realize, however, is the centrality which this theme came to play in Gerson's *De consolatione theologiae* (1418); see below, Ch. 5, especially section B.1. Otherwise, however, his discussion of Gerson's »conservatism« is excellent, surveying not only theological themes in his thought but the practical measures he advocated or implemented as University chancellor at Paris. It is within this broader program, based on what Hübener calls his »konkordistischer Grundtendenz« applied in the hortatory voice, that we must understand his strident criticism of the divisive tendencies and idle speculation or »vain curiosity« of scholastic theology. »Der ... Konservativismus,« pp. 172 ff., and pp. 197–200. Finally, see also Christoph Burger, *Aedificatio, Fructus, Utilitas. Johannes Gerson als Professor der Theologie und Kanzler der Universität Paris* (Tübingen, 1986), pp. 110–24.

[12] See below, Ch. 6. A.1.

[13] This is a conclusion shared among Gerson scholars, though the conclusion is perhaps most eloquently phrased by Delaruelle. In his study of the period of the schism and conciliar crisis, he concludes in almost eulogistic style that »Gerson est – peut-être essentiellement – un pasteur. Il n'a pas entendu faire de la société qu'il décrit un tableau désinteresse; il diagnostique les maux de son temps; il critique ou condamne, il propose les remèdes et

shall later argue in greater detail, but of conversion, of a progressive reforming of the church in her pilgrimage *ad Deum*.

To speak of Gerson as reformer within a church badly deformed by schism and dissent, therefore, requires something more than the metaphors of mirrors and harvests: this task demands that we delineate the conservative and progressive dimensions of Gerson's program of reform, and that we interpret the theological and ecclesiological foundations of his thought within this tension. In this sense it is possible to discern in his writings »a fully unified pattern of reform,«[14] particularly in terms of how individual and social dimensions coalesce in his thought, but this unity of purpose must account for his deeper ambivalence of method. The contribution of this study, therefore, will not lie in considering once again the question of »decline« or »harvest,« this time vis-à-vis Gerson, nor in seeking to discern the outward unity of his thought; rather, our interest here is to explore the deliberate tension of progressive and conservative tendencies by which he structures his thought — both ecclesiological and theological — at every point. This ambivalence shapes the pastoral moorings upon which he constructs his »edifying« theology and his »ordered« ecclesiology, both in order to guide *ecclesia militans* upon its pilgrimage, or *regressus*, toward God. And, as we shall subsequently suggest, it might well be this decisive tension rather than either more specific theological emphases or his broadly acknowledged eclecticism that should discourage any simple identification of Gerson with a »school« label. He is, of course, a syncretistic theologian, and the breadth of his early thought does place him within the orbit of what has been called the »pastoral nominalism« of this age.[15]

---

embrasse d'un large regard toute l'Eglise de ces années décisives. Il est souvent dans cet examen étonnamment moderne; dans le domaine de la religion populaire il fait date par ses analyses et par ses initiatives.« *L'Eglise*, p. 838. One wonders, of course, exactly what he means by »modern,« though this is a question better explored in another context.

[14] This is the conclusion which Steven Ozment reached in a short essay, »The University and the Church. Patterns of Reform in Jean Gerson,« *Mediaevalia et Humanistica. Studies in Medieval and Renaissance Culture*, ed. P. M. Clogan, n. s. 1 (Cleveland, 1970), p. 121. He concludes in this study that the unity within Gerson's distinctive »pattern« of reform has to do with the coalescence of ecclesiology and anthropology, such that the *via mystica* and *via concilii* are but two expressions of the same spirit-led reform.

[15] For a more precise discussion of this phrase, see E. Jane D. Douglass, *Justification in Late Medieval Preaching. A Study of John Geiler of Keisersberg* (Leiden, 1966), p. 205. Douglass identifies Geiler with this characterization, though the parallels to Gerson are quite suggestive since Geiler considered the *doctor consolatorius* as »the most important single authority . . . on the spiritual life« (*ibid.*, p. 37). Furthermore, Herbert Kraume has pointed to the links between Gerson and Geiler in his recent study *Die Gerson-Übersetzungen Geilers von Kaysersberg. Studien zur deutschsprachigen Gerson-Rezeption* (München, 1980). He builds upon this general thesis of dependence, exploring Geiler's use of German translations of select homiletical and pastoral treatises of Gerson's, and thus also aligns the two within a tradition of fifteenth-century nominalism. Finally, Oberman has also argued that Johannes Altenstaig's *Vocabularius theologie* (Hagenau, 1517), which he calls »essentially an inventory

As a general term this characterization adequately locates Gerson in the late-medieval theological spectrum. But the breadth of this term, on the one hand, and the peculiar soteriological development of his later thought, on the other, warn against using such labels without due caution. Indeed, it appears that Gerson has reconstructed his theology in fundamental ways after Constance: at this juncture we find him orienting his soteriology along a different axis altogether, one which abandons the Ockhamist approach to justification by blending elements of the Scotist view of predestination with an anthropology redolent of an extreme Augustinian position.[16] And, because this theme is

of the nominalist theological vocabulary,« links Gerson and Biel as the preeminent authorities in the supposed »school« of Ockhamists within the broader tradition of fifteenth-century nominalism. See his early study, »Some Notes on the Theology of Nominalism,« pp. 49 ff., and *idem*, »Gabriel Biel and Late Medieval Mysticism,« *Church History* 30 (1961), p. 280, n. 25. These theses are certainly quite fruitful in suggesting how later theologians perceived Gerson's legacy within a nominalist tradition. And, of course, it is quite true that the general outline of Gerson's early thought supports an alignment which places him within the »main current« of nominalism, to recall the metaphor which emerges in Oberman's *Harvest*; from this vantage point Gerson does seem to represent the rough mid-point of the nominalist trajectory from Ockham to Biel. But for reasons we shall subsequently explore, it is not entirely accurate to interpret Gerson's thought as a whole with this label, since his later writings show a marked movement away from this position. In this sense we would label Gerson's theology, particularly in its later development, as pastoral without being »nominalist« in any strict sense, not only because the chancellor's theological preferences blurred any meaningful adherence to the logical and epistemological bases of that philosophical tradition (cf. here Hübener, pp. 196–200; more recently, Courtenay has argued, with regard to the English scene, that all such »schools« largely disappeared during the later fourteenth century due to what he has called »the revolutionary innovations in philosophical and theological *methods*«; see his *Schools and Scholars in Fourteenth Century England* [Princeton, 1987], pp. 190–92, 198 ff., 216–17), but more importantly because the shape of his mature soteriology distanced him altogether from the so-called Ockamist »school« within that broader tradition. We use the term »nominalism,« in other words, in guarded fashion following the usage established by Oberman and others, a perspective which as Ozment has noted »deals with nominalism almost exclusively from its theological side, in terms of its soteriology«; see his »Mysticism, Nominalism, and Dissent,« in *The Pursuit of Holiness*, p. 69. In other words, Gerson's thought in its later form no longer fits the broader pattern of this tradition, considered in its theological shape.

[16] The question of the compatibility of Scotism and nominalism considered as a *theological* tradition has not been resolved without debate. The principal disagreement has been well expressed in the position first advanced by Werner Dettloff, who perceived a close connection between Scotism and nominalism, grounded above all in the *acceptatio* doctrine; see his *Die Entwicklung der Akzeptations- und Verdienstlehre von Duns Scotus bis Luther mit besonderer Berücksichtigung der Franziskanertheologen* (Münster i. W., 1963). Against this position Oberman has more recently argued that »the differences between nominalistic and scotistic traditions in the later middle ages should not be minimized«; he disputes Dettloff's basic approach above all by pointing to the pivotal role of *predestinatio*, the doctrine which, as he argues, determines the *context* of the doctrine of justification. Cf. »*Iustitia Christi* and *Iustitia Dei*: Luther and the Scholastic Doctrines of Justification,« *Harvard Theological Review* 59 (1966), p. 5. This is finally a more sufficient and convincing

embedded within the Ockhamist concept of covenant, which has been recently designated as the key to this theological »system,«[17] we cannot underestimate the significance of this shift as an index of broader and deeper theological convictions. As we shall subsequently suggest, this reorientation appears to reflect not merely the outer structure of a theological change of mind, but rather a foundational shift of perspective shaped by pastoral convictions as well as specific polemic concerns emerging from his anti-Hussite vision of reform. All of this, at this introductory juncture, stands merely as a general orientation to the complexity facing us in this study, and as an early announcement that Gerson research has not yet finished its work; these are themes that we can only sketch in barest detail at this early point, however, promising a more complete analysis as this study progresses.

A superficial review of the recent flurry of respectable Gerson studies might suggest that enough has been said to grasp the nuanced character of his complex and varied theological contribution, or at least to discern the basic outline of his thought and work. Alongside André Combes's impressive series of studies on Gerson's mysticism, which represent the energies of an entire career devoted to his thought, and to which we shall return later in this chapter, four recent studies bear particular mention in providing an orientation to the state of research. The first three of these, works by Steven Ozment, Louis Pascoe, and Christoph Burger, focus primarily upon the early, pre-conciliar writings of the chancellor, and deal with Gerson's anthropology in terms of his mystical writings, his ecclesiology, and his program of theological and ecclesiastical reform, respectively; the final and most recent contribution of Catherine Brown treats Gerson's pastoral efforts in a more comprehensive sense, though with particular attention given to his vernacular sermons. None of these, in other words, devotes sustained attention to the later Gerson, and none suggests that Gerson's thought demonstrates the kind of development we have alluded to earlier. Each testifies to the complex character of Gerson's work, but the suspicion nonetheless remains that we have not yet grasped this dominating theologian and churchman in the *full* breadth and nuance of his thought.

The first of these, Steven Ozment's *Homo Spiritualis. A Comparative Study of the Anthropology of Johannes Tauler, Jean Gerson and Martin Luther (1509–16) in the Context of their Theological Thought* (Leiden, 1969), devotes a major section to the analysis of Gerson's »anthropology.« Yet the thematic and textual focus of this analysis falls primarily upon Gerson's early writings on mystical theology;[18] as such, Ozment's »comparative« study does serve to update

---

argument. And, as our study of Gerson suggests, this focus upon predestination enables us to identify the later Gerson's unexpected preference for the »Scotistic« rather than »nominalistic« doctrine of justification.

[17] See Courtenay, »Nominalism and Late Medieval Religion,« p. 59.

[18] Ozment focuses primarily upon a cluster of early mystical treatises, and above all

Combes's early and groundbreaking work on the mystical themes of Gerson's
oeuvre, particularly by focusing not upon his formulation of *theologia mystica*
itself but rather upon how this mysticism shaped his image of the person. The
work, therefore, accomplishes what it promises to do, and thus accepts the
general characterization of Gerson the »semi-Pelagian« nominalist which
Ozment's mentor, Heiko Oberman, had earlier explored in *The Harvest of
Medieval Theology*. Yet this thematic focus and the historiographical
assumptions upon which the work builds necessarily preempt any broader
appreciation of Gerson's own theological development, and as such render this
otherwise suggestive study of limited use for our purposes. The second piece,
Louis Pascoe's *Jean Gerson. Principles of Church Reform* (Leiden, 1973), appeared
in the same series (Vol. VII of Studies in Medieval and Reformation Thought,
edited by Heiko Oberman) and scrutinized Gerson's contribution from a
different vantage point altogether: viz., that of his ecclesiology, and
particularly what Pascoe calls »the ideological principles that motivated and
directed that program.«[19] Yet Pascoe's work also focuses quite narrowly upon
the early writings – and particularly those leading up to the Council of
Constance – since the Great Schism provided the problematic stimulating
much of his thought on ecclesiology and reform. As a consequence this study
largely ignores the post-conciliar period of Gerson's life, an era during which
not surprisingly his earlier pragmatic and »ideological« interests in church
reform shifted to other matters. The third work, Christoph Burger's
*Aedificatio, Fructus, Utilitas. Johannes Gerson als Professor der Theologie und
Kanzler der Universität Paris* (Tübingen, 1986), attempts to update Johann
Baptist Schwab's original monograph of similar name (Würzburg, 1858).
Unlike Schwab, however, Burger restricts his attention to those writings
leading up to the Council of Constance (1414–1418), and concentrates his
attention primarily upon Gerson's »pastoral« intentions, both theoretical and
practical, which dominated those writings from his professional career

---

Gerson's *De mystica theologia speculativa* (1402/3) and his *A Deo Exivit* (1402). He published
in the same year an anthology – with extracts from both of these texts, along with a section
of the *Contra curiositatem studentium* – as *Jean Gerson. Selections from ›A Deo exivit,‹ ›Contra
curiositatem studentium,‹ and ›De mystica theologia speculativa‹*, intro., ed., and trans. Steven
Ozment (Leiden, 1969).
[19] Pascoe, *Jean Gerson*, p. 3. Pascoe's work, despite its differing thematic interest, does
yet serve to build upon that of Combes and Ozment, for he inquires about the »spiritual
orientation« underlying Gerson's »concept of reform.« Although Pascoe's thematic
concern holds his focus for the most part upon the writings pre-dating the Council of
Constance (1414–1418), and hence diverts attention away from the chancellor's later
works, his study will nonetheless prove quite helpful to our own inquiry, particularly in
our concluding chapter on ecclesiology and reform. As we shall there argue, the Dionysian
ecclesiology which Gerson accepted early in his career continues to inform and shape his
later thought, though within a quite specific context as the theoretical foundation
undergirding his anti-Hussite polemic.

antedating Constance.[20] In a manner which anticipates our own study of Gerson, Burger interprets the chancellor's theological oeuvre principally as an expression of pastoral interests and a resolution of ecclesiastical problems — viz. as an edifying theology in service of the church. The textual basis of his study is certainly broader than Ozment's, and more focused than Pascoe's; he works systematically through a series of primary texts, and above all Gerson's extended lectures on Mark's gospel, in order to offer what he calls »a grasp of Gerson's entire person and legacy. «[21] The particular strength of Burger's piece is the comprehensive scope of his analysis, at least up to Gerson's departure for Constance, and this in terms of both the themes he explores and the textual basis upon which he draws. His work alone among recent studies discerns the conservative/progressive ambivalence of which we have earlier spoken, and he rightly points us to the »altered scheme of values« by which the chancellor promoted with determination a grasp of *theologia* as a »science of the church. «[22] Yet the focus of this study only occasionally strays beyond the texts Gerson produced in fulfillment of his active teaching duties in Paris — that is, before his journey to Constance — and the few cross-references to treatises from the last decade of the exiled chancellor's life do not substantiate Burger's hypothesis that these later writings only reiterate or further expand upon the earlier theological emphases and themes. For this reason his expressed hope that the work might offer a grasp of the *entire* Gerson remains unfulfilled, to say the least; Gerson's later writings, while remaining firmly committed to »pastoral« issues, yet move decisively away from earlier theological positions he had embraced. The final chapter at least of a truly comprehensive study remains to be written.

Finally, we must mention D. Catherine Brown's *Pastor and Laity in the Theology of Jean Gerson* (Cambridge, 1987), particularly since this work promises to offer a broad overview of Gerson's thought regarding pastoral issues. As the title suggests, Brown's aim is to offer an extensive survey of Gerson's theology insofar as he intended it either *for* the laity as direct recipients of the vernacular homilies and writings, or for pastors in their vocational

---

[20] Burger addresses this theme by speaking of Gerson's »seelsorgerliche Intentionen,« his contribution to pastoral issues related to the *cura animarum*; see *Aedificatio*, pp. 21 ff.

[21] In this regard, Burger assumes that these lectures, offered as a sustained expression of Gerson's sense of responsibility for his teaching office (»Lehramt«), provide a condensed yet comprehensive portrait of themes and concerns which he later developed more fully: »Gerson hat in seinem Lehramt viele der Anschauungen entwickelt, die er später in Konstanz, im bayerischen und österreichischen Exil und in Lyon entfaltete. Deshalb bietet sich eine Konzentration auf diesen Quellenkomplex, ergänzt durch Ausblicke auf erhaltene Schriften verwandter Zielsetzung, an, um einen neuen Ansatz zu einer Würdigung Gersons zu unternehmen.« *Ibid.*, p. 22. As we shall here argue, this thesis no longer appears tenable; Gerson has altered his theology in decisive points, such that we must now set theological divergences of a fundamental character against abiding thematic continuities.

[22] *Ibid.*, pp. 40–42.

responsibilities *to* the laity. Her efforts are largely successful in this regard. While quite self-consciously disavowing any attempt to reconstruct a social history from these sources, her work seeks to evaluate Gerson's »pastoral teaching« in terms not only of its *content*, but of its explicit or implicit pastoral *context*, and particularly insofar as he has constantly before him the situation of *les simples gens*. As such her focus is quite different from Burger's and complements it rather well, since her interest lies less in the character of Gerson's »professional« theology within the academic arena than in the matter and manner of his pastoral work. Yet a serious methodological difficulty which weakens what is an otherwise competent study is the random manner in which Brown cites Gerson's works. References tumble from the sermons in a style controlled only by theme, and thus her wide acquaintance with Gerson's sermons does not yet fully integrate these texts within the specific historical circumstances of the day. We look in vain here for a sustained analysis of thematic developments – textual or more broadly contextual. Furthermore, Brown has here accepted, perhaps unwittingly, the same mistaken principle of selection which weakens Delaruelle's otherwise insightful work: viz. the assumption that one might distinguish in Gerson's oeuvre the occasional and pastoral writings intended for a broader public from those esoteric texts meant for theologians and dealing with »eternal truths.«[23] Several sections of this

---

[23] Cf. Delaruelle, *L'Eglise*, p. 838: »Nous nous en tiendrons strictement aux oeuvres de circonstance, d'ailleurs multiples, plus qu'aux oeuvres soucieuses de vérités éternelles.« Of course, one wonders which Gerson texts Delaruelle would cite as »oeuvres soucieuses de vérités éternelles,« since he nowhere specifies which these were. In the same manner as Delaruelle, apparently, Brown designates as her chief focus »that part of Jean Gerson's teaching intended for the laity, either directly as it appears in his vernacular sermons and tracts, or indirectly as in his Latin works for pastors.« See *Pastor and Laity*, p. 1. Such an approach underrates Gerson's intention to reform »academic« theology – particularly in the exaggerated extremes to which he felt scholastic theology had devolved – as itself of significant if indirect import for the laity. In point of fact, even those texts intended for a learned audience, such as his university sermons, bear the imprint of his unwavering concern for pastoral issues of the day, such that Gerhard Ritter has spoken of Gerson's writings as »erbaulich-gelehrten Schriften,« perceiving in them »das Vorbild einer ausgedehnten halbpopulären, synkretistisch gestimmten theologischen Literatur, die für das ganze 15. Jahrhundert charakteristisch ist.« See *Studien zur Spätscholastik*, Vol. II: *Via antiqua und via moderna auf den deutschen Universitäten des XV. Jahrhunderts* (Heidelberg, 1922), p. 133. The more recent suggestion in the works of Douglass and Kraume of a line of dependence linking Gerson with Geiler, as noted above (n. 15), is a further instantiation of this claim; Gerson was surely heard and read during the fifteenth century as a »popular« theologian, though distinctions were not always made between the occasional and the more formal academic treatises. Hence, Brown's delineation of Gerson's writings on the basis of pastoral intention ignores the full texture of his theological reform, above all by dismissing the point which is apparently so vital to Gerson's works that audience may not significantly influence his thematic approach. That is, a consideration of audience (or readership) may not even alter his manner of speaking or writing, particularly since he insisted that the reform of academic theology required a concentration upon the »useful« questions of

study, however, despite these methodological shortcomings, offer an advance over the earlier and more recent Gerson literature. We shall draw upon these as our our work progresses, noting in particular Brown's recognition that a soteriological groundshift has occurred in Gerson's later writings vis-à-vis the doctrine of predestination.[24] This study as a whole, however, does not move us far beyond the point from which we started. We now know something more concerning the pastoral issues which occupied this academic theologian to such an extraordinary degree, and we hear from another vantage point the thesis that Gerson's thought was highly eclectic. But this contribution, along with the others mentioned above, still leaves us with at best a vague sense of the later Gerson, and almost no recognition of the development found in these writings. In other words, these works considered together have given us a greater sense of the complexity of Gerson's thought, primarily by providing insight into

---

doctrine; certainly he did not intend to speak of a utility accessible only to the academically trained theologians, a point which he reaffirms in *De consolatione theologiae* through his high regard for the *idiotae* who might only have a »simple« faith but often enough rooted that faith *in affectum* (see below, 4. C. 1). Of course, this criticism does not yet mention the further point that a preference for Latin and for an academic style over a simple vernacular form might only reflect his desire for a *broader* rather than narrower readership, particularly given Gerson's awareness of professional obligations within the international horizon presented by the church in his day. Latin was still at this juncture the common basis for the wider dissemination of texts and ideas, and consequently authors such as Gerson often found themselves obliged to undertake *Latin* translations of their own vernacular writings to accommodate this fact. This was a period in which a startling number of Latin texts – and among them a cluster of Gerson's with particular frequency – were translated into European vernaculars. Kraume cites the conclusions of a Würzburg philology colloquium on »Spätmittelalterliche Prosaforschung« that this peculiar form of translation records »die Ausformung lateinisch geprägten Wissens in die Volkssprache,« a process through which a new »lay culture« manifests itself »aus der universalen Schriftlichkeit des Lateinischen«; see *Die Gerson-Übersetzungen Geilers von Kaysersberg*, pp. 10 f. The rise of vernaculars, in other words, did not always stand in opposition to the use of Latin, nor did the mere use of Latin signal an esoteric intention alienated from a more popular use. On the contrary, Latin as a universal language in western Europe still made of it an essential conduit for the otherwise elite literature of the church and academy, and this often caused authors to write in Latin precisely in order to broaden their appeal and thereby enrich the various vernacular literatures.

[24] Brown, *Pastor and Laity*, pp. 114 f. Unfortunately, however, her analysis does not go beyond this realization in bare form, and she resigns herself to retreat behind the argument of complexity; having noted that some of Gerson's views seem reminiscent of Thomism, some of Scotism, and some of Bonaventure's thought, she abruptly concludes that »it is not surprising that [Gerson] has had attached to him so many different labels.« *Ibid.*, p. 115. In this question, as more generally as we have suggested, her study otherwise ignores the historical factors which helped to shape such theological developments. What a more differentiated approach might yield on precisely this point, and this is a deficiency which the present study will address in the fifth chapter, is a more nuanced portrait of Gerson's progressive movement *away* from a rigid »nominalist« soteriology. For a more detailed discussion of this point, see below, Ch. 5, and my essay, »Gerson after Constance«.

various aspects of his earlier pastoral writings, but we are left with little beyond general impressions of his later writings and few clues as to the historical circumstances which apparently reshaped his thought at this juncture.

Hence, the time is ripe for a careful study of the later Gerson, one which accounts for the writings *after* Constance and explores developments in his thought in terms of the specific historical circumstances he faced once the papal schism had been healed. In this regard we shall suggest, beyond the ascription of »eclectic,« that the shifting contours of Gerson's thought are not fortuitous, but reflect a quite different approach to theological, pastoral, and polemic concerns than we find in his earlier writings; these represent, moreover, not so much a change of convictions as an altered theological strategy demanded by the crises which he confronted within the church at this point. Of course, such a contribution, if it is also to broaden and deepen our present understanding of the late-medieval theological horizon more generally, must situate Gerson's thought in context, historical and theological. We must, in other words, discern the shape of his thought in terms of his own wider oeuvre, but also in regard to the complex panorama presented by the early fifteenth-century church. This will require that we proceed in conversation at some level with voices interpreting not only Gerson, but later medieval theology and culture more generally.[25] This study, then, will not dispute the work already accomplished on the younger Gerson which in its essential shape provides an adequate survey of his thought, nor will it adopt as its organizing method »a comprehensive view of [Gerson's] person and work.«[26] What it will offer is an initial exploration into the curiously neglected chapter of Gerson's later life, a chapter which advances a revisionist approach to Gerson studies in specific, and to surveys of late-scholastic theology more generally. To accomplish this reorientation, this study abandons the broad thematic scope which has characterized recent Gerson research — and particularly the contributions of Pascoe, Burger, and Brown — in favor of a sharper and more focused approach, taking as its centerpiece the treatise which Gerson wrote at the close of the Council of Constance: *De consolatione theologiae* (1418).[27]

---

[25] Again, cf. Delaruelle, *L'Eglise*, pp. 837 ff.

[26] Burger has rightly noted at the outset of his *Aedificatio* that previous studies of Gerson, aside from Combes's series of studies with their narrower focus on Gerson and mysticism, have failed to provide such a »Gesamtschau von Person und Werk.« *Aedificatio*, p. 21. His own contribution does address this need, particularly by providing a broad orientation to Gerson's work as university chancellor. Yet Burger's suggestion that the theological interests and convictions which Gerson expressed as university chancellor — i. e., before his departure for the Council of Constance — announce the full breadth of his thought no longer appears adequate, and thus stumbles short of accomplishing a truly »comprehensive« study of Gerson.

[27] The question of Gerson's exact location during the composition of this treatise has evoked considerable debate. Glorieux has settled upon Rathenberg as the place and July,

This choice of texts offers an appropriate and even compelling foundation for such a reorientation for several reasons. First, this text certainly provides one of the most sustained treatments of *pastoral* themes to be found in Gerson's later writings — academic or occasional, Latin or vernacular. And, of course, it is this text which Gerson devotes to a theme which had long occupied his thought, and for which he later came to be known as *doctor consolatorius*. It is moreoever curious enough, given the recent interest in this dimension of Gerson's thought, that this text should have been largely ignored in the recent literature,[28] but this curiosity becomes quite perplexing when we discover that Gerson here advances a soteriology — identified as one of the keys of nominalist theology because this theme structures the covenant model[29] — markedly different from the Ockhamist perspective we find in his earlier thought. What will this theological groundshift entail for other themes which are related to it, either directly or implicitly, and how will this reshape the pastoral themes characteristic to the earlier Gerson? And, of course, what will all this mean in assessing the full complexity of Gerson's contribution to theology in the early fifteenth century? A reorientation of the current view of the theological undergirding for Gerson's pastoral thought, and perhaps of that thought itself, appears necessary. But is this the text by which we should articulate a revisionist approach to Gerson's work?

The second of these considerations answers this question quite directly, since this text, as we shall subsequently argue in greater detail, offers a compre-

---

1418, as the date of composition; see »Essai biographique,« G 1, p. 133. Combes, on the other hand, although initially accepting this view, later retracted his position, deciding on the basis of extant correspondence in favor of a later date, the early fall of 1418, when Gerson took up temporary residence in Melk (Austria), as the invited guest of the Benedictine abbot there; see *La théologie mystique de Gerson. Profil de son évolution* (Rome, 1964), 2:306—11. Combes's argument appears the most convincing of the two, though what is at stake in this debate would not, in either case, alter significantly the interpretation of this treatise.

[28] Recent studies — and above all those of Burger and Brown — have built upon Delaruelle's widely accepted claim that »Gerson est — peut-être essentiellement — un pasteur.« Cf. L'Eglise, p. 837. Because this mature treatise conveys Gerson's pastoral concerns persuasively and in non-technical language accessible to a broader audience than the limited realm of trained scholars (see below, 3. B. 3), it is quite surprising to find that Brown's study largely ignores this work. Furthermore, several recent Gerson scholars, including Delaruelle, have defended Gerson as a theologian still »relevant« for the church of today, yet ignored *De consolatione theologiae* altogether; in this regard, see *ibid.*, pp. 837 f., where Delaruelle concludes that Gerson »est souvent dans cet examen étonnamment moderne.« In the same vein, and with deliberate reference to this text, Combes concluded a brief discussion of the treatise by arguing that »la leçon n'a rien perdu de son actualité.« See his »La consolation de la théologie d'après Gerson,« *La pensée catholique*, 1 (1945): 26.

[29] See above, n. 17.

hensive survey of Gerson's theological concerns. If Gerson himself intended to express his fundamental theological convictions in different form or in an altered framework, then such a text would certainly be well-suited to the task. The metaphor which structures the treatise as a whole, the *peregrinatio ad Deum*, provides an arena in which Gerson explores not only fundamental themes of theology, soteriology, and ecclesiology, but the themes which are more specifically characteristic of his thought: viz. the relation of theology and philosophy, the function of scripture, the role of the theological virtues, the place of despair and tribulation in the Christian life, etc. Furthermore, the dialogue form which Gerson here utilized reflects a broad tendency of the Renaissance to prefer unsystematic, literary forms over the more rigid academic conventions that had dominated medieval scholasticism.[30] As a style which was both »graceful« and »unsystematic,«[31] the dialogue allows Gerson to convey many of the themes which concerned him within a flexible structure and in relatively condensed form. Hence, when we find within this »comprehensive« treatise themes either not to be found in the earlier treatises or articulated in a fashion uncharacteristic of his earlier writings, the largely untested hypothesis that the chancellor's earlier thought set the agenda for his entire career is no longer tenable. Gerson himself, in other words, announces in this text a significant groundshift in his own theological perspective, a development which requires a reorientation of the general historical reception he has received.

These considerations alone, however, might not provide sufficient cause to call for a »reorientation« to Gerson studies as a whole, but they do not stand alone. Third, and perhaps most importantly, it appears that Gerson chose both

---

[30] This tendency needs no elaboration, though the lingering tendency to treat »the Renaissance« as a predominantly Italian phenomenon obscures the fact that northern theologians such as Gerson also favored the »occasional« forms of dialogue and poetry. Indeed, James Connolly has even argued that Gerson's dialogues, written during a period of ferment and experimentation in the area of liturgical drama, may have been intended for public performance; cf. *John Gerson. Reformer and Mystic* (Louvain, 1928), pp. 227–29. This suggestion is somewhat difficult to imagine with regard to this particular dialogue, though the form certainly offered a more colloquial articulation of traditional theological problems and a version of the school debates which would have been more readily accessible to a lay audience untrained in the theological schools (i. e., the *idiotae* of this treatise); see below, 3. B. 3.

[31] This is the characterization offered by William Bouwsma; cf. »The Two Faces of Humanism: Stoicism and Augustinianism in Renaissance Thought,« in *Itinerarium Italicum. The Profile of the Italian Renaissance in the Mirror of its European Transformations*, ed. Heiko Oberman (Leiden, 1975), p. 17. Bouwsma is not, of course, referring to Gerson's specific use of this form, but is speaking more broadly of the humanist reliance upon Stoic sources, texts which he argues held an attraction for Renaissance writers because of their genre; it is this »graceful and unsystematic form of the sources,« Bouwsma argued, which disguised from them Stoicism's conservatism.

the form and subject matter of the *De consolatione theologiae* for quite deliberate and personal reasons, reasons which should dissuade us from assuming that this treatise merely stands as another in a literary contribution of prodigious dimensions. He apparently chose to write a dialogue based upon Boethius' *De consolatione philosophiae* not only because this literary form provided a comprehensive vehicle of expression, nor because the textual precedent enabled him — implicitly at least — to draw the Boethian voice, along with something of the rich overtones of its translators and imitators, into an already established dialogue upon some of the classic themes of scholastic debate. Nor did this textual precedent suggest itself only because it provided a literary form deeply engrained in the medieval imagination through this rich trajectory of translations, commentaries, and glosses,[32] a tradition to which Gerson's

---

[32] The significance of Gerson's contribution both to the literary tradition based upon this Boethian text and to the broader genre of *consolatio* literature represents a curious lacuna still awaiting critical treatment. This is particularly strange given the several recent studies devoted to *consolatio*, both vis-à-vis the Boethian tradition and as a subject of literary interest more generally. In the massive and critically detailed undertaking of Peter von Moos, an impressive three volume study entitled *Consolatio. Studien zur mittellateinischen Trostliteratur über den Tod und zum Problem der christlichen Trauer* (München, 1971), we find no discussion of the Boethian tradition in its broad spectrum and no mention of Gerson's work; this omission reflects von Moos' decision, either arbitrary or anachronistic, that philosophical (and, by implication one supposes, theological) arguments cannot offer a legitimate *consolatio mortis*. See *ibid.*, p. 32. In Courcelle's *La Consolation de Philosophie dans la tradition littéraire. Antécédents et posterité de Boèce* (Paris, 1967), the discussion of the Boethian trajectory in the later Middle Ages is superficial and finally altogether inadequate; cf. *La Consolation*, especially Ch. 4, »Les commentaires des XIVe et XVe siecles.« Courcelle restricts his focus exclusively to the commentaries and glosses upon the text, thereby eclipsing altogether from his purview the category of »imitations.« Among these, of course, he includes Gerson's treatise, since as a deliberate theological variation upon the Boethian precedent it stands in a primarily formal relationship to *De consolatione philosophiae*; as an imitation, in other words, this treatise is part of what Courcelle dismisses, not without contempt, as a »diffuse and frequently contestable influence upon the *consolatio* genre« (*ibid.*, p. 10). This decision, however, seriously weakens Courcelle's study as a whole, since he removes from his vision contributions to the genre, such as Gerson's »imitation,« which tell us much about the vitality and flexibility with which later medieval authors used Boethius (and other »classical« texts) and thus about the lingering intersection of Boethius' with their *own* concerns. On this same point, though without specific regard to the Boethian tradition, Sem Dresden has concluded that »a kind of secondary literature« developed during the Renaissance, »by which phrase is meant neither a qualitative judgment nor a body of literature about literature. On the contrary, I mean literary works that developed out of already existing works. In a certain sense, Renaissance literature was conditioned by the works available to its writers. It developed out of them, and wanted to be, in its own way, what the original was.« See »The Profile of the Reception of the Italian Renaissance in France,« in *Itinerarium Italicum*, p. 148. This is precisely what Gerson intended his *Consolatio theologiae* to be: namely, a further echo of the Boethian text, but in a style and with concerns more directly related to his audience; that is, Gerson's text attempts *in its own way*, to borrow Dresden's language, to speak to his age as Boethius' treatise had spoken in an earlier period. Indeed, Gerson tells us as much at the opening of his

mentor, Pierre d'Ailly, had himself offered a youthful contribution.[33] All of these reasons, of course, suggest themselves to us as possible explanations for Gerson's choice, and each might have satisfied our curiosity under other circumstances. But we must reckon with another factor which apparently motivated Gerson to write his own *Consolatio theologiae*, a matter having to do not with the literary structure of Boethius' text but with the historical circumstances under which it was written: in the tradition and mood of Boethius' »deathbed« prototype, Gerson appears to have written his text under the impression that it would stand as his final theological contribution. We know, at least, that he wrote it during a period of depression and anxiety, overwrought as he was with the disturbing news from France which left him exiled from his homeland; it even appears, judging from the extant cor-

---

dialogue, where one of his characters remarks that it is his intent »to continue the argument regarding consolation from the point where Boethius left off«; *De consolatione theologiae* I pr. 2 (G 9, p. 188). In terms more specifically related to the Boethian legacy in the fifteenth century, Dresden's article does not help us further, but the question has been addressed in Anthony Grafton's short essay, at least with reference to the Italian Renaissance; see »Epilogue: Boethius in the Renaissance,« in *Boethius. His Life, Thought, and Influence*, ed. Margaret Gibson (Oxford, 1981), pp. 410–15. I have explored this question more fully, with specific attention to Gerson's contribution, in a yet unpublished paper entitled »Re-Imaging Boethius in the Fifteenth Century: Jean Gerson's *De consolatione theologiae* at the End of a Tradition.«

[33] D'Ailly's text, called by its author »tractatus utilis supra Boetium ›de consolatione philosophiae‹«, is loosely based upon the Boethian *consolatio* and surveys many of the themes which interested Gerson as well — viz. the question whether philosophy can discern the end of human beatitude; the themes of divine foreknowledge and human freedom; the nature of the sacraments, and particularly the eucharist, etc. And while his own »imitation« moves far beyond d'Ailly's more formal use of scholastic argument and his deferential use of *auctoritates*, Gerson might have at least found inspiration for his own piece in d'Ailly's choice of the Boethian treatise as the basis for one of his early works. D'Ailly's text, which is still only available in manuscript form (*Paris. lat.* 3122), has received a brief and unsympathetic review in Courcelle's *La Consolation*, pp. 324–25. He dismisses this treatise as »a peine un commentaire« which finally offers »une effrayante compilation,« a work which »montre bien les défauts de l'enseignement à cette époque« and obscures all interpretation of Boethius »dans ce fatras prétentieux.« But what he fails to appreciate is the reason why Boethius no longer served as a voice capable of resolving the serious questions of his day; Courcelle also ignores the careful nature of the eclecticism he finds in d'Ailly's compilation, the peculiar editorial selection by which d'Ailly draws heavily upon the works of the *auctoritates* — and we should note that d'Ailly himself opens the piece by admitting that »ego namque considerans me iuuenem et indoctum coram uobis patribus meis et elegantis sapientiae uiris ... erubesco.« Here we find that he sets »modern« theologians alongside the classical Greek and Roman philosophers as well as their more recent Jewish and Arabic commentators, a compilation which itself merits a closer and more detailed analysis. Courcelle's dismissive review of d'Ailly's treatise, in other words, remains superficial at best; the work still requires a more sustained and appreciative analysis, particularly in setting this work within the broader scope of d'Ailly's oeuvre as well as its late-medieval context.

respondence of this period, that he had resigned himself much in the spirit of Boethius to the inevitability and imminence of his own death.[34] It is thus reasonable to assume that the themes articulated in this late treatise stand not merely as a glimpse into his mature thought, but a quite intentional effort to say what still needed to be said *in extremis* and offer his final theological legacy to those surviving him. If Gerson here provides a quite different approach to the theological questions which had occupied him throughout his life, then we might assume that this is no minor caveat nor a merely accidental detour. In this case, of course, the need for a reorientation to his work becomes of pressing concern. Combes has quite suggestively described the inherent texture of Gerson's work as »une sorte de syncretisme d'essence théologique, «[35] and this is certainly true as far as it goes, but we shall suggest on the basis of a sustained analysis of *De consolatione theologiae* that the character of this syncretism, the precise nature of the complex eclecticism which others have pointed to in Gerson's thought, has changed in fundamental ways from that of his earlier writings.

The significance of *De consolatione theologiae* for Gerson studies is thus clear enough, announcing a reorientation of how we should perceive his later

---

[34] Cf. his letter »à ses freres Nicolas et Jean, « which Glorieux dates August 10, 1418, a piece of correspondence which is significant not only for its proximity to the writing of *De consolatione theologiae* but because he addressed this letter to the same brother (Jean) represented in that dialogue as »Monicus« (see below, Ch. 2); G 2, pp. 216–17: »nostra conversatio in coelis est, nolite quomodolibet solliciti esse qualis in peregrinatione mea sit corporalis aut futurus status meus, sed existimantes me quasi mortuum et perditum super terram, totam vestrae recogitationis aciem vertite ad rogandum ea pro me quae ad pacem sunt Jerusalem, tam internam quam supernam, quae est mater et patria nostra.... Sunt autem innumerabilia verborum piorum genera huic articulo mortis accommoda.... Quid multa dinumero, qualia utique placent et placere debent mihi, et in omnino eamdem recidunt sententiam ut Deus pure gratis agens nobiscum sit misericordia nostra, refugium, susceptor in die mortis inevitabilis quae januam aperit ad patriam ut non confundatur spiritus noster dum loquatur inimis suis in hac porta. «
[35] See *Essai sur la critique de Ruysbroeck par Gerson*, Vol. III/1 (Paris, 1959), p. 223. Combes is here speaking of the earlier Gerson, and specifically of the sermon *A Deo exivit* (1402) and the university lectures *Contra curiositatem studentium* (1402/3); he concludes in this regard that Gerson developed his thought in direct opposition to Ockham, and utilized the Venerable Inceptor only when convenient as a counter-measure against the extreme speculative interests of the Scotists (i. e., *formalizantes*). Already before Combes published this work, however, Gilson had reached similar conclusions but with an added level of specificity, arguing that Gerson had »never adhered to nominalism except against a certain realism and, more precisely, against what in realism ran the risk of leading to the doctrines of Scotus Erigena, of Wyclif, of Jerome of Prague and John Hus« (*Christian Philosophy in the Middle Ages*, p. 529). This is a perceptive point, and one which the detailed analysis of Gerson's later works after Constance supports in striking ways. Yet neither Gilson nor Combes after him noticed the theological groundshift in the later Gerson, above all in terms of his soteriology; this point causes us to delineate more carefully exactly how Gerson abandoned what does appear to be an Ockhamist position in his earlier writings. See below, Ch. 5.

thought in its altered contours and suggesting that this text adds an important and hitherto neglected insight into the theological horizon of the early fifteenth century. But it still remains for us to survey studies that devote specific attention to this treatise in the older Gerson literature, since we have noted that the most recent contributions have largely ignored this text along with Gerson's later works more generally.[36] On this point as well the need for a fresh analysis of this text will be seen to be great. Here, then, we must bring our consideration of the state of research to a close by considering the earlier contributions to Gerson scholarship, and particularly those works which broke fresh ground in successive generations spanning the last century: i. e., the studies of Schwab, Connolly, and Combes, which in their own ways kept the figure of Gerson in the textbook discussions of late-medieval religion. Does this general assessment of the incomplete state of current Gerson research, and the particular neglect of the later Gerson, also hold for these studies, particularly regarding their treatment of *De consolatione theologiae*? This question must be settled before we set forth the exact shape of our own study.

The first of these works appeared more than a century ago, the product of Johann Schwab's lifelong *Quellenstudium* of Gerson's life and work, entitled *Johannes Gerson. Professor der Theologie und Kanzler der Universität Paris. Eine Monographie* (Würzburg, 1858). As the first modern historical analysis of Gerson's work, a study which has not yet been surpassed in terms of its sweeping scope and careful scrutiny of historical detail, Schwab succeeded in avoiding what he rightly perceived as »the tiresome breadth and monotony as well as the predominantly rhetorical character which characterize most previous studies« devoted to issues involving »the western schism.«[37]

---

[36] We have already suggested that recent Gerson studies — above all, Ozment's *Homo Spiritualis*, Pascoe's *Principles of Church Reform*, Burger's *Aedificatio*, and Brown's *Pastor and Laity* — have ignored this text, apart from occasional reference. When these studies have drawn from this text, they have done so without exception in a haphazard manner; either the choice of thematic interest or the chronological (or textual) scope has not permitted these studies to delve more deeply and carefully into the intricacies presented by Gerson's treatise. Careful study of the later Gerson, therefore, remains a curious lacuna in the field of late-medieval studies, such that the recent flurry of Gerson research has not yet obviated Delaruelle's remark, published in 1964, that »le monde gersonien est donc actuellement un chantier, où tout est matière à discussion.« See *L'Eglise*, p. 865. This remark occurs in an appended note on the »current state of Gerson studies« under the heading »doctrine de Gerson« (see pp. 861—69, and particularly pp. 864 f.).

[37] Schwab, *Johannes Gerson*, pp. iii—iv. Burger's criticism of Schwab serves as a useful reminder that Schwab's weakness lay in the historical reliability he accorded to Gerson's observations in general. But Burger readily concedes that this early »Gerson-Biographie ist noch immer brauchbar, weil sie aus den Quellen erarbeitet wurde.« See *Aedificatio*, p. 12. It must also be said that Schwab's work alone merits the description as a »comprehensive study« (*Gesamtschau*) of Gerson's life and work, though one which later studies have corrected both in detail and in more substantial terms.

Schwab's work provided exactly what his title would lead one to expect: a detailed monograph surveying Gerson's life and work as chancellor and professor, attending principally to biographical and secondarily to textual detail. As such, it is Gerson himself who stands out in this study, with his literary works cited to portray the concrete character and personal circumstances of his work as chancellor, conciliarist, and theologian. The focus of the study, as a consequence, falls upon the earlier Gerson; while Schwab does not terminate his study with the Council of Constance, his regard for the post-conciliar Gerson — the man whose immediate influence as either chancellor or professor had become negligible, since during the final decade of his life he remained an »exile« from Paris — wanes considerably. In a short concluding chapter devoted to »Gerson's last years, his character, and his writings,« Schwab offers a terse review of the salient events of these latter years, a sketch that includes only a cursory review of the broad themes Gerson announced in *De consolatione theologiae*.[38] Written of course without the benefit either of the sustained manuscript research of later generations of Gerson scholars[39] or any familiarity with the more recent blossoming of work devoted to the field of late-medieval theology in general and nominalism in specific,[40] Schwab's work can offer little assistance with regard to the textual and contextual appreciation of the later Gerson which we are here undertaking. Once Schwab had staked out this ground, the task has fallen to others to cultivate those fertile though for many generations fallow fields.

---

[38] Schwab, *Johannes Gerson*, pp. 759—61.

[39] This has been an arduous labor carried out, for the most part, by Combes and Glorieux and his students; for a bibliographical essay of work completed before 1964, see Delaruelle, pp. 862, 863—64 (»Editions generales, sigles« and »La question des manuscrits«). Apart from this, the edition of Glorieux has now reached the tenth volume, with a detailed »index« still outstanding. The usefulness of this re-edited series lies primarily in making Gerson's texts once again more readily available than has been the case since Du Pin's edition of 1706, and in improving upon the textual shortcomings of that earlier edition; cf. here Combes's preface to Louis Mourin, *Six sermons français inédits de Jean Gerson: Étude doctrinale et littéraire, suivie de l'édition critique* (Paris, 1946). As a critical edition, however, Glorieux's *Œuvres complètes* suffers considerably both in method and final result, and this for two principal reasons: first, because of the absence of a critical textual apparatus, which leaves the reader completely ignorant of editorial decisions in cases of textual variants, either in the manuscripts or in later printed editions; and, second, because of the extremely uneven editing by which references within Gerson's texts — biblical, theological, biographical, etc. — are noted in rather haphazard fashion. For a similar critical view of this edition, see Burger, *Aedificatio*, pp. 7—9; and, for further bibliographical references to this question, see Brown, *Pastor and Laity*, p. 258, n. 16.

[40] That is, scholarly studies of nominalism during the past generation, and particularly those which have accepted Oberman's orientation to this question, have understood this tradition primarily in its theological dimensions; the attention has shifted away from the older focus upon epistemology, with its attendant assumption that the truly significant contributions of the *via moderna* were philosophical. On this question, see Ozment, »Mysticism, Nominalism, and Dissent,« pp. 69—71.

Connolly's study, *Jean Gerson. Reformer and Mystic* (Louvain, 1928), was the
first major effort to succeed Schwab's pioneering work. This piece, too,
attempts to survey Gerson's work in a comprehensive manner, though the
whole project — accomplished, not insignificantly, under the lingering cloud of
the Roman anti-modernist campaign — is marred by what we must now
consider a tendentious approach to nominalism, a defense of Gerson as anti-
nominalist and even anti-Lutheran which finally tells us more about the
confessional dogmatism and exaggerated polemic of Connolly's age than about
Gerson himself. With regard to *De consolatione theologiae* in specific, and the
later Gerson more generally, Connolly does not advance the scholarly
discussion in any appreciable sense.[41] This is perhaps the result of his stated
thematic focus, which apparently prevented him from discerning much in this
later text that was pertinent to the themes of »reform« or »mysticism.« His
interest, along with more recent students of Gerson, lay primarily with the
chancellor's earlier, pre-conciliar works. Connolly's concluding remarks are
quite suggestive in this regard, for he here tells us that his initial intent had been
to survey only Gerson's mystical teachings, »as in some cloistered nook,
engrossed only with teachings on the Way to Perfection,« only to discover that
»the mysticism that we wished to study had been organized as a remedy; it
came as the high point of a whole programme for reform.«[42] Despite the
obvious historiographical limitations of this study, this is a perceptive insight,
though apparently for reasons he had not fully envisioned, since Connolly
rightly recognizes that Gerson evaluated *theologia mystica* in terms of its
functional usefulness to the church as a whole, and by offering it as a
»programme for reform,« criticized forms of mysticism which resulted in
quietism. What remains to be said, however, is that this is true not only
regarding the earlier treatises devoted specifically to mystical theology, but
with reference to the later texts as well. *De consolatione theologiae* is no exception
to this: while not a text focused upon mysticism per se, this treatise does
approach *theologia mystica* as the »summit« of theology toward which all *viatores*
aspire, interpreting mysticism as a vital part of the reform initiative. In general
terms, however, Connolly's work tells us as much about the strained
atmosphere in which Roman Catholic historians labored during the early part
of this century as about Gerson's work, and offers no notable insight into the
later stages of the chancellor's oeuvre.[43]

---

[41] In this regard he dismisses *De consolatione theologiae* as »either the fruit of a nervous
crisis or [a text] meant to dispel such.« *Ibid.*, p. 363.

[42] Connolly, *John Gerson*, p. 381.

[43] In this sense, the confessional bias of Connolly's work seems to dominate his
orientation, not toward fifteenth-century nominalism in general which he is willing to
dismiss as essentially heterodox, but toward Gerson's work which he is intent on absolving
from any incriminating association with Luther. His position must be interpreted within

Finally, we must consider several of the myriad writings of André Combes, particularly because he stands as the single Gerson scholar to devote any sustained discussion to this treatise. Here we must turn first to an early essay devoted specifically to this text[44] and subsequently examine the pertinent section of his later *La théologie mystique de Gerson. Profil de son évolution.*[45] In the earlier essay, published in the wake of a distinguished series of studies devoted to Gerson's mystical writings, we find surprisingly little more than a detailed paraphrase of the text itself bracketed by general comments of comparison to Boethius' exemplar. Gerson's treatise is, he argues, »a work which is at once both radically new and deliberately traditional,«[46] though his reference never strays beyond these particular texts. Perhaps as a consequence of this narrow approach, what Combes here cites as both »traditional« and »original« avoids any regard either for the broader literary genre of medieval commentaries on Boethius and above all the manner in which Gerson's own contemporaries read this »last Roman,«[47] or the critical question of how this text reflects the complex historical and theological scene contemporaneous with Gerson.[48] In this sense, the principal shortcoming of his analysis lies not in what he has said,

---

the polemic horizon of Reformation research in the early decades of this century. Following the strident attack upon Luther's orthodoxy advanced by Grisar and Denifle (cf. *Luther*, 3 Vols. [Freiburg i.B., 1911−12] and *Luther et lutheranisme*, 3 vols. [Paris, 1913−16], respectively), A. V. Müller offered a Lutheran counter-attack in his *Luthers Werdegang bis zum Turmerlebnis, neu untersucht* (Gotha, 1920). It is in the wake of this specific historical debate and in the general atmosphere of the anti-modernist campaign that Connolly's study of Gerson must be interpreted. Thus, for instance, he intends the piece to offer a useful spiritual guide for »a troubled world,« drawing »applications of [Gerson's] wisdom to the needs of an age that is groping to find a path to a world, cut off by the dictums of materialistic Philosophy and the pretensions of false Science«; Connolly, *Jean Gerson,* pp. 356−64, 381, 390−92.

[44] See »La consolation de la théologie d'après Gerson,« *Pensée catholique* 14 (1960), pp. 8−26.

[45] See especially 2:304−66 (Rome, 1964), pp. 304−66.

[46] »La Consolation,« p. 9. What he apparently intends by this is to link Gerson (the »new«) and Boethius (the »traditional«), but in a manner which emphasizes the quite unexpected freedom Gerson assumes vis-à-vis the medieval literary tradition surrounding Boethius' *Consolatio philosophiae*; the later work is »à l'imitation de Boèce, sur le type même de sa *Consolatio* mais de façon très originale.« *Ibid.,* p. 10. With this insight Combes anticipates Dresden's general thesis about the Renaissance use of classical texts; see Dresden, »Profile,« pp. 145−46.

[47] This phrase derives from Martin Grabmann, *Die Geschichte der scholastischen Methode,* Vol. I: *Die scholastische Methode von ihren ersten Anfängen in der Väterliteratur bis zum Beginn des 12. Jahrhunderts* (Freiburg i. B., 1909), pp. 148ff., where he describes Boethius as »der letzte Römer, der erste Scholastiker.«

[48] This omission causes much of Combes's discussion to remain focused mainly on the text's surface, exploring themes within the treatise in contrast to Boethius' prototype. He does, however, contend that despite the obvious textual similarities between the two *consolationes* there remains a »formal difference« between the two, arguing that Gerson's

which is little enough, but in what remains to be said — a weakness of omission, as it were. When he does stray beyond this rigid textual comparison he insists on reading the text principally in terms of its mystical teaching, thereby pressing it to fit his general interest in Gerson; any discussion of other theological themes set within a broader contextual basis is noticeably absent. Hence, »La Consolation« provides little direction for anything other than a rather narrow reading of the text alongside Boethius' original.[49]

In Combes's subsequent comprehensive study of Gerson, *La théologie mystique de Gerson. Profil de son évolution* (Rome, 1964), we find a more vigorous interpretation and in many respects a more penetrating analysis of this text. In the lengthy discussion here devoted to *De consolatione theologiae*, Combes presents a narrative tapestry of sorts, a portrait of this text which weaves together threads of a biographical nature with strands of Gerson's argument set within the context of his broader oeuvre. This is a clear advance upon his earlier discussion, though Combes continues to evaluate this text principally as an index to Gerson's *théologie mystique*. Yet from this vantage point, Combes's analysis makes a breakthrough not seen by other interpreters, earlier or later. Here he acknowledges that this text stands as a turning point for Gerson, not precisely as a »crisis of mysticism,«[50] but rather as a more strident criticism of

---

text »ne s'agit ni de dialectique ni de conversion. Ici, c'est seulement à la fin que la Théologie intervient en personne, et sa tâche est tout autre que celle de la Philosophie. Gerson lui même ne paraît pas directement. Les interlocuteurs ne sont pas les personnages pris par l'épreuve et, par contre coup, objets de consolation. Ce sont des témoins d'une réalité déjà acquise, à savoir l'état d'âme de l'éxile. C'est une âme déjà consolée. L'oeuvre n'a plus pour raison d'être de décrire, ou plutôt de procurer l'illumination progressive d'une âme qui passerait de la désolation à la paix et à la joie. Elle n'est rien d'autre que l'inventaire des ressources propres à une âme déjà enrichie de la foi chrétienne, et qui vit de sa foi.« *La Consolation*, pp. 11–12. In *La théologie mystique* Combes retracts several aspects of this early discussion, admitting that this essay exposed him as the »victime d'une analyse trop rapide. . . .« *Ibid.*, 2:364, n. 182. But he did not retract this broad theme, and repeated his insistence that Gerson's text offered »no conversion« in almost exact form in his later *La théologie mystique*, 2:317: »Du côté de Gerson, la situation est tout autre. Sans doute, pour lui aussi, il s'agit de construire un dialogue, mais un dialogue qui ne vise aucune conversion . . .« etc. We shall subsequently call this conclusion into question, since the entire dialogue brings the skeptical Monicus to an affirmation — through a conversion of perspective — of *consolatio theologiae*; see below, Ch. 2.

[49] Burger rightly criticizes Combes's style on this point, commenting that despite the »imposantes Bild« which Combes provides for us, the reader nonetheless »kann aber nicht sicher sein, zu welchem Teil es in Gersonschen Texten verankert ist und wieviel davon er der selbstbewußten Interpretation Combes' zu verdanken hat.« *Aedificatio*, p. 17. In the case of the present article, most of the »discussion« is actually a mere paraphrase of the original text itself, though even this point is not borne out in the accompanying notes which Combes provides.

[50] Cf. *La théologie mystique*, 2:339–42.

any conceptualization of mysticism as »a total passivity.«[51] *De consolatione theologiae* is not, however, a treatise addressing the question of mystical theology in any strict or sustained fashion; indeed, Combes concedes with rhetorical force bordering on hyperbole that this treatise »is not mystical« at all, not at least in terms familiar to readers of Gerson's earlier works.[52] Rather, he contends that the treatise offers a two-fold critique, directed toward any theology content to be either mystical or speculative; that is, he opposes, on the one extreme, any mysticism which so emphasizes *absorptio* that it neglects altogether any attentiveness to *charitas*, while countering, on the other, any speculative theology devoted to an abstract knowledge and thus devoid of an affective dimension. Thus, although Combes's discussion does not yet place this text squarely within the complex horizon of late-medieval theology, it does represent a considerable advance upon his earlier article and serves to correct Daniel-Rops's dismissive assessment of the piece.[53]

But Combes is clearly at his best, and penetrates more deeply into the heart of this treatise, when he observes here that the treatise is »a preparation,« and as

---

[51] *Ibid.*, p. 349; see also pp. 162–64, »Passivité et activité mystiques.«

[52] As he here argues in considerable detail, and with characteristic rhetorical flourish, this work »ne décrit pas l'union mystique. Il n'en évoque ni les douceurs ni l'amertume. Il n'en élabore pas la théorie. Qui plus est, ce qu'il ne fait pas, il ne veut pas le faire. C'est très déliberément, et de toute la force de sa structure même, qu'il refuse l'épithete qu'on a voulu lui attribuer. Contrairement à ce qu'a pu penser l'historien qui a réduit à cette oeuvre l'héritage gersonien méritant, à son sens, ›de survivre‹, ce dialogue n'est à aucun degré un ›dialogue mystique‹, mais un dialogue très humain, volontairement limité a l'ordre de la raison. Ce refus, à un tel moment, est, nous le verrons, éminemment caractéristique de Gerson. ... Le *De consolatione theologiae* est un oeuvre rationnelle, et même, dirais-je volontiers, puissamment rationnelle.« *Ibid.*, 2:305–306. This final claim, exaggerated to say the least, appears to bolster Combes's well-intended but ultimately ill-grounded attempt to describe Gerson in terms of »the birth of humanism«; see *idem*, »Gerson et la naissance de l'humanisme: Note sur les rapports de l'histoire doctrinale et de l'histoire littéraire,« *Revue du moyen-âge latin*, 1 (1945): 259–84. In this essay, Combes rightly argues that Gerson cannot be adequately portrayed as hostile to classical letters, but his claim that he speaks as »en humaniste plus humaniste que l'humaniste lui-même« belongs in the realm of hyperbole; *ibid.*, p. 267. But to return to *La théologie mystique*: when Combes continues his introductory remarks regarding *De consolatione theologiae* by asserting that »c'est une réflexion méthodique sur une expérience,« one is by no means prepared for his subsequent conclusion that »c'est une psychanalyse.« Here, as in his earlier essay, his analysis suffers from his penchant at convincing the reader of Gerson's relevance for the modern age; his conclusion to »La Consolation,« set forth in an abrupt argument *ad hominem*, claims that »la leçon n'a rien perdu de son actualité« (p. 267), a conclusion which might well be true but which he has not established on the basis of any substantial *historical* analysis.

[53] Cf. *L'Eglise de la renaissance et la reforme* (Paris, 1955), 1:168: »Le seul livre de lui [i. e., Gerson] qui mérite de survivre est son dialogue mystique sur la *Consolation par la theologie*. Mais il est encore écrit en marge de Boèce.« Cited by Combes, *La théologie mystique*, 2:305, n. 5. Needless to say, this is hardly a flattering review, nor one which demonstrates a significantly critical appreciation of Gerson, to say nothing for the moment of his theological contribution to the early fifteenth-century horizon.

such is not a speculative work but a quite practical guide to the *itinerarium in Deum*, »a spiritual guide which occupies itself with truth only in order to attain a more elevated degree of love. «[54] This is no new Gersonian theme, of course, but it does properly recognize what we shall call the »paideutic« nature of this treatise: the text designates the function of *theologia* in terms of character formation, such that his primary concern settles not upon the reform of theology per se but upon the reform of the *viator*. Furthermore, and more importantly, Combes advances beyond his earlier analysis of this treatise — and here he stands alone among Gerson interpreters — by suggesting that *De consolatione theologiae* reveals a decisive shift in Gerson's thought: the exiled chancellor here conceives the human »journey« *ad Deum* not primarily in mystical terms as a pathway toward ecstasy, but as the road to martyrdom.[55] And this, Combes here argues somewhat tentatively, signals a distinct development in Gerson's thought, or so he initially suggests. As his argument progresses it becomes clear that he is unwilling to concede quite this much, concluding with greater reserve that while Gerson had been extremely troubled because of the ordeal he had undergone at Constance, *De consolatione theologiae* instructs us only with regard to »the state of his mind« and leaves us »exceedingly ignorant regarding the state of his thought. «[56] But is this really the case? A closer analysis of this treatise than Combes provides, and one which sets Gerson's decidedly original treatment of *doctrina* within the broader horizon of late medieval scholasticism, suggests a quite different conclusion: the theological shift which Combes suggests occurred only at the end of Gerson's life (ca. 1425) as part of a personal conversion is already essentially intact in this treatise of 1418. Indeed, the shift even at this earlier stage represents a much more ambitious development of fundamental theological themes than Combes had suspected, a point which will become particularly clear when we read *De consolatione theologiae* within the historical context of the recently concluded Council of Constance.[57] Hence, although Combes's

---

[54] *Ibid.*, 2:343–44.

[55] As he phrases it, the *viator* »n'est donc pas sauvé par la mystique, mais par l'ascèse. Ce chemin ne conduit pas à l'extase, mais au martyre. « *Ibid.*, 2:364. Combes does not develop this theme, however, and nowhere suggests how this theme functions within the thematic structure of the treatise more generally; it would appear that this emphasis is part of his anti-Hussite polemic, which becomes a sustained if discrete polemic in the final books of the text. For a detailed analysis of this question, see below, Ch. 6.

[56] *Ibid.*, 2:364–66. Later in the same study, Combes suggests with less hesitation that the real shift in Gerson's thought, a development in which the still exiled chancellor abandoned the doctrine of *synderesis* in favor of a more thorough-going emphasis upon divine grace, occurs in the final years of his life (i. e., from 1425). He even suggests in this discussion that Gerson offers at this late juncture »a Thomist doctrine of grace, « a point which might well be made in terms of the earlier treatise, *De consolatione theologiae*; see *ibid.*, 2:465 ff., 557–68.

[57] This is no small point, and herein lies the weakness of Combes's analysis: although he

analysis in *La théologie mystique* does not yet grasp the full significance of this treatise, his work nonetheless serves an important function by pointing to decisive theological shifts in the later Gerson, a development which a closer contextual study of *De consolatione theologiae* delineates already as early as Gerson's departure from Constance.

This survey of previous Gerson research suggests, therefore, that another chapter still needs to be written, and it is precisely this need which the present study undertakes to fulfill. The later Gerson remains a subject of considerable significance, not only for a more critical appreciation of the decisive development in his own thought, but for a more nuanced perspective than is presently available of the complex horizon of theological thought and religious life during the early fifteenth century. It should be equally evident from the preceding discussion that this is largely unexplored or hastily charted territory. While the early studies — above all those of Schwab, Connolly, and even Combes — did not yet penetrate beyond the surface in interpreting the later Gerson, and particularly his major treatise *De consolatione theologiae*, more recent contributions have either ignored this period of Gerson's work or have blended it without hesitation or discretion into his thought as a whole, assuming apparently that the elder churchman would not have deviated from his earlier positions. Combes's studies should have suggested the danger of this assumption. Indeed, we have drawn upon them in considerable detail for this reason, for we find in Combes's magisterial study, *La théologie mystique*, an announcement of the shifts in Gerson's later works which has remained without answer in the subsequent scholarship. For this reason Combes's work remains quite useful as an initial guidepost, even if we shall have to rework the basic design of his analysis and move beyond his cautious and ultimately insufficient thesis.

To accomplish this reorientation with requisite academic *discretio*, we shall of course utilize, where pertinent, earlier studies devoted to Gerson's thought. The focus of this study, however, is on the treatise *De consolatione theologiae* as a watershed marking a new departure from his earlier, and a decisive pointer toward his later, writings. By focusing upon this text in particular and subjecting this treatise to a detailed, critical reading, we begin to perceive a quite different Gerson than previous studies have disclosed: *doctor consolatorius*, as he came to be called later in his century, offers a view of consolation and a

---

begins his discussion of this text by speaking of the traumatic impact of the council upon Gerson, arguing that »*De consolatione theologiae* nous oblige donc à penser que l'épreuve de Constance a bouleversé Gerson de façon beaucoup plus radicale qu'on ne le croyait jusqu'ici,« his analysis has ignored this particular context almost completely. Absent in Combes's treatment is any mention of the Hussite controversy, a theme Gerson apparently intended — admittedly, in a veiled manner — much of this treatise to address; see below, Ch. 6.

revised model of the covenant which become the very foundation of his larger
program of reform, ecclesiastical and theological, a »patient« reform as we shall
suggest which Gerson roots within the Dionysian structure and dynamics of
his ecclesiology. It should thus be evident that a reorientation to Gerson's
thought, particularly with regard to his later works, can no longer be post-
poned; it should be equally clear that this approach to Gerson will contribute
not only to the perspective of Gerson specialists, but also to our appreciation of
his thought as a *speculum* of his age more generally, to recall Delaruelle's metaphor, a mirror reflecting the play of images from the recently concluded Council of Constance as indeed from the wider horizon of fifteenth-century religious
thought and ecclesiastical life.

Chapter II

De Consolatione Theologiae:
An Introduction to the Text as Literature

And just as [Gerson] imitated Boethius' *Consolation of Philosophy* in the literary form of the work, so he tried also to continue the argument regarding consolation from the point where that author left off.[1]

With these words of preface, the Du Pin edition of Gerson's *De consolatione theologiae* introduces the reader to the problematic lying at the foundation of the treatise. This explanatory note alerts us to Gerson's intention in writing his »consolation,« yet it suggests more than this: this claim goes to the very heart of his constructive view of how theology functions — and of the nature of philosophy as propaedeutic for this task — in directing the »pilgrim«[2] through life. This initial vantage point already tells us much about Gerson's grasp of the theological task, and of its intended »audience.« That is, we see that Gerson measures both philosophy and theology here — against the tide of strictly

---

[1] »Et sicuti Boetium *De consolatione philosophiae* in forma scribendi imitatur, ita etiam consolationis argumentum ubi ille dimisit, hic continuare conatur.« So reads the concluding remark of the editor's *monitum*, or explanatory note, at the outset of the Du Pin edition (Antwerp, 1706), I: 129B. Indeed, this claim echoes Gerson's own point, expressed in a key debate between his interlocutors (I pr. 2), where Monicus wonders aloud why »Philosophy's famous dialogue with Boethius [would not] suffice?« Volucer's careful response, which we shall examine in greater detail below (4.B.2), argues that »theology begins her consolation of the pilgrim from the vantage point of that wisdom set forth by philosophy.« In the earlier Köln incunabulum (1471), we find another editor's introduction which paraphrases this argument in order to introduce Gerson's text squarely within the bounds of the Boethian literary tradition.

[2] Gerson speaks throughout this treatise, apparently without intended distinction, of the human person variously as *peregrinus, viator,* and *advena.* What is of significance in this designation, as we shall see, is his reluctance to distinguish priests or monks from laity, since all finally were *in via* and shared a common destination *in Deum.* This is a thematic concern already evidenced in his earlier mystical writings and in his defense at Constance of the Brethren of the Common Life, and one which would later acquire the force of a »programmatic« emphasis within the broad phenomenon known as *devotio moderna.* On the former point, see Burger, *Aedificatio,* pp. 159–60; on the latter, see Oberman, *Masters of the Reformation. The Emergence of a New Intellectual Climate in Europe,* trans. Dennis Martin (Cambridge, 1981), pp. 62–63.

academic circles, particularly those following in the Scotist tradition whom he refers to disparagingly as *formalizantes* – not primarily as professional fields requiring specialized training and the acquisition of an esoteric vocabulary, but as common interpretive tools accessible to every *viator*.[3] Everyone needs consolation in the pilgrimage *ad Deum*, and *theologia* is particularly well-suited for this task through its reliance upon scriptural instruction, a medium of instruction accessible not only to those tutored in scholastic theology but to all *peregrini*. In a word, theology alone is able to offer the hope which every pilgrim needs because she alone offers, *per scripturam*, a vision of »the way« to God. In what might initially appear to be a startling claim for a university chancellor to make, Gerson here reminds his reader that the audience places the burden of performance upon theology, rather than vice versa.

But who, then, is *peregrinus* of this dialogue? If we would take Gerson at his word, and this is clearly the wisest starting point in answering such an apparently straightforward question, we must first say that this pilgrim is none other than the author himself, one who became »like an exile in an unknown and distant region where he hears a language he does not know.« In this sense the text is never far from autobiography, standing as a peculiar dialogical narrative through which Gerson offers glimpses of his own plight and comments, often in an oblique way, on the recent events which transpired at the Council of Constance and in his native France. One of the two main interlocutors of the dialogue (Volucer) reports to the other (Monicus) that he had been at Constance »for the General Council,« whereupon his listener inquires after information concerning this *peregrinus*, described in intimate terms as »the favorite of my soul, the love of my heart.« Moreover, Gerson presents this pilgrim with what is an only slightly veiled autobiographical reference in the imagery of key biblical figures: he interprets his own situation through the prophetic archetype of Jeremiah who lamented the desolation of Jerusalem, and in the posture of Mary who »rejoiced in the Lord« and magnified God through her spirit.[4] In the first instance, then, Gerson himself is *advena*, the pilgrim interpreted according to biblical models whose fate it was to wander in exile from his native land after the council's close.

---

[3] Gerson carries this theme even further late in this treatise, arguing that »the spirit of catholic judgment« might finally lie with the simple but pious Christians (*simplices* or *idiotae*), rather than with the educated but too often morally corrupt among the theologians; see also below, 4. C. 1,3. On Gerson's approach to *les simples gens*, see Brown, *Pastor and Laity*, p. 1, 257 (n. 2). For a thorough discussion of his indictment of the *Formalizantes*, see Zénon Kaluza, *Les querelles doctrinales à Paris. Nominalistes et realistes aux confins du XIVe et du XVe siècles* (Bergamo, 1988), pp. 35–86.

[4] Cf. I pr. 1 (G 9, p. 186): ». . . gaudet potius in Domino, magnificans eum, et exultat spiritus ejus in Deo salutari suo. . . . Miserabilem denique Civitatis celeberrimae desolationem (tanquam Jeremias ruinas Jerusalem) lamentatur. «

But such an answer to this question of the pilgrim's identity, as unambiguous as it at first appears, does not yet penetrate beneath the surface of the matter. As the text unfolds we quite quickly realize that *peregrinus* functions not merely on an autobiographical level, but rather more broadly as the representative of every human person. *Homo viator* stands on the level of personal narrative as one who must »bear calmly everything that has happened« at the recent council, but this self-portrait is only Gerson's point of departure as an author: on a deeper level *peregrinus* is the prototype of every person who like Gerson must face life's vicissitudes. In a word, he is »everyman.« The literary precedent for this is not difficult to discern. Just as Boethius had described the prisoner's »remedy« in figurative language as a return from self-imposed exile to the *patria*, or homeland,[5] and had thereby defined the human predicament in universal terms, so also does Gerson's »wanderer« come to exemplify the person in general, an exile in this life whose plight he envisions with that most medieval of metaphors, viz. the pilgrimage.[6]

---

[5] This is no invented theme, but rather a conventional literary topos, an image which structures Boethius' text as the orientation of human life: »But how far from your homeland [*a patria*] have you strayed!« he argues, adding that »you must remember what your native country is« (cf. I pr. 5, *CCSL* 94:13); characterizing the human condition in general terms, he argues that »because you are wandering, forgetful of your real self, you grieve that you are an exile« (I pr. 6, *CCSL* 94:15); at a midpoint of the treatise Lady Philosophy suggests that »there is only a little more left for me to do for you to come back to your homeland [*patriam*] safely, capable of grasping happiness« (III pr. 12, *CCSL* 94:60); later she adds that »I shall afix to your mind wings, whereby it may raise itself aloft, so that with all disturbance dispelled, you may return safely to your homeland [*in patriam*], under my guidance, on my path, and in my carriage« (IV pr. 1, *CCSL* 94:65); and, finally, she concludes that »I am hastening ... to make good my promise and open the way to you by which you may be brought back to your homeland« (V pr. 1, *CCSL* 94:88). Boethius does not, of course, refer to his »prisoner« as *peregrinus*; his language settles more consistently on the epithet »exile« (*exul*) — a descriptive word which Gerson also applies to himself in *De consolatione theologiae* — and language expanding upon the medical imagery he so frequently uses.

[6] This theme derives in large measure from biblical language as well as from the medieval imagery found throughout its literature which described human life as penultimate, a temporary »wandering« to be lived amidst shadows and fractured glimpses of a vision to be fully manifest only after death. In this regard, several biblical passages played a prominent role in shaping theological anthropology, particularly the Old Testament references to the Israelites wandering in the wilderness (Ex. 12ff.) and, in the New Testament, Heb. 11.13 (»quia peregrini, et hospites sunt super terram«) and 1 Cor. 13.12 (»Videmus nunc per speculum in aenigmate; tunc autem facie ad faciem«). By the fifteenth century *peregrinus* had become a commonplace for describing human beings. The theme also reflects Gerson's use of neo-Platonic imagery, particularly his preference to speak of all reality in terms of the cycle of *processus a Deo* and *regressus in Deum*; for a discussion of this theme, see below, 6. B. 4. In more general terms, Evelyn Underhill has suggested that the pilgrimage motif came to represent in medieval literature »a transparent allegory« of our progress »from the unreal to the real,« providing »an image as concrete and practical, as remote from the romantic and picturesque, for the medieval writers who used it, as a symbolism of hotel and railway train would be to us.« See *Mysticism. A Study in the Nature and Development of Man's*

With this metaphor before us, we begin to see Gerson's broad intention in presenting this treatise not merely as a technically demanding piece with a theological or literary readership in mind nor as an ad hoc text focusing upon some disputed question or ecclesiastical problem. This is rather a text with a broader and more general purpose, intended to serve as a handbook for life, an *enchiridion* for all *viatores* seeking guidance and consolation for their life's journey. Considered from this vantage point, we also discern a clue as to why Gerson chose the dialogue form for this text: aside from the obvious pattern set by Boethius' treatise, this literary genre offered him a useful device which exchanged academic prose for popular idioms and cast abstract problems debated in the schools into the more generally accessible language of conversation. It was, moreover, a literary form quite well adapted to the comprehensive, if also decidedly unsystematic, scope of his thought here;[7] the conversation ranges quite freely across a wide spectrum of topics, moving forward through the device of Monicus' relentless interrogation and frequent cross-examination of his counterpart. All of this is to say that he has here embraced a form particularly suited to his readership and to his subject matter, since the vivid and colloquial dialogue we find here seems quite well disposed »to insinuate the truth into the lives of the crowd,« to recall one historian's characterization of Gerson's general rhetorical tactic.[8] It is expansive in scope, though by no means systematic in the ordered form of a *summa*, as we have earlier suggested. More specifically, the Boethian precedent upon which this treatise draws placed Gerson's thought within the orbit of a broad and resilient

---

Spiritual Consciousness (New York, 1911), pp. 129–30. Gerson utilizes the metaphor with just this emphasis, fusing throughout this treatise the theoretical and practical dimensions of this image.

[7] Anne Crabbe has pointed to this stylistic feature in Boethius' *Consolatio*, noting that his range was »comprehensive rather than divisive«; see »Literary Design in the *De consolatione philosophiae*,« in *Boethius. His Life, Thought, and Influence*, ed. Margaret Gibson (Oxford, 1981), p. 240.

[8] Cf. Connolly, *John Gerson*, p. 119. Of course, Gerson was not in any sense original in this; it was quite conventional during this period to choose this form. On this development within the broader horizon of the quattrocento Renaissance, cf. Bouwsma, »The Two Faces,« p. 17; cf. also, Trinkaus, *In Our Image and Likeness*, 1:307. Both Bouwsma and Trinkaus suggest that the rise of dialogue had to do with the resurgence of classical forms of rhetoric. Bouwsma goes further to suggest that the rise of Stoicism during this period, as one of the »faces« of fifteenth-century humanism, had to do in part with a stylistic question, viz. the »graceful and unsystematic form of the sources in which it was chiefly available,« including of course dialogues, and thus provided »an alternative to scholastic habits of thought« (»The Two Faces,« p. 17). Both of these points are useful in suggesting why Gerson chose this particular literary form for his purposes. In terms of the former, however, we must also point out that we find explicit references in this text not to classical models of the dialogue, though he apparently reads Boethius in this vein, but to the early Augustine's use of this form in his *Soliloquies* (i. e., Bouwsma's »other face« of humanism); for a detailed discussion of the latter, see below, 3. B. 4.

literary tradition, one which had dominated the educational curriculum of medieval society and was still very much in circulation during his lifetime. Within the wide trajectory of this textual tradition with its well-established thematic emphases and arguments, Boethius' text became a fitting point of departure upon which Gerson launched his own theological argument. In other words, by crafting his »consolation« within a literary trajectory of such magnitude, Gerson's discussion of particular questions acquires, to those familiar with the Boethian textual tradition, a profound depth and complexity of character.

The question of the literary focus of this text, and the universal role played by *peregrinus*, reminds us of a theme found already earlier in Gerson's writings: namely, his attack upon the long-debated medieval presumption that the monastic life alone could lead to perfection. This contention had prompted his writing of *De consiliis evangelicis et statu perfectionis* (ca. 1400), a *quaestio determinata* in which he had argued, against the presumption of contemporary mendicants and a deeply engrained monastic tradition, that *all* persons regardless of the question of religious vows could seek after perfection — the *vita apostolica*,[9] to recall the terminology used since the disputes surfacing late in the eleventh century.[10] Yet this theme, which Gerson early applied as a specific

[9] On this question, see E. W. McDonnell, »The *Vita apostolica*: Diversity or Dissent?« *Church History* 24 (1955), pp. 15–31; also, see E. Werner, *Pauperes Christi: Studien zur sozial-religiösen Bewegungen im Zeitalter des Reformpapsttums* (Leipzig, 1956).
[10] Cf. G 3, pp. 10–26; Glorieux dates this work before 1401. In this treatise Gerson argued that although the *consilia evangelica* offered useful *instrumenta* to attain perfection, these were by no means necessary: »Et ita patet etsi consilia evangelica plurimum expediant et valeant ad perfectionem vitae spiritalis conquirendam, non tamen necessario requiruntur ad eam, *quoniam in omni statu, sexu, ordine, gradu, perfecti viri inventi sunt.*« *Ibid.*, pp. 15, 20 (my emphasis); for a detailed discussion of the medieval usage of *ordo* and *status*, see M.-D. Chenu, *La théologie au XIIᵉ siècle* (Paris, 1957), pp. 241–43. This particular argument Gerson aimed at those who presumed that the monastic life was more perfect than that of secular priests, but clearly the implications of his defense range further than this question. Luise Abramowski offers an extensive discussion of this treatise in her essay, »*De consiliis evangelicis et statu perfectionis,*« in *Studien zur Geschichte und Theologie der Reformation: Festschrift für Ernst Bizer* (Neukirchen, 1969), pp. 63–78. These implications came to the surface again and again in Gerson's later thought. Thus, for example, during the decades following the writing of this treatise, Gerson opposed any narrow monastic definition of *religio*, arguing against the Dominican, Matthew Grabow, who opposed the validity of such religious movements as the Brothers and Sisters of the Common Life. On this point, see Gerson's *Contra conclusiones Matthaei Graben* (April, 1418), G 10, pp. 70–72; texts related to this controversy, including Grabow's *Conclusiones et Articuli* and later *Revocatio et abjuratio* as well as Pierre d'Ailly's response, are included in the Du Pin edition (see Vol. I, pp. 467 ff.). This remained a constant concern of Gerson's throughout his life; after the Council of Constance (ca. 1422), he addressed himself to this theme once again in *De perfectione cordis*, here echoing the thesis he had stated against Grabow's conclusions (see G 10, p. 70, *propositio* 3a). His argument here is as impressive for its sheer simplicity as for its rhetorical force: recounting the decision against Grabow of the *doctores theologi*, he argued

counter-argument against what he viewed as a presumptuous and faulty ennoblement of the monastic life over against that of the secular clergy, receives an even broader interpretation later in his career: here we find the same theme loosed from the narrower professional question of the relative status of the secular and religious vocations, and applied to the nature and status of the Christian life more generally.[11] Indeed, on the basis of this aspect of the treatise it is proper to delineate within the broad scope of Gerson's later writings a »democratization« not only of mysticism, as Oberman has argued with regard to the later work of Gabriel Biel, but of the »religious« life (i. e., *religio Christiana*) itself.[12] This claim may sound peculiar from a modern vantage point, but when we set it within the framework of the early fifteenth-century church and the hierarchical ecclesiology which dominated not only Gerson's thought but that of conciliar theologians more generally, we begin to see the progressive force of his perspective. Gerson's *viator* is nowhere burdened with the obligations of academic degrees or ecclesiastical vows; indeed, *viator* represents »everyman,« not however in the quest for ecclesiastical (i. e., hierarchical) status in order to live a truly »religious« life, but in the universal

---

that neither Christ, nor the apostles and disciples, nor the virgin Mary, nor the Christians in *ecclesia primitiva* had taken religious vows, and yet these were surely »perfect.« On the basis of this reasoning, he concluded that all people owed obedience to »Christ, the supreme abbot,« regardless of who it was standing directly above them within the ecclesiastical hierarchy of authorities. See G 8, p. 118 ff.; for a discussion of this theme, see Burger, *Aedificatio*, pp. 159, 182−83, and Brown, *Pastor and Laity*, pp. 46−48.

[11] See especially his propositions 1−4, which he advanced against the conclusions of Matthew Grabow; *Contra Conclusiones Matthei Graben*, G 10, p. 70. The terminology *religio christiana* which Gerson here uses captures the terms of this debate, since the Brothers and Sisters of the Common Life interpreted *religio* to include alongside those bound by monastic vows other forms of Christian life ordered by resolutions and intentions. On this point, see John van Engen, »Introduction,« in *Devotio Moderna. Basic Writings*, trans. and intro. John van Engen (New York and Mahwah, NJ, 1988), pp. 14 f. and 29.

[12] See above, n. 10. Oberman first suggests this thesis in one of his early studies of Gabriel Biel, »Gabriel Biel and Late Medieval Mysticism,«, pp. 268−69. In his later works he returned to this point, identifying this »democratization of mysticism« as one of Biel's unique contributions; see *Harvest*, pp. 341 ff., and *Werden und Wertung*, p. 68, n. 39. On the basis of my reading of Gerson's later writings, and particularly those of the Constance period, this emerges as a fundamental theme; if this is correct, then we must interpret Biel here too as following »in the footsteps of Gerson,« to recall Oberman's apt characterization (*Harvest*, p. 340), particularly in terms of the conceptualization of mysticism found within the writing of the Parisian chancellor after Constance. In these post-conciliar texts, as we shall subsequently argue in greater detail, we still discern Gerson's abiding concern with mystical theology, though he here expresses it in terms accessible to a broader audience. This thesis would explain why Combes finds it so difficult to see in this treatise anything resembling the mysticism of the earlier Gerson. The point Combes rightly makes is that *De consolatione theologiae* presents an approach to this theme quite different from his earlier mystical treatises; what he fails to see, however, is that Gerson has not here abandoned mysticism per se, but interprets *theologia mystica* as an avenue accessible to *all* Christians. See below, 4. C. 3.

pilgrimage toward God. In this sense Gerson defines his audience in theory at least without qualification, such that *theologia* itself becomes the »way« to God, the path of the pilgrim accessible to *all* Christians — professed or »religious« and lay, educated and simple. Every *viator* becomes in this sense »religious.« Against the esoteric tendencies of the scholasticism of his day, which the chancellor had earlier criticized for holding theology captive to unedifying subtleties and useless abstractions,[13] Gerson here goes further by »democratizing« theology itself, an accomplishment which as we shall see becomes a »de-professionalizing« of it as well.

Yet this concern demonstrates another, hitherto neglected facet of Gerson's thought. Giles Constable, following the lead of Augustin Renaudet, has argued persuasively that Gerson must be understood as an »heir of St. Bernard and the Victorines,« and that this twelfth-century spirituality established above all through the writings of Gerson and Pierre d'Ailly a continuity between these ages.[14] But this realization obscures a vital modulation of this thematic continuity, for Gerson's use of Bernard's spirituality occurs in the midst of a significant disjunction of audience. Gerson writes for all *peregrini*, not merely for the *periti* destined for a monastic (or, for that matter, secular) vocation in the church, the *status perfectionis* of which he had earlier written. Here he has deliberately removed this monastic spirituality from any explicit religious profession, and set it rather within the framework of the pious life available to all persons. Not the continuities of theme but the intentional broadening of

---

[13] In his *Contra curiositatem studentium*, a series of lectures delivered before a university audience in 1402, Gerson had identified curiosity and singularity as the two leading threats to the state of theological teaching in his day. *Curiositas* he here defined as the »vitium quo dimissis utilioribus homo convertit studium suum ad minus utilia vel inattingibilia sibi vel noxia,« calling *singularitas* »vitium quo dimissis utilioribus homo convertit studium suum ad doctrinas peregrinas et insolitas.« He added that »although by reason of their different subjects their faces are distinguished by various individual features, curiosity and singularity as is the custom with sisters are alike in many ways. Each is guilty of forsaking the more useful things . . ... Curiosity does it in order to know what is improper; singularity in order to excel over others.« For this translation and the accompanying Latin text, see *Jean Gerson. Selections from ›A Deo exivit‹, ›Contra curiositatem studentium‹, and ›De mystica theologia speculativa‹*, trans. and ed. Steven Ozment (Leiden, 1969), pp. 28–29. On the broader history of the theme *contra curiositatem* in Christian thought, cf. Oberman, *›Contra vanam curiositatem‹. Ein Kapitel der Theologie zwischen Seelenwinkel und Weltall. Theologische Studien* 113 (Zürich, 1974), and the opening chapter of E. P. Meijering, *Calvin wider die Neugierde. Ein Beitrag zum Vergleich zwischen reformatorischem und patristischem Denken* (Nieuwkoop, 1980).

[14] See Giles Constable, »Twelfth Century Spirituality and the Late Middle Ages,« *Medieval and Renaissance Studies. Proceedings of the Southeastern Institute of Medieval and Renaissance Studies: Summer, 1969*, ed. O. B. Hardison, Jr. (Chapel Hill, 1971), pp. 32, 43, 50. Constable intends here, in agreement with André Wilmart and against Émile Male, to establish a continuity of »feelings« and »an affinity of religious temperament« between the twelfth and fifteenth centuries.

audience is what is so impressive about the nature of Gerson's dependence upon his twelfth-century predecessors; indeed, this is the fundamental characteristic distinguishing the essentially differing shape of his anthropology from that of his monastic predecessor.[15] For Gerson transforms what might be called a strictly »professional« spirituality linked with a religious vocation into more comprehensive terms, transposing Cistercian piety into broader cadences accessible to *all* pilgrims. Thematic continuities, deliberately modified by being addressed to a universal audience, in this case suggest a spirituality of considerably altered texture and proportions.

If Gerson intends to address this treatise on consolation to *peregrinus*, who comes to represent *every* Christian, what can be said of the central *dramatis personae* whom he has named Monicus and Volucer? Do their identities disclose anything about his intended audience, or about the leading concerns Gerson here explores? In other words, do the characters themselves and the perspectives they come to represent already sketch the contours of Gerson's intentions as critic and reformer within the disordered church of his day? Here we can raise these questions in an only introductory fashion, but the point demands further comment for a significant reason: it is no accident but rather part of a careful literary strategy that Gerson attributes such evocative names

---

[15] Here, then, we must correct the fundamental thesis upon which Constable has grounded his provocative argument. He does concede that »by isolating such individual themes, there is a danger of exaggerating the overall resemblances between the two ages« (*ibid.*, p. 50). This is certainly correct, as far as it goes, and he rightly resists the temptation to discern continuities strictly in terms of doctrine; too much water has passed under the bridge separating these centuries for such an approach to prove of much help. Yet Constable fails to apply this cautionary note regarding *content* to the widely differing *contexts* which these theologians addressed, overlooking without comment the decisively different audience to whom Bernard and such twelfth-century monastic theologians, on the one hand, and Gerson, on the other, directed their writings. What is most remarkable about Gerson's use of Bernard, beyond any continuity of themes, is the very different application of those themes by which he had »democratized« the »religious« life by broadening their accessibility. This is, of course, precisely the basis of his adament defense of the Brethren of the Common Life against Grabow's attack. In his recent Gerson study, Burger identifies more critically this modulation of audience which he discusses under the rubric of »Gersons Bernhard-Rezeption und Bernhard-Modifikation«; Burger is entirely correct in pointing to Gerson's early dependence upon Bernard's *De praecepto et dispensatione* in his own *De vita spirituali*, and he is perceptive in suggesting that Gerson's »modification« of this message had to do with his audience – i. e., Gerson »richtet sein Augenmerk nicht allein aufs Kloster [as Bernard had done], ja nicht einmal vordringlich aufs Kloster. Er bedenkt vielmehr die Frage nach Gottes Recht und menschlichen Anordnung für *alle* Christen. Allen Christen ist ja nach seiner Überzeugung das geistliche Leben angeboten und aufgetragen, das Bernhard als den Vorzug der Klöster gepriesen hatte. Er wendet sich also an Weltpriester, Mönche und Laien gleichermaßen.« *Aedificatio*, p. 188. Burger does not, however, go further to consider what this change suggests about Gerson's flexible use of this tradition, nor does he suggest how this »modification« reflects – or, perhaps, helped to shape – the theological and ecclesiastical scene during the early fifteenth century.

to his characters, and herein we discern a critical dimension of Gerson's theological and ecclesiastical perspective. Yet already on this basic point the editorial introductions which preface both Johannes Koelhoff's early incunabulum (Köln, 1483) and the later Du Pin edition (Antwerp, 1706) offer little instruction; they accept what appears *prima facie* to be the conventional interpretation of these characters, such that the names come to represent expected points of view. Thus, Du Pin identifies Monicus as the »hermit« who portrays Gerson's brother Jean, prior of the Celestine community in Lyons, and further characterizes him as »the meditative and inquiring intellect«; Volucer is the »messenger« who embodies »the discursive or reasoning intellect«; and, finally, Peregrinus portrays »the human person at once active and contemplative.«[16] Nor does Gerson's own terse description expressed at the opening of the text — viz. that Monicus is »one who lived in religious life,« as his name itself implies, and that Volucer is »a nimble messenger plying his ways« — extend beyond the verbal force of the« names themselves. With such predictable introductions the reader is hardly prepared for what follows: with what can only be interpreted as deliberate irony Gerson's Monicus vigorously challenges the legitimacy of the »solitary« life, while it is left to Volucer to defend this not in the form of any quietism but as the effective means of effecting a reform of church and society. Given such an inversion of perspective, the matter of interpretation must take account of literary voice within the dialogue itself, and thus grasp Gerson's authorial strategy on a level deeper than the text's plain surface.

This point demands a more detailed explanation, particularly since recent Gerson studies which have dealt with this text have ignored the question of literary form and as a consequence often misread statements by isolating them from the movement of his argument. The dialogue genre, however, should discourage such indiscretion, since as a literary form it allows the author to argue a question from several sides. This strategy carries a similar overall effect as the disputation, though in informal style: both enable an author to develop an argument through contrasting or even opposing points of view. Thus, any use of this text must attend carefully to the context and not merely the content of the argument.[17] Furthermore, Gerson's use of irony in this treatise, often

---

[16] Cf. *Opera omnia*, ed. Du Pin, Vol. I, 129/130: »Volucer est Intellectus discursivus et ratiocinativus; Monicus est Intellectus meditativus et inquisitivus; Peregrinus est homo contemplativus simul et activus.« The latter, therefore, embodies the *vita ambidextra* or what he elsewhere calls *vita mixta ex utraque* (i. e., the active and contemplative life), a theme which is characteristic of Gerson's reform strategy already during his earlier career as university chancellor. On this point see Gerson's *De comparatione vitae contemplativae ad activam*, G 3, pp. 71 ff.; Burger discusses this theme in his *Aedificatio*, pp. 184–87;

[17] Combes, alone among Gerson interpreters, has devoted a sustained treatment to this text, though even his analysis only begins to take literary voice into account in discerning Gerson's strategy. Thus, for example, his failure to recognize what we have called his

exercised through his choice of which character in the dialogue argues on
particular sides of an issue, becomes critical in determining his theological
perspective. This point also discourages us against reading this text in an
unnuanced manner as recent Gerson studies have tended to do. Interpreting
such a dialogue properly cannot be accomplished by a mere recitation of texts:
it is necessary to take into account « the literary context of both questions and
responses, the broad movement of the argument, and the subtle force of
narrative voice in order to grasp the theological perspectives toward which
Gerson steers the reader. The nature of dialogue as a genre, in other words,
requires of the interpreter of *De consolatione theologiae* a careful attentiveness to
literary issues in delineating authorial intent.

In turning from such formal questions to the substance of the dialogue itself,
we find that Gerson informs the reader in the opening lines as to the supposed
occasion of this treatise: it is to have been a conversation in which Monicus
inquired of Volucer, who had left the Council of Constance »after the final
departure of the pope,« concerning his brother, called only by the name
peregrinus. This pilgrim, as we have earlier suggested, apparently represents
Gerson himself, since he like Boethius had become »an exile in an unknown
and distant region where he hears a language he does not know.«[18] Yet this is
finally little more than a literary convention. On a deeper level *peregrinus* stands
as the archetype of every person, and as such represents all *viatores* who are
exiles from *patria*: with strains reminiscent not only of Boethius but more
decisively of Bonaventure, Gerson envisions life as a journey *ad Deum*, toward
God who is *humanae peregrinationis refugium*.[19] This theological context rather
than the autobiographical perspective ultimately comes to structure the

---

inversion of perspective leads him to conclude that this is »un dialogue qui ne vise aucune
conversion,« and he adds that »elle consiste dans l'inventaire des ressources dont jouit une
âme sincèrement chrétienne, qui sait vivre de sa foi.« Cf. *La théologie mystique*, 2:317. Such
a sweeping conclusion may suggest something of the contrast of this text to Boethius' *De
consolatione philosophiae*, with its formally different dialogical approach, but it is an
untenable thesis when one analyzes Gerson's literary strategy with greater nuance,
particularly regarding Volucer's careful leading of his interlocutor in the course of the
dialogue; the movement of the conversation, and the perspectives which the characters
represent, suggest that this is much more than a mere »inventory of resources.« As we shall
suggest later in this study (pace Combes) the text is quite deliberately intended as a »manual
of conversion«; see below, 3. A. 2 and 6. B. 4.

[18] G 9, p. 182.

[19] The question of Gerson's relation to Bonaventure has been frequently noted in the
secondary literature; see for instance Burger, *Aedificatio*, pp. 2, 16, 49, etc. In one of his
treatises, in fact, Gerson cites Bonaventure as one of the seminal authorities to be studied *de
contemplatione*, and points to the *Itinerarium mentis in Deum* above all. Combes renders this
text in his »Études gersoniennes. I: L'authenticité gersonienne de l'*Annotatio doctorum
aliquorum qui de contemplatione locuti sunt*,« *Archives d'histoire doctrinale et littéraire du moyen-âge*
14 (1939), p. 292. It is this treatise in particular which seems to provide the precedent for
Gerson's conceptualization of life as *peregrinatio ad Deum*.

dialogue as a whole — or, as the case may be, Gerson here interprets his own life *theologically*, such that theology and autobiography coalesce in his literary strategy.[20] In this regard the treatise opens as a conversation between the leading characters of the dialogue — Monicus and Volucer — on the meaning of Rom. 15.4 (*super hoc verbo*). As the »inquiring intellect« (*intellectus inquisitivus*), Monicus shows himself at the very outset to be a skeptic, the provocative voice in the dialogue intent on raising problems and doubts concerning the vexing matters of faith and life. Volucer, on the other hand, speaking with the voice of the »discursive intellect« (*intellectus discursivus*), presents the magisterial voice of one well versed in scriptural wisdom and facile in probing beneath his counterpart's questions to uncover the deceptive motivations of pride and doubt.[21] Indeed, his voice apparently carries Gerson's pastoral convictions as he responds in one voice (i. e., Volucer) to the pastoral questions raised by the other (i. e., Monicus),[22] and the discursive voice of the former develops added

---

[20] In this regard, the explicit references to Gerson's circumstances, or those which prevailed more generally within the church and his homeland in the wake of the Council of Constance, are relatively scarce. This does not mean, however, that autobiography does not exert a strong influence over the piece; as we shall argue in greater detail below, in fact, the concrete horizon — and particularly the threat posed by the Hussite circle — provides the decisive clue which explains the striking development we find here in Gerson's thought. Context, in other words, shapes the substance of his thought even where explicit autobiographical references are lacking. On this point, for example, see below, 6. B.

[21] As we have earlier suggested, the dialogue form may have been intended for public performance, or, more cautiously, we might discern Gerson's frequent use of it because of its suitability for broad pedagogical purposes. This form, in other words, enabled him to use a popular idiom more suited to a broad audience. Yet there may be a polemic intent suggested by this form as well, at least when considered from the peculiar vantage point by which Paul Saenger has examined the shifting styles of reading during the Middle Ages. Saenger has argued that the high Middle Ages experienced a marked shift toward silent reading, a trend which »provided a new dimension of privacy [which] emboldened the reader, because it placed the source of his curiosity completely under his personal control,« such that this form of reading became unintentionally perhaps »a conduit for heresy«; in reaction to this, »the new spiritual literature that emerged in the 14th and 15th centuries was consciously composed to be read aloud.« In other words, Saenger interprets this shift, particularly in the hands of church leaders, as an effort to control doctrinal orthodoxy. See »Silent Reading: Its Impact on Late Medieval Script and Society,« *Viator* 17 (1982): 387–400. If Saenger's analysis and conclusions are correct, then we might understand Gerson's use of this dialogue form as a »publicizing« of church teaching — i. e., not merely so that the language might be more understandable, but so that the very form might accommodate itself to a public use. Following such an interpretation, Volucer as a mediating character could be apprehended as the voice of authority articulating the church's position, while Monicus raises the doubting perspective — even to the point of offering in explicit terms the heretical Hussite challenge to the church's authority, a challenge which had escalated into a crisis during the conciliar proceedings at Constance (for detailed discussion of this point, see below, 6. B).

[22] In this sense Combes has misread the text, since he can nowhere find Gerson's own voice in the dialogue (cf. *La théologie mystique*, 2:319); while it is true that Gerson

conviction and a more differentiated response to his interlocutor as the dialogue progresses. Here literary structure in general, and narrative voice more specifically, are the media of Gerson's theological intentions: the magisterial voice of the dialogue, Volucer, depends for the nuanced articulation of his ideas on his counterpart, Monicus, who spurs the argument forward with his brash and often cynical interjections. The mood and methods of the latter are decidedly skeptical, since he appears overwhelmed with despair and as a good empiricist subjects to doubt all which cannot be ascertained through experience. Thus, for example, he inquires in a style not unfamiliar to readers of Boethius how *peregrinus* is to arm himself »against the unfair assaults of savage fortune, lest the sorrow of the world which brings death deject or preoccupy« him.[23] »Nihil difficile est volenti,« Volucer concludes, echoing in mood if not also substance the voluntarist admonition Boethius' Lady Philosophy had initially proferred the sorrowful prisoner in her charge.[24] Volucer's voice thus carries the full force of the »consoling« pastoral argument, for it is this magisterial voice through which Gerson articulates his functional view of *theologia* as itself the *via* leading *in Deum*. From this vantage point we begin to understand that this treatise, far from a *summa theologiae* meant to explore doctrinal *loci* or discrete *quaestiones*, functions rather as an edifying text, a treatise carefully designed to facilitate the transformation of character (*paideia*). Gerson here shows himself as an astute cartographer not of an esoteric mysticism relegated to self-professed athletes of the spirit, but of the human journey toward God common to all *viatores*.

With the principal *dramatis personae* introduced, the stage is now set for our examination of the dialogue itself. The treatise proper begins with Gerson's recitation of Romans 15.4, a citation which Gerson attributes to »that great

---

does not appear as directly as did Boethius in his *De consolatione philosophiae*, who is both partner in the dialogue with *philosophia* and the subject of what Combes rightly calls »une dialectique de la conversion, d'une conversion difficile« (*ibid.*, p. 317), this should not obscure the fact that he interjects in the voice of Volucer his own perspective – admittedly not as one in need of consolation, but rather as one able to offer it. Fifteenth-century readers recognized this by calling Gerson the »doctor of consolation« (*doctor consolatorius*), not the doctor in need of it.

[23] *De consolatione theologiae*, G 9, p. 187: »... quibus insuper armis spiritualibus adversus iniquos fortunae saevientis impetus congredi solitus est, ne tristitia saesuli, quae mortem operatur, ipsum vel dejiciat, vel absorbeat.«

[24] Cf. in this regard *De consolatione philosophiae*, I pr. 2, the early scene in which *philosophia* chides her patient for his self-indulgent sorrow: »But now is the time for cure rather than complaint. ... He is in no real danger, but suffers only from lethargy, a sickness common to deluded minds« (*CCSL* 94:4). Or, again, I m. 7, when Lady Philosophy responds, in an admonishing tone of voice, to the lengthy outpouring of self-pity displayed by the weary prisoner: »You too, if you want/ Clearly to see the truth/ And to walk the right road straight,/ Cast out joy,/ Cast out fear,/ Rid yourself of hope and grief« (*CCSL* 94:16–17).

disciple of theology«: »Whatever things have been written have been written for our instruction, that through the patience and consolation offered by the Scriptures we might have hope.« This biblical text articulates in direct fashion a theme often found in the chancellor's earlier writings, since he identified scripture in its consolatory function frequently throughout his earlier works.[25] In this specific context, however, this starting point should probably not be read as the consequence of Gerson's own exegetical ponderings, nor as the outcome of his personal ruminations upon this theme. In an earlier treatise bearing the same title, Johannes of Dambach (d. 1372) had introduced his subject with the same scriptural citation (i. e., Rom. 15.4). The further fact that Dambach's text had gained wide circulation by Gerson's day discourages any suggestion of originality on his part.[26] Although we have no incontrovertible proof that Gerson was familiar with this treatise, the circumstantial evidence suggesting this is at least quite strong: we now know that Dambach's treatise gained an extensive circulation during the late fourteenth and early fifteenth centuries, spreading through translations and textual traditions to such an extent that it had acquired widespread use by Gerson's day as a pastoral tool.[27]

---

[25] See for example, *La mendicité spirituelle* (1401), in which Gerson speaks at considerable length about scripture's role as a source of consolation: »Que diray je de la table planteureuse de la saintte escripture ou vous me donnes refeccion, ou je treuve medicine contre toute maladie, ou est toute saveur el doulceur pour ma consolacion?« G 7, pp. 266 f.

[26] For a detailed discussion of Dambach's treatise, and its role within the broader history of consolation literature, see Albert Auer, O.S.B., *Johannes von Dambach und die Trostbücher vom 11. bis zum 16. Jahrhundert*, Beiträge zur Geschichte der Philosophie und Theologie des Mittelalters, Vol. 28/1 (Münster i. W., 1928). This study, which began as a more focused dissertation called »Studien über Johannes von Dambach,« eventually took the shape of presenting Dambach's *Consolatio theologiae* within the broader framework of other works discussing this theme. The strength of the study is Auer's ability to interpret both a narrow literary tradition based upon Boethius (i. e., »Consolatorien im strengen Sinn,« pp. 237–63) and other expressions of the same theme (as found in diverse genres such as letters and sermons, which he interprets under the categories »Consolatorien im weiteren Sinn,« pp. 263–73, and »Consolatorien im uneigentlichen Sinn,« pp. 273–88). This approach has clear methodological advantages over that followed later by Moos and Courcelle, both of whom set artificial boundaries upon their studies which preclude the exploration of such »variations« upon either the Boethian treatise itself (Courcelle) or the epistolary form (Moos). See also above, p. 17, n. 32.

[27] See H. R. Patch, *The Tradition of Boethius. A Study of His Importance in Medieval Culture* (New York, 1935), pp. 92–93. Also, Auer argues that the significance of this treatise does not lie in its theological originality or weightiness, since it is primarily a »compilation« of other sources; rather, »seine Bedeutung liegt in der weiten Verbreitung im 14. und 15. Jahrhundert.« By the beginning of the fifteenth century, in fact, it circulated in a variety of vernacular translations and textual traditions; Auer contends that already during the century of its authorship it had found its way into most of the northern European languages. See »Das Fortleben der Consolatio theologiae in den Exzerpten« in *Dambach*, pp. 188 ff. In addition to the widespread circulation of Dambach's text, Pedro de Luna (later, Benedict XIII, deposed during the Council of Constance) had written a *Consolatio* of

It appears quite likely, therefore, that Dambach's treatise may have inspired not only Gerson's notion of such a project, but perhaps even his conception of the title and the biblical starting point of his treatise. A coincidence in both cases would seem unlikely. Beyond this similarity, however, Gerson's version demonstrates no further signs of dependence. What, then, might we glean from Gerson's use of this biblical citation, one by which he frames the treatise on both ends and organizes the text thematically into the four books of his design?

The first point we must notice is his characterization of Paul as »that great disciple of theology« (*magnus ille discipulus theologiae*), an ascription not uncommon among scholastic theologians but here anticipating a peculiarly Gersonian theme: namely, his understanding of scripture as the fundamental substance of theology. That is, Paul is *magnus discipulus theologiae* precisely as the (human) author of scripture, and not as a theologian in any more elaborate sense. But as we shall subsequently argue in greater detail this terse ascription already announces one of the determinative theses of Gerson's theological method. In describing Paul as a theologian precisely in his capacity as biblical author, Gerson prepares the reader for his broader approach to the theological task: »the scriptures« become for him the matrix of theology itself, such that *sacra pagina* functioned as an essentially undifferentiated theological source. This emphasis should not be mistaken with the *scriptura sola* of the later Protestant reform; we shall note in due course that Gerson viewed scripture not as an independently functioning authority but as dependent upon *traditio*, the interpretive horizon of the historical church. On this point at least Gerson is no forerunner to later Protestant exegesis and theological method, but a distinctively conservative voice: we must interpret Gerson's theological approach within the horizon of earlier medieval scholasticism which defined *theologia* largely as commentary rooted in »tradition« upon the scriptural text (*sacra pagina*).[28] We shall return to this theme in a later context. At this early juncture of our study, we must limit our focus to more modest questions, particularly those related to the literary structure of this treatise.

Returning to this introductory biblical text — viz. Rom. 15.4 — we find that Gerson informs the reader at the outset that the treatise focuses upon four

---

his own, which Patch has described as »one of the compilations from Johannes of Dambach, with few differences from the original«; *The Tradition of Boethius*, p. 95. It is possible, though no external evidence survives to verify this thesis, that Benedict XIII's text served to familiarize Gerson with the content of Dambach's *Consolatio theologiae*; this seems highly plausible, particularly given Gerson's close association with »Papa Luna,« as he was affectionately known. On this point see Burger, *Aedificatio*, pp. 24—25.

[28] Cf. Beryl Smalley, *The Study of the Bible in the Middle Ages* (Notre Dame, 1964), pp. 76 f. Henri de Lubac identifies this tendency in broader terms; cf. *Exégèse médiévale. Les quatre sens de l'écriture* (Aubier, 1964), I/1: 59 ff. We shall return to this theme and offer a more detailed analysis in a later chapter; see below, 4. A.

themes delineated in this Pauline passage, with the dialogue expounding an elaborate theological examination of these distinct themes:

The dialogue to follow will set forth [Monicus'] questioning and [Volucer's] response. Their conversation, which lasted four days, also proceeded by means of a four-sided consideration. They discussed, in order, the consolatory themes which are here appropriately listed: first, the consolation of theology which comes by considering through hope [*per spem*] the divine judgments; second, that consolation which through scripture [*per scripturam*] reveals the order of the world; third, the consolation offered by moderating zeal through patience [*per patientiam*]; and fourth, the consolation of theology through teaching [*per doctrinam*] which calms the conscience. »May then the God of patience and of consolation comfort us in all our tribulation,« (Rom. 15.5) and grant to both men's lips proper speech.[29]

With this explanatory preface to the text, Gerson turns directly at this point to the subject matter of the treatise proper. Immediately the formal similarity to Boethius' *Consolatio philosophiae* becomes apparent, as Gerson follows his precedent by opening his treatise with an elegy as the *primum metrum*.[30] This is a text which laments the desolation of Volucer's (i. e., Gerson's) native France,[31] portraying the situation facing him in the civil realm at the close of the

---

[29] G 9, p. 185. The four-fold structure is apparently suggested by these four themes found in Romans 15.4: hope, scripture, patience, and doctrine or teaching; this might also reflect the medieval preference for »four« as a complete number, since this already represents a striking deviation from Boethius' five-fold structure.

[30] In the Du Pin edition, the editor adds an explanatory note for this as for each succeeding poem. Here the terse commentary simply identifies this as the »elegy of the first book, in which the misery of civil dissension is lamented. This corresponds in the form of its song to the first poem in Boethius' *Consolation of Philosophy*.« In this case, as often throughout the work, Gerson's poem approximates themes as well as metrical forms found in the corresponding poetry of Boethius, usually by transforming according to his theological approach the philosophical issues as found therein. In this particular case, whereas Boethius' opening poem is an elegy sung by the prisoner, lamenting his condition and calling for a timely death, Gerson takes as his theme – sung, appropriately, by Volucer, envoy at the General Council of Constance – the civil, political, and even religious desolation to be found in the France to which he is returning:

Heu, quid id est? Saevo Bellonam cerno tumultu
Civili surere, sanguine cuncta replet.
Spiritus in medium missus vertiginis errat,
Obtrucant gladiis mutuo se propriis . . .
Clerum, militiam, cives sine lege reclusos
Carcere, plebs rabida sicut aves jugulat.
Nullus adest noster respectus religionis . . .
Nulla fides pietasque manet, confunditur omne
Pasque nefas, regnat horrida Tesiphone . . .
Advena tu felix, alia te parte receptans,
Namque patent oculis non mala tanta tuis.

[31] For a terse discussion of this history, see Lewis Spitz, *The Renaissance and Reformation Movements*, Vol. I: *The Renaissance* (St. Louis, MO, 1971), pp. 71–75. It is important to

44   *De Consolatione Theologiae*

Council in a mood not unlike Boethius' opening elegy in his *Consolatio philosophiae*. Yet the poem also sets the stage for the treatise as a whole by describing the desperate situation facing Gerson himself as a more than adequate ground for consolation. Indeed, Monicus realizes how bleak were the prospects confronting the pilgrim; with driving rhetorical force he portrays Gerson's plight as »an exile from country, parents, neighbors, acquaintances, and friends,« and sets the stage for the treatise by inquiring how it is that this *peregrinus* is not »distressed in heart« and »disturbed in mind«?[32] The treatise opens, in other words, on the plane of autobiography, affording a glimpse into the »desolation« confronting Gerson in his day.[33] We discern in this portrait the

---

recall that Gerson did not know a time when France and England were not locked in war, and this treatise bears a string of references to this sustained political and military strife; furthermore, during the decade leading up to the Council of Constance, France had been torn asunder by civil war between the houses of Orleans and Burgundy, a struggle in which Gerson had become embroiled through his opposition to the »tyrannicide« question. In this matter, which led to a heated debate which spilled into the Council at an advanced juncture, he had opposed Jean Petit's position which stood with the Burgundian house in defending *homicidia* on exegetical grounds; against this position Gerson argued his case in *De sensu litterali sacrae scripturae* (G 3, pp. 333–40). We find lingering allusions to this controversy at the close of *De consolatione theologiae*, where Gerson speaks of »homicidia sine legitima auctoritate perpetrata« (see G 9, p. 228). Karlfried Froehlich offers a penetrating discussion of Gerson's exegetical arguments in the broader context of late-medieval exegesis in a study entitled »›Always to Keep the Literal Sense in Holy Scripture Means to Kill One's Soul‹: The State of Biblical Hermeneutics at the Beginning of the Fifteenth Century,« *Literary Uses of Typology from the Late Middle Ages to the Present*, ed. Earl Miner (Princeton, 1977), pp. 27 ff.
[32] G 9, p. 186: »Qua ratione fieri potest, o Volucer, quod exul a patria, a parentibus, a propinquis, a notis et amicis non angustietur in corde, non in animo conturbetur?«
[33] After citing as a parallel to his own times the prophetic indictment of Judah's transgressions found in Isaiah 59.14–15, Volucer responds that »compared with this one sees the falsity, not just of any sort whatsoever, but of the heretical wickedness which lies in the way of God's commands; roaming the streets and holding its head up high, it insults the Catholic truth along with its defenders, trampling upon them with shameful feet and, like a most victorious mistress glories in its triumph over them.« Cf. G 9, p. 187: »Quo contra, videre est falsitatem, non qualemcumque sed haereticam pravitatem in via mandatorum Dei, quae perambulat vicos et plateas erecta cervice, insultans Catholicae veritati cum defensoribus suis, proterit eos pedibus sordidissimis, ac de ipsis tamquam domina victoriosissima triumphare gloriatur.« This view of man as the one animal who »holds his head up high« was a commonplace in Cicero's rhetoric (e. g., *De natura deorum*, II. lvi), emerging again and apparently under this influence in the twelfth and fifteenth centuries. See R. W. Southern, »Medieval Humanism,« in *Medieval Humanism and Other Studies* (Oxford, 1970), pp. 38–41; also, Bouwsma, »The Two Faces,« p. 15. It is probably no accident that Gerson borrows this specific terminology (i. e., *plateas erecta cervice*), since Boethius had drawn upon precisely this metaphor (*De consolatione philosophiae*, V m. 5; CCSL 94: 100). Yet Gerson invokes this image for a quite different purpose, utilizing it as part of a polemic argument with a more immediate and concrete referent: viz. as an assault directed principally at »the heretical wickedness« which obstructed »the way of God's commands.« In other words, he has inverted this classical metaphor by translating it from

concrete horizon facing Gerson in the wake of the council, and thus the treatise opens by identifying his own plight as *peregrinus*. As we have suggested, however, this focus quickly fades into the background as *peregrinus* comes to represent in the first instance not Gerson himself but the situation facing all *viatores*. In contrast to Boethius' treatise, in other words, Gerson writes not to console himself. Rather, he intends his work as a manual describing how theology had offered him consolation, and thus offers the piece as a pastoral treatise to be »edifying« and »useful« for all those like himself who were exiled *viatores*, seeking consolation on their pilgrimage toward their ultimate »refuge« in *Deum*.

It remains for us to move beyond the bare outline of the text which Gerson offered at the outset, and survey in brief form at least the thematic contours of his *De consolatione theologiae*. This is a task complicated by the form of the text itself: as a dialogue this treatise is comprehensive yet at the same time far from systematic, wandering from theme to theme much as a sustained conversation might do, with occasionally abrupt intrusions of material and seemingly inexplicable changes of topic. For this reason a detailed interpretation of this text seems better served by a thematic treatment, an analysis which occupies the major portion of this study, rather than an annotation of the text; among such alternatives the former has the distinct advantage of discerning developing themes more coherently, both in terms of this treatise itself and within the broader scope of Gerson's oeuvre. This thematic approach also enables us to examine the text from several distinct perspectives, concentrating upon the theological problematic as he himself understood it and placing this analysis within the wider conversation in the secondary literature on Gerson and late-medieval theology more generally. As a consequence of this approach, this study promises to advance the historiography of this period above all by contributing a much needed and more critically nuanced discussion of the later Gerson than has been hitherto available. Although this approach cannot yet attempt a general survey of Gerson's thought, it does offer a detailed theological exegesis of this particular text and thereby suggests the manner in which his thought shifted later in his life. In the remaining pages of this chapter, however, our attention must settle upon other matters of more modest proportion, fulfilling a preliminary but important purpose by orienting the reader to this text as literature. It remains for us to introduce this treatise in terms of its broad

---

a description of the human condition at its best to a foreboding portrait of *homo viator* after the Fall; more specifically, this characterization portrays those heretics who »roamed the streets« and »insulted the Catholic truth along with its defenders,« probably a direct reference to the Hussite circle as we shall suggest later in this study (see below, 6. B). It is this pride, in other words, which is the inner cause and the outer sign of heresy; in an earlier treatise he described this phenomenon through an analytical echo to Augustine, concluding that »superbia facit haereticum, non ignorantia« (*De sensu litterali sacrae scripturae*; G 3, p. 339).

thematic contours, providing an initial survey of themes and concerns similar
to an aerial view of the topography before lowering our vision in the following
chapters to engage in a detailed and systematic analysis of the terrain at close
range.

As already noted Gerson prefaces the treatise by dividing the dialogue as a
four-day conversation between these characters, with each day constituting a
book and each book devoted to a particular theme. The organizing principle is
suggested to him by the various themes he delineates in Romans 15.4: first,
hope and divine judgment (*per spem*); second, scripture and providence (*per
consolationem scripturarum*); third, patience and zeal (*per patientiam*); and, fourth,
doctrine and serenity of conscience (*per doctrinam*). When we turn to the first
book, devoted to the »consolation of theology« that comes »through hope in
contemplating the divine judgment,« Gerson points out that this is precisely
the question which could not be penetrated by *philosophia*, and hence eluded
Boethius in his quest for consolation. This admission leads to a brief digression
in which Gerson considers the role played by theology as »companion« (*comes*)
for the pilgrimage. In a form which parallels Boethius' view of *philosophia*,
theology as personified by Gerson stands as an instructor in consolation for the
viator: »The pilgrim receives this consolation from his teacher, Lady Theology,
who has given herself as the companion of his pilgrimage,«[34] an image he later
expands in the vivid language of poetry:

> Happy that theologian whom fair wisdom
> Wants as her spouse from his boyhood;
> She binds him, chaste, to herself with love.
> Pledging to be his sister,
> Always she offers herself as companion:
> Lightening the tedium and gloom of life,
> And comforting through echoing the songs of Zion. . . .
> Thus no one has extolled enough
> The praises of Theology . . .,
> By whom cares flee away, and the mind is made glad.[35]

---

[34] See G 9, p. 187: ». . . quod eam accipit doctrice theologia, quae comitem se dedit
peregrinationi suae.« Combes has suggested that this is a reference to 2 Cor. 8.19 −
»Ordinatus est ab ecclesia comes peregrinationis nostrae« − but the context is so decidedly
different that any parallel seems accidental (cf. *La théologie mystique*, 2: 317, n. 32). On a
much more straightforward level, however, this appears to reflect Gerson's reliance upon
the Boethian precedent: although *theologia* only acquires a voice in the dialogue during the
final pages of the treatise, her presence is felt throughout the text in terms of Gerson's use
of scripture, which he here identifies with theology as »revealed« or »supernaturally
infused« (cf. G 9, p. 189). In this specific sense scripture represents the voice of *theologia*,
and vice versa; see below, 4. A.

[35] G 4, pp. 28−29:

The consolation offered by theology, therefore, has a quite personal and even intimate quality to it, for in this personified form *theologia* extends to *viatores* consolation by offering nothing less than herself. In a wonderful and apparently original allegorization of the Book of Wisdom, Gerson interprets the »spouse« as »Lady Theology« herself, identifying her as our lover who becomes the companion *ab infantia* throughout life's pilgrimage: »Her have I loved,« he concludes, »and I have sought her out from my youth, and have sought to take her for my spouse, having become a lover of her form. . . . Going into my house, I shall find rest with her, for her conversation has no bitterness, nor her company any tediousness, but only gladness and joy.«[36] This, then, stands as the general framework within which *theologia* is to be understood throughout the treatise: not in scholastic terms as an object of knowledge nor as an academic discipline, but in the intimate language of this biblical allegory. Gerson thus alters the mood almost immediately — and hereby departs quite dramatically from Boethius' style — from the elegiac opening, and this image and mood carry the discussion throughout the treatise.

As the dialogue progresses in this first book Gerson offers an extended consideration of the nature and function of philosophy, interpreting *philosophia* as propaedeutic for theology proper. Philosophy has a role to play as the »foundation« for theology, but it is a limited utility at best. This excursus on method is no mere digression, as Gerson uses it both to justify his literary intention and at the same time to clarify his point of departure: »we represent the first word of theology as beginning at that summit where philosophy terminated its consolation of Boethius.«[37] Once theology has been suitably

---

Felix theologus, pulchra sophia
Cui vult a puero se dare sponsam
Quam castum tenero stringit amore.
Ejus se vocitans jure sororem
Casus se sociam praebet in omnes
Ac vitae relevat taedia moestae
Solatur resonans cantica Sion . . . .
Ergo nemo satis theologiae
Laudes extulerit tanta patrantis
Qua curae fugiunt mens hilarescit . . . .

Gerson often draws upon the vivid domestic imagery of wisdom literature, as in this poem; indeed, he frequently refers to the church as *sponsa Christi*, though this reference to theology as *pulchra sophia*, our spouse and lover, is otherwise not found in his writings. This usage is quite different, in other words, from the earlier medieval tradition following Bernard of Clairvaux which had utilized such language from the Song of Songs in articulating a »bridal mysticism« in which the bride, representing the church or the soul, found union with Christ the bridegroom.

[36] G 9, p. 187; the biblical reference, in which Gerson interpets *sapientia* as *theologia*, is Wisdom 8.1, 2, 16.

[37] G 9, p. 188.

introduced, and contrasted with philosophy, Gerson moves from methodological prolegomenon to his task proper, proclaiming his intention to
illustrate how theology leads »miraculously, as it were, to our embracing
through love the God of all consolation, to whom we also cling as if to a place
of sure refuge.«[38] This image of the pilgrimage *ad Deum*, which he describes
here *velut in locum refugii*, becomes the principal metaphor which dominates the
remainder of the first book and indeed the treatise as a whole: his entire project
stands as a sustained response to Monicus' question, »I would like to hear by
what arrangement this miraculous leading, from fear to hope and love, takes
place,« and the momentum of the dialogue moves the discussion persistently
toward his final acclamation of the *pax Dei*.[39] On this account it becomes clear
at the very outset and again at the close that Gerson's intention is to offer this
treatise as a practical *enchiridion*, a sort of »manual of conversion« by which
viatores might find consolation and aid as they make progress on their
pilgrimage toward God, a destination which Gerson here describes not in what
he considered the heretical terms of an essentialist mysticism which dissolved
the mind in God[40] but in Augustinian terms which safeguarded the distinct
individuality of the subject in what he describes as a »loving embrace« of God.

In the remainder of this first book Gerson articulates a cluster of themes
which dominate his theological approach in fundamental ways, all of which
relate to the general themes of hope and judgment. Among such topics he
devotes particular attention to the following: the role of »seeking« God, based
upon the biblical promise in Heb. 11.6, as the juncture of divine and human
initiative; the *ordo judiciorum* by which divine mercy precedes judgment, and the
relation of Christology to this »order«; the consideration of predestination as
the basis of soteriology, a perspective on this doctrine which follows the Scotist
approach in its broad outline; the inescapable power of sin, such that
soteriology is not a pursuit of holiness but an abandonment of one's own
righteousness in favor of the *iustitia Dei*; and, finally, Christ's role as *mediator
Dei et hominum* and as the bearer of »sufficient« grace which becomes
»effective« *per fidem*. Here, too, he announces his advocacy of *via media et regia*,
a mediating course by which he joins together the general nominalist emphasis
upon divine omnipotence and freedom with an insistence on human freedom
and responsibility, a paradoxical union which he effects in terms of the biblical
covenant that »God rewards those who seek him« (Heb. 11.6). As a »theology

---

[38] *Ibid.*, p. 189.

[39] *Ibid.*, pp. 190, 245.

[40] For his early warning against this strain of mysticism, see *De mystica theologia
speculative conscripta*, cons. 41.6, ed. André Combes (Lugano, 1958), p. 106 f. It is this
caution which undergirds Gerson's attack upon the third book of Ruysbroeck's *De ornatu
spiritualium nuptiarum*; on this point see Combes, *Essai sur la critique de Ruysbroeck par Gerson.*
Vol. I: *Introduction critique et dossier documentaire* (Paris, 1945), pp. 615 ff., and the terse
discussion in Burger, *Aedificatio*, pp. 139—43.

of seeking, « however, Gerson refuses to place any confidence in human works (*fiducia de propriis operibus*); the *viator* seeks God through an utter desperation in self (*desperes volo, sed de te et in te*) and a corresponding trust in divine righteousness — as he later summarizes, *per desperationem ad spem*, through desperation (in self) to hope (in God). It is finally this soteriological approach, unexpected for a supposed nominalist of the Ockhamist »main current« because of the bleakness with which it characterizes the human potential, which returns again and again in an almost fugue-like pattern, establishing this theme through various melodic developments as the structuring focus of the treatise as a whole. It is on this basis that his dialogue leads *viatores*, as he expresses this dynamic, upon the course of life leading »from highest desperation in man to highest hope in God, and up through an inestimable and intolerable desolation to a solid consolation.«[41]

The second book Gerson devotes to the broad topic of the revelation of the world's governance (i. e., providence) through scripture. It is here that Gerson announces the outline of his voluntarism, a theological approach which shapes both his soteriology and his anthropology. With this fundamental emphasis upon the will, and first of all upon the divine will, Gerson utilizes biblical language, and that above all from the Psalms, to argue that the divine will accomplishes all that it purposes, and all that it accomplishes is thereby just: »Just as it is always efficacious,« he contends, »so also is it always just, and without it nothing is done.«[42] Gerson's voluntarism, however, is not a matter of a free and omnipotent divine actor who somehow incapacitates the human will and thereby preempts all accountability *coram judice Deo*, to recall the forensic context Gerson holds before us; here we must recall the balanced structure of his *via media et regia*. On the contrary, this becomes the arena in which Gerson draws upon what has been called the »nominalist mystical ideal« in contrast to the Eckhartian view of an essentialist union between God and the human soul: viz. the theme of *conformitas voluntatis*.[43] Our wills are to be

---

[41] These particular themes will be identified more fully, and discussed in their appropriate contexts, in the following chapters. The final citation derives from the final prose section of this first book (I pr. 4; G 9, p. 198): »Non aliter vult eadem theologia, per summam desperationem de homine, trahere ad summam de Deo spem, et per desolationem inaestimabilem et intolerabilem, sursum ducere ad solidam consolationem.«

[42] G 9, pp. 203—204: »sicut semper efficax sic et justa est, sine qua factum est nihil.«

[43] Cf. Oberman, »A Nominalistic Glossary,« in *Harvest*, pp. 463—64. He also calls this theme, without further explanation, »the golden rule of nominalistic ethics«; this could be said of Gerson's thought as expressed in this treatise, but only if one qualifies this to insist that ethics for Gerson cannot be understood outside of a soteriological schema. That is, Gerson speaks of *conformitas voluntatis* primarily here in terms of *imitatio Christi*, but he refuses to sever this theme as an ethical concern from his insistence on the salvific character of Christ's role as *mediator Dei et hominum*. For a more detailed discussion of this question see below 5. D. 1—2.

conformed to the divine will itself: *peregrinatio ad Deum* is finally nothing other than a matter of *conformitas voluntatis*.

But is this a »mystical« theme, strictly speaking, in Gerson's thought? Apparently not, a conclusion Combes also offered in his study of this text, at least not in terms familiar to readers of Gerson's earlier treatises in which he directed his attention explicitly and exclusively to *theologia mystica*. But viewed from a broader angle this conclusion is not as convincing: indeed, Gerson appears to be here intent upon expanding considerably the horizon of mysticism itself, such that the mystical life comes to characterize at some level the progress or at least the culmination of the pilgrimage *ad Deum* which all *viatores* must undertake. Gerson here conceives of the Christian life as ultimately flowering in a mystical apprehension of God, a »stable« state in which the mind itself arrives »through contemplation . . . at a pure and simple understanding.«[44] This suggestion thus points to a fascinating development in Gerson's thought, since he hereby expands the context of mystical theology while at the same time integrating it within the broader contours of *theologia* in general since as he here notes it is theology itself which persuades *viatores* to »aspire to this [mystical] state.«[45] But elsewhere in this text he avoids any prolonged discussion of mystical themes, even noting in the passage just cited (i. e., II pr. 4) that this issue »should be discussed in another place.« And thus he devotes his efforts to considering other themes, discussing for example in terms of his general psychological model of the »three-fold will« the configuration of Jesus' inner nature. Here we find that Gerson interprets the familiar *imitatio Christi* theme not in ethical terms, but in the more abstract psychological terms of *conformitas voluntatis*: that is, we are to conform our wills to God's, just as Jesus conformed the »highest« part of his human will to the divine. He quickly concedes, however, that all human effort in this regard is ultimately futile, and this because of the power sin — original, actual, and habitual — holds upon *viatores*. *Imitatio Christi*, yes, but Gerson insists that the incapacity which sin inflicts upon us requires more than natural effort: in the final analysis we are to »cry out with the apostle, ›Unhappy man that I am! Who will deliver me from this body of death?‹, whereupon let us answer, ›The grace of God through Jesus Christ our Lord.‹ (Rom. 7.24–25).« Ethics and soteriology meet upon the common ground of his Christology, a doctrinal merger which Gerson locates not in a speculative discussion *de providentia Dei* but within the horizon of the peculiar divine covenants of scripture.

The remainder of this second book treats a variety of themes related only tangentially to the general topic of *regimen mundi*. This is particularly true of the extended discussion Gerson gives to human psychology, with a quite detailed

---

[44] G 9, p. 211 f.

[45] *Ibid.* For further discussion of this point, see below, 4. C. 2, where we consider this question in terms of mysticism and the »democratization« of theology.

analysis of human cognition; here he discusses the role of »phantasms« and »intelligible species« as vital aspects which, if disordered, disrupt the »harmonious disposition« upon which the use of free choice (*usus liberi arbitrii*) depends. It is an excursus, in other words, which is necessary for Gerson's defense of human freedom, though he advances this argument with little regard for the topic at hand but rather wanders into a detailed analysis of the human psyche itself. From this he returns to the theme on the basis of which he styles his theological perspective as *via media*: viz. the confluence of divine providence and human freedom. As he advances this characteristically Boethian question, he promotes what appears to be a Thomist solution by suggesting that God »co-operates« in all matters emanating from (free) rational minds such that these are called »contingent« rather than »necessary.« On the basis of this argument Gerson attempts to blaze a mediating path between those theologians and philosophers who attributed *regimen mundi* exclusively to either divine or human initiative. To support this mediating position he avoids the characteristic arguments through which scholastic theologians had debated this point; instead of this he draws upon the »historical narratives« of the scriptures, and particularly the Old Testament, to demonstrate God's »ruling providence [*providentia regitiva*] of all that is done, both in heaven and upon the earth. « The book closes in this same vein with a defense of prayer,[46] a theme to which Gerson had devoted considerable thought during the council,[47] since prayer itself presents the purest expression of *conformitas voluntatis*: that is, the providence of God is such that it beckons us to participate in the processes of

---

[46] It should be noted that Gerson's approach to this theme offers a remarkable approximation to Boethius' formulation in *De consolatione philosophiae*. Boethius had addressed this theme several times in the final book (V pr. 3), arguing that a thorough-going determinist interpretation of divine providence would obviate altogether the rationale of prayer which he described as *inter homines deumque commercium*. In the final lines of the treatise he returns to this theme with a different argument, contending that our prayers (*preces*) and hope (*spes*), when they are proper, cannot be ineffective (*cum rectae sunt, inefficaces esse non possunt*). Boethius based this formulation upon his insistence that »human reason should submit to the divine mind« (V pr. 5; *CCSL* 94:100), an approach which fuses his emphasis upon divine *and* human freedom. In much the same manner Gerson's *via media*, which sought to establish a similar balance of freedoms, articulates a similar view of prayer; the single difference is that Gerson locates the confluence not in terms of reason but as a matter of the will (*conformitas voluntatis*), an emphasis which underscores from another angle the voluntarist bent of his thought.

[47] This theme emerges in unusual prominence in the correspondence of this period; see particularly letters 38 and 39, in G 2, pp. 175–98. Each of these conveys a mature and measured analysis of prayer, and in the precision and extent of expression represents what Glorieux aptly has called »lettre-traité« bearing only the minimal characteristics required by the epistolary form.

causality, a perspective which echoes Thomas Aquinas's conviction that God
shares with us the »dignity of causality.«[48]

In the third book Gerson proposes to explore how *viatores* receive
»consolation through patience by moderating zeal,« a discussion that
demonstrates the correlative nature of pastoral and polemical concerns in
Gerson's theological method. Much of this treatise, as we shall later argue,
stands as a direct response to the Hussite heresy, and this on a cluster of issues:
e. g., the role of zeal, as necessarily moderated by patience, in removing
»scandal« from the church; the necessity of discretion and the seeking of advice
within the hierarchical church rather than proceeding according to one's own
judgment; the requirement of legitimate »judicial authority« for the
undertaking of any act within the church or society; the defense of the
cloistered life or monastic orders; the defense of the benefice system against the
charge of simony, when used moderately; the distinction of »fraternal« from
»judicial« correction; and the need for toleration, since the church remains an
imperfect body in this »interim« age. In each of these cases the Hussite position
stands as the foil over against the church's official response, an interrogation
that Gerson sets within the deliberate logic of this dialogue. Yet he moves his
argument beyond a merely defensive posture. As we shall see, Gerson here
addresses himself point by point to the central charges levelled by Hus and
members of his circle, offering in each case a constructive exegetical counter-
argument to this criticism. Indeed, an analysis of the conversation found in this
book, compared with a sampling of Hus's writings and particularly the
historical records of his trial at Constance, suggests that this treatise offers a
dialogue – hypothetical or real? – between the chancellor and the Czech
preacher: Monicus' voice offers Hus's argument in general outline as in specific
points of detail, while Volucer's nuanced responses apparently present
Gerson's own magisterial position. We do not know whether Gerson actually
articulated his side of this debate in the council proceedings; it is at least
plausible, and we do know that this perspective was well represented since his
argument follows in emphasis as in particular points the responses advanced
by Gerson's colleague and friend, Pierre d'Ailly.[49] We also know, on the basis of
the correspondence which has survived from this period, that these issues
occupied Gerson's attention before the council even convened at Constance.[50]

---

[48] See also below, 5. D. 3; the reference to Thomas Aquinas, which we shall discuss later
in greater detail, is *Summa theologiae* Ia q. 22 a. 3 resp.

[49] For the detail of this argument see below, 6. B. Mladoňovice's account of these
proceedings is rendered in *Relatio de Mag. Joannis Hus causa*, in *John Hus at the Council of
Constance*, trans. and ed. Matthew Spinka (New York and London, 1965). See also Spinka,
John Hus: A Biography (Princeton, 1968), pp. 248 ff., an account quite sympathetic to Hus's
position.

[50] See, for example, his exchange of letters with Conrad de Vechte, the Archbishop of
Prague, spanning the period from May through September, 1414 (G 2, pp. 157–66. In the

The issue of this debate, which we shall subsequently explore, was not only a matter of external criticisms levelled against the disorder within the church and the apparent corruption of the pastoral office. The differences run much deeper than this. Beneath the surface of these admittedly differing views of reform lie varying ecclesiologies and quite distinctive approaches to the matter of eschatology and apocalypticism. But this must be the subject of a later discussion; for the moment we can only announce this feature of the dialogue in bare outline, and promise a more detailed analysis in a succeeding chapter.

Following this contextual interpretation of the themes found in this third book, we shall also suggest that this discussion only appears to be unrelated to his decisively altered soteriology. Why is it, in other words, that Gerson moves away from the traditional Ockhamist appropriation of the *facere quod in se est* doctrine, substituting in its place a striking emphasis upon the sheer futility of all human works and the utter desperation which these must bring upon *viatores*?[51] Can this offer a »theology of hope,« as he sets out to do? And, furthermore, what prompts the abrupt development in his soteriology by which Gerson now despairs of any human contribution to the process of salvation, a shift to the »right« by which he now aligns himself with the Scotists in defending predestination *ante praevisa merita*?[52] The focus of this third book provides the vital clue to interpreting the motivation undergirding this shift, since Gerson here argues against the presumption of human reform — of

final letter which survives from this correspondence, Gerson appends the condemnation advanced by the Paris faculty which censured twenty articles taken from Hus's *De ecclesia*, theses in which the Parisian theologians linked Hus to Wyclif; G 2, pp. 163 ff.

[51] Adolar Zumkeller traces the theme of the abandonment of any emphasis upon human merit in a broad Augustinian tradition which influenced Luther, thereby interpreting the impulse of his reform within a late-medieval continuum; see »Das Ungenügen der menschlichen Werke bei den deutschen Predigern des Spätmittelalters,« *Zeitschrift für katholische Theologie* 81 (1959), pp. 265–305. Against this view, Oberman has questioned the sufficiency of Zumkeller's textual basis, since he bases his thesis upon the Lukan text (Lk. 18.10 ff.) about the Pharisee and the Publican which Oberman argues is »the traditional place to stress the importance of humility and God's grace.« *Harvest*, pp. 181–82, n. 112. Douglass has challenged Zumkeller's conclusion from another angle, arguing that these themes need not be exclusive of one another and that late-medieval nominalist preachers often emphasized the utter unworthiness of human merit alongside the need *de potentia Dei ordinata* to act trusting in God's covenants of grace; *Justification in Late Medieval Preaching*, pp. 162–63, 176–78. What sets Gerson's view apart from that of Geiler of Keisersberg, as Douglass portrays it here, is that Gerson abandons altogether any emphasis upon *facere quod in se est*, and retools the Ockhamist model of divine covenant by substituting what we shall call a covenant of »seeking« for one of »doing«; on this point see below, 5. C.

[52] On this point, therefore, Gerson dissociates himself from his earlier Ockhamism, joining at this late juncture of his life with what Oberman has called »the predestinarian trend« advocated by the more extreme Augustinian voices of this period (i. e., his so-called »right-wing nominalism«), and thereby abandoning what Oberman has characterized as the at least »semi-Pelagian« theme of the *viator*'s »responsibility for his own salvation«; see *Harvest*, pp. 205–206, 245, 423 f., and below, 5. B.

society, the church, and even the self — as part of his argument against the apocalypticism and misplaced zeal he discerned in the Hussite demand for reform. In contrast to this approach Gerson offers what might be called a reticent eschatology, one which relied finally upon the divine work — which he here calls *opus Dei* — as the key to reform, and counselled tolerance and patience in order properly to moderate the zeal bent on removing *scandala*. In the »interim« such patient reform was not only advisable but necessary; and, of course, all of this Gerson sets within the framework of the »divine law and order«[53] with its corresponding hierarchy of authority. His advocacy of toleration and discretion, in other words, arises out of his Dionysian ecclesiology,[54] and this he bases in turn upon his moderate eschatology. Patience, therefore, is only the outward consequence of his understanding of the church's structure as itself *in via*.

In the final book of this treatise, Gerson turns to the theme of consolation offered »through instruction« (*per doctrinam*) which establishes serenity of conscience. Already at the outset, however, we stumble upon a terminological problem, viz. the difficulty of interpreting exactly what Gerson means with the word *doctrina*. On the first level, of course, it is enough to point to the source where he derived this word: in this case, his citation of Rom. 15.4 in its Vulgate rendering as »quaecumque enim scripta sunt *ad nostram doctrinam* scripta sunt. . . .« In other words, scripture itself serves as the »instruction« (*doctrinam*) we need in order to attain what he here calls, in contrast to what philosophy can »know« (*cognovit*) or philosophical teaching attain, the »true and solid consolation.« Thus, Gerson again points to the close relationship between *scriptura* and *doctrina*: scripture is the conduit of *theologia* and therefore indistinguishable from *doctrina*, such that scripture is instruction in its character as »revealed« or »supernaturally infused« theology (i. e., beyond philosophy).[55] Similarly, theology *is* scripture according to Gerson's approach, an

---

[53] Cf. G 9, p. 188, where Gerson articulates this theme of the *lex divinitatis et ordo*: »Est autem lex divinitatis et ordo ut suprema inferiorum jungantur ad superiorum infima, more concatenationis, veluti Plato loquebatur, quae in corporalibus argentea, in spiritualibus aurea vocabatur. Et plane hanc in scala Jacob graduum figurationem accipimus.« This is an extremely telling passage, since here Gerson identifies the hierarchical approach to reality which he embraces not in terms of the Dionysian model, but on a more fundamental level as a reflection of the Platonic view as well as that exemplified in the biblical metaphor of Jacob's ladder. We shall return to this theme later in this study; see below, 6. A. 1.

[54] Gerson often invoked what he understood to be the heart of this ecclesiology, the »divine law« whereby ». . . ad suprema reducantur infima per media«; see for example G 2, p. 171, a letter written in Constance to his brother Jean.

[55] In this sense Gerson apparently utilizes *doctrina* and *theologia* as interchangeable terms; it is simply not the case that he distinguishes them according to identity or function. For a discussion of Aquinas's quite different use of these terms, with specific nuance given to each because of diverse functions, see Per Erik Persson, »*Sacra doctrina*«: *Reason and Revelation in Aquinas* (Philadelphia, 1970), pp. 71–77. Persson also notes that Aquinas utilized the term

identity which he demonstrates throughout this dialogue not only in theory but in his practical use of scripture in its *sensus litteralis* to articulate and develop theological arguments. As we later suggest his theological method recalls the tendency found in the earlier monastic and cathedral schools to conflate theology and biblical exegesis: it is in this sense *theologia biblica*. In this manner his approach, which has been recently characterized as that of »a sophisticated fundamentalist,« offers a biblical theology solidly based upon *sacra pagina*, to the extent that theological argument often becomes little more than citation of the relevant scriptural texts, often in traditional glossed form.[56]

But does Gerson stay within this broad interpretation of *doctrina* in this final book? This appears to be the case as long as we interpret this theme as Gerson did, which means without a more specific connotation and principally in terms of his theological use of scripture according to its *sensus litteralis*. Yet we must say more than this, particularly since it is in this section that Gerson advances an idea of broad significance in terms of late-medieval hermeneutics: his contention that scripture, if it is to be rightly understood, must be interpreted within the historical tradition of the church — or, as he here puts it, according to the *sensus a sanctis patribus traditus*. Thus, his discussion focuses not only upon the content of the consolation offered *per scripturam*, but ranges further to establish the context in which scripture is to be interpreted. We shall discuss this later in terms of the perspectival dimensions of Gerson's hermeneutics, a two-fold requirement by which he insists that the proper interpretation of the biblical text depends upon the moral life of the exegete as well as the historical tradition conveyed »by the holy fathers.«[57]

The remainder of this final book Gerson devotes to themes related to this use of *doctrina*. Thus, he returns in the opening pages of the book to the fundamental question of soteriology that had occupied his attention at the outset of the treatise: namely, the contrast of human and divine *iustitia*, by which he argues that our fear of past sin does not cause us to »despair of God's mercy« but raises us to »a more solid hope.« This movement he here calls

---

theologia infrequently in contrast to *doctrina*, a point which further distanced his use of the term from Gerson's; indeed, Gerson utilizes *theologia* in this treatise much as Aquinas had used *sacra doctrina* primarily in order to establish its distinct relationship to *philosophia*.

[56] For this characterization, see Froehlich, »Fifteenth-Century Hermeneutics,« p. 44. A thesis remaining to be tested with regard to this work concerns the relationship of the frequent glosses Gerson provides to particular biblical texts. Some of these we have traced to traditional sources, though it might be quite useful to analyze these with specific reference to a standard version of the gloss which Gerson must have had before him — the *Glossa ordinaria*. This must remain a thesis for exploration in another context, particularly once the history of the gloss as well as its textual transmission and use in the later Middle Ages become more accessible.

[57] See below, 6. A. 3.

iustitia fidei, since it depends not upon human effort but solely upon faith in the mercy offered to *viatores* through the *ordo judiciorum*. He also distinguishes the various levels of certitude, delineating not only moral and civil from supernatural certitude but a three-fold structure of supernatural certitude as well. In this sense it is the third or lowest level of certitude which most occupies his attention, probably since this is the knowledge which accompanies *viatores* through life: this is the form which *viatores* receive *per fidem*, a certitude which one has not through evident reason (i. e., »tunc autem facie ad faciem«; 1 Cor. 13.12) but by divine authority (»non evidentiae rationis innititur, sed auctoritati divinae«). This is the admittedly »dim« knowledge available to *peregrini*, those *in via* who do not yet have »the clear and intuitive« knowledge found *in patria beatorum*; as such it is a certitude grasped *per speculo et in aenigmate*, an obvious reference to 1 Cor. 13.12. But he is quick to add that this »interim« knowledge is entirely trustworthy since »through no power, not even the absolute power of God, is it able to deceive us,« the single instance in this treatise in which he invokes the theme of the »two powers of God« familiar to late-medieval nominalist theology and underscores the inviolability of the covenants of knowledge and grace *de potentia Dei ordinata*. In this we sense the »strong eschatological emphasis« which has been identified in Gerson's thought,[58] but Gerson adds to this an ambitious theme which sets him against a dominant scholastic tradition. This dim but trustworthy knowledge, which is available to »all the faithful [*fidelibus omnibus*] as they journey on their way [*peregrinantur in via*],« places a broad responsibility upon *viatores*: Gerson here insists that all persons, regardless of hierarchical status, must possess a faith both implicit and explicit, directed not only toward the *articuli fidei* but *toti sacrae scripturae*. This thesis distances Gerson from the classic Thomist perspective, widely accepted during the later Middle Ages, which applied the Dionysian view of the mediated revelation to the various offices or levels within the ecclesiastical hierarchy. As such it offers us a critical insight into the qualified use Gerson here makes of the Dionysian framework, and the more aggressive role he attributes to the laity (*idiotae*) who he suggests might well bear »more fruitfully« (*fructuosius*) the »spirit of catholic judgment« than the learned. In this context Gerson insists that the character of the true theologian is *bonus vir in sacris litteris eruditus*, with the clear emphasis falling less upon an abstract or speculative erudition than upon an »experienced« knowledge of the heart and the corresponding goodness of the person.[59] This, then, represents an aggressive development of his characteristic concern for the *simplices*, since he here attributes the »tradition« of theology not to the educated but to the pious,

---

[58] Oberman, *Harvest*, pp. 339—40.

[59] For an excellent discussion of this theme in Gerson's earlier mystical writings, see Burger, *Aedificatio*, pp. 129—43.

those *viatores* in whom *theologia* is integrated »not only through the intellect [*per intellectum*] but much more in the heart [*in affectum*].«[60]

The closing prose section of this fourth and final book introduces *theologia* in her own voice, a soliloquy which the Du Pin edition prefaces with the title »personification of theology« (*prosopopaeia theologiae*). In this lengthy monologue, introduced by Volucer as »the teaching of theology sent from heaven« (*doctrina theologiae coelitus immissae*), Gerson's focus ranges across a wide spectrum of themes: the manner of divine election and providence, discerned above all »from the prophetic and historical books« of scripture; the punishment which sin merits, even »hidden« offenses unnoticed by civil or ecclesiastical authorities; the »will to power,« to anticipate a later Nietzschean theme, by which he attributes the desolation of his day to »the lust for dominating and ruling« over others; and, finally, an extended discussion of martyrdom, those who »struggled for the law of God even unto death« (»qui pro lege Dei sui certaverint usque ad mortem«). Again, the optimism to be found in Ockhamist nominalism is conspicuous by its absence; not only is Gerson's view of the human condition an unambiguously bleak one, but this pessimism extends to his consideration of the social and political arena. In this context his identification of the martyr's cause with the divine law is no accident: indeed, this theme structures the final pages of the treatise which read as a kind of capsulary martyrology. Here Gerson offers a chronology of the various manifestations of the *lex Dei*, together with those martyrs who died in defense of that law: he begins by identifying Abel as »the first martyr under the law of nature« (*primum martyrum in lege naturae*); the seven Maccabaean brothers who died in defense of »the written law« (i. e., *lex vetus*); John the Baptist whom he identifies as a martyr standing »at the boundary [*limes*] between the law of Moses and the law of Christ«; and, finally, more recent martyrs from the church's history, among whom he includes »Thomas of Canterbury« (à Becket), Leodegard of France, and Agatha, Agnes, and Lucy of the pre-Constantinian era. This appears to be a strange finale, until we recall the force of Gerson's anti-apocalyptic and anti-Hussite message. This »martyrology« accentuates, in other words, the definition of martyrdom in terms of *lex divina*, which in this case leads toward an identification of *lex Dei* and *lex ecclesiastica*: against those disposed to interpret Hus and his followers as the present-day martyrs, Gerson insists that the *defensio catholicae veritatis*, far from »the cause of desolation« as apparently »some impudent people« held (those of the Hussite circle?) who were »thereby condemned for their stubbornness,« stood as the invitation to true martyrdom. It was the defense of *lex divina*, interpreted as the advocacy and not the critique of the established *ordo ecclesiasticus*, which finally represented the cause leading to martyrdom.

---

[60] G 9, p. 237.

58 De Consolatione Theologiae

The treatise concludes with a brief summary of the consolation offered for
»all kinds of tribulation,« a device meant to reinforce earlier themes through a
»brief epilogue« for the text as a whole:

Let us aspire with all our heart to raise our eyes to the heavens, saying: »God is the father of
mercy and all consolation; in his compassion we should hope, conforming ourselves to his
will. From him we receive the virtue of patience, and in him is the serenity of conscience.
In the meantime [*interim*] let us endeavor to carry in our hearts [*in affectum*] that which we
have discussed intellectually [*per intellectum*] during these four days.«[61]

In affectum: this treatise thus ends on a characteristic Gersonian theme, the
emphasis upon the »heart« and its affects rather than the intellect alone. In this
sense he varies the familiar Anselmian theme as if to read *fides quaerens affectum*,
since faith even if it is only *fides simplex* must finally root itself in the human
heart, demonstrating his contention that the »erudition« in sacred scripture
demanded of the theologian is »not a matter of the intellect alone, but much
more of the heart.«[62] With this thesis Gerson aligns himself with the
Augustinian tradition of exegesis that read the grammar of scripture as love and
not mere knowledge, and by which theology itself became the science of *fides
formata* or a faith formed by acts of charity. What finally mattered was not the
acquisition of intellectual understanding alone but the »transfer,« as Gerson
here puts it, of this »unformed« knowledge (*intellectus*) to the heart's affects and
to the execution of good works. »Formed faith,« or the *fides quae per charitatem
operatur* (Gal. 5.6) of which he had earlier spoken, characterizes the end to
which all *viatores* should aspire, just as it also identifies the character of the true
theologi. *Theologia* must be »mixed« with the theological virtues if it is to »build
up« (*aedificat*) rather than »puff up« (*inflat*), a Pauline theme which saturates his
university writings.[63] And with this he brings the text to a close by citing once
again, this time as a benediction rendered by Monicus, the biblical text which
had been his point of departure: »... so that through patience and the
consolation of scripture we might have hope« (Rom. 15.4).

With this overview of *De consolatione theologiae* as literature, a discussion
which has explored in general terms both the form and the matter of this
treatise, we are now in a position to examine with greater nuance the detail of
his theological arguments as well as the broader problematic of this text. In
doing so our analysis focuses primarily though by no means exclusively upon
this text, setting the themes Gerson here articulates within a broader spectrum
— both that of his own oeuvre and that of theological traditions of the period.

---

[61] G 9, p. 244.

[62] This is a definition he develops as a variation upon a Ciceronian theme: namely, his
definition of the philosopher as *vir bonus dicendi peritus*.

[63] G 9, p. 237. The biblical reference earlier is 1 Cor. 8.1. For a general discussion of this
theme with regard to his university writings, see Burger, *Aedificatio*, pp. 48–49, 55 ff.
Indeed, Burger rightly identifies *aedificatio* as one of the central themes in Gerson's works.

In this sense, our study of this treatise serves as a window through which we survey something of the wider horizon and variegated terrain of the church during the later Middle Ages. This text is particularly suited to serve as such a vantage point, above all because of its comprehensive character: Gerson's treatment of the motif of the *peregrinatio ad Deum* offers a penetrating and at the same time expansive vista of the concerns, both pastoral and more properly theological, that dominated this period. Our analysis commences by looking first at the basic approach Gerson follows in this dialogue, exploring the pedagogy he employs in relation to theological method, and suggesting that he here devises a »paideutic« approach to the theological task.

Chapter III

Pedagogy and Theological Method:
A Paideutic Approach to Theology

The broad purpose of Gerson's *De consolatione theologiae* is, as we have
suggested, to be discerned on two distinct though interrelated levels. In the first
place, it must be read in terms of its autobiographical intent, for it is replete
with allusions if often of an indirect nature to the events which Gerson and his
contemporaries had experienced during the years of the Council of Constance.
Yet it is much more than autobiography, and as a dialogue is clearly something
altogether different from traditional literary forms utilized by scholastic
theologians. Although comprehensive in scope, and sprinkled with questions
which move the argument forward, this is a piece far removed in form at least
from the genre of a theological *summa*,[1] since Gerson intends this text to offer
consolation as a kind of practical handbook for *homo viator*. That is, this
dialogue functions not unlike a sermon as a kind of »manual of conversion.«[2]
The broad shape and progressive thematic developments of this treatise mark it
with a paideutic function, lending it the character of an enchiridion aimed at
forming — or, more precisely, »re-forming« — the human person. The text
accomplishes this function by guiding *peregrinus*, who represents »everyman,«
on an interior pilgrimage from despair to hope. In the preceding chapter we
spoke of the treatise as autobiographical narrative, and *advena* as in a funda-

---

[1] A contemporary literary critic has recently described these *summae* as texts which
function as »attempts at total containment,« an accurate description which is useful in
accentuating the quite different character of Gerson's treatise. This treatise is admittedly
»comprehensive,« as we have earlier noted, but it is anything but systematic; it functions as
a »program« for life rather than as an effort to achieve some sort of »absolute containment«
in doctrinal terms. Cf. George Steiner, »The Retreat from the Word,« in *Language and
Silence. Essays on Language, Literature, and the Inhuman* (New York, 1982), p. 14.
[2] On this point we must correct Combes's suggestion that Gerson's text, in contrast to
Boethius' *Consolatio philosophiae*, »ne s'agit ni de dialectique ni de conversion.« Cf. »La
Consolation,« p. 11. He later repeated this thesis without variation in *La théologie mystique*,
2:317. As we have earlier argued, Gerson's *Consolatio theologiae* does function *differently*
from Boethius' treatise, a point which Combes rightly perceives. But Combes fails to
recognize the reluctant »conversion,« if we might call it that, of Monicus within the
dialogue, just as his perspective also ignores the pedagogical function of the text to lead the
reader on an inner journey »from desperation to hope«; see also below, 5.C.2.

mental sense Gerson himself. In this chapter we now turn directly to the second level, exploring the theological contours of *De consolatione theologiae* in
terms of the pedagogical logic undergirding his consolatory argument. At this
level of the treatise we find that Gerson raises questions and offers a »way« for
the pilgrim bound on the human quest for solitude, peace, and *stabilitas*, an
interior journey which he finally interprets here as *peregrinatio ad Deum* leading
ultimately to the *pax Dei*.

But why is it that Gerson chose precisely this literary form, a dialogue which
he fashions quite intentionally after the literary precedent of Boethius' *De
consolatione philosophiae*? How does Gerson himself understand this relationship, and why is it that he offers a *theological* consolation? With these
questions we intrude upon the quite complex matter of literary genre, of
Gerson's deliberate choice of a textual precedent — i. e., the Boethian original
and its rich tradition of commentaries, translations, and imitations — which
had served as a cornerstone of medieval pedagogy.[3] Yet the genre question
cannot command our attention within the parameters of this study, since the
focus of our analysis of this text is not upon the literary trajectory of the
Boethian tradition with its quite varied history of reception during the later
Middle Ages,[4] but upon Gerson's appropriation of it for his own purposes.
This disclaimer notwithstanding, we must at least inquire into the general

---

[3] In a short but penetrating study which analyzes the »the medieval image« as expressed
in the literature of the period, C. S. Lewis comments that »To acquire a taste for [the
Consolation of Philosophy] is almost to become naturalised in the Middle Ages.« *The
Discarded Image. An Introduction to Medieval and Renaissance Literature* (Cambridge, England,
1964), p. 75. Lewis is surely correct in pointing to the quite central role which this treatise
played in medieval teaching and in the process of »bringing Greece to Rome,« to echo
Boethius' own stated intentions; on the genre question, cf. also Courcelle's *La Consolation*,
a magisterial study devoted to analyzing the literary trajectory by which this treatise was
transmitted and reinterpreted throughout the Middle Ages.

[4] Again, cf. Courcelle, *La Consolation*, especially pp. 7–14. Grafton has a terse but
suggestive examination of how fifteenth-century humanists read Boethius, though the
focus of his treatment falls upon quattrocento Italian circles; see »Epilogue: Boethius in the
Renaissance,« *Boethius*, ed. M. Gibson, pp. 410–15. The particular value of this essay lies in
Grafton's expansion of Courcelle's work on the *literary* trajectory of Boethius in medieval
commentaries upon the text; that is, Grafton does not restrict his interest to the narrower
question of the textual history of medieval commentaries upon this text, but discusses how
fifteenth-century readers perceived Boethius more generally. At the same time, his essay
does not yet explore Boethius' reception outside the Italian orbit of fifteenth- and early
sixteenth-century scholars; he makes no reference to those northern Europeans, like
Gerson, who made important use of the Boethian literary tradition. This is a striking
omission, particularly because this might have provided further insight into the continuities
which transcended the Alpine divide. In this regard we can only suggest that Gerson's view
of Boethius approaches Valla's, since he, too, concluded that Boethius had »overestimated
the power of philosophy to solve the great problems of providence and free will«; Gerson
went much further than Valla, however, in constructing an elaborate rebuttal of sorts to the
Consolatio philosophiae; cf. *ibid.*, p. 411.

purpose of this treatise, considering how Gerson utilized Boethius – and, in particular, the »paideutic« nature of the *Consolatio philosophiae* – in order to articulate his quite different theological message. As we shall subsequently see in greater detail, Gerson understood this variant not as *imitatio* but as *aemulatio*, and in this reflects a broad humanist tradition of this period. For this reason we must recognize that Gerson intended his *consolatio* as something other than a literary imbellishment, and in any case one cannot adequately account for his treatise by dismissing it, as Courcelle has done, as a pale version of the Boethian »original,« and hence as a merely derivative construct.[5] Rather, Gerson presents his *Consolatio theologiae* as a necessary sequel to Boethius, a text which exemplifies in its literary form and thematic substance the fundamental Thomistic logic by which theology »surpasses philosophy, not casting it aside but taking it into service.«[6]

---

[5] On this point of interpretation, we must at least call attention to the shortsighted scope of Courcelle's study, since he dismisses from his survey any text which moves beyond the commentary tradition but asserts at the same time that Boethius' thoughts »n'est plus aussi vivante« in the examples from this literary genre of the fifteenth-century. As he goes on to conclude, »le triomphe de l'humanisme sur la scolastique marquera le terme de ses succès.« *La Consolation.*, p. 337. See also above, p. 17, n. 32. The genre limits he places upon his study, however, eclipse from consideration Gerson's text since it is an »imitation« rather than commentary; this is an unfortunate omission, since such an editorial decision prevents Courcelle from recognizing the vitality of Boethius' text for this age – i. e., not in the commentary tradition, which had admittedly run its course by the fifteenth century, but in the Renaissance tradition of literary imitation. It is precisely this genre, within which Gerson's text stands, which Dresden has identified as one of the leading characteristics of the Renaissance: viz. the penchant for imitating classical models. As he suggests, »*imitatio* thus acquired a very different meaning and turned easily into *aemulatio*. Within the rigid framework of rhetorical literary tradition, the reader and above all the creator was to compete with the text which he read. He endeavored to reach the same level, to attain the same degree of perfection, as his model.« This point raises the much-disputed question of Gerson's relationship to fifteenth-century humanism, a topic which we can only announce in this study as meriting further discussion. See Dresden, »The Italian Renaissance in France,« p. 144.

[6] See G 9, p. 188. This point offers crucial assistance in unravelling the eclecticism often attributed to Gerson; as we shall subsequently suggest, *De consolatione theologiae* provides ample evidence for revising Combes's tentative suggestion that Gerson's »théologie thomiste de la grace« can be delineated only after 1425, since already in *De consolatione theologiae* we see clear evidence of such a theological position; cf. *La théologie mystique*, 2:546 ff. Of course, this point should also caution us against naming Gerson as a nominalist, since the epistemology he here advanced distances him from this tradition; on this point Courtenay's suggestion should not go unheeded when he argues that Ockhamism rather than nominalism serves as »the least undesirable term« to speak of the heirs to the Venerable Inceptor; see »Nominalism and Late Medieval Religion,« p. 53. More recently, Shank has defied the use of such labels altogether, concluding that »given the inevitable ambiguities of these terms in current historiography, it has seemed preferable to describe the positions of individual thinkers rather than to give them labels that only spread confusion.« *Logic, University, and Society*, p. xiii.

Before we turn to this theme, however, we must first establish how it is that Gerson delineates not only the legitimacy but the necessity of consolation. By introducing *theologia* not with an abstract discussion of epistemology or soteriology, which would set the issue within the academic horizon of scholastic debate, but with a consideration of the *tentationes* confronting every *viator*, we recognize his pastoral point of departure here: Gerson addresses his readers' experience and thus speaks first of all not as academic theologian but as pastor obligated by the *cura animarum*. Consolation is a necessary theme for *viatores* not as an abstract or professional question of scholastic disputation but because all wayfarers must confront life as a situation of despair. Gerson's approach throughout the dialogue discerns the theological task as at once a pastoral duty, identifying »Lady Theology« as the guide who leads pilgrims »through the highest despair in ourselves to the highest hope in God, and through an inestimable and intolerable desolation upward to a firm consolation.«[7]

A. What is consolation?

On first reading *De consolatione theologiae*, Gerson's emphasis of desperation as the very form of life appears closely allied with the mood of much popular preaching during this period,[8] and at the same time congruous with the portrait of this period as a time of heightened anxiety and despair. As an era in which »a sombre melancholy weighs on people's souls,« to recall Huizinga's view of the later Middle Ages, the fifteenth century appears as a time of the decay of »an overripe form of civilization,« a gloomy era which leaves the reader of its surviving documents with »the same impression of immense sadness«: »Always and everywhere in the literature of [this] age,« Huizinga concludes, »we find a confessed pessimism.«[9] Yet we must inquire whether Gerson himself, together with other contemporaries who struck this note in their preaching, meant to use desperation as the final context of life and whether this theological perspective was one of thorough-going pessimism about the human predicament *coram Deo*, or whether this theme functions for him as the

---

[7] G 9, p. 198.

[8] Again, see Zumkeller, »Das Ungenügen der menschlichen Werke,« *passim*. Douglass has criticized this thesis by arguing that the theme of human unworthiness leading to desperation *coram Deo* is »merely part of the common medieval tradition and will be found in the writing and preaching of men holding very different theological positions«; *Justification in Late Medieval Preaching*, pp. 176 f. What heightens the desperation, as Gerson expresses it in *De consolatione theologiae*, however, is the complete absence of the *facere quod in se est* doctrine which other Ockhamist theologians – and the younger Gerson himself – had linked to the ordained covenant of salvation (i. e., *de potentia Dei ordinata*).

[9] Huizinga, *The Waning of the Middle Ages*, pp. 31 ff.

prelude to a careful pastoral strategy meant to transform *viatores* in their
journey »from desperation to hope.« By inquiring how it is that this theme
functioned both in terms of the broader context of Gerson's works and with
more specific attention to *De consolatione theologiae*, we shall examine how this
emphasis upon desperation serves as the necessary starting point of a careful
pastoral strategy rather than the pervasive context of his thought.

To approach this broad question we must first examine Gerson's aggressive
examination of *tentationes* to describe the desperate situation facing *viatores*. In
this regard we shall have occasion to suggest that Gerson was aware of but at
the same time sought to transcend what Huizinga has identified as the
melancholy and despair of this period. And, more importantly perhaps,
Gerson's theological strategy in this treatise stands as a critical voice over
against Tentler's controversial interpretation of the church's sacramental
system as the basis for a »culture of guilt.«[10] It appears that Gerson's pastoral
convictions after Constance prompt him to articulate a soteriological view of
theologia which bears no reference to the sacramental system. Theology itself
stands as the interior guide leading *viatores* on their pilgrimage toward God, and
this is a path which offers consolation in the midst of *desperatio* facing all
viatores.

1. *Desperatio* as the context for *consolatio*

Throughout this treatise, as in his earlier writings as well,[11] Gerson addresses
the problem of *tentationes*, the temptations facing all *viatores* throughout their
pilgrimage.[12] Indeed, this theme articulates the desperate texture of human

---

[10] Cf. Thomas Tentler, *Sin and Confession on the Eve of the Reformation* (Princeton, NJ, 1977), p. 46.

[11] The *tentationes*, or *temptacions* as he calls them in the vernacular treatises, became a particularly prominent theme in Gerson's sermons. See Brown, *Pastor and Laity*, pp. 90–91. Summarizing this material, Brown poses the question which Gerson addressed again and again in the sermonic material: »What sweetness can there be, what mercy when all goes ill, when all goes ›from worse to worse, from affliction to affliction, from torment to torment‹? ... Tribulations of mind and body, miseries and adversities, both public and private, are all sent from God but for a good end: for example, to encourage us to turn to God in our troubles, to humble us, to make us patient, to correct us.« Brown lists, without further explanation, a series of references to *temptacion* in the vernacular sermons (*ibid.*, p. 288, n. 90); elsewhere she suggests, perhaps too hesitantly, that »Gerson seems to be among those who place a good deal of emphasis upon obstacles« (*ibid.*, p. 192). Hence, her work offers an adequate survey of Gerson's approach to *tentationes* in his vernacular works, though the discussion is lacking in interpretive nuance; absent, for example, is any reference to the fundamental question of what this thematic emphasis implies within the context of Gerson's soteriology.

[12] In his study of Gabriel Biel and late-medieval nominalism, Oberman noted that »a special study on Gerson's understanding of temptations and their remedies would be most

life as our natural condition: »troubles and trials,« he here argues, »are the common lot of all who are living.«[13] *Viatores*, therefore, should not expect to avoid either *tentationes*, which are the external condition of life, or *peccata* which constitute the inner human condition. Echoing the proverbist, he cautions at the outset of this treatise that no one should expect an exemption from this condition, since »even the just person [*justus*] falls seven times each day« (Prov. 24.16),[14] and he adds to this the assertion that it is ultimately God who »wills that *viatores* be plagued with many troubles.«[15] God not only »allows« bad things to happen to good people, but rather actually wills that these occur in order to instill humility and hence drive away self-confidence and pride. In another passage which bears unmistakable Pauline echoes (i. e., to 1 Cor. 1.21 ff.), Gerson defines »the method and approach of theology« as a journey »to wisdom ... through foolishness,« contending that *theologia* brings us »through the greatest despair about humanity and leads us through inestimable and intolerable desolation,« only in order to »lead us upward to the highest hope in God ... and to the firm consolation above.«[16] Desolation and despair, then, become the ineradicable context of human life, fulfilling the biblical dictum that »man is indeed born to labor.«[17] Yet they also prod us forward — or rather »upward,« to recall his use of conventional medieval imagery — driving us to seek a »higher« beatitude than we might find in natural terms.

Gerson thus grounds his discussion of *consolatio* not with a theoretical analysis of the human predicament, nor with a scholastic definition of the Fall or of original sin; rather, he identifies the experience common to all *viatores*, the sense of human abandonment in the *tentationes* of life and the utter despair to which this leads, not as the problem confronting theologians but as what he terms the very *modus* and *ars* of theology. *Viatores*, according to Gerson, are to expect nothing more nor less than that life itself will become a »spiral« of despair, »warfare« (*militia*) leading them into an ever greater desolation. And

---

welcome,« identifying *tentationes* as a central concern of Gerson's. *Harvest*, p. 231, n. 129. While this theme can be treated here in only cursory fashion due to the limitations of our focus, our analysis sketches the outline of a more critical and nuanced approach to Gerson's understanding of the positive function of *tentationes*, with regard both to his anthropology and more significantly his later soteriology.

[13] G 9, p. 227.

[14] G 9, p. 195; both Du Pin and Glorieux fail to note this biblical reference, which is significant since with it Gerson builds his pessimistic view of the human condition not merely on an experiential basis but in terms of the sure authority of a scriptural precedent.

[15] G 9, p. 205.

[16] G 9, p. 198.

[17] Cf. Job 5.7; G 9, p. 227. He goes on in this passage to cite the later reference from Job as well, reminding the reader that life is in no way lived without trials, for it is »warfare« (Job 7.1: »militia est vita hominis super terram ...«).

here already we find the basis for his caution against an overly ambitious quest for mystical experience: he warns against presuming that one might escape from »the struggles of human beings« or »the scourge of tribulations,« deciding not to live in hope but »in beatitude itself.«[18] But this is only Gerson's first word on the subject of *tentationes*, since these experiences which indeed lead *viatores* to a sense of desolation become at the same time the matrix in which we are to seek consolation. And, as he goes on to argue, these are the experiences through which theology is to lead us, guiding us beyond the limits of our innate knowledge, abilities, or experiences toward a »firmer« consolation. Indeed, Gerson elaborates this spiraling dynamic of desolation leading to consolation by articulating what he himself acknowledges is an unprecedented theological argument, a rationale which »will probably seem surprising« to his counterpart:

> Thus it occurs to a person who, by however many tribulations he is besieged, however much he struggles against them and is often overcome by them − either by voracious desires, sleepy lethargy, or frequently endured stings of the flesh, or by other such trials − so much the more frequently, certainly, and thus forcefully, because humbly, does he yield himself to God, hoping and trusting in God.[19]

Tentationes, then, serve to goad restless *viatores* to abandon any vestige of pride in themselves and their own works precisely by driving them beyond self-confidence and into this »spiral« of desperation. In this he follows the ancient medical maxim, »contraria contrariis curantur,«[20] applying this rule to the psychology of salvation. As he concludes in a particularly poignant passage,

---

[18] G 9, p. 202. Often in this treatise Gerson addresses himself to this theme, describing the mystical experience with echoes to the Psalms as a »tasting« of *dulcedo Dei*, or the »sweetness of God«; in this case he argues that some despair in the goodness of God (*bonitas Dei*) if they do not attain this experience: »Quid quod desperant alii de Dei bonitate, si non suavitatem dulcedinis suae experimento jugi gustent; quasi jam esse velint non spe, sed ipsa re beati, et possidere haereditate sanctuarium Dei, neque esse in laboribus hominum, neque cum hominibus per tentationes flagellari.« This section presents a broad criticism of deviant forms which mystical desire could take, not in order to dismiss mystical experience altogether but as a reminder that this experience as *donum Dei* could not be acquired by force. On this theme see also G 9, p. 201. Oberman rightly points to the »strong eschatological emphasis« which flavors Gerson's thought, not only in general terms but specifically with regard to his mysticism; he also notes that it is this eschatological dimension of Gerson's works which has brought upon him the charge that his was not a true mysticism. See *Harvest*, pp. 339−40, and especially n. 53.

[19] G 9, p. 198. Gerson reiterates this theme in more vivid metaphoric language in a later passage, concluding that »though you have been conquered a thousand times, you will be crowned a thousand times; and the more fully and surely the more you relinquish all trust in your own works.« And, as he goes on to say in the same vein, »the love of self in [the condemned] works to the contempt of God, just as in [the elect] the love of God works to the contempt of self.« *Ibid.*, pp. 199−200.

[20] See here Wilfrid Werbeck, »Voraussetzungen und Wesen der scrupulositas im Spätmittelalter,« *Zeitschrift für Theologie und Kirche* 68 (1971), pp. 343−44.

»I wish you to despair — but of yourself, and in yourself, since you are man, and you are flesh.«[21] This emphasis upon *tentationes* provides a curious echo to Huizinga's portrait of this period, though only in the most superficial sense: these tribulations represent the point of departure for the human pilgrimage toward God and not its final context, standing as the inevitable predicament of life for which theology offers its consolation. Its *modus* is distinctively dialectical,[22] since it roots itself within the maelstrom of human desperation in order to lead *viatores* »upward« in hope toward God.

It is striking to note that Gerson's approach here, in distinct contrast to his pastoral tactic in earlier treatises, identifies the guiding and consoling role of *theologia* in terms that he had earlier reserved following medieval practice for

---

[21] G 9, p. 199. Gerson prefaces this passage with a theme of similar proportions, offering a »four-sided« meditation through which he guides *viatores* through various stages of contemplation. The first three have to do with God's nature, as revealed in scriptural commands, while the final addresses the theme of the self-denial necessary to find true consolation: »and the fourth meditation has to do with one's own frailty, lest you hope in yourself or in your own powers.« The clear inference is that all human effort to establish oneself *coram judice Deo* is in vain, and that the first and last step of the human approach to God is through claiming God's promises as revealed in scripture: »Say in answer [to any doubts about your own salvation] that you are obeying the commanding God who, in a thousand places in holy scripture, enjoins that you hope in him.« *Ibid.* This emphasis upon the biblical covenants has been rightly identified as one of the keys to the entire system of Ockhamist theology (see Courtenay, »Nominalism and Late Medieval Religion,« pp. 58–59). Yet as we will subsequently argue (see below, Ch. 5), how this »pact« functions for Gerson in this treatise is quite different than other Ockhamists, since he abandons human effort or merit (i. e., *facere quod in se est*) and emphasizes a covenant of despair in self and corresponding trust in God as the key to hope.

[22] Once again, this realization steers us beyond Combes's mistaken suggestion that there is no dialectic in Gerson's (i. e., in contrast to Boethius') *consolatio*; cf. »La Consolation,« p. 11; it is perhaps not insignificant, therefore, that Combes drops this assertion in his later discussion in *La théologie mystique*, an analysis of this treatise which otherwise follows his earlier essay. It is also worth noting that this theme distinguishes Gerson in general terms from the Ockhamist soteriology with its emphasis upon *facere quod in se est*; he does *not* suggest that *tentationes* are to be overcome through the confidence gained by works of love, but rather *per fidem* in the *fiducia de Deo* (see below, 5.C). Gerson does not presume, in other words, that *tentationes* drive us to seek confidence in our own works of love; rather, he portrays these trials and faith itself in a dialectical relationship. These are the goading force driving us to *fides*, a faith *de Deo* rather than *de propriis operibus* since the latter only consigns us to spiraling despair. This is a peculiar deviation from Gerson's earlier Ockhamist position, a point we shall subsequently discuss in greater detail; it does suggest that Gerson understood *Anfechtungen* in a manner which anticipates Luther, a point which the later reformer himself noted: »Gerson allein hat vor dieser Zeit von geistlichen Anfechtungen geschrieben (alle Andere haben allein leibliche oder fleischliche Anfechtung gefühlet) . . .« (see *Tischreden, WA*, 1:495). In this sense we must at least acknowledge Gerson's movement away from the late-medieval emphasis upon works (or »congruous« merit) as the means of gaining assurance of salvation and thereby quieting the conscience. We might also suggest that Luther's approach to *tentationes* is closer to Gerson's in this case than has been earlier

the sacrament of penance.[23] As he establishes at the very outset of the treatise, it is theology and not the sacraments which lead us through life, for she »gives herself as companion [*comes*] on the pilgrimage, «[24] thereby functioning as the means God ordained so that *viatores* might resist these *tentationes* and the sins that ensued from them. Theology, rather than these sacramental acts of reconciliation, fulfills the central role in consoling *viatores* by leading them *ad Deum*.

The absence throughout this treatise of any direct reference to the sacraments – and particularly that of penance – can hardly be accidental, nor is it insignificant since this omission buttresses Gerson's conviction that one must abandon all trust in self and in one's own works, including the sacramental works of penance. Indeed, he draws attention to this point by underlining the stark contrast of *fiducia de Deo* with *fiducia de propriis operibus*, including among the latter what he calls the sacramental acts of reconciliation;[25] human effort, even when bound to this penitential system, is unable to cope with the accumulating weight of sin and tribulation, for such trials establish the context of – and the need for – consolation. *Tentationes*, in other words, overwhelm us in the very midst of our works. Here, then, we come upon a peculiar development in Gerson's thought, since he had devoted much of his attention in earlier treatises to the matter of combatting or at least coping with scruples, often by applying ourselves with due moderation to the regular channels of grace accessible via the sacraments. In this case his pastoral tactic had been to moderate anxiety over one's sins by lightening penances imposed and insisting

---

supposed, such that Oberman's description of Luther's uniqueness is no longer as convincing: »In the tentatio one does not therefore transcend the state of faith by the evidence for the presence and security of one's faith found in the actual works of love, but it is through tentatio that one appropriates this faith« (see his essay »Luther and the Scholastic Doctrines of Justification, « in *The Dawn of the Reformation. Essays in Late Medieval and Early Reformation Thought* [Edinburgh, 1986], p. 113). The same could be said of Gerson's dialectical approach to this theme in *De consolatione theologiae*, as we here see.

[23] Cf. for example his affirmation in a vernacular treatise of 1401, *La mendicité spirituelle*: »I want you to know, presumptuous pride, by what title or right you always wish to reign in me and all that which I have done; in good faith humility should rather reign there, for I have nothing in me which is mine except evil. And if anything good has been put there by the kindness of my Lord, I have lost or corrupted it – as, for example, the pure white garment of innocence or righteousness [*de innocence ou de justice*] which has been often given to me, as in my baptism or at the holy sacrament of penance. But alas! What have I done with it? Mortal sin has quickly torn it apart and discarded it, or venial sin has stained it with black, disgusting marks so that I could never show it to my Lord.« Even at this early juncture, however, Gerson recognized the inefficiency of penance in compensating for human sin, since our penchant for sinning quickly overcomes even this medium by which we might be restored to a state of innocence or righteousness. It is in this context that we are to understand his vigorous opposition to scrupulosity; on this point, see Werbeck, »Scrupulositas im Spätmittelalter, « pp. 327 ff.

[24] G 9, p. 187.

[25] G 9, p. 200.

at the same time on the reasonable and reliable character of God's expectations of us.[26] This approach emphasized in traditional terms the priest's role as arbiter of sacramental grace, a stance which has been lately characterized — though with peculiar anachronism — as one of »strong paternalism,«[27] demonstrating a »concern for penitents« by accentuating the priestly role corresponding to the church's sacramental system. But this emphasis is nowhere present in *De consolatione theologiae*, and in its place we find at the very heart of this treatise a theme uncharacteristic of the younger Gerson: here he insists on emphasizing rather than diminishing scruples, since these reflect the inevitable human response of desperation to a *fiducia de propriis operibus*. Human achievement, even in terms of the sacrament of penance apparently, cannot lead us out of this spiral of despair. On the contrary, knowing that our sins are »a great abyss and darkness beyond measure,« »more numerous than the sands of the sea,«[28] we are to »collapse in complete desperation of [our] own defense,« taking the part as if in a trial not of the defendant but rather that of »accuser, witness, and judge« against ourselves, and thus »exaggerating [the charges against us] as much as we are able.«[29]

Indeed, his decision here to emphasize tribulation and sin, even to the point of encouraging *scrupulositas*,[30] may paradoxically plumb the true depths of what

---

[26] On this point, for example, see Brown, *Pastor and Laity*, pp. 68–72. Brown concludes, on the basis of vernacular treatises Gerson wrote before the Council of Constance, that »in this way Gerson attempts to allay doubts that might arise from the *facere quod in se est* doctrine. How widely he and pastors who followed his methods were successful in this and in consoling others whose anxieties and scruples had their roots in other aspects of the theology of the sacrament of penance it is impossible to say. But his attempts show a deep psychological sensitivity and insight, and he demands a similar sensitivity from all pastors in their role as confessors.« *Ibid.*, p. 71.

[27] *Ibid.*, p. 70.

[28] This phrase is perhaps a deliberate inversion of Ps. 139.18 (Vl. 138.18): »dinumerabo eos et super harenam multiplicabuntur. . . .«

[29] G 9, p. 232. Can it be that Gerson utilized this imagery in reference to the heated trial of John Hus at the recent council? This appears quite likely, since much of this treatise stands as an answer to the challenges — exegetical, theological, and ecclesiological — raised by Hus (on this point see below, Ch. 6). As we shall later suggest, this concrete polemic against the Hussite position may well have reshaped in basic outline at least Gerson's soteriology. In this sense, a theme which is conspicuous in this treatise by its absence, and which had played a role in his earlier treatises as what one recent study has called »a rider to [Gerson's] reliance on the mercy of God,« is the *facere quod in se est* doctrine; cf. Brown, *Pastor and Laity*, p. 71. We shall discuss this in considerable detail below, but it is significant to point out at this early juncture that Gerson's skepticism vis-à-vis human acts, and his apparent refusal to invoke this argument with its reasonable emphasis on human responsibility, suggests something more than a change of mood in these later writings, and is probably not unrelated to his response to the Hussite problem.

[30] Gerson devoted numerous early treatises, written both for the laity and for the clergy, to the pastoral problem of scrupulosity; for a detailed and balanced discussion of these, see

has been recently called with reference to his earlier, traditional reliance upon the sacraments a »deep psychological sensitivity and insight.«[31] No longer do we find him identifying and analyzing sin, on the one hand, and counseling against scrupulosity through a moderate use of the sacraments, on the other, a duplicity which this same study of Gerson's earlier vernacular treatises has astutely suggested »does not exonerate him from the charge of helping to create the disease [i. e., *scrupulositas*] he sought to cure.«[32] In this treatise his uncompromising concern is rather that of identifying the human »disease« of sin and desperation in its most acute stage, but precisely in order to offer a proper if unexpected diagnosis: by encouraging a vigorous application of scruples to one's past sins[33] Gerson here counsels *viatores* to succumb to scruples and self-despair in order that the *tentationes* and *peccata* which besiege them might have their proper effect of driving them toward a proper trust in God. Not the sacraments but theology itself leads us »per summam desperationem de homine . . . ad summam de Deo spem, et per desolationem inaestimabilem et intolerabilem sursum . . . ad solidam consolationem.«[34] This is also the framework in which Gerson interprets the dialectical *ars* and *modum* of theology as *scandalum crucis*, a clear dependence upon Pauline language: *tentationes* are for *viatores* the inner identification with the cross of Christ, and in this sense establish the constructive shape of the Christian life.

This vivid portrait of desperation, with its accompanying and quite intentional rhetoric of self-accusation, is not then the problem (i. e., as *scrupulositas*) but is itself part of the solution to the human predicament. *Desperatio* alone constitutes the proper matrix for consolation. It would be too much to conclude from his avoidance of any reference to penance that he is here intent on developing an anti-sacramental position; indeed, Gerson's conserv-

---

Werbeck, »Scrupulositas im Spätmittelalter,« pp. 331−49, Brown, *Pastor and Laity,* pp. 68 ff. and Burger, *Aedificatio,* pp. 98 ff.

[31] Cf. Brown, *Pastor and Laity,* p. 71.

[32] *Ibid.,* p. 170.

[33] Here Gerson invokes the counsel of Gregory, who called it »the mark of good minds to recognize fault where none exists«; in this treatise Gerson affirms this advice, though he carefully qualifies this to be relevant only for one's *past* sins. Regarding those which have not yet happened Gerson explicitly alters this claim, noting that »about things still in the future« we should »not impute fault where none lies« lest »an erroneous conscience [*erronea conscientia*] results« (i. e., scruples); G 9, p. 235. This positive though qualified use of Gregory's dictum advances beyond the use Gerson had earlier made of it; see *De vita spirituali, aegritudine et morte animae,* G 3, p. 195. Burger cites this passage, along with the first reference from *De consolatione theologiae,* but he does not yet recognize how Gerson alters his own earlier use of this passage, nor does he appreciate the constructive force of Gerson's emphasis upon *desperationes*; cf. *Aedificatio,* p. 103. See also below, Ch. 5, n. 99.

[34] G 9, p. 198. This is the dialectic which Gerson aligns with the Pauline language of *per stultitiam . . . ad sapientiam*: »sicut per stultitiam et scandalum praedicationis crucis salvos fecit credentes, sic per insipientiam trahit ad sapientiam, dicente Apostolo« (cf. 1 Cor. 1.21 ff.).

ative churchmanship warns against an interpretation expressed in such aggressive terms. But this striking thematic omission in a treatise specifically devoted to consolation, together with his peculiar defense of a heightened scrupulosity in self-accusation and distrust vis-à-vis one's own works, suggests that Gerson's appreciation of his pastoral responsibilities has shifted at this juncture. No longer is he simply content to advocate the sacraments as the pastoral means of dealing with sin or its inward effect, scrupulosity.

This is an intriguing point, particularly when measured against Tentler's analysis of the functional role of the sacramental system during this period.[35] His thesis concentrates above all on the sacrament of penance and the genre of *summa confessorum*, pastoral handbooks quite popular during the later Middle Ages which offered guidance for those hearing confession, indicting the popular use within the church of the sacramental system as a means of maintaining what he calls »social control.« With this thesis Tentler characterizes the later Middle Ages in a manner corresponding to Huizinga's bleak portrait of this period, though he approaches this question from another vantage point altogether: he describes the brooding melancholy of the age from the other side, as it were, identifying the church's deliberate manipulation of penance in order to promote and subsequently control a heightened »culture of guilt.« This thesis has not been without its critics who have suggested a more nuanced reading of the practices surveyed by Tentler.[36] But what interests us here moves beyond the scope of Tentler's critique and the discussion surrounding it, since this thesis and its rebuttal accept the *summae confessorum* as representative for this period of the pastoral »management« of sin and guilt. In contrast to this discussion, which does at least point to the officially sanctioned institutional means of handling sin during the medieval period, our analysis of Gerson's *De consolatione theologiae* suggests that voices not only outside but within the established church were already offering alternatives to this arrangement. Can it be that Gerson, whom Tentler himself describes as »the greatest voice in the cure of souls,«[37] moves *beyond* the sacramental system in

---

[35] Cf. Tentler, »The Summa for Confessors as an Instrument of Social Control,« *The Pursuit of Holiness*, pp. 103–26, and his »Response and Retractatio,« *ibid.*, pp. 131–37; also, his lengthier treatment of this theme in *Sin and Confession*.

[36] For example, Leonard Boyle has vigorously disputed the basis of Tentler's thesis not in terms of the external evidence cited but on the basis of the interpretive approach to the documents (*summae confessorum*) themselves; see »The Summa for Confessors as a Genre, and Its Religious Intent,« *The Pursuit of Holiness*, pp. 126–30. Boyle reads these practical handbooks as means of forming »an educated clergy,« particularly in areas remote from »any contact with scholastic circles«; he interprets these, consequently, in a much more positive light, identifying these pragmatic *summae* as the pedagogical means by which the lower clergy became familiar with »the law of God« and its practical implications for pastoral oversight.

[37] Tentler, *Sin and Confession*, p. 46. He suggests here that Gerson's authority can be measured by »the ubiquity of his opinion and the authority accorded it« later in this

addressing the question of sin and despair? This appears to be the case in this treatise. The problem of this system, in other words, lay not so much in its strength as in its weakness, since not even the sacramental act of penance could resolve the underlying problem of human desperation *coram Deo judice*. The way to a merciful God, as Gerson here perceives it, is not through meritorious works set within the penitential system but through *tentationes*, the *Anfechtungen* which lead us first to *desperatio* and only then to a confidence in God's mercy. *Theologia* and above all the biblical promises of grace *per Jesum Christum*,[38] rather than the sacrament of penance, establish the signposts leading *viatores* toward hope *in Deum*. In this regard we find at least the essential structure of Luther's later insight that we must »spring over« (*transilire*) from our sins to Christ's righteousness, finding our righteousness not in our own works but in Christ who is himself »the sacrament of our reconciliation.«[39] Gerson's view of *desperationes*, consequently, functions as the critical side of his assault upon confidence in human works, and apparently even tempers the quite traditional reliance he had earlier placed in the sacramental system. As we can only suggest at this juncture, this development signals a shift not only in Gerson's thought but in the sacramental focus of pastoral care during the later Middle Ages.

2. The character of theology as *paideia*

Our discussion of the nature of consolation now proceeds in its proper horizon, with Gerson's view of the positive function of *tentationes* and the necessary role of *desperatio* clearly before us. We now understand why it is that Gerson held consolation to be necessary for *viatores*, since desperation and desolation stood as the unavoidable form of human life. The first question we must explore requires us to consider more precisely what exactly Gerson understood as the consolatory nature of the theological task. Gerson himself did not entertain such a question, at least not in such stark terms; he simply assumes that the nature of theology is nothing other than that of »consolation,« a thesis he

---

century. Brown cites this conclusion without further comment in *Pastor and Laity*, pp. 116−17.

[38] See for example G 9, p. 209, where he cites Rom. 7.24. He addresses this theme in another passage earlier in the treatise: »Denique spes velut anchora, quanto minus in arenulis fragilibus et fluidis humani auxilii figitur, tanto solidius et certius supra firmam petram, quae Christus est, defixa stabilitur«; *ibid.*, p. 200.

[39] See G 9, pp. 190, 195, etc. This is a point which does not occur in any of Gerson's earlier treatises, as far as I have discovered, but its presence here would at least qualify Werbeck's conclusion that »Gerson hat nicht bis dahin gelangt, die Gewissen unter Hinweis auf Christus und die Verheißung zu trösten.« Cf. »Scrupulositas im Spätmittelalter,« p. 350. See also below, 5.C.

advanced as authoritative by framing the treatise on either end with Rom. 15.4: »Whatsoever has been written ... has been written for our instruction [*ad nostram doctrinam*], so that through patience and the consolation of scripture we might have hope.« Gerson assumes, in other words, that the nature of theology as consolatory needs no explanation beyond the recognition that *theologia* fulfills its function in terms of sacred scripture. Indeed, his fundamental conviction about the functional identity of *scriptura* and *theologia* discloses a critical step in the development of late-medieval exegesis, the consequence apparently of his nominalist tendency to isolate scripture in its unique revelatory character as the foundation and guiding norm of the theological task itself.[40] In this sense, Gerson utilized sacred scripture as the context as well as the content of the theological enterprise, and with this offered both a retreat and an advance in the medieval history of biblical exegesis. As a retreat, Gerson's contribution must be understood against theological and exegetical developments during the high Middle Ages, a period in which the theological task was increasingly grasped not simply as commentary upon *sacra pagina* but as the discrete domain of *sacra doctrina*.[41] In this sense he retreats, in terms of theological method, to an early approach to *theologia* as biblical commentary such that *sacra pagina* determined the contours of theological discussion. But this is only one facet of his exegetical practice: Gerson's hermeneutic theory stands as an advance in terms of his progressive accentuation of the »literal« sense, a theme we shall explore more fully later in this study.[42] This is not yet to suggest that Gerson anticipates as a »forerunner« the later Protestant notion of *scriptura sola*, since his views on the necessary ecclesiastical *context* of biblical interpretation bracket his hermeneutic theory and practice squarely within the horizon of church tradition — viz. the *consensus patrum et doctorum*.[43] But with

---

[40] In his analysis of fifteenth-century hermeneutics, Froehlich has pointed to this facet of his thought, concluding that »in [Gerson's] nominalist tendency toward separating the Bible from all other literature, Gerson was against extending to any other writing the positive privilege of biblical ›truthfulness‹ ... [and] he was against extending to Holy Scripture the negative privilege of universal doubtfulness or equivocation so freely used to cover up dubious moral intentions of human authors.« See »Fifteenth-Century Hermeneutics,« p. 44. Pascoe has also pointed to Gerson's identification of scripture and theology, concluding that Gerson already early in his university career had described the theologian's task principally in terms of scriptural exegesis; see *Jean Gerson*, p. 92.

[41] Cf. Smalley, *The Study of the Bible in the Middle Ages*, pp. 271 ff. Cf. also, G. R. Evans, *The Language and Logic of the Bible. The Road to Reformation* (Cambridge, England, 1985), pp. 7−8; J. de Ghellinck, »›Pagina‹ et ›Sacra Pagina.‹ Histoire d'un mot et transformation de l'objet primitivement designe,« *Mélanges August Pelzer* (Louvain, 1947), pp. 23−59. It is in this vein that his exegesis has been characterized as »the attempt of a sophisticated fundamentalist to keep the unity and uniqueness of the Bible,« since Gerson insists on defining the theological task principally within »the orbit of scripture itself.« Froehlich, »Fifteenth-Century Hermeneutics,« p. 44.

[42] See below, 6.A.3.

[43] On this point see below, 4.A.4, 6.A.3

Gerson we are at least on the road toward a conceptualization of theology within the limits not of the logic of scholastic argument, but of a logic peculiar to the biblical language itself. As he had earlier argued, scripture has »its own logic and grammar, just as the moral sciences have for their logic rhetoric.«[44] This conviction results in an »exegetical« or »biblical« theology which appropriates the text as the horizon both *from* which and *toward* which one works as a theologian.

In recognizing the close proximity of *scriptura* and *theologia* and the peculiar authority accorded to biblical language in Gerson's later writing, therefore, the identity of theology cannot be either extracted or abstracted from *scriptura sacra*. Thus it is no small point when he opens his treatise by honoring Paul as »the great disciple of theology,« nor is it insignificant that he chose as the scriptural framework for this treatise Paul's claim, following the Vulgate reading, that the biblical texts were written »for our instruction« (*ad nostram doctrinam*). Scripture itself becomes the source for *doctrina*, the matrix out of which theology arises; it extends to all *viatores*, moreover, and not simply to professional theologians, guidance as the companion (*comes*) upon life's pilgrimage, and in this capacity offers consolation while leading us *ad Deum*. As Gerson expands upon this text and unfolds the manner in which theology offers this consolation, he identifies *doctrina* simply as »instruction« rather than in its more technical definition as theological explication.[45] In this less technical sense Gerson enunciates the doctrinal function of *theologia*, which thus depends upon the substance of scripture, as a matter of character formation, the guidance of *viatores* from despair to hope: in a word, as Christian *paideia*.

This interpretation of Gerson's literary and theological intent in *De consolatione theologiae* as paideutic becomes more convincing when we ask about his view of philosophy, and more specifically about how he viewed Boethius whom he distinguished from earlier sources since his predecessor though a philosopher lived »in the time of grace« and was thus »established in a higher light.«[46] That is, he understands this bearer of philosophical consolation not

---

[44] Gerson had begun to formulate this thesis already during his sojourn in Constance, shortly after Hus's death in 1415; see his »Réponse à la consultation des maîtres,« in G 10, p. 241: »Sed habet scriptura sacra suam propriam logicam et grammaticam, quemadmodum scientiae morales habent pro logica rhetoricam.«

[45] For a good discussion of the force which *doctrina* had in Aquinas's thought, see Persson, *Sacra Doctrina*, pp. 71 ff.

[46] G 9, p. 204. It is intriguing to note that Gerson distinguished Boethius' philosophic superiority primarily because other philosophers were only acquainted, he assumes, with Jewish prophetic literature; and, as a consequence of this limitation, such thinkers devoted themselves to discussions of »the perpetuity of the world.« The contribution of *Christian* thought, in other words, refuted this »heretical« doctrine. This point reflects his careful reading of Boethius (see *De consolatione philosophiae* V pr. 6, *CCSL* 94: 102 f.), who rejected the theory of the »coeternity« of the world. But is there another level of polemic to be heard in this affirmation? It is quite possible that the respect Gerson here lavishes upon Boethius

as a philosopher of noble »pagan« ideas, nor as an archetype of Christian humanism, views given in several recent efforts to resuscitate Boethius.[47] Rather, Gerson's view of Boethius identifies him among the great advocates of *paideia* in the classical philosophical tradition, broadly speaking. As Gerson read Boethius — and he offers an interpretation of his predecessor which remains remarkably faithful to Boethius' stated intentions — philosophy was the nurse (*nutrix*) who announced the *medicinae tempus*, thereby bringing the ailing person from lethargy or despair back to the good life of virtue. *Paideia* in its classical form had to do with a theory of the growth or transformation of human personality, yet Gerson did not embrace such a philosophical program without further comment. Rather, his intentions in this treatise emulate the program of the Cappadocian fathers, a theological *paideia* which Werner Jaeger has described as preserving »certain basic tendencies of the classical mind around which the ideas of their own age could crystallize.«[48] Like his Cappadocian predecessors in this regard, though probably under the more immediate influence of Boethius, Gerson defined the theological task in terms of a Christian *paideia*, an approach to theology as a »conversion« of the human person which clearly moves beyond the »moral and religious content« offered by the »pagan« *auctoritates* while nonetheless preserving the functional shape of their thought.[49]

This theme of *paideia*, interpreting Gerson's grasp of theological consolation as a program aimed not at an abstract notion of *doctrina* but at the trans-

---

reflects at the same time his condemnation of the later Boethius of Dacia, whose thought Bishop Tempier had condemned in 1270 and again in 1277. This appears to be a concern of Gerson's already in his early lectures *Contra curiositatem studentium*; see *Selections*, ed. Ozment, pp. 34–35. On the question of Boethius of Dacia's thought on this subject, see *On the Supreme Good, On the Eternity of the World, On Dreams*, trans. and intro. John Wippel (Toronto, 1987), pp. 9–19. And, finally, on Tempier's condemnation of Averroistic Aristotelianism, see Gilson, *History of Christian Philosophy in the Middle Ages*, pp. 402–10.

[47] E. g., in Courcelle's *La Consolation* and Henry Chadwick's *Boethius. The Consolations of Music, Logic, Theology, and Philosophy* (Oxford, 1981), *passim*, respectively.

[48] Cf. Werner Jaeger, *Early Christianity and Greek Paideia* (Cambridge, MA, 1961), p. 85. This final contribution of Jaeger's life-long study of the history of *paideia*, which focuses primarily upon the contribution of the early Alexandrians and the later Cappadocians, called for an ongoing analysis of how this classical theme continued to exert an influence upon medieval Christian theologians. Jaeger sketches the direction such a study might take by pointing in the closing pages of this work to the influx of Greek thought into the west during the mid-fifteenth century, an expansion of the »available« ideas brought about by the fall of Constantinople and the migration of Greek scholars and texts to the west. This is surely a vital part of this history. But it is not yet the whole story, since this thesis only accounts for the impact of *paideia* in the Renaissance; surely this influence exerted itself through other textual channels during earlier centuries, including Boethius' *Consolatio philosophiae* in its medieval reception. This must be a question settled elsewhere, but we can suggest here that Gerson's close attention to Boethius' text might well be at least one source through which he derives his paideutic approach to theology.

[49] *Ibid.*, p. 81.

formation of the human person, is not to suggest that he deliberately set about
to extend this classical legacy for his own day. On this point we must say, at the
very least, that he himself nowhere announces this as his intention. Yet his
dependence upon Boethius — not only in the literary construction of this
treatise, in the most obvious sense, but in the subtler aspect of having studied
the text »from his youth«[50] — is what shapes this treatise as »paideutic,« a
theological denouement of the constructive role first introduced by
philosophy. Of this purpose, both literary and theological, the treatise bears
ample witness. For instance, Gerson infers in the opening pages that the
justification of theological *paideia*, above and beyond what philosophical
knowledge can do for us in this regard, is that philosophy »has not the means
. . . to confer either the virtues or the formal acts« by which we might
»objectively attain to this state« — viz., the ultimate goal of the *peregrinus* as
being »perfected by the inclusion of every good thing.«[51] Theology alone
recognizes our true destiny, which Gerson calls again and again »our
supernatural goal« (*finis supernaturalis*), and she alone can direct us in the way of
the virtues — i. e., the highest, or theological, virtues of faith, hope, and love
which are necessary to attain to this end.[52] Elsewhere he also addresses this
theme of virtue theory, describing *theologia* again in personified form as our
»companion« on the human journey, or again as a wise »sister« who comforts
us and restricts our steps »within safe bounds.« That journey finds its structure
and direction from the virtues:

---

[50] Gerson notes in the opening pages of this treatise (I pr. 2), here speaking through
Monicus' voice, that he had »labored over this book from [his] youth, brooding upon it
strenuously« (»memini, Volucer; et quali principio exordiens, quali praeterea medio
progrediens, hucusque processerit, retineo, nimirum qui studio libri illius ab adolescentia
vehementer incubuerim«; G 9, p. 188). Curiously, and probably not accidentally, we might
note that Boethius had also admitted to having frequented the dwelling (*lares*) of philosophy
ab adulescentia (*De consolatione philosophiae* I pr. 3, *CCSL* 94: 5); furthermore, though along
another line altogether, it is probably not insignificant to note that Gerson also mentions in
this treatise his acquaintance with the Bible from an even earlier age, or *ab infantia*,
suggesting that that *theologus* is truly happy (*felix*) whom fair wisdom wants for her spouse
a puero. These distinctions appear to reflect not only pedagogical but theological
convictions, since Gerson insisted that even children should hear the Bible being read and
thereby begin their formation as »theologians« (*theologi*) before being trained to read and
study texts belonging to the liberal arts curriculum, as Boethius' *De consolatione philosophiae*
was utilized throughout the Middle Ages.
[51] G 9, p. 189: ». . . sed neque virtutes neque actus formales, quibus attingatur iste status,
objective quidem, in Deo intuitive cognito, philosohia tradere non valuit.«
[52] See G 9, p. 196: »Est autem humani cordis desiderium et pondus in Deum sicut in
locum suum et centrum ferri; est supremum post quod non relinquitur aliud humanae
peregrinationis refugium. Superest igitur nihil infra quod, vel ultra quod possit humanum
se cor deflectere vel fugere dum pondere suo se constituit adhaerere Deo, nunc interim per
spem, fidem et amorem; neque enim sibi dat aliter status praesens.« As we shall later argue,
this emphasis upon the theological virtues *nunc interim* articulates the constructive side of
Gerson's anti-apocalyptic argument; see also below, 6.B.

... Hope and true faith and divine love
Accompany [the pilgrim], and virtue four-fold:
Prudence, moderation, bravery, and justice ... .[53]

The classical and theological virtues combine, in other words, to form an uninterrupted structure guiding *viatores* not only in mundane terms but with regard to their final destination *ad Deum*. In a later reference to these virtues, he identifies these as containing the »cleansing of penance« as well as providing a »refuge of immunity,«[54] a description which is replete with echoes to the sacraments, and he goes further to argue that these are the means by which an inner peace, disrupted through human fear, might be re-formed (*reformetur*).[55] Once again, this shift in emphasis portrays the theological virtues as functioning in a similar manner as had the sacraments in the scholastic theory and ecclesiastical practice during this period, a further clue to soteriological developments in Gerson's thought. According to his broad grasp of *doctrina* in this treatise, it is theology which ultimately conveys these virtues *nunc interim*, and these serve as the indispensable instruments (*media*) by which *viatores* are to be re-formed to their original state as they journey through life.

In a similar sense, and here we can only mention a theme to which we shall subsequently return, Gerson contends that the theologian like Cicero's orator must be a »good« person, in this case not one who is »an expert in speaking« (*vir bonus dicendi peritus*) but who is rather »learned in the sacred writings« – not in the education of the intellect alone, »but much more of the heart« itself.[56] In

---

[53] G 4, pp. 28–29.

[54] See G 9, p. 240. It should be noted that this is the single reference to penance found throughout the treatise, and here the theological virtues rather than the varieties of divinely ordained *media* – including, apparently, the sacraments – come to offer the penitential cleansing. Elsewhere, as earlier noted, he identifies Christ as our »sacrament of reconciliation«; see G 9, p. 190, and below, 5.C.1.

[55] On this point Gerson's paideutic view of theology extends themes explored by Gerhart Ladner in *The Idea of Reform. Its Impact on Christian Thought and Action in the Age of the Fathers* (Cambridge, MA, 1959) and *idem*, »Reformatio«, in *Ecumenical Dialogue at Harvard. The Roman Catholic-Protestant Colloquium*, ed. S. Miller, G. E. Wright (Cambridge, MA, 1964), pp. 172–90. Ladner rightly points to the broad use of this concept through the patristic and well into the medieval period, but he steers his survey toward a final consideration of monasticism. Our study of Gerson would suggest that such ideas achieved, at least at the hands of this particular late-medieval theologian, a significant modulation, insofar as he drew upon this and related themes of earlier monasticism yet did so by extending their applicability to *all* Christians. We shall subsequently speak of this as his »democratization« of the monastic spiritual tradition, though we might better say that he democratizes the very profession of theology by broadening both its function and its »audience.« See below, 6.C.

[56] See G 9, p. 237. Combes rightly notes regarding this citation that the source should stand as Quintilian rather than Cicero, and argues that this is what he calls »un geste d'humaniste impénitent«; cf. *La théologie mystique* 2: 354, n. 152. Combes also reminds us in discussing this particular passage that Gerson has borrowed this language primarily from scripture (e. g., Ps. 77.7, Eccli. 6.23), though he also acknowledges thematic parallels, if not

other words, the theologian like the philosopher must be »formed« by the virtues of »the good life,« each as his respective discipline teaches. In the case of the theologian, this requires *viatores* to integrate theology in life, to »form« theology through exercising the theological virtues. This is, of course, a characteristic Gersonian claim by which he often insisted that *theologia* is a matter one must grasp not only *per intellectum*, but much more *in affectum cordis*.[57] This theme appears at first glance strangely out of character since with it Gerson seems to embrace the »neo-Donatist« position as expressed in the Hussite critique of the »unworthy« priest.[58] Upon closer scrutiny of the context, however, one detects that Gerson's intention steers in another direction altogether: he intends to draw out in didactic rather than polemical terms the integrated nature of theology in human life, and the implications this carried for the tasks confronting not only professional theologians (*magistri, theologi*) but the common people (*idiotae*) as well. All *peregrini* are to have a »formed« faith, though the »simple« will necessarily have a *fides simplex* alongside *suavis charitas*; at issue is not the quantity of knowledge, since this varies according to the person, but its quality. Gerson demands of clergy and laity an erudition of the »heart« by which faith was formed in the virtues.[59] This variation upon the medieval theme of *fides formata*, which Gerson

---

also more suggestive verbal echoes, to texts of Bernard of Clairvaux, Thomas Aquinas, and Nicolas de Clemanges. *Ibid.*, pp. 354–55, nn. 153, 154, 155. For further analysis of this text in terms of Gerson's ecclesiology, see below, 6.A.3.

[57] See G 9, p. 237: »... non quidem eruditione solius intellectus, sed multo magis affectus; ut ea quae per theologiam intelligit, traducat per jugem ruminationem in affectum cordis, et executionem operis.« In other words, one must be a theologian not only in terms of one's doctrinal knowledge, but through having *fides formata*, or faith formed through works of love, a conviction he supported by reciting Gal. 5.6. This is not yet to suggest, however, that Gerson advocated »formed faith« as a means of gaining an assurance of salvation, a view which characterized the Ockhamist soteriology more generally; in contrast Gerson insisted that the »weight« of sin – original, actual, and habitual – finally overcame our better intentions to live guided by *all* the virtues. In a sharp exchange upon this point, it is Monicus who defends the traditional Augustinian anthropology, warning against any naïveté in this regard; Volucer responds with the Pauline treatment found in Rom. 7.24, »Infelix ego homo quis me liberabit de corpore mortis hujus ...« adding, »Gratia Dei per Jesum Christum!« G 9, pp. 208–209.

[58] On this question, see also below, 6.A.2. Jaroslav Pelikan addresses the phenomenon of neo-Donatism in *Reformation of Church and Dogma (1300–1700)*, vol. 4: *The Christian Tradition. A History of the Development of Doctrine* (Chicago, 1984), pp. 92–98. This was clearly on Gerson's mind as early as 1414, when he entered into a prolonged correspondence with Conrad de Vechte, Archbishop of Prague. In a letter dated September 24, 1414, in which he offered advice on how to counter the Hussite heresy, he isolates as »the most pernicious« of all Hus's errors the denial of hierarchical authority to prelates who were thought to be in a state of sin; see G 2, p. 162 f.

[59] See G 9, p. 238: »Confido in Domino quod apud idiotas sollicitos de salute sua, in quibus est simplex fides, certa spes et suavis caritas, insidebunt fructuosius in animo catholicae sententiae, ideo non frustra sunt, quam apud repletos litteris gignentibus scientiam illam quam inflare dicit Apostolus.« We shall later explore this theme in greater

enunciates in an unusual phrase as *theologia formata*, reinforces his conviction about the essentially paideutic nature of theology. *Theologia* as »formed« faith thus has little to do of necessity at least with the professional guild, since theology as »life-instruction« conveys to every *viator* the knowledge both of their destination and of the means of attaining this goal. With this theme Gerson carefully extends his model of the theologian, portraying *theologus* as *viator* — whether *idiota* or *peritus* — who is »wise in sacred scripture,« though with a learning rooted in the affective dimension of the person. His point is not that each person should enter into academic training to become a theologian by profession; rather, he offers an alternative model of *theologia* itself, de-professionalizing it by portraying theology as »a companion [*comes*] on life's pilgrimage« (cf. I pr. 1) which functions to guide all *viatores* in the task of formation in the virtuous life. Theology, in other words, is *paideia*, and as such stands as an obligation falling to all people.

A theme related to this point is the role of law in Gerson's works, a vast and intricate issue which we can only mention at this juncture.[60] In Gerson's articulation of theology as paideutic discipline, we find him constructing a »history of salvation« in which he conceived various dispensations which progressively manifested faith — viz. »the time of grace« when faith was fully manifest; »the time of the written law« when faith was »less explicit«; and »the time of the natural law« when faith was »even less« accessible.[61] Yet this »Heilsgeschichte« did not dispel but rather accentuated the continuity underlying the corresponding dispensation of this divine »law.« That is, it is the *lex divinitatis et ordo* which undergirds this historical structure of a progressive revelation — i. e., the natural law (*lex naturale*); the old law (*lex vetus*); and, finally, the new law (*lex nova, lex evangelica*, etc.) — in order that human actions might be governed in each historical epoch and the human character progressively re-formed. Thus, the theme of the paideutic function of

---

detail, since it appears that Gerson attributes the prospect for »formed faith« to be greater among the *idiotae* than the *eruditi*. See also below, 4.C.

[60] See below, 4.B.1; for a discussion surveying Gerson's thought more broadly, see also Posthumus Meyjes, *Jean Gerson et l'Assemblée de Vincennes (1329). Ses conceptions de la juridiction temporelle de l'église* (Leiden, 1978), pp. 92–101; Pascoe, *Jean Gerson*, pp. 49–79; and, finally, Burger, *Aedificatio*, pp. 84–97.

[61] G 9, pp. 196–97; see also *ibid.*, p. 237, where Gerson describes the threefold succession by which God »imprints« the principles of the moral law: namely, first, upon nature itself; second, on tablets of stone (i. e., the Mosaic law); and, finally, »in the gospel by the tradition of faith« (*per fidei traditionem in evangelio*). This emphasis upon the continuity of *lex Dei* is a characteristic of Gerson's thought in general, and stands at the very center of this dialogue — perhaps, as we shall later point out in greater detail, because the events which had transpired during the Council of Constance as well as »the turmoil which split apart the famed kingdom of France« during his day (G 9, p. 228) drove him to emphasize with particular force in this treatise the inviolability of the *lex divinitatis et ordo*. See below, 6.A.1, and, on the threefold succession, 4.B.1, esp. n. 61.

law coalesces with Gerson's grasp of *theologia*, serving as the guide and companion for *viatores* through history conceived here *coram judice Deo*. This proximity of theology and law reminds us that Gerson interpreted of the theologian's task less in terms of relaying information about God than in charting the path by which *peregrini* were to approach God.

3. *Consolatio* as the texture of *scriptura sacra*

We have already pointed to Gerson's use of Rom. 15.4 as the literary frame of this treatise, a programmatic text which organizes the structure of his treatise. At the same time, as we have earlier suggested, this scriptural text articulates his conviction that biblical language has a formative utility which we have termed its paideutic function: it is meant to instruct us, to teach us patience, to offer us true consolation. This instrumental character of scripture, in other words, is that of *aedificatio*, one of the principal Pauline themes which exercised Gerson's thought and writing during the decades preceding the Council of Constance.[62] Yet as we explore the question of what constitutes *consolatio*, and how this theme relates to what we have called his paideutic use of scripture, we begin to discern how insistently Gerson introduces *theologia* also as the vehicle of consolation — in short, as itself the source of edification. The original question regarding the character of consolation thereby becomes an inquiry into the nature of theology and of its close relation to scripture.

Gerson accomplishes this identity most clearly in his persistent fusion of theological argument and biblical text, creating in the process a literary treatise saturated with scriptural citations and allusions — at times a key phrase, but more often whole sentences culled from the scriptures, and above all from the Psalms and Pauline literature.[63] The modern editors of Gerson's *œuvres*

---

[62] On this point see Burger, *Aedificatio*, pp. 48–49, 55–62. Burger rightly identifies this as one of the central Gersonian themes.

[63] One might detect in Gerson's frequent if often oblique use of scriptural phrases or images an instance of the manner in which quotations were handled more broadly speaking during the Renaissance. In this regard Dresden has argued that »the quotation is obviously connected with and is, in a sense, the consequence of paraphrase. In the paraphrase, the words of a text are replaced, while the meaning is retained. A form of quotation develops when a few words of the text remain, while others and, ultimately, the sense of the whole text, are altered. As we know, humanist literature — poetry, philosophical tracts, and every other type of literature — was full of quotations. What was the point of this practice? Initially, we must consider the admiration of the humanists for venerable, ancient models, and then the authority with which they tried to clothe their own writings by recalling what ancient writers had said on the subject.« »The Italian Renaissance in France,« pp. 145–46. Dresden goes on to cite Erasmus' admiring description of Origen, for whom biblical texts »flowed quite naturally from his pen,« and adds that this could be applied to many medieval writers. It is probably in this sense, rather than in the humanist tradition of emulating the

complètes, from Du Pin's early eighteenth century edition through Glorieux's more recent efforts, have only begun to identify the full extent of this dependence on biblical argument and language. In this project what remains undetected is the breadth of such references as well as the flavor these bring to the paideutic function of theology: scripture itself provides the theological substance of the consolatory argument found in this treatise. One notices this functional character of *scriptura* in Gerson's use of a subtle literary technique throughout the treatise: he personifies *theologia* by giving her a voice, and she uses this voice in an insistent manner to »reveal« scripture: »Among those truths [revealed by God], though by no means against the dictates of reason [*non irrationabiliter*], *theologia* offers this one: that God ›rewards those who seek him. . . .‹«[64] The truth, of course, which *theologia* announces bears no original thought, nor does it offer arguments from the arsenal of scholastic disputation. Rather, theology — or perhaps we should read »Lady Theology« — articulates the plain scriptural text (Heb. 11.6) in the logic of its literal sense. Later in the treatise »faith« assumes the same personified role, for it »says to him again that ›for those who love God‹ and hope in him ›all things work together for the good,‹ just as the apostle teaches« (Rom. 8.28).[65] Scripture stands as a text written *ad nostram doctrinam* and thus teaches the way in which we should proceed through life. It is meant to educate and guide all *viatores*, effecting an erudition not merely of the »intellect« but »much more of the heart,«[66] an allusion to Gerson's portrayal of faith »formed« through the virtues (*fides formata*) and hence integrated into the texture of human life. And, in a surprising affirmation which moves beyond the medieval teaching regarding the hierarchy of faith which existed in the church, Gerson extends in this treatise the responsibility which the laity assumed toward scripture: here he demands of all *viatores*, the laity (*idiotae*) along with the higher clergy, a »certitude« and »explicit faith« (*fides explicita*) not only of the creed's twelve articles but of »the whole of sacred scripture.«[67]

---

great classics, that Gerson's use of scripture is to be understood. Biblical language saturated his thought not for rhetorical effect, but because he understood this as the very basis of *theologia revelata*; see below, 4.A.1.

[64] G 9, p. 189. In this sense, *theologia* speaks in an indirect voice throughout the treatise, even though entering as a formal voice in the dialogue only in the final pages; Combes failed to recognize this, and concluded that »la théologie n'y prend la parole qu'à la fin, et sa tâche ne ressemble en rien à celle de la Philosophie.« *La théologie mystique*, 2: 317. We should also notice the force of Gerson's comment that this language »revealed« by theology is offered *non irrationabiliter*. Although he did define scripture in nominalist fashion as the special language of revelation, and hence distinctive when contrasted with other literature, he also held what appears to be the Thomist position that theological language merely brought to perfection what nature offered. Thus he argued at one point, ». . . sic theologia philosophiam exsuperat, quam non abjicit, sed in obsequium sumit« (G 9, p. 188).

[65] G 9, p. 197.

[66] See above, 3.A.1.

[67] G 9, p. 231. For further discussion of this point, see below, 4.C.

82 Pedagogy and Theological Method

4. Theology and teleology: *peregrinatio ad Deum*

Alongside Gerson's attentiveness to the task theology serves as *paideia* stands his conviction that theology is necessary to offer us true consolation since it alone steers us toward our ultimate destination. Theology alone defines the final end facing every *viator*. In this sense the general theme of pilgrimage — i. e., »from fear to hope« — which structures the treatise can indeed be read in terms of an interior journey *ad Deum*, a journey in which *viatores* make their way through life's struggles »de timore in spem et amorem.«[68] Yet theology leads on this inner pilgrimage not only toward the theological virtues and hence beyond »nature.« This path directs us finally toward the ultimate goal of human life, toward God himself, since it leads »miraculously, as it were, to our embracing through love the God of all consolation, to whom we also cling as if to a place of sure refuge.«[69] The search for security is finally nothing other than the quest for God.[70] Somewhat later in the treatise Gerson approaches the same theme from a related vantage point, though here he articulates it in a manner redolent of a neo-Platonic cosmology. Noting that »the condition of things« is to tend toward their established end (*in suos fines tendant*), Gerson argues that »the desire and weight of the human heart is to be carried to God, as toward its proper locus and center.«[71] God stands as the *humanae peregrinationis refugium*, the final refuge of the human pilgrimage; not to know the character of this goal is to misinterpret, and hence mis-live, that journey. Just as theology *conveys* a knowledge of that end, its proper identity is itself

---

[68] Cf. G 9, p. 190: »Vellem audire quo pacto fieri habet haec inductio vere mirabilis, de timore in spem et amorem.«

[69] *Ibid.*

[70] This language, which betrays what has been called a »search for new security,« has been used by Oberman to describe late-medieval life in a general sense, though his thesis is that this period witnessed a progressive lessening of the gap separating the sacred and profane. See »The Shape of Late Medieval Thought: The Birthpangs of the Modern Era,« reprinted in *Dawn*, pp. 25—29. More recently Berndt Hamm has returned to this theme in order to establish the context in which Johannes of Paltz's theology should be understood; cf. *Frömmigkeitstheologie am Anfang des 16. Jahrhunderts. Studien zu Johannes von Paltz und seinem Umkreis* (Tübingen, 1982), pp. 216 ff. If this is an accurate description of late-medieval piety and theology in general terms, as it certainly appears to be, then Gerson's articulation in *De consolatione theologiae* of an anthropology which he shapes in terms of an Augustinian soteriology (i. e., *praedestinatio ante praevisa merita* which Scotus advanced) cuts against this tendency. As we shall subsequently argue in greater detail (see below, 6.B), this shift in Gerson's thought appears to be in response to the Hussite position with its striking emphasis upon moral rectitude as one of the outward signs of membership in the *ecclesia invisibilis*.

[71] G 9, 196. This echoes Augustine's view of the human condition, of course, but it is probably a reflection of the abiding influence of Dionysian thought on Gerson; see below, 6.B.4.

nothing short of the guide toward this end, a teleological function which distinguishes it from philosophy.

With this theme Gerson identifies the ultimate source of our humanness, an inner compulsion which projects human reason itself as the centering force of all creation in its *regressus* toward God who is both source and goal of the human pilgrimage.[72] It is in part at least a polemic theme as well, since this conviction disallows for the adequacy of any anthropological model conceived in what Gerson understood to be »natural« terms. This is not merely a choice between a natural and supernatural world-view, but rather the demand that anthropology be properly grasped within a »theo-logic.« Defined in this manner, the question of anthropology or psychology could not be settled without reference to the revealed knowledge offered by theology, a principle leading Gerson to qualify the ultimate efficacy of philosophical knowledge: philosophy can know that we are to be judged, as Boethius had argued in the closing paragraph of his *Consolation*, but philosophy of itself cannot know the nature and demands of those judgments.[73] Gerson inserts this qualification again and again in response to diverse questions raised in this text, usually with the refrain *philosophia non cognovit*.[74]

This theme of the insufficiency of philosophy moves the reader beyond the bounds of classical virtue theory, and this in two ways. First, Gerson criticizes the cogency and efficacy of any instruction which bases itself on a purely inner-worldly approach, which he assumes is the extent to which philosophy can lead us: »It is not enough to say with the Stoics that virtue is its own reward, just as vice is its own punishment; people should be drawn to the toilsome works of virtue and kept from their pleasurable vices by something different and greater, whether as reward or punishment.« Continuing this argument he adds that »because philosophy cannot reach this, here philosophy is deficient in the consolation it offers.« Philosophy with its »natural« grasp of virtues cannot, Gerson contends, lead us *ad finem aeternae beatitudinis*.[75] To attain to this end the

---

[72] See also below, 6.B.4, for a discussion of Gerson's use of the dynamic, hierarchical cosmology of Dionysius. His use of this theme would align Gerson's thought at this juncture with Philotheus Boehner's characterization of Ockham's thought; see his »The Metaphysics of William Ockham,« in *Collected Articles on Ockham*, ed. E. M. Buytaert (St. Bonaventure, NY, 1958), pp. 373 ff. In reviewing this position, Courtenay has cautioned against portraying nominalism as disallowing any form of metaphysics or »natural theology« in principle; see »Nominalism and Late Medieval Religion,« pp. 45–46.

[73] Cf. for example I pr. 2; G 9, p. 188: »Credere enim oportet accedentem ad Deum quia est et inquirentibus se renumerator sit. At vero Deus ipse qualis judex existeret, qualem insuper renumerationem daret quaerentibus se, non potuit philosophia, neque discipuli sui, ductu rationis invenire.«

[74] See for example G 9, pp. 189, 190.

[75] G 9, pp. 213–14. The final aim of Gerson's teleological view of theology, in other words, is *altior felicitas* (G 9, p. 226), the heavenly peace gained beyond the *viator*'s earthly pilgrimage; this is the point for which the human heart yearns, and it is *theologia* alone which

»divine gifts« of faith, hope, and love — viz., the *divina charismata* which he usually refers to simply as the theological virtues — are necessary. Yet these function according to Gerson's treatment in *De consolatione theologiae* precisely in the place where we would expect to find a discussion of the sacraments: these virtues constitute the »security« which *viatores* seek, standing as the »three cities of refuge« described allegorically in Joshua 20 and »containing the cleansing waters of penance« and »an asylum of immunity.« These virtues, finally, are the means by which *viatores* attain to beatitude, the state of perfect *pax*. *Theologia* thus discerns the proper »goal,« establishing the broad eschatological framework within which the virtues are to be understood as efficacious. This approach places the question of theological *consolatio* in a teleological horizon, one that clearly exceeds the reach of philosophy as Gerson understood it. *Viatores* could not find true or what he here calls »solid« consolation without knowledge both of this goal and of the means to attain it, demands that depended upon the proper application of the theological virtues.

His second critique moves in an altogether different direction, toward what he would have called »theo-logy« proper: i. e., the discussion of God's nature as judge, or to be more specific the *ordo judiciorum supremi judicis Dei*, an order of judgment which philosophy »could not distinguish.«[76] Given the final scope of Gerson's grasp of this teleology — namely, the judgment of God — this is finally the essential outline of Gerson's eschatology; we shall return to this thesis later in this study, in order to establish the contrast between Gerson's approach to this theme set against the more radical apocalyptic views of his day. Yet it is significant to note that in moving »beyond« philosophy with its limited grasp of the human destiny Gerson by no means eclipses philosophy altogether; it is still useful, if limited, since it stands as the necessary *fundamentum* for theology with its more extensive eschatological horizon. To put it in simple terms, Gerson recognizes that philosophical knowledge has a limited role not only for what it offers but perhaps even more importantly for what it cannot attain: *philosophia* finally functions as the foil by which he defines *theologia* in comparative terms — as »a *higher* happiness,« »a *more solid* consolation,« and so forth. He defends this complementary relationship, by which philosophy accentuates by contrast the broader contours of theological *paideia*, in a manner which is reminiscent of a Thomistic epistemology: he describes philosophy and theology as »the gradations in the story of Jacob's ladder,« invoking as well Plato's metaphor of the »chain« (*more concatenationis*) by which »the highest of a lower order« is linked to »the lowest order of a higher.«[77]

---

can both discern this goal and offer the means to attain it. And, of course, it is probably not accidental that Gerson's treatise ends not with an admonition, as had Boethius' *Consolatio philosophiae*, but with a biblical promise of peace (Phil. 4.7).

[76] G 9, p. 190.

[77] G 9, p. 188; it is not without significance that Gerson seeks a biblical metaphor to

5. *Stabilitas*: mystical variations on a Boethian theme

This emphasis upon God as the ultimate goal of the human journey, a theme which circumscribes Gerson's broad grasp of theology as a paideutic discipline, correlates with one of the central emphases of Boethius' *Consolatio philosophiae*, though with several important differences. For Gerson, as for Boethius before him, God is conceived as a stable center of reality, the »intelligible center« which »remains still and grants motion to all else. «[78] With this formulation we find Gerson borrowing an essentially philosophical (neo-Platonic) image of God which has been interpreted, among readers medieval and modern, as one of the most enduring if also controversial passages from this treatise as a whole: namely, *Consolatio Philosophiae* III m. 9, the poem which Courcelle has identified as the text around which the medieval debate regarding Boethius' orthodoxy ranged.[79] And yet Gerson sets this theme in a markedly different framework, as we might well expect, than had his predecessor. For Boethius, motivated by his very different methodological axiom that »no comparison is possible between the infinite and the finite, «[80] had drawn quite different implications from this characterization of God than did Gerson. Indeed, this conceptualization of God's nature and relation to the created order led Boethius to set forth a fascinating and exquisitely beautiful description of contingent reality and »the infinite motion of temporal things«: this motion »imitates the immediate present of [God's] changeless life, and, since it cannot reproduce or equal [this] life, it sinks from immobility to motion and declines from the simplicity of the present into the infinite duration of future and past. «[81] In other words, all motion is the inevitable result of the utter incapacity of creation — including, of course, human beings — to imitate or approach God.

---

support his view of reality as a graded hierarchy, here again demonstrating his willingness to exegete Old Testament images or stories through traditional forms of allegory. It is in this sense that we later find Gerson defining a »theological literal sense, « a formulation by which he intends to legitimize the allegorical sense within the supposedly »intended« meaning of the text. And, because Gerson assumed that God was the true author of the biblical text, his grasp of how this »theological literal sense« operates echoes Aquinas's conclusion: because God is capable »not only of adapting words to convey meanings ... but of adapting things themselves [*res ipsas*], « allegory functions as part of the newly expanded literal sense. See Aquinas, *Summa theologiae* Ia q. 1, a. 10 resp.; and, on Gerson's formulation of this *sensus*, see Froehlich, »Fifteenth-Century Hermeneutics, « pp. 42 ff.

[78] G 9, p. 212; cf. Boethius, *Consolatio Philosophiae* III m. 9, CCSL 94:51.

[79] See Courcelle, *La Consolation*, »Troisième partie, « pp. 159–200. As he here notes in summary fashion, »ce chant 9 du Livre III, substantiel et concis, est obscur et presque intraduisible; dès le Moyen Age et le XVIIᵉ siècle il a ete un sujet de litige entre adversaires et partisans du christianisme de Boèce. « *Ibid.*, p. 163.

[80] Cf. *De consolatione philosophiae* II pr. 7; CCSL 94: 33.

[81] *Ibid.*, V pr. 6, CCSL 94: 102. This translation is from *The Consolation of Philosophy*, trans., intro., and notes by Richard Green (Indianapolis, 1962), p. 116.

The contrast in emphasis and purpose to Gerson's later utilization of this Boethian — or perhaps we should rather say neo-Platonic — conception of God is striking, revealing how differently he conceived the paideutic impact of *theologia* in contrast to philosophy in shaping the Christian life. For Gerson the human pilgrimage itself stands as the approach to God, and consequently this journey meant approaching and eventually participating in the divine *stabilitas* by entering ever more fully into God's »stillness.« Admittedly, Boethius' *Consolatio* is not without such a concept, since he also punctuates his discussion of the divine nature by arguing that we must »submit human reason to the divine mind,« and thereby be »raised up, if we can, to the height of that highest intelligence.«[82] But this is a theme which stands in isolation without further thematic development in Boethius, while for Gerson this admonition discloses a different preference, an »inverted« approach which stands at the very center of his thought: the conclusion he reaches does not vary the theme but the emphasis, since *theologia* in contrast to *philosophia* »does not stand content in considering only the mutable, transient things here below.«[83] In other words, Gerson here limits the utility of philosophy in discerning *how* the pilgrim might »submit« to the divine presence precisely as an apology of the theological task, which »raises herself higher, gazing upon the true form of beauty rather than some image or idol of happiness.«[84] Theology thus answers Boethius' »Lady Philosophy« in her call to »raise up the mind to right hope,«[85] beyond the unstable horizon of this changeable world. In doing so Gerson delineates the human path toward God in terms that can only be described as *via mystica*.

This consolation and the stability it promises is the working out of Gerson's theological *paideia*, and in the process offers a distinct variation — theological, but also mystical — upon one of Boethius' central themes. By inverting the focus of this Boethian conceptualization, he stresses unlike his predecessor not the necessary falling from God's »eternal present,« but the human aspiration to enter into that divine simplicity. As he suggests later in the second book of this treatise in a passage saturated with Platonist imagery and terminology, »theology persuades [*viatores*] to aspire« to that state in which

the mind, through contemplation ... arrives through an understanding pure and simple (*ad intelligam puram et simplicem*), without motion or activity (*sine motu vel discursu*), at the ›idea‹; this understanding, though very imperfect, contemplates by the simplicity of the divine understanding and in a single intuition what is present, past, and future. And,

---

[82] *Ibid.*, V pr. 5, *CCSL* 94: 100.

[83] Cf. G 9, p. 226.

[84] *Ibid.* We can only point to this neo-Platonic language at this juncture; for a more detailed discussion, see also below, 4.B.3.

[85] Cf. *De consolatione philosophiae* V pr. 6, *CCSL* 94: 105: »... ad rectas spes animum sublevate.«

remaining still, as the equivalent of the intelligible center itself, this understanding grants movement to all else such that, simple and unchanging, it gazes upon and grasps all that is subject to motion.[86]

Gerson's emphasis upon this contemplative experience by which *viatores* enter into the stillness of the divine »center« elucidates another theme which emerges in this treatise. Later in the text the voice of Volucer — and not, interestingly, Monicus — defends the necessary status of the *solitarius* within the church, a further argument against Combes's suggestion that Gerson has in this text abandoned his earlier interest in *theologia mystica*.[87] Those »cloistered« in this vocation, and thereby committed to a life of prayer, nonetheless serve a vital function within the hierarchical church, because it is their prayers that ultimately support the pastoral work undertaken by the minor prelates who had to busy themselves »in the world« with the tiring work of »preaching, admonishing, and correcting. «[88] This is hardly a dismissal of the active *cura*, the *vita activa* of the clergy bound by pastoral duties, but rather serves as a cogent defense of the *utilitas* within the ecclesiastical hierarchy offered by the secluded life of prayer. As we shall later explore more fully, this emphasis may be one expression of Gerson's response to the Hussite indictment of the monastic

---

[86] G 9, p. 211 f. In what otherwise appears to resemble a mysticism of the »essentialist« variety, which Gerson had earlier denounced in no uncertain terms, we must underscore his qualification here — against such a view, apparently — that this understanding enters into the »eternal presence« of God *licet imperfectum valde*, and not through an absorption of the human mind with the divine. Combes has argued that Gerson moved toward such a position at the end of his life, but this text in *De consolatione theologiae* would suggest that the propensity at least is earlier. See *Essai sur la critique de Ruysbroeck par Gerson*, Vol. 3/1: 316 ff.

[87] On this question, his exegesis of the biblical story of Mary and Martha as a defense of the *vita contemplativa* merits mention; cf. G 9, p. 224, and below, 4.C.1. This theme would qualify Combes's thesis that Gerson's concerns in *De consolatione theologiae* have eclipsed mysticism altogether; cf. *La théologie mystique*, 2: 339 ff.

[88] Cf. G 9, p. 224: »Tolle orationes timentium Deum quid proderit, obsecro, labor fatigantium se vel praedicando vel monendo, vel corrigendo. . . .« Gerson had described in an earlier French sermon the general responsibilities of these secular clerics again with another triplicate description, pointing to their duty to »purify,« »illuminate,« and »perfect,« the triad which structured Dionysius' view of how both the celestial and ecclesiastical hierarchies functioned. Cf. *Quomodo stabit*, G 7, p. 982. Yet he more commonly spoke of these duties in terms descriptive of specific pastoral responsibilities, and he particularly underscored the significance of preaching as »the natural means chosen by God to illuminate us and to make his will known to us«; cf. Brown, *Pastor and Laity*, p. 19. As he argued in an earlier vernacular sermon: »Et pourquoy Jhesu Cristi ne monstra tantost sa gloire a tout le monde. Il souffisoit que par ses messaigiers et par luy aussi il se monstra a tous par predicacion. « Cf. *Gloria*, G 7, p. 643; also, *Non in solo pane*, G 7, p. 746. In other words, while Gerson had earlier insisted on the centrality of preaching and the concrete pastoral responsibilities falling to prelates, a view which he does not here retract, he does nonetheless qualify this emphasis in order to recall the significance of prayer in supporting or even effecting reform within the church. See also below, 6.B.3.

life,[89] since the monks were »set apart« to pray in order to uphold the secular clergy in their pastoral responsibilities. In this sense *stabilitas* is not only a goal of the mystical life, though it is clearly also this to Gerson's mind: it is at the same time the goal in concrete terms of pastoral work within the church. This theme discloses, therefore, his conviction that theology serves a paideutic function not only on an individual but also on a social plane, since it is finally theology which delineates the goal of life and offers means by which *peregrini* might advance toward this goal on the *via mystica* and thereby assist others in their journey *ad Deum*. *Aedificatio* is once again the norm of his theology, in this case in terms of the social responsibilities facing pastors and *solitarii* in their work for reform within the church.

B. Theology and literary method: »Re-forming« scholastic theology

Thus far we have explored Gerson's *De consolatione theologiae* only in terms of its broad paideutic intention, considering the manner in which he viewed *theologia* as the guide (*comes*) for *viatores* upon their journey *ad Deum*. It now remains for us to turn from theoretical themes, by which he orients us to the theological task, more directly to the matter of theological method itself. Our concern in this section settles upon the manner in which this treatise articulates a theological reform. Yet here we find that his approach is quite different than that of his earlier treatises: we need only recall, by means of contrast, the pragmatic nature of his several earlier detailed letters sent from Bruges to d'Ailly and his colleagues at the College of Navarre in which Gerson outlined his proposal for reforming the theological curriculum,[90] or his lectures *Contra curiositatem studentium* which he delivered before the university audience upon returning to Paris in order to clarify these themes.[91] In these treatises, *reformatio ecclesiae* was a quite practical affair involving such matters as changes in the academic curriculum, modification of the rancorous school loyalties exhibited by the masters, a proper respect of tradition, and an attentiveness to biblical study.

The mood and approach in *De consolatione theologiae* is decidedly different: here Gerson offers a more broadly defined and one might even say more

---

[89] See below, 6.B.3.

[90] Cf. G 2, pp. 23–28 (to d'Ailly) and especially the »Memoire sur la reforme de l'enseignement théologique« (pp. 26–28), which Glorieux suggests Gerson had appended to this letter; pp. 29–43 (to his colleagues at Navarre).

[91] G 3, pp. 224–49. Both these lectures and the earlier letters have been thoroughly discussed elsewhere; see for example, Burger, *Aedificatio*, pp. 110–24; Schwab, *Johannes Gerson*, pp. 671 ff., and *Selections*, ed. and intro. Ozment, especially p. 6.

thorough-going reform of the practice of theology, not as a strictly academic discipline but as a »life discipline.« It is in this treatise that we meet Gerson no longer speaking as university chancellor per se, but as *theologus ecclesiae catholicae* in a broader sense. This different perspective, the result perhaps of his altered professional role as an exile from France, brings him to articulate his call for reform in a manner which is at once fundamental and radical: Gerson here utilizes a theological method which corresponds to his more extensive vision of reform, the consequence of his view of theology as *paideia* which carried implications for the entire hierarchy, including the laity.[92] This broadened view of theology thus has decisive implications for Gerson's otherwise hierarchical ecclesiology. In the final section of this chapter we shall consider the question of theological method, postponing for the moment a discussion of how his commitment to the ecclesiastical hierarchy tempered his views of reform.

1. The use and user of the Bible: correlation of text and reader

In the foregoing discussion it has become evident that Gerson's theological method brought *theologia* and *scriptura* into close connection, not only in a theoretical sense but in practical terms as well. When *theologia* speaks, or when Gerson poses and resolves a theological question through the voices in this dialogue, we confront an argument far removed from the academic form of theological disputation and much closer to the approach of a sophisticated biblical fundamentalism: in the final analysis, the biblical text in its plain meaning (*sensus litteralis*) often comes to stand as the theological argument itself, with little of embellishment beyond the occasional gloss which Gerson

---

[92] We must at least announce at this point a theme which appears in this treatise, and suggests a quite different approach to reform than Gerson had earlier demonstrated. Both Pascoe and Brown point to the priestly vision of the church which Gerson advocated in his earlier writings; Pascoe concludes that for Gerson »the laity . . . does not possess hierarchical power« to the extent that »the church . . . becomes essentially a church of prelates« (*Jean Gerson*, p. 32); Brown echoes this conclusion, claiming that »from one point of view, he can be said to have seen the church as made of ordered ranks of clerics only, with the laity as outsiders, inferiors to be helped towards their spiritual end by the church, but not true members of it« (*Pastor and Laity*, pp. 38—39). In a certain sense, of course, these claims are true: Gerson did hold that the active *leadership* within the hierarchy fell not to the laity (*inferiores*) but strictly to the priests (*superiores*). But to exclude them from this particular hierarchical function, as Gerson explicitly does, is not to exclude them from the church: indeed, the function of the priests depends upon the presence of the laity, such that there would be no church without both of these together. We shall see Gerson apply this conviction in even more forceful terms in *De consolatione theologiae*, as he suggests that the »spirit of catholic truth« finally resides »more fruitfully« in the *inferiores* or *idiotae* than the learned but morally corrupt among the clergy. The laity here inherit the theologian's role, since they embrace the theological life through what he here calls »an erudition . . . of the heart.« For further discussion of this matter, see below, 4.C.1.

has added.[93] Thus, he introduces many of his points with such clauses as »Theology says,« or »Faith says,« and it is scripture itself which constitutes the substance of his theological argumentation.

In a passage from the treatise in which Gerson addresses the logic underlying his deliberate and close identification of theological with exegetical method, his Volucer announces through a gloss upon a biblical text that »in the scriptures ›God speaks once,‹ says Job, ›and does not repeat the same thing a second time.‹« As he goes on to note in this passage, the scriptures are »sufficient« to »teach and offer us counsel, providing that they are read over with a pure, faithful, and open heart.«[94] In the broader context of this passage, in which Gerson is offering an explanation of how to find »a moral certitude sufficient for acting,« the emphasis falls not only on his identification of scripture but on the accent he gives to this theme: namely, his insistence that the Bible is a sufficient form of teaching and guidance, but that one must approach the text in the right spirit in order to receive its proper counsel. The use of the biblical text, in other words, offers us sufficient instruction to get on with the tasks of living, but this is only part of the hermeneutical circle: we must read it in the right perspective if we would grasp its message. Our obligation is thus not that of moving beyond the text, nor that of finding a purely objective truth »behind« it: rather *viatores* must limit their attention to the scriptural *doctrina*, and learn to read it in the correct spirit (i. e., *puro fideli et integro corde*). This demand places the reader in a vital relation to the text, a situation which Heidegger and following him Gadamer have characterized as a hermeneutical circle, since Gerson assumes that a false approach to the text — the inevitable result of those who read »with a bad will«[95] — will obliterate the text's proper paideutic character and drive the reader toward what he calls »a thicker darkness of errors.«

The »re-forming« of theology as a matter of biblical exegesis is at the same time, according to Gerson's hermeneutic theory, a matter of personal conversion, of »re-forming« ourselves as biblical readers. The reform of theology is thus in the first instance dependent upon the reform of the theologian. In other words, the perspective of the reading subject determines whether the text will be read faithfully, and in this case that means whether one will be led into »darkness« or discern its consolatory and reforming character. This single qualifying adverb *sufficienter* establishes the methodological ra-

---

[93] As earlier mentioned, I owe this characterization of Gerson to Froehlich; see »Fifteenth-Century Hermeneutics,« p. 44.

[94] G 9, pp. 236–37: »Itaque semel in scripturis suis locutus est Deus, et idipsum, ait Job, non repetet, quoniam sufficienter erudiunt et consulunt; tantummodo relegantur puro fideli et integro corde.« The biblical reference is to Job 33.14.

[95] *Ibid.*: »Malevolis autem et incredulis, tenebrosior inde nascitur erorum caligo quod in haereticis olim.« For a more detailed discussion of this point in relation to Hans-Georg Gadamer's work, see below, 6.A.3.

tionale for Gerson's reliance upon the biblical text in doing theology, and as such articulates as theory what he elsewhere simply accomplishes in practice as a biblical theologian.

2. *Scriptura cum experientia*

It is but a short step from this theme of the symbiosis binding text with reader to Gerson's coordination of scripture with *experientia*. Just as the proper function of the biblical text depends upon the manner of approach, such that the way of *living* informs the prospect of a faithful *reading* which in turn reforms the way of living, so also Gerson assumes that human experience and the scriptural texts form a cohesive whole.[96] This is not simply to repeat what we have already observed about the prescriptive role of the biblical text as paideutic, as shaping life through instruction and counsel, but rather to suggest that Gerson also presupposes a reciprocity between scripture and experience in this paideutic dimension. This conviction allows him to identify the language of experience and that of scripture from another vantage point within the hermeneutical circle, in this case by informing how the text is to be read through experience — *scriptura cum experientia*[97] — by moving between biblical and experiential narratives.

This dimension of Gerson's thought is anything but peculiar within the varied horizon of medieval theology. *Scriptura cum experientia* could have stood as a programmatic outlook deriving from either of two broad and occasionally intersecting streams which flowed through medieval thought: the Augustinian tradition, broadly understood, which placed high value upon *experientia* since the creation was itself a *speculum* reflecting at every level God's (trinitarian) image; or Aristotelian influences which ennobled the constructive dimensions of experience, since the knowledge gained through the senses offered a reliable view of reality. These varied approaches to *experientia* establish what stands as

---

[96] This realization cautions us against accepting de Lubac's analysis of Gerson's thought; he concludes in this regard that »exégèse, construction dogmatique et organisation de l'expérience intérieure sont bien pour [Gerson] trois disciplines, qui sans doute communiquent entre elles, mais sans se compénétrer, ou à peine.« See *Exégèse médiévale*, 2/2: 492. De Lubac is here speaking of Gerson's approach in the mystical writings, though even in this case his conclusion appears exaggerated.

[97] G 9, p. 218. This phrase occurs in a discussion of how one ought to govern; in such matters, both scripture and experience offer instruction. He pursues this by identifying scriptural precedents in the Old Testament, from both the wisdom literature (Prov. 29.12, etc.) and the pentateuch (Ex. 18.17 ff.), alongside practical observations from experience. The entire section reaches its crescendo when Gerson seals his argument with a reference from »tradition,« citing the experiences of Pope Gregory the Great who yearned to be free of »the chains of public rule.«

a widely favored theological and epistemological axiom by the later Middle Ages. Although it is difficult to speak with certainty of sources when an author remains silent on the subject, as Gerson does in this case, and particularly when the source question must contend with a theme as commonplace as this one was by the fifteenth century, we might safely point to Cistercian piety as one conduit through which this Augustinian influence reached his writings.[98] Another would be the influence of his mentor and colleague, Pierre d'Ailly, for whom the twin phrases *experientia docet* and *patet inductive* stand out as dominant formulations guiding the theologian and aligning this discipline within the empirical realm.[99]

3. *Theologia velut humano more loquens:* toward a metaphorical theology

With this methodological theme *scriptura cum experientia* before us we must now consider how it is that Gerson applied this theory, which as we have suggested is a theological conviction that shapes the contours of his literary style. Throughout *De consolatione theologiae* we find Gerson drawing upon *experientia* in order to integrate scripture and life, often by translating theological discourse into metaphorical language in order to render it more accessible to those outside the narrow guild of professional theologians.[100] Literary method and the choice of genre in this case represent Gerson's conviction that pedagogical considerations ought to determine the broad accessibility of theological rhetoric, that *theologia* was meant to be grasped not only by the *periti* among the academicians but by *idiotae* as well.[101] This raises the question,

---

[98] The influence of Bernard's affective mysticism on Gerson has been widely discussed in recent studies, most recently and perceptively by Burger, *Aedificatio*, pp. 187–90.

[99] On this point, see Oakley, *The Political Thought of Pierre d'Ailly. The Voluntarist Tradition* (New Haven and London, 1964), pp. 25–26. Caroline Bynam addresses the role of *experientia* in Cistercian piety in »The Cistercian Concept of Community,« *Jesus as Mother. Studies in the Spirituality of the High Middle Ages* (Berkeley and Los Angeles, 1982), pp. 78 ff. Finally, both Oberman and Oakley have made much of this theme in considering the broader contours of the nominalist tradition, the former by arguing against H. Blumberg that we should locate the origins of natural science within late-medieval theology because the nominalist advance of the *potentia Dei ordinata* theme established the foundation for empiricism. Cf. Oberman, »*Contra vanam curiositatem*« (Zürich, 1974), and *idem, Masters of the Reformation*, pp. 6–7, 10; Oakley, *Omnipotence, Covenant, and Order: An Excursion in the History of Ideas from Abelard to Leibniz* (Ithaca and London, 1984), see esp. Ch. 3. Finally, cf. Hamm, *Frömmigkeitstheologie*, pp. 156 ff.

[100] This propensity stands in line with the broader convictions of many early humanists, for whom dialogue represented both an inevitable literary development given the resurgence of classical forms of rhetoric and a literary alternative to the established scholastic modes of thought. See Bouwsma, »The Two Faces of Humanism,« p. 17.

[101] See Burger, *Aedificatio*, pp. 71 ff., 98 ff., 191 ff.; also, Brown, *Pastor and Laity*, pp. 183 ff.

once again, of readership or audience. Even though Gerson wrote *De consolatione theologiae* in a language inaccessible to his unlettered contemporaries, and
hence produces a treatise probably aimed at the lower clergy exercising *cura
animarum*, he develops a theological approach which interpreted such duties
through the questions and issues raised and the responses given.[102] Indeed, the
style of theological discourse, above all in its experiential basis and dialogical
form, would have lent itself without difficulty to a simple translation for such
purposes.

How, then, does Gerson apply metaphorical language to the theological
task? Here we can only select several examples of this style, references which
demonstrate both the diversity of expression and the centrality of theological
theme which he reforms in such language. For instance, at an early juncture of
De consolatione theologiae Gerson sets about to explain how it is that *theologia*
leads *mirabiliter* to »our embracing, through love, the God of all consolation.«
In so doing he avoids altogether the use of scholastic terminology in explaining
this process, choosing rather to translate this explanation into the vivid
language of metaphor. It is here that Gerson describes, in a methodological
aside of sorts, the proper manner of theology which speaks »as if in a human
manner . . .« (*velut humano more loquens*). In this context he goes on to offer an
extended metaphor of the »three-fold tribunal« and »triple throne« by which
God »indulges« us with grace, »corrects« us with mercy, and only then
»condemns« us with justice. Absent is the complex scholastic terminology
about the technical manner in which grace functioned, or what he here calls
the *ordo judiciorum*. He has re-cast the esoteric possibilities of a technical
theological language into metaphor as a more widely accessible form of
rhetoric, translating academic concepts into experiential images. In another
instance Gerson draws upon the biblical metaphor of the parables, extending
Jesus' explanation of God's providence with the imagery of the preservation of
the sparrows (Mt. 5.29) to add that even the leaves falling from the tree are
within the orbit of God's care.[103] Again, Gerson is fond of drawing upon the
Pauline explanation of *figura*, following the Vulgate reading of 1 Cor. 10.6, by
which Paul derives through an allegorical reading of the Exodus narrative the
equation that the »rock« was Christ (cf. 10.1−7). Gerson broadens this allegory

---

[102] On this point we would do well to remember the genre question, as Gerson styled the
piece quite deliberately as a complementary treatise to Boethius' treatise. There is even
reason to assume that he intended that this piece be read alongside Boethius' *Consolatio
philosophiae*, not only by those of advanced education but by students like the young Gerson
who would have received Boethius in their early arts curriculum.

[103] Cf. G 9, pp. 203−204. This is perhaps an entirely inconsequential reference, though
it is possible that this allusion to autumn would place the writing of this text later in 1418,
as Combes has argued against Glorieux's July date; at best, however, such an allusion
would only help confirm the firmer evidence which Combes has mustered. See *La théologie
mystique*, 2:306 ff., and above, Ch. 1, n. 27.

to function as a metaphor descriptive of Christ's character *pro nobis*: Christ is »the steadfast rock« upon which hope sets itself »like an anchor« (*spes velut anchora*). *Theologia velut humano more loquens*: Gerson's application of this theory to construct a metaphorical theology lends a vitality and accessibility to theological themes he here explores, translating potentially abstract concepts such as forgiveness, grace, or justification out of scholastic terminology into the vivid language of human experience.

Finally, we must at least mention one of the more extensive and hence obvious areas in which theology speaks, under Gerson's pen, »in a human way«: namely, the poems which punctuate the sections of dialogue in this treatise. Here, as in Boethius' *Consolatio philosophiae*, metaphoric language fills literary form. Thus, for example, in drawing upon the language of the Psalms which speak of »tasting« God's sweetness, Gerson adds the curious metaphor describing God as *mel nobis sapidum*, »our sweet honey«;[104] he describes hope as an »oak, standing on the high mountain ridge,« which does not fear the trials (*tentamina*) of stormy weather;[105] he portrays life as a journey upon the high seas in which we struggle to avoid »shipwreck« and »raging storm,« ending the scene with a sailor's fervent prayer to Christ;[106] or, again, he describes the quest for »firmer« hope beyond the trials of this present life through the metaphor of a woman giving birth to a son, a struggle which is »not without sorrow.«[107] In assessing these poems Combes has suggested that they stand as a pioneering effort to transcribe within the historical trajectory of ecclesiastical Latin the mystical experience in poetic form.[108] This may well be the case. But in less ambitious terms, and with regard to his literary style within the broader scope of this treatise as a whole, what is striking about these Gersonian poems is the continuity of metaphor which identifies them with the prose sections. The presence of metaphoric language in the poetry only represents a difference in degree, not in form, when set alongside his vivid metaphoric dialogue in the prose sections. Metaphor stands as the vehicle of theological instruction, and in this sense appears to have much to do with Gerson's broadening of the horizon in which *theologia* was comprehensible.

---

[104] See G 4, pp. 127–28; once again, this language translates into vivid metaphor his more technical handling of the *dulcedo Dei* theme, a phrase which was a commonplace in the writings of the affective mystics such as Bernard. On this point see also below, 4.C.3. Also, the reader of this treatise in the Glorieux edition will stumble immediately upon the awkward format in which the text is rendered: the editor has chosen to extract the poems from this treatise and has inserted them − not seriatim, but alphabetically by first word! − within a separate volume devoted to Gerson's poetry (G 4), a clumsy format which further detracts from the usefulness of this edition.

[105] *Ibid.*, p. 156.

[106] *Ibid.*, pp. 173–74.

[107] *Ibid.*, p. 168.

[108] Cf. *La théologie mystique*, 2: 314.

The preponderance of metaphoric language found throughout this treatise distinguishes this as one of the hallmarks of Gerson's pedagogical commitment. Yet this preference raises, beyond the question of projected audience, the matter of the character of the theological enterprise more generally. That is, although it is not incorrect, as several recent studies of Gerson have pointed out,[109] to point to his references to *les simplices* or *idiotae* in his various vernacular and Latin works in establishing the breadth of audience he felt theology should have, Gerson suggests another perspective on audience in this treatise. Here he draws directly upon Paul's language to articulate »the manner and art of theology,« echoing the apostle in saying that *theologia* brings us »to wisdom through foolishness,« and thus saves those who believe »through the folly and stumbling block of preaching the cross.«[110] *Per insipientiam . . . ad sapientiam*: does this phrase not also provide the rationale for the theory undergirding Gerson's authorship, and thereby express at the same time the character of the *ars theologiae*? This suggestion explains why it is that Gerson depends in such persistent fashion upon the simplistic language of metaphor; this choice of language is, therefore, not to be construed as a »theology of the cross,« as one historian has recently suggested,[111] but rather represents Gerson's grasp of what theology is and how the very nature of its expression reflects its identity. Its task is to mediate the divine revelation in understandable form, a theory which Aquinas had already defended in inquiring whether »sacred scripture should employ metaphorical or symbolical language.«[112] In other words, Gerson's consistent effort to translate the technical depth of scholastic disputation into vivid, ordinary speech redefines the theological enterprise in terms of its audience and, consequently, also in terms of its formal expression.

But does metaphor carry the day for Gerson in this treatise, or is this merely a literary gown to dress up the real work of theological discourse? In surveying this text as a whole, one is quite hard pressed to find much beyond a rudimentary use of technical theological terms. These are of course present

---

[109] See above, Ch. 1, n. 23.

[110] Cf. 1 Cor. 1.21–25.

[111] Cf. Oberman, *Harvest*, pp. 231–35.

[112] Cf. *Summa theologiae* Ia q. 1 a. 9. Of course, Aquinas concluded that scripture *should* employ such language, since it »fittingly delivers divine and spiritual realities under bodily guises, for God provides for all things according to the kind of things they are.« Aquinas continues this discussion by noting that scripture is not the domain of the elite or learned alone, but uses such images so that »the uneducated [*rudes*] may then lay hold of them.« This is the same approach Gerson adopts in *De consolatione theologiae*, even to the point of concluding that not only *scriptura* but *theologia* itself should utilize metaphoric language, another instance of the close identity he projected between scripture and theology. Gerson follows Aquinas in quite close style in arguing that »God wanted others besides the philosophers to be made participants in this most salutary knowledge«; cf. G 9, p. 204 and *Summa theologiae* Ia q. 1 a. 1, resp.

when Gerson deliberately builds upon the philosophical problems posed by Boethius, and hence we do find mention of the broadest and most familiar themes: e. g., *providentia Dei, liberum arbitrium, massa peccati, fomes originalis*. But the relative infrequency of such technical terms is finally impressive, particularly given the Boethian textual precedent; these remain the occasional signposts, rather than the detailed roadmap, by which Gerson directs the *viator* on life's pilgrimage. His clear preference is to translate such terminology and the problems set forth by the technical jargon of the schools into the common speech of metaphor. Consequently, as we have suggested, this is not merely a matter of literary style but represents Gerson's more ambitious commitment to »re-form« theological discourse — not only because this is better suited to a broader audience, but because popular idiom (*insipientia*) is a more suitable vehicle than scholastic jargon to reach our destination (*sapientia*). The »scandal« of the cross, therefore, suggests to Gerson a biblical legitimation for his articulation of a metaphorical theology.

4. *Modus loquendi*: from scholastic *disputatio* to *dialogus*

The most cursory examination of *De consolatione theologiae* suggests that Gerson borrowed not only the prosametric structure of Boethius' text, but the Boethian use of dialogue in the prose sections. With this, however, the similarities end, or remain on only the most superficial level. Gerson, unlike Boethius, does not offer a conversation between a prisoner or exile and *theologia*, although theology does intrude at the very close (cf. IV pr. 5) to render an extended address to *homo viator*, a speech which the Du Pin edition introduces as *prosopopaeia theologiae* and which Glorieux simply notes with the phrase *hic theologia loquitur*. Rather, Gerson's text has altered the literary structure of the dialogue itself, offering an extended dialogue between two characters, Monicus and Volucer, who meet to speak *about* another person, named simply *peregrinus*. The entire dialogue concerns this absent character, who as we have earlier suggested stands in the first instance as Gerson himself,[113] though as Volucer unfolds Gerson's own story as *viator* he delineates

---

[113] This point is evident within the comments Gerson himself prefaced to the text, introducing the characters by noting that Monicus sought to question Volucer »about many things, but even more about a certain pilgrim, his own brother.« Somewhat later, in the opening lines of the treatise's first prose section, Volucer reports to Monicus that he had been »at Constance for the General Council with your brother, until the final departure of the Pope.... He left at that time, preferring to become a sojourner in a foreign land, in accord with the name *peregrinus*, rather than returning here to his own people.« Gerson's identification of himself as *peregrinus* was no novelty; indeed, he was quite aware of the root of his name, derived from the Exodus story (cf. 2.16 ff.) regarding the naming of Moses' first son as »Gershom, because, he said, ›I am a stranger in a foreign land‹« (Ex. 2.22,

much more than autobiography, describing in the process *peregrinus* as a model of the quest for consolation.

If this particular dialogue describes the human quest for God, we must also add that this literary form addresses itself to a broader audience than had been the case within the technical genres of scholastic theology. The dialogue becomes important, therefore, as a more flexible and universal means of communication: Gerson's use of this form alters the *modus loquendi* which had dominated scholastic theology in general, replacing the academic disputation which allowed for a dialectical resolution of particular questions or problems with the dialogue form. With this formal shift the *context* if not also the *content* of the theological task became a quite different one, a development which apparently corresponds to Gerson's revised sense of *theologia* as a paideutic guide for all *viatores*, not simply those with appropriate academic opportunities or professional credentials. The reforming impact which Gerson's use of this genre exerted upon the fifteenth century is only now becoming more apparent,[114] and this treatise in particular represents a genre which is a curious hybrid between academic form and popular style: the dialogue here continues to carry the dialectic qualities of the *disputatio*, though it conveys this in a much more broadly accessible conversational medium.

The paideutic structure of the treatise, of which we have earlier spoken at some length, thus functions on two levels of the narrative. In the first instance, Volucer leads his skeptical and troubled companion Monicus in what often resembles a therapeutic encounter leading toward wholeness. And, because this is a personal encounter rather than an abstract wrangling over ideas and terminology, the conversation translates the pastoral problems much disputed

---

Vulgate). Gerson used this reference in a sermon delivered at Constance, which Glorieux dates to April 21, 1415: »... quod a longe prospicientes olim Moyses et Levi non sine mysteriorum quodam involucro primogenitis imposuerunt nomina Gersan et Gerson quae interpretati sonant idem quod advena vel peregrinus.« G 5, p. 398.

[114] Ritter already suggested this influence in his *Studien zur Spätscholastik*, where he argued in general terms that Gerson's use of »erbaulich-gelehrten Schriften ... wurde das Vorbild einer ausgedehnten halbpopulären, synkretistisch gestimmten theologischen Literatur, die für das ganze 15. Jahrhundert charakteristisch ist.« *Ibid.*, vol. 2, pp. 133–34. In a more recent study Hamm has returned to this theme, this time in describing the »Frömmigkeitstheologie« which he argues dominates the fifteenth century as a whole. He remarks in this study that »Denk- und Sprachstil sind [für die spätmittelalterliche Frömmigkeitstheologie] kaum voneinander zu trennen. Allerdings sind die Grenzen zwischen den ›erbaulichen‹ Darstellungsformen der Frömmigkeitstheologie und dem spezifisch scholastischen Modus loquendi fließend, und zwar gerade dort, wo das Bemühen lebendig ist, zwischen der Theologie der Universitäten und dem Ruf nach einer Reform christlicher Lebensgestaltung aus dem Geist der Buße zu vermitteln.« He goes on to speak of the »›halb-akademischen‹ oder ›popularscholastischen‹ Stils, der sich im 15. Jahrhundert zwischen der scholastischen Quästionenliteratur und der populartheologischen Erbauungsliteratur ansiedelte,« and although he does not mention Gerson in this regard the inference is clear. See *Frömmigkeitstheologie*, pp. 175–76.

in the schools[115] into a different idiom. In other words, Gerson has taken the
external structure of the *disputatio*, based as it was upon the posing of a *quaestio*
and its resolution through careful use of logic and syllogistic argument, but he
has refashioned it as dialogue, and in this manner integrates the issues of
scholastic debate into more immediately personal dimensions.

    This point could be illustrated from almost any page of the text: thus, for
instance, Monicus asks at the very outset by what means *peregrinus* could
»restore« himself, and how he could arm his spirit against »the unfair assaults of
savage fortune,« and Volucer responds by leading him toward »the true and
lasting consolation of the wayfarer.« In charting this journey Volucer describes
the means by which *peregrinus* advanced toward this goal: *theologia* is the one
who gave herself as a companion (*comes*) for his pilgrimage, while the young
pilgrim »knew« the sacred scripture from his youth. As if to dispute this point
Monicus turns almost immediately upon Volucer's recitation of a scriptural
text (i. e., as an argument from authority) to expound »the spirit of salvation«
— viz. »Now the fear of the Lord is the beginning of wisdom« (Prov. 1.7) —
and demands to know, with a skeptical tone of voice, how it is possible »that
any delight come out of fear.«[116] The dialectic, then, is set first within the
experiential level, but quite quickly becomes an exegetical argument at the
same time. In *sic et non* fashion Gerson builds his dialogue, with Volucer leading
Monicus step by step, point by point, beyond the various doubts and
challenges he had raised — in this case from a skeptical »philosophical«
standpoint with its limited reach to the »loving embrace« of God through the
leading of theology. In other words, literary form facilitates the deeper
paideutic function of Gerson's text. Through a carefully crafted dialectic
argument which the dialogue accommodates, Gerson steers Monicus — and,
we must presume, those readers who shared this character's skepticism and fear
— beyond the restricted horizon of philosophy and finally toward the »true«
and »solid« consolation that only theology can bring. In this sense, literary
strategy and theological intention coalesce, such that the voice of Monicus also
functions on two levels: insofar as the questions this character raises belong to
the *viator* who is also searching for the *humanae peregrinationis refugium*, and thus
in quest of consolation on the journey *ad Deum*, the literary structure serves the
paideutic function of re-forming the reader as well on this journey from fear to
hope. It functions on this level as a »manual of conversion,« leading the reader
from doubt to faith, from despair in the self to trust in God.[117]

    Yet this is to point to only one level of how narrative structure establishes the

---

[115] On this point, Leonard Boyle has demonstrated how the quodlibets as an academic
forum disclose the pastoral interests of the student audience who themselves posed the
questions for disputation. See »The Quodlibets of St. Thomas and Pastoral Care,« in
Pastoral Care, Clerical Education, and Canon Law, 1200–1300 (London, 1981), esp. pp. 340 ff.
[116] G 9, pp. 188–90.
[117] In this regard Combes's conclusion that Gerson's *De consolatione theologiae* is »un

paideutic function of this text. On another level the contribution Volucer makes to this dialogue moves stylistically within the orbit of Gerson's homiletical voice, such that this leading character speaks to Monicus not in the »second« but »first« person plural. He speaks to *us*, about *our* condition, and thus we hear in his rhetoric not the abstract language of theological disputation but the personal cadences of the sermon: »Let *us* cry out, Monicus, with the apostle, ›Unhappy person that I am! Who will deliver me from the body of this death?‹ and thereupon let *us* answer, ›The grace of God through Jesus Christ our Lord.‹ Let *us* say to him, ›Be it done to us, Lord. . . .‹«[118] In this case, which is characteristic both of Volucer's contribution to the dialogue as a whole and of Gerson's sermonic method more generally, scripture has become the vehicle for upbuilding or edifying *viatores* since it offers promises to grasp on the pilgrimage to God.

In another example of the homiletic tenor of the dialogue, Gerson introduces at regular intervals into Volucer's speech a sermonic device which might best be described as guided meditations. These are practical digressions of a sort, standing as interruptions of the conversation proper, added apparently both to illumine some potentially abstract theological question and to provide a coherent means of integrating the advice offered by *theologia* into one's own life. Once again we discern in these meditations Gerson's keen interest in accentuating the paideutic function of theology, since he relies upon these digressions to lead Monicus, and with him the reader, in a progressive reflection aimed to »re-form« the human person.[119] Thus, for instance, in a passage in which Gerson's Volucer explores the nature of divine election and predestination (cf. I pr. 4), one is struck by the relative absence of theological

---

dialogue qui ne vise aucune conversion« is simply a shallow reading of the text. Cf. *La théologie mystique*, 2:317. The narrative movement of this text manifests a deliberate and progressive movement — in a word, the *dialectique* which Combes had found lacking — as Gerson's Volucer responds point by point to his interlocutor's doubts and fears. And, as we have already suggested, the dialogue traces a protracted and difficult conversion of this character, who closes the treatise by offering a benediction of sorts: Monicus has the last word, and that word is an invocation of a biblical promise for peace, as well as an affirmation of Rom. 15.4 with which the text opened.

[118] See G 9, p. 209: »Exclamemus, Monice, cum Apostolo: ›Infelix ego homo, quis me liberabit de corpore mortis hujus.‹ Subinde respondeamus: ›Gratia Dei per Jesum Christum.‹ Dicamus eidem: ›Fiat nobis, Domine, secundum judicium atque desiderium‹« (my emphasis).

[119] In Brown's study of Gerson, we find a good survey of the overall shape of this preacher's homiletical theory and practice and the study recognizes the striking »richness of doctrinal content« to be found in his sermons (see *Pastor and Laity*, p. 23), yet we find no mention here of this particular facet of the chancellor's homiletic method. Schwab comes closer to the mark, concluding in what remains the most comprehensive discussion of »Gerson as preacher« that »es ist das christliche Leben in seiner Gesammtheit, das den Kern aller homiletischen Thätigkeit Gersons bildet, theils nach seiner Grundlage in den Wahrheiten des Glaubens, theils nach seiner Gestaltung in Sitte und Recht, und zwar letztere Seite beinahe überwiegend. Denn nicht blos behandelt ein großer Theil der auf uns

terminology and scholastic argument, in place of which Gerson offers a series of *exempla*[120] which leads to a »paideutic« meditation — in this case, a *quadruplex meditatio* — by which Volucer guides us through four steps meant to root hope more firmly in our lives. This *meditatio* offers in each step biblical promises to build confidence in God's faithfulness, since Gerson claims in typical nominalist fashion that while God »is not obliged by any rational creature,« nonetheless God has bound himself (i. e., *de potentia ordinata*) to the divine promises conveyed in scripture. The Bible, then, as *theologia revelata*, cannot mislead us *de potentia ordinata*, since its irrevocable and thereby reliable covenants become the pathway by which *viatores* find their way to God. But Gerson carries this argument a step further than this: he here moves beyond the traditional use of the nominalist argument *de potentia Dei* to affirm that the certitude of faith which *viatores* hold, a certitude which must be applied to the entire biblical canon, cannot be deceived under *any* circumstances — not even *de potentia Dei absoluta*, since »God cannot deny himself« under any circumstances. *Scriptura sacra* establishes the covenantal matrix of Gerson's broader paideutic enterprise, and he utilizes scripture in order to advance this cause. The meditations themselves, in other words, are not only a matter of literary style: they represent another aspect of his effort to guide *viatores* by directing his readers toward such biblical signposts, in this case by applying scriptural covenants as the inviolable source of consolation and assurance.

Another literary technique found throughout this dialogue, which is at the same time a frequent device used in his sermons, is the presence of biblical *exempla*, examples drawn from biblical history meant to convey concrete models of proper living which illustrated or defended diverse theological arguments.[121] We find one such cluster of examples in the same discussion of divine election previously mentioned. In order to illustrate that God chooses *us* regardless of the quality of our present life, and hence *ante praevisa merita*, he mentions the cases of such biblical heroes and heroines of piety as Peter, Mary Magdalene, and Paul, none of whom God chose because of the sanctity of their lives and all of whom were elected while yet sinners.[122] Through the use of this technique Gerson roots his arguments in historical and at the same time intentionally personal terms. *We* as the reader, in other words, might well grasp Paul's intention in echoing the theological affirmations of his scriptures

---

gekommenen Predigten Gersons rein ethische Themate, auch die dogmatischen Vorträge gehen durch allegorische Behandlung der biblischen Texte immer wieder auf das Leben und seine sittliche Entwicklung über.« *Johannes Gerson*, p. 381.

[120] On this stylistic aspect of his sermons, cf. Brown, *Pastor and Laity*, pp. 28−29.

[121] Again, see *ibid.*, pp. 28 ff.

[122] G 9, p. 197 f. In this sense God not only »brings good from the sins of the elect« (*ex peccatis electorum*) but elects those who are yet sinners; this demonstrates, he is quick to point out, the depth of God's mercy, since »the kindness of mercy is even more prominent in the restoration of the lost.« *Ibid.*

(e. g., Volucer's use of Rom. 7.24 above), but in any case we can identify with the apostle on the biographical level: that is, »the grace of God through Jesus Christ« did not depend upon the holiness of Paul's (or, by inference, the *viator's*) life, but upon God's choice. So, too, must we grasp God's election in *our* case, not on the basis of human merit but as sinners in need of forgiveness.

Finally, Gerson adds to the conversation between these two characters a further level of dialogue, one which he conveys principally through Volucer's contribution: namely, a dialogue between the reader and God. He accomplishes this on one level, as we have just noticed, through utilizing scripture to teach *us* how to speak with God. Scripture becomes the language we can use with confidence to address God, and here we can only note that the Psalms function in a particularly prominent manner in this treatise. These texts become the language of the soul addressing God, a thoroughly natural application for one like Gerson who would have been rooted in the daily rhythms of the church's liturgical life. On another level Gerson articulates this dialogue of the pilgrim with God through the addition of fervent prayers at key points in the text, and particularly at the close of various poems (e. g., I m. 5; II m. 4; III m. 4; IV m. 3). These prayers, in other words, extend his technique of introducing the »first person« into the dialogue, in this case by inserting prayers into the text which because of their form and their strategic placement easily become the reader's own.

Through these various literary techniques, many of which parallel Gerson's homiletic style as we have noted, the dialogue brings the reader to identify with *peregrinus* quite generally, and perhaps even with Monicus in his doubting and fearful moods. In both cases the reader ultimately becomes the object of the dialogue and the recipient of its dialectic argument: the reader is the one who is in need of a »companion« while maneuvering through life's trials (*tentationes*) in search of »firm hope« and ultimately in quest of God. In this sense, the reader becomes actor upon this stage, entering into the dynamic movement of this narrative structure in the pilgrimage *per desolationem ad spem*. By thrusting the reader *into* the narrative, Gerson thus draws the reader within the paideutic horizon of this theological *consolatio*, thereby altering the Boethian literary structure in a subtle but extremely significant manner: here we have no dialogue, as we might have expected given the literary archetype established by Boethius, between »Lady Theology« and an ailing exile, nor does Gerson's text yield increasingly to the lone voice of *theologia* as did Boethius' to *philosophia*. Rather, here the dialogue sustained between the two main characters establishes a constructive paideutic framework by which Gerson leads the reader himself as *peregrinus* on the journey *ad Deum*. It is not only that the *dramatis personae* differ from Boethius' archetype: the dialogue itself functions as a kind of enchiridion, or what one might well call a »manual of conversion,« designed to re-form *viatores* as they moved toward the *pax Dei*, the immediate embrace of God at the end of life.

Chapter IV

Foundations of the Theological Task

In turning from our survey of how Gerson's *De consolatione theologiae* functions as paideutic text, an approach to this treatise which considered the coalescence of literary structure and theological intention, we shall focus in this chapter on the theological foundations of Gerson's thought. Here, then, our attention falls upon three fundamental concerns which the chancellor articulates in this treatise: his theological use of scripture; the relation of philosophy and theology; and, finally, his integration of *theoria* and *praxis*. These broad themes do not exhaust the detail of his argument in this text, but they do point to the general theological concerns which guided his thought. As we shall subsequently note, each of these concerns presents an array of issues which show marked development from his earlier writings; the focus he devotes to each suggests that these were methodological issues which exercised his thought to a considerable during this later period of his life.

In the final two sections of this chapter we shall explore the manner in which Gerson discerns the relation of philosophy and theology, as well as the implications this movement entailed for his deliberate integration of *theoria* and *praxis*. Our analysis begins, however, by returning to the question of how Gerson used scripture, in theory and in practice, in order to structure the theological task; here we shall suggest that while this is no *scriptura sola* in the later Protestant sense, his approach constructs what we might well call a *theologia biblica* since he argues that »the tradition of theology« (*theologiae traditio*) has been revealed through scripture (*per scripturam*). On this question we find a sustained and vigorous discussion of theological method; indeed, what is quite striking about this treatise in general is how central his discussion of methodological issues becomes. This is no merely »occasional« piece, despite its unsystematic character; the wide range of topics he here treats and the theoretical detail of his discussion suggest that Gerson intended this treatise to chart the shape of his theology in a comprehensive sense.

A. The construction of a *theologia biblica*

To accomplish this we must discuss, first of all, Gerson's construction of what might appropriately be called a *theologia biblica*, or »biblical theology.« In the foregoing chapter we have already suggested that Gerson brings *theologia* and *scriptura* into such close connection that theological argument is often little more than a recitation, often in glossed form, of biblical texts; similarly, when *theologia* finally addresses the reader in the text's closing pages, she does so by spinning a largely biblical narrative. *Consolatio theologiae*, in other words, is ultimately — and here he simply follows Paul's lead, as rendered by the Vulgate reading of Rom. 15.4 — a scriptural consolation, the presentation of biblical texts which lead *viatores* on a dialectical pilgrimage from desolation to hope. If as he argues in the opening pages *theologia* is the »companion« on this journey, then *scriptura* stands as the detailed roadmap guiding the pilgrim step by step toward life's destination *ad Deum*. Yet this is not to say that Gerson advocates a method *scriptura sola*, or as he himself put it *scriptura nuda*: his reliance upon scripture — and his argument in this connection appears to be a direct refutation of the Hussite argument on authority, as we shall later demonstrate — always places the biblical text within the church as interpretive context. In this sense he is quite traditional by medieval standards, articulating a theory of biblical hermeneutics which is set within an ecclesiological framework. We shall have more to say on this matter later in this study.[1]

Our inquiry into his conception of the theological task must first explore the specific use Gerson makes of scripture as the »revealed« basis for the »tradition of theology.« We must also inquire, second, about the concrete function of scripture within the church. Only then will we be in a position to raise the crucial question of the »sufficiency« of scripture in constructing this *theologia biblica*, an issue which has evoked considerable debate among historians of this period. And, finally, we must examine in a preliminary fashion how Gerson's biblical hermeneutic intersects both in theory and practice with his ecclesiology, a topic to which we shall return in the sixth chapter of this study.

1. *Theologiae traditio per scripturam revelatam:* the horizon of theology

According to Gerson *sacra scriptura* is the ultimate horizon of the theological task, a claim he bases upon his assumption that scripture is revealed by God and thus conveys a knowledge which is beyond natural reason (i. e., his refrain that »philosophia non cognovit«). In the preceding chapter we pointed out that Gerson avoids almost altogether in this treatise the terminology and formal

---

[1] See below, 6.A.3.

disputational structure which established the basic medium of scholastic theology, choosing rather to translate theology out of its esoteric technical forms into the less precise but colloquial and metaphorical rhetoric of conversation.[2] This stylistic preference is the constructive side of his strident criticism, expressed in an early letter to Cardinal d'Ailly in which he outlined a program for reform[3] as in his subsequent lectures *Contra curiositatem studentium*,[4] of the propensity demonstrated by the theological faculty to focus upon »useless doctrine« which was »without fruit or solidity,« and to emphasize obscure questions with vague terminology to the neglect of that teaching which was »necessary and useful for salvation.«[5] In his choice of themes to be considered in this dialogue, as in the literary style by which he discussed such matters, Gerson identifies *theologia* as an edificatory enterprise; in this sense literary form becomes the suitable medium of theological intent. Thus his development of a metaphorical theology was not merely a stylistic point, as we have suggested, but stood as the natural implicate of the close relation he maintained between *scriptura sacra* and *theologia*. That is, since Gerson had earlier maintained that the logic proper to scripture was »rhetoric,« and consequently that it should be interpreted »not . . . in terms of the power of logic or dialectic but rather according to the modes of expression used in rhetorical speeches,«[6] and because theology for him »spoke« this scriptural

---

[2] This is particularly true of the homilies delivered to common people (i. e., *idiotae*); as Connolly has rightly noted, »before the congregations in the churches he was sure to make a practical approach to his subject and to enliven his talk by anecdotes drawn either from the *Books of Examples* or from his own experience. . . . With graphic imagery and keen analogy he helped the people to understand their duty.« See *John Gerson*, p. 155. Combes has attributed this stylistic characteristic in *De consolatione theologiae* less to the intended audience (or readership) than to the directly personal or autobiographical nature of the piece, describing the treatise as »une réflexion méthodique sur une expérience. . . . C'est une psychanalyse.« This is an intriguing idea, but Combes fails to explain it in the subsequent discussion, and »psychoanalysis« remains as a description of the text a novel but unconvincing notion. His conclusion, however, is more balanced and penetrating: »A moins de supposer que tout effort créateur doive, pour être puissant, engendrer des *Sommes*, il me paraît évident que, tant par son objet que par sa nouveauté, la vigueur de son enquête, la rigueur de sa méthode, la valeur de ses résultats, la qualité de sa forme littéraire, la portée de son témoignage, une telle oeuvre ne se relie à la scolastique du XIIIe siècle que comme un sommet se rattache à la chaîne dont il fait partie et qui permet de mieux mesurer sa hauteur.« *La théologie mystique*, 2: 306.

[3] G 2, pp. 23 ff.

[4] G 3, pp. 224 ff.

[5] Indeed, this critique stands as the first thesis in the program of reform he outlined in his letter to d'Ailly (G 2, p. 26), and comes early in his first lecture *Contra curiositatem studentium* (G 3, p. 230).

[6] Cf. *De sensu litterali sacrae scripturae*, G 3, p. 334: »Sensus litteralis sacrae scripturae accipiendus est non secundum vim logicae seu dialecticae, sed potius juxta locutiones in rhetoricis semonibus usitatas. . . . Habet enim scriptura sacra, sicut et moralis et historialis

language, his articulation of theology in a metaphorical or rhetorical vein in *De consolatione theologiae* comes as no surprise. Throughout this treatise the rhetoric of scripture blends in an almost seamless manner with the language of theology, with *scriptura* and *theologia* often meeting on the common ground of metaphor. It is this close connexion which prompts him to affirm »et amplectanda theologiae traditio per scripturam revelatam«: the tradition of theology must be embraced through revealed scripture.[7]

Yet if it is true that Gerson often uses scripture in a quite straightforward manner and relies upon the biblical text in its plain or literal sense in constructing theological arguments, this is not always the case. At several junctures of the dialogue he does resort to the *doctrina* commonly used »in the schools,« usually acknowledging this as an explicit departure from the norm.[8] In such cases, however, *exceptio probat regulam*: the exceptional character of this use of scholastic argument proves the general rule, and thus represents a deviation but not a thoroughgoing revision of his reliance upon scripture as the normal rhetoric of theological discourse. Nonetheless, these exceptions may tell us much about Gerson's grasp of *theologia* more generally, particularly by alerting us to what it is in these cases which prompts him to rely upon these methods.

How, then, and when does Gerson resort to scholastic forms of argument? There are only several occasions in this treatise where Gerson informs the reader in certain terms that the resolution of some disputed question – in almost every case involving the interpretation of a biblical passage – cannot be

---

scientia, suam logicam propriam, quam rhetoricam appellamus. « Later Gerson defines the unique character of scripture in different terms, this time declaring that scripture has »its own proper logic and grammar« just as the moral sciences claim »rhetoric« as their own »logic.« Yet this claim should not be read to contradict his earlier emphasis upon the rhetorical dimension of scripture. Indeed, in this later text his intention is to oppose an exposition of scripture »according to the power of logic or dialectic which serves the speculative sciences, « and he deliberately aligns his approach with Augustine's argument in *De doctrina christiana* (*De doctrina christiana* (I.2.2, 2.1.1–2.4.5; *CCSL* 32: 32:7–8, 32–34) which interprets »the literal sense« to consider »the mode of speaking through figures, tropes, and rhetorical qualities« (see »Réponse à la consultation des maîtres«; G 10, p. 241). Rhetoric rather than the logic used by the speculative sciences functions as the norm in reading and interpreting scriptural language.

[7] For this text I follow the early incunabulum of Joh. Koelhoff (Cologne, 1483) and the Du Pin edition (Antwerp, 1706); Glorieux's text reads »et amplectanda theologiae traditio per scripturam revelatum, « without further reference to this textual discrepancy. Cf. G 9, p. 204. Combes has come to the same conclusion regarding this theme which he rightly interprets as a matter of both style and method: »On se tromperait donc du tout au tout, si l'on voyait en ce dialogue un exposé didactique de théologie scripturaire par lequel Gerson aurait voulu dégager de quelques textes bibliques, soigneusement choisis et techniquement interprétés, une notion complète et complexe de l'espérance. « Cf. *La théologie mystique*, 2: 344.

[8] Thus, for example, he adds at one point that he must consult »the teaching« of the schools: »doctrinam consulit quam theologica tradit schola.« G 9, p. 229.

attained without recourse to scholastic teaching. In one such case (III pr. 3), the question under consideration happened to be the source of considerable debate during this period: the matter of simony. As we have earlier noted Gerson utilizes the voice of Volucer in this treatise to set forth the magisterial position on a variety of disputed questions of the day, many of which Monicus advocates to provoke debate. Throughout this treatise, as in this particular passage, the immediate events of the recently concluded Council of Constance apparently dominate his thought: here he directs his argument in quite specific terms against Hus and his supporters, who following the Wyclifite tradition had taken a strong and outspoken stand against simony. Against such strident criticism which equated any monetary gifts received for pastoral services as simony,[9] Gerson insists that the mere act of receiving such gifts – including benefices – was beyond reproach, as long as one's intentions were only to gain »the means to be sufficiently supported« and the incumbent pastoral duties were actually performed.[10] As the dialogue proceeds, Monicus counters this explanation by arguing that this justification appears too lenient and does not meet the criticism advanced by »some people« (presumably Hus and his circle) who viewed simony as »so widespread that almost none of the clergy would be found uninfected« by it.[11] Yet this disputed question breaks off rather abruptly

---

[9] Gerson had earlier forwarded the list of articles taken from Hus's *De ecclesia*, which the Paris masters had censured, to the Archbishop of Prague, Conrad de Vechte. This list includes Hus's attack against simony: »Quod omnis datio pecuniae ministris ecclesiae facta in ministratione spiritualium quorumcumque reddit ecclesiasticos hujusmodi Simoniacos vel Gezitas.« The Paris faculty condemned this thesis, calling it »error scandalosus et temerarius; quoniam potest aliquid dari talibus ecclesiasticis titulo sustentationis ministri, absque venditione vel emptione spiritualis rei.« See G 2, p. 165.

[10] G 9, pp. 221–22: »Nec est leviter hoc imputandum simoniacae pravitati; sicut nec dum frequentantur in ecclesiis horae canonicae ad recipiendum destributiones quotidianas et solitas; aut dum vicarius deservit uni curae suspiciens inde stipendium: ›Dignus est operarius mercede et cibo suo.‹ [Lk. 10.7] Dicam amplius. Si profitetur aliquis vitam claustralem, rationabiliter intendens illic sufficienter sustentari alioquin non intraturus, neque tamen simoniacus est, dum intentio principalis sit servire Deo, et sustentatio suae vitae est ad illum finem, et sub illo: ubi autem unum propter aliud, jam non duo, sed unum sunt.« Gerson argues, in other words, for the »sufficient compensation« of priests, considering their salary an allowance for what was necessary to sustain them so that they might perform their pastoral duties properly. The key is that their *intentio* was to be the service of God, not the reception of wages; this was »accidental,« as it were. This is a more detailed and intriguing defense than we find in the brief rebuttal included in the earlier censure by the Paris faculty (see preceding note). Throughout this prose section (i. e., III pr. 3), Gerson devotes his attention to answering various criticisms levelled by Hus and his followers.

[11] G 9, p. 222. Hus addressed this theme in extenso in his treatise *On Simony*; see *Advocates of Reform*, ed. and trans. Matthew Spinka (Philadelphia, 1953), pp. 196–97, 201, and especially 260–78.

at this juncture, with Monicus concluding that this particular problem must be pursued »more in accord with the scholastic method.«[12]

It seems at first glance curious and something of an anomaly given Gerson's manner of reliance upon scripture throughout this treatise that the dialogue reaches this impasse as quickly as it does. Yet the broader context of this debate, considered as we have earlier suggested in its historical form rather than this limited literary representation of it, provides a clue which explains this abrupt shift from *scriptura* to scholastic argument: Gerson found himself in the debate over simony pressed into the awkward position of countering one scriptural argument – in this case, Hus's use of Jesus' statement, »freely have you received; freely give« (Mt. 10.8)[13] – with a conflated text gathered from the wider synoptic parallels of this pericope. Gerson simply builds his rebuttal by following the first rule he had earlier identified as the key to interpreting »the literal sense«: namely, one must consider literary context, »the circumstances of what precedes and follows« a given text.[14] Thus, he qualifies the force of this disputed text with a conflation of the statement which immediately follows: »for a laborer is worthy of his reward [Lk. 10.7] and his bread [Mt. 10.10].« But at this juncture, recognizing that this was a bitterly disputed case which pitted not only theologian against theologian but scripture against scripture, Gerson could not hope to establish the legitimacy of the benefice system simply through resorting to one particular text. Scripture was apparently ambivalent in this case, supporting both sides of the argument if cited with one emphasis or another.[15] It is in such cases that we find Gerson admitting that scripture might usually but did not always provide for the resolution of theological disputes, particularly in circumstances in which one text apparently spoke against another. In such exceptional circumstances, he proposes that one should argue

---

[12] G 9, p. 222: »Sed hoc interim omisso, cum multis quae magis scholastice tractanda sunt.«

[13] Cf. Hus, *On Simony*, in *Advocates of Reform*, p. 203: »Thereby Saint Gregory means that whenever anyone confers a spiritual gift improperly either himself or through another, either openly or covertly, either in consideration of service, of material gift, or human favor, he thereby commits simony, contrary to the scriptures and Christ's command, ›Freely have you received, freely give.‹« For the moment we shall not examine this argument more closely, since our intent here is to suggest how such exceptions still affirm Gerson's general rule that theology is a matter of exegesis pure and (usually) simple.

[14] G 10, p. 241; Gerson is here deliberately paraphrasing Augustine's *De doctrina christiana* III.2.4, III.3.6, *CCSL* 32: 78–81.

[15] It is intriguing to note in this regard that Gerson did not ignore or fail to recognize this ambivalence in his harmonization of the gospels (i. e., his *Monotessaron*), but placed each of these differing emphases in immediate proximity. His »harmony,« in other words, did not flatten out such scriptural inconsistencies, but merely offered a full statement of each pericope in its parallel readings; on this particular text in its synoptic parallels as he renders them, see G 9, p. 283.

»in the scholastic manner,« apparently intending by this the church's authoritative exegesis as established by the university masters.

As we have suggested, the exceptional character of these cases confirms the general principle governing Gerson's approach regarding both literary style and theological method. Gerson utilizes scripture in its plain or literal sense to shape his theological argument and indeed to create a theological rhetoric. He thus aligns theology, here following his elder colleague Henry Totting of Oyta quite closely,[16] directly with exegesis: the text itself establishes the arena of theological discussion, though in areas of exegetical dispute one must finally resort to the authoritative position as articulated by the university theologians »in the scholastic manner.« *Theologiae traditio* usually derives, however, directly from the literal sense of the revealed scriptures themselves; these are the horizon *in* which theological discourse finds its bearings and *into* which it constructs its arguments, since the revealed text establishes both the matter and the form of theological argument.

2. *Per eruditionem sacrae scripturae:* the teaching function of scripture

This point raises the broader methodological question, which Gerson also addresses in this treatise, regarding the practical matter of how the scriptures are to be used within the church. In other words, for whom is this rhetoric intended? If *scriptura sacra* represents the horizon of theology, is its rhetoric suited principally for the professional theologians, those granted the degree of *baccalarius biblicus* and commissioned to teach the Bible on the theological

---

[16] Albert Lang has argued that »Heinrich von Oyta der Heiligen Schrift die grundlegende Bedeutung für die Theologie und den Glauben zuerkannt hat. In den von der Schrift dargebotenen Wahrheiten sah er die unentbehrliche Prinzipiengrundlage für die theologische Wissenschaft.... Letzlich und wesentlich müssen alle theologischen Aussagen auf die Heilige Schrift sich stützen können.« See »Das Verhältnis von Schrift, Tradition und kirchlichem Lehramt nach Heinrich Totting von Oyta,« *Scholastik* 40 (1965), pp. 216–18. Here Lang aligns Oyta within the Augustinian tradition which included Alfons Vargas of Toledo, Gregory of Rimini, Hugolin of Orvieto, etc.; we know from citations found in various passages throughout his works that Gerson held Oyta in high esteem and positioned his own view of scripture squarely in line with his predecessor at Paris. On this point see G 10, p. 241, in which Gerson builds his approach to scripture on the basis of Oyta's position as expressed in the prologue to his *Quaestiones sententiarum*. It should be noted that Oyta completed this work during the period in which Gerson was teaching on the arts faculty at Paris, and just before he commenced with his theological training (1382). Several decades later, in writing his own university lectures *Contra curiositatem studentium*, Gerson spoke of »venerabilis et venerandus doctor Henricus de Hoyta, qui pro suo merito veteribus aequari et inter eruditissimos logicos, metaphysicos et theologos numerari potest, dum hanc materiam tractaret, ad concordiam conatus est extrema reducere ....« G 3, pp. 241–42. See also Burger, *Aedificatio*, pp. 54, 118.

faculty as well as minor prelates who used scripture for preaching and guidance in the
cura animarum?

By approaching this question Gerson's »democratization« of the theological
task — or in this case the matter of biblical exegesis — becomes apparent once
again.[17] If scripture is indeed the horizon of theology, then it presents a
panorama accessible to all *viatores* regardless of formal academic training — i. e.,
the *idiota* stands on an equal footing with the *peritus*, because both are pilgrims
to whom *theologia* gives herself as companion on the journey *ad Deum*. Thus, in
the early pages of this treatise he points out that *theologia* accompanies us
throughout the human pilgrimage, and from an early age, since we know *sacrae
litterae* from our infancy (*ab infantia*).[18] Moreover, he viewed biblical language
not as an esoteric domain for speculative or »subtle« questions — indeed, one
was not to apply the logic used by the »speculative sciences« in exegesis[19] — but
as what he here calls *bullae*, or edicts, given for all those *in via* to God, so that
these *peregrini* might address themselves »confidently« to God.[20] As the source

---

[17] In *Pastor and Laity*, Brown has also pointed to this »anti-elitism« of Gerson's writings,
a point which might have suggested that his ecclesiology be treated with greater
appreciation; as I have earlier noted, Brown's study follows Pascoe's interpretation of
Gerson's hierarchical model (cf. *ibid.*, pp. 38—39, and Pascoe, *Jean Gerson*, p. 32). Although
Brown's primary focus in terms of this observation has to do with Gerson's treatment of
theologia mystica, there is nonetheless a distinct and important parallel to his ecclesiology:
already in the earlier mystical treatises Gerson contrasts mystical from »scholastic«
(academic?) theology, in part because »simple uneducated people (*simplices idiotae*) reach
theologia mystica more quickly and sublimely than those learned in scholastic or discursive
theology. It is because their faith is not disturbed by contrary opinions which they have not
heard and therefore do not think about.« Brown, *Pastor and Laity*, p. 187, citing Gerson's
Élucidation, G 8, pp. 158—59. We shall return to this theme below; see 4.C.3.

[18] G 9, p. 187. This is a conviction arising from Gerson's own upbringing, a point which
Schwab identified in another passage from his writings in which he places upon the lips of
a young child the claim that »laudo quod ad pauca te revocas quae possint tractari per sacras
scripturas, quas ab infantia, non adulans loquor, nosti . . .« etc. See Schwab, *Johannes
Gerson*, p. 380, n. 1. This conviction emerges from another angle because of Gerson's
attentiveness to the education of youth and their need to claim the companionship of
theologia in order that they might themselves learn the rhetoric of scripture. Indeed, he
placed considerable emphasis upon the pedagogy of children, devoting the last years of his
life to this pursuit, since he was convinced that *ecclesiae reformatio* must begin with the young
(*a pueris*). See Connolly, *John Gerson*, pp. 86—87, who cites this passage from *Rememoratio
per praelatum quemlibet agendorum* (p. 87, n. 4).

[19] See G 10, p. 241.

[20] G 9, p. 233. Here, too, we must correct the sweeping claim made by Henri de Lubac,
when he concludes that Gerson holds as three distinct disciplines »exégèse, construction
dogmatique et organisation de l'expérience interieure« (cf. Exégèse médiévale, 2/2: 492); on
the contrary, Gerson sought quite consistently to integrate scriptural exegesis not only with
doctrine but with inner experience, a point which is ably demonstrated in his conviction
expressed later in this treatise that one must claim the biblical promises of hope not only *per
intellectum* but *in affectum* as well. Cf. G 9, pp. 237, 244.

of instruction for the journey to God (*humanae peregrinationis refugium*), the scriptural text becomes the matrix of paideia, the context in which the human person is formed into the image of God. We have already pointed in general terms to this feature of the treatise, since Volucer often lapses into the »first person plural« in recommending scriptural texts by which »we« — and he intends with this *all* persons as *viatores* — should speak to God.[21] Scripture thus becomes not only the language of human formation, but the rhetoric of access to God, the medium by which *peregrinus* approaches God with petitions. In this sense theology instructs and guides the wayfarers by giving them a scriptural language of prayer — a quite practical and concrete example of Boethius' *commercium inter homines Deumque*. This functional view of scripture, which utilizes the text as paideutic for all who are journeying toward God, thus represents a deliberate program of »democratization,« in that this text belongs within the common domain of the church. By establishing the proper horizon for *theologia*, scripture comes to chart the way in which all pilgrims — both the young and the old, the simple and expert — journey toward God. Just as the literary form of this treatise establishes its function as a »manual of conversion,« therefore, it is finally scripture which fulfills this function in a concrete sense, »converting« or »re-forming« the human person on this pilgrimage. Scripture *is* paideia.[22]

Along similar lines Gerson is not at all naive about the varying grasp diverse persons will have of scripture, according to differing levels of human ability and educational experience.[23] His »anti-elitism« does not blur such differences nor does it ever eclipse the hierarchical structure of his ecclesiology by ignoring the pastoral offices within the church through which those who teach and preach explicate scripture for the laity. In this treatise he argues that in contrast to »the few« (*pauci*) who grasp the *eruditio sacrae scripturae* on their own (*ex propria eruditione*) and thus need no teachers, »the many« must be instructed by others, »receiving from them an understanding of the scriptures.«[24] Gerson

---

[21] See above, 4.A.1.

[22] In this regard we must once again point to Jaeger's work on paideia, in which he suggests that for the Cappadocians »the Christian paideia is the Bible.« Cf. Jaeger, *Early Christianity and Greek Paideia*, p. 92. This is not to suggest that one might draw any direct lines of influence from the Cappadocians to Gerson; indeed, we have already dismissed such a dependence, above all because his knowledge of the Greek fathers appears to be meager and derivative. But it may suggest that Boethius functioned as a vital link in the story Jaeger only begins to outline in this study. See also above, 3.A.2.

[23] For example, Gerson argues that the manner in which one grasps, through faith, particular points of the *eruditio sacrae scripturae* varies according to talent and experience; G 9, p. 229.

[24] G 9, p. 236: »Pauci per seipsos dociles sunt propter claram suae complexionis harmoniam, addo vel aliam gratiam gratis datam, qua faciliter agenda concipiunt, scripturas ut Augustinus intelligunt. Multi per alios erudiuntur, recipientes ab eis intelligentiam scripturarum.« The reference to Augustine recalls his admission that »one who is supported by

concedes, in other words, that diverse abilities and levels of training modulate the manner in which scripture is utilized, though without dimming his conviction that its purpose is *eruditio* for all. However, his concern to underscore the breadth of this function, and hence to democratize the paideutic task of theology, did not overlook basic pedagogical considerations: these required him to defend the established means within the church's order by which »the many« are either taught, or, if they cannot grasp such teaching, »submit« by »obeying those who teach them.«[25] Normally, therefore, the church's hierarchy could be conceived in Dionysian fashion as a channel of descending revelation, such that the task of teachers was to convey and interpret the *theologiae traditio* to those beneath them.

But this model gives us only part of the story, since Gerson does qualify this application of the hierarchical model with its varying degrees and descending structure by which *inferiores* received moral certitude *per eruditionem sacrae scripturae*. In so doing he offers a subtle but decisive criticism of earlier scholastic views of the nature of faith and its function within the church, a point which he articulates with peculiar force in this treatise. At stake here is the question of accountability, and particularly the character of the faith for which the *idiotae* found themselves responsible. In a formulation which became widely accepted during the later Middle Ages, Thomas Aquinas concluded that all within the church were not bound to believe everything »explicitly«: those of higher degree within the ecclesiastical hierarchy (*superiores*) who had a duty to teach *inferiores* were »bound to believe explicitly more things than others are.«[26] The key word here is »explicit,« since all were bound to believe, but those who were taught (i. e., the laity) could rely upon the church's »implicit« faith — a kind of »treasury« of faith. But this concession which accurately recognized that those with formal academic training had a different and more

---

faith, hope, and charity, with an unshaken hold upon them, does not need the scriptures except for the instruction of others.« See *De doctrina christiana*, I.39.43; CCSL 32:31. Gerson, following Augustine once again, calls these »few« the »perfect« ones, at least »insofar as perfection is possible in this life.« G 9, p. 236.

[25] *Ibid.*: ».. . aut si nequeunt credunt saltem dicentibus et obediunt.« This emphasis of submission must be understood within the hierarchical concept of church which Gerson held; he draws upon this theme to interpret what he understands to be the principal function of religion: »Puto quod religionum instituendarum principalis causa fuit auctoritas regiminis, cui magis obedientia praestaretur, quam propriae rationi, quae in plurimis dubia valde est, debilis et incerta.« *Ibid.* For a detailed discussion of this point, see below, 6.A.1.

[26] Cf. *Summa theologiae* IIaIIae q. 2 a. 6. This thesis was nothing more than the logical outgrowth of Aquinas's conviction that »divine revelation reaches those of lower degree through those who are over them, in a certain order,« a conviction which is an essentially Dionysian point. Cf. for instance *The Ecclesiastical Hierarchy*, PG 3:373; in *Pseudo-Dionysius. The Complete Works*, ed. and trans. Colm Luibheid (New York, 1987), pp. 196–97: »Subordinates ... are to pursue their superiors and they also promote the advance of those below them, while these too, as they go forward, are led by others.«

sophisticated faith — at least, understood in the cognitive dimension[27] — could easily become either the justification for passivity on the part of those of »lower degree« (i. e., the laity) or an occasion for pride on the part of those who taught. Against any such understanding of faith Gerson held here that whatever might be understood *per theologiam* must be integrated through »constant rumination in the affects of the heart and by the execution of good works.«[28]

For this reason Gerson applies his democratizing perspective to explain the purpose of scripture's *eruditio*. He insists, as if to qualify his earlier argument regarding the varying levels of certitude, that a »general credulity« (*fides implicita*) does not suffice »in many things,« and certainly not in those which are held to be certain *per eruditionem sacrae scripturae*: all these should be held »by explicit faith« (*explicita fide*). This appears to be addressed to the laity, who are here admonished to expand the scope of their certitude over against the minimalist attitude which stressed the vicarious nature of their faith. Gerson bolsters this claim in a later passage (IV pr. 2):

> It is necessary for all the faithful [*fidelibus omnibus*], as they journey along life's way, that they believe with this certitude [viz. ›a third kind of supernatural certitude‹ which ›faith possesses in the hearts of believers‹ and which ›is based on an adherence to what is seen obscurely, as in a mirror,‹ and hence is ›supported not by reason but by divine authority‹] not only the twelve articles of the creed, but the whole of sacred scripture — both actually and habitually, implicitly and explicitly, so that they are certain in their belief and cannot be deceived.[29]

----

[27] Here we must point again, however, to Gerson's qualification of faith as a matter not merely of knowledge, but of affection. Thus he insists, for example, that the faith held by *theologus*, who was a »good man learned [*eruditum*] in sacred letters,« was »not only the learning of the intellect but much more of the affects.« He even goes so far as to suggest that »the spirit of catholic judgment« (*animus catholicae sententiae*) will »root itself among the simple [*apud idiotas*] more fruitfully [*fructuosius*], concerning their salvation, since they have a simple faith, sure hope, and sweet charity, than among those filled with learning which, as the apostle says, brings forth the knowledge which ›puffs up.‹« See G 9, p. 237. Consequently, we should not expect Gerson to conclude that *theologi* have an »explicit« faith which exceeded that of the laity; indeed, he suggests that if anything the *fides simplex* of the laity, if rooted in the affects more effectively than in the intellect, stands as the better way when contrasted with those »learned« theologians whose high learning fills them with pride. In his earlier lectures *Contra curiositatem studentium*, Gerson had argued in a similar vein that pride prevents scholastic theologians from repenting and having »living faith«: »Superbia scholaticos a poenitentia et fide viva praepediens . . .«; G 3, p. 230. See also his *Élucidations*, in which he makes the same case for the laity vis-à-vis *theologia mystica*, arguing here that academic learning introduces too many qualifying arguments into the minds of the learned. G 8, p. 158.

[28] G 9, p. 237; this assertion paraphrases the Pauline formulation of Gal. 5.6, ». . . fides quae per charitatem operatur.«

[29] G 9, p. 231. Several years earlier (ca. 1416) Gerson had written a treatise entitled *Quae veritates sint de necessitate salutis credendae*, in which he announced the same theme: »Primus gradus veritatum credendarum est *canon totius scripturae sacrae* et singulorum quae in ea litteraliter asserta sunt . . .« G 6, p. 181 (my emphasis).

This argument offers a quite calculated and specific critique of Aquinas's conclusion that not all were »equally bound to have an explicit faith,« a view of faith as the property of the church as a whole in which those lower in the hierarchy could rely upon an »implicit« faith in all matters beyond those fundamental doctrines (*articuli fidei*) announced in the creed.[30] In contrast to such a position – and in proximity to the viewpoint earlier articulated by both Henry Totting of Oyta and John Hus[31] – Gerson insists that the faith of all *viatores*, and not merely those within the church's teaching ranks, must affirm the *eruditio* of scripture, not only regarding selected texts which correspond to the »articles of faith« as Aquinas had argued but in terms of the entire biblical canon. All are to believe »everything in the biblical canon,« not only by implicit or »habitual« faith but by explicit as well as »actual« faith.[32]

---

[30] Cf. *Summa theologiae* IIaIIae, q. 2 a. 6. He addressed this theme in the preceding article, »Whether a person is bound to believe explicitly in anything«: ». . . Just as one is obliged to have faith, so too one is obliged to believe explicitly in its primary tenets, i. e., the articles of faith. With regard to other points, no one is bound to an explicit but only to an implicit belief or a readiness to believe, i. e., to be prepared to believe whatever is contained in Scripture. Even so, one is held to explicit belief in such matters only when it is clear to him that they are in truth contained in the teaching of faith.« *Ibid.*, IIaIIae, q. 2, a. 5, resp. (trans. Blackfriars edition, Vol. 31, p. 83). This thesis goes back, as Aquinas points out, to Gregory the Great's allegorical interpretation of Job 1.14: »There is a text in Job, ›The oxen were feeding and the asses were feeding beside them,‹ on which Gregory comments to the effect that in matters of faith the simple people, symbolized by the asses, must stand by their teachers, symbolized by the oxen.« *Ibid.*, IIaIIae q. 2 a. 6, sed contra; see also Gregory, *On Morals in Job* 2.30, *PL* 75: 578. For a discussion of this theme vis-à-vis Geiler of Keisersberg who, unlike Gerson, follows Aquinas, see Douglass, *Justification in Late Medieval Preaching*, pp. 66–68.

[31] On this question see Lang, »Das Verhältnis von Schrift, Tradition und kirchlichem Lehramt,« pp. 216–23. Lang argues that in terms of the argument regarding those matters which the church was necessarily to believe for salvation, Oyta pointed to the sufficiency of scripture – of those matters which were »either explicitly asserted in the biblical canon or were able to be formally inferred as necessary consequences from these«; see *ibid.*, p. 223. Gerson's respect for Oyta has been well documented elsewhere; it suffices here to recall that in his »Réponse à la consultation des maîtres,« delivered at Constance in 1415, Gerson instructed his audience to refer to Oyta's *Quaestiones Sententiarum* regarding the proper exposition of scripture in its literal sense. See G 10, p. 241 f. It is worth noting that Hus also esponsed this claim: »Et isto modo tenetur quilibet christianus credere explicite vel implicite omnem veritatem, quam sanctus spiritus posuit in scriptura.« See *Tractatus De Ecclesia*, ed. S. H. Thomson (Cambridge, 1956), p. 56.

[32] As a historical excursus on this point it is important to note that this theme (i. e., *fides implicita* of the medieval doctrinal tradition) played a key role in the later Protestant reformers' criticism of what they understood to be the dominant medieval teaching on this point. Luther's criticism of the mass rested above all on his conviction that the divine promises required the active and hence explicit response in faith of each believer; see *The Babylonian Captivity*, in *Three Treatises*, trans. A. T. W. Steinhäuser (Philadelphia, 1982), pp. 162–67. This theme becomes even more central, and is articulated with considerable emphasis, in Calvin's *Institutes*, and this already in the earliest edition. See especially the

Per eruditionem sacrae scripturae: this phrase places a demanding task not only upon the theologians but upon the entire church, because with it Gerson means to widen the purpose scripture should play in the life of all believers, *idiotae* and *periti*. This also offers a considerable revision of the Thomistic doctrine of implicit faith, since for Gerson this *eruditio* demanded the full certitude of »all the faithful« who were to utilize their faith in engaging the entire corpus of scripture. Thus, Gerson's explication of the purpose of scripture correlates with his understanding of faith: beyond the concrete practice of utilizing scripture in constructing theological arguments he here establishes scripture as the context in which faith is *formed* and the human person *transformed*. *Dum peregrinantur in via*: scripture is finally the instrument by which *viatores* make their way *ad Deum*. As such Gerson's conviction is once again evident that scripture belongs in the common domain; it is not − and, indeed, may not be interpreted as − the exclusive property of the »professional« theologians. Nor is its function somehow greater for those of advanced academic training, since all are to have a level of what he calls »supernatural certitude« by which the entire corpus of scripture functions in an edifying manner within the church. Thus, when we read Gerson's ambitious claims that no one should doubt that which is held *per eruditionem sacrae scripturae*, and that »all the faithful« are to believe »the entire biblical canon« by both »explicit« and »actual« faith, we realize that he has attributed to scripture an exalted function within the church. The instruction of scripture has become the »erudition,« as he calls it, of the entire church.

3. On the »sufficiency« of scripture

Earlier in this study we had occasion to mention Gerson's emphasis of the singular manner by which God »speaks« in scripture: »For [the scriptures] are sufficient,« he argued, »to teach and counsel us, providing that they are read with a pure, faithful, and open heart.«[33] With this claim of »sufficiency« Gerson delineates the functional role of scripture as a foundational authority governing both theological method and pastoral practice.[34] In context this claim has to do with the sufficiency of scripture as the basis not only for believing, but for

---

»Prefatory Address to King Francis,« and III.2.2−5; *Institutes of the Christian Religion*, ed. J. T. McNeill, trans. F. L. Battles (Philadelphia, 1960), I: 14,544−48.

[33] See above, 3.B.1.

[34] Connolly has argued the point that Gerson's sermons draw chiefly upon scripture; see Connolly, *John Gerson*, p. 154: »... the sermons of Gerson were scriptural from the *thema* to the conclusion.« This finally only states the obvious, however, since Connolly does not inquire more deeply into how Gerson conceived the relation of scripture and tradition, or the question of how scripture and theology itself were to be understood.

finding »a moral certitude sufficient for acting«: *scriptura* stands as the sufficient
guide not merely for thought but for life, the process by which the faith of
viatores must be »converted« into »the works of love« (*executio operis*). The
substance of faith must be »formed« through such acts (*fides formata*), just as he
insists that *theologia* itself must be »formed« by being »joined« to the
theological virtues of faith, hope, and love lest it »puff up« and finally »kill.«[35]

The theologian, as he goes on to say in this passage, is a »good man learned
in sacred letters« (*bonus vir in sacris litteris eruditus*), a *viator* for whom this
scriptural erudition becomes »not indeed an erudition of the intellect alone, but
much more of the heart.«[36] Scripture is sufficient not only for instruction in the
faith — and as he here contends *all* scripture is useful for this purpose and must
be believed »explicitly« by all — but for the formation of the *viator* whom he
here calls *theologus*.[37] Yet as we have earlier pointed out the scriptural text for
Gerson, though sufficient in itself, never functions by itself: he insists that the
perspective of the reader plays a critical role in determining the functional
utility of the biblical text, a theme we have earlier characterized under the
rubric of the »correlation« of text and reader.[38] And yet precisely on this point
Gerson insists that the *reader* is not sufficient as biblical interpreter, or, to put
this in a positive form, the reader must interpret scripture within the context of
the church. This insistence, accentuated apparently by the sharp conflict with
the Hussite faction at the Council of Constance, prompts Gerson to qualify his
view of scripture's sufficiency, and here we find ourselves in the midst of a
complex late-medieval debate regarding theological authority: namely, the
relation of scripture to another source of authority, usually referred to under
the ambiguous term »tradition.«[39] On this point we find ourselves faced with

---

[35] G 9, p. 237: »... hoc unum credidi, propter quod et locutus sum, quod Theologia non
admixta fidei, spei, et charitati, inflat et officit. ...« For a detailed discussion of this theme,
see Froehlich, »Fifteenth-Century Hermeneutics.«

[36] G 9, p. 237.

[37] *Ibid.*

[38] See above, 3.B.1.

[39] On this much disputed issue, not only in the sixteenth-century debates but also among
historians both Protestant and Catholic since then, our discussion here can only survey the
issues in a most cursory fashion. Joseph Geiselmann launched the most ambitious attempt
to reconstruct the Tridentine debate on this point in a series of essays during the late 1950s,
among them his contribution entitled, »Das Mißverständnis über das Verhältnis von
Schrift und Tradition und seine Überwindung in der katholischen Theologie,« *Una Sancta*
11 (1956), pp. 131–50. In this essay, which outlines the essential thesis of his argument,
Geiselmann contends on the basis not of the final conciliar statement on scripture but rather
of his reconstruction of the Tridentine debates leading up to that document that the final
choice of the hinge-word *et* — i. e., *scriptura et traditio* — was a rebuttal to the *partim-partim*
proposal. See *ibid.*, pp. 138–39. Oberman has subsequently disputed this interpretation;
Harvest, p. 407, n. 136. Indeed, Oberman's criticism of specific historical points found in
Geiselmann's argument on Trent is convincing, but the constructive argument he provides

a historical argument of considerable complexity: viz., what »sufficiency« meant not only in the immediate circumstances in which Gerson wrote his *De consolatione theologiae* but in the broader medieval horizon. In addressing this issue Gerson set the hermeneutical question within an ecclesiological framework; the church is finally the arbiter of exegetical disputes, functioning as the tradition within which scripture is to be interpreted. The irony here is that Gerson's position stands in proximity to Hus in that both held scripture to be the norm in settling theological questions; both accepted what we might call the *material* sufficiency of scripture as the fundamental theological norm. But Gerson distanced himself from the Hussite position by also invoking the church as the *formal* medium of interpretation,[40] not because the church added anything to scripture in this process but because the church as the historical community of biblical interpretation (i. e., tradition) held a position of singular authority vis-à-vis scripture.[41] Whereas Hus's view of scripture tended to restrict severely the concept of tradition, Gerson insisted that the church was the normative interpreting community; hermeneutics becomes a function of the church, since scripture as a sufficient authority is neither self-authenticating nor self-interpreting, particularly in disputed passages, as we have seen. We shall return to this question later in this study, when our attention turns to the ecclesiological dimension of Gerson's thought.[42]

---

in *Harvest* on »Tradition I« and »Tradition II« does not yet explain Gerson's position correctly, as we shall argue later in this study (see below, 4.A.4, 6.A.3).

[40] We must be quite precise with this language, as these theologians themselves were: to say that scripture was »sufficient« for salvation is not to exclude extra-scriptural revelations which might also be believed. The failure to recognize this subtle point has caused considerable confusion vis-à-vis Ockham's formulation in the *Dialogus* and its subsequent use by later medieval theologians, including Gerson; we shall return to this point in the following section of this chapter. Here I acknowledge my dependence upon the work of Yves Congar and others on this theme of scripture's »sufficiency« in medieval theology; see e. g., Yves M.-J. Congar, O.P., *Tradition and Traditions. An Historical and a Theological Essay* (New York, 1966), pp. 111–18; George Tavard, *Holy Writ or Holy Church. The Crisis of the Protestant Reformation* (New York, 1959), pp. 52 ff.; and, finally, Gabriel Moran, *Scripture and Tradition. A Survey of the Controversy* (New York, 1963), pp. 54–56. The use of the Aristotelian language of »matter« and »form« to distinguish scripture from tradition is first suggested by Johann Adam Möhler, who used this terminology to explain this relationship in his early work *Die Einheit in der Kirche oder das Prinzip des Katholizismus, dargestellt im Geiste der Kirchenväter der ersten drei Jahrhundert* (cited in Geiselmann, »Das Mißverständnis,« pp. 146–47); Congar returns to the same language in order to suggest that patristic and medieval theologians used this language as we have noted, while later Protestant reformers inverted this usage to stress the »formal« guidance of scripture as well – i. e., against the Roman view which would increasingly view the present magisterium as *traditio*. See Congar, *Tradition*, pp. 116–17.

[41] On this point, cf. Oberman, *Harvest*, pp. 385–90. Oberman is right in concluding that Gerson defended »the sufficiency of Holy Scripture as containing all the truths necessary for salvation,« and he is correct in suggesting that for Gerson »the doctrine of the Church is the final standard ...«; *ibid.*, pp. 385–86. But his conclusion that »through the ongoing

But what is the foundation upon which Gerson builds this argument for the sufficiency of scripture? In exploring this question we come upon a fundamental dimension of Gerson's *theologia biblica*, since the argument for sufficiency is for Gerson first of all a theological and not merely hermeneutical question, or perhaps we should say that hermeneutics depends upon his view of divine revelation. Gerson, agreeing with Ockham, does not argue that divine revelation is limited to scripture, such that God could not reveal divine truth directly in another manner and another place. But he does insist that God limits himself in faithfulness to those declarations which are revealed in scripture, and he goes further than Ockham in insisting that *only* these are necessary to be believed by the whole church. This is a critical distinction for discerning how it is that Gerson speaks of scripture's sufficiency: it is the reliable source of the divine promises which are binding upon the entire church. In this sense, God speaks, God commands, God instructs through scriptural texts; these are *verba Dei*, as he here puts it, and for this reason *scriptura* becomes the sufficient norm not only for theological argument but for guidance in pastoral matters as well. This is on the deepest level a theological affirmation, since he conceives of scripture in nominalist terms as a *pactum*, a self-limitation of God in the covenantal promises and commandments (i. e., *de potentia Dei ordinata*). Furthermore, and this is apparently an unexpected argument within the broad nominalist tradition, Gerson utilizes the biblical commandments *not* as we might expect to declare the contingency of the created order — in this case in terms of the *lex divina* which regulates *human* conduct — but rather to underscore the character of the divine nature.[43] These promises and commands function as »law« governing the divine will, and thus guarantee the reliability of *divine* acts: in binding himself to scripture, God gives *viatores* a sufficient language that they might utilize in their journey *ad Deum*, a theological affirmation which offers a consoling pastoral argument. Scripture is covenantal language, in other words, which grants pilgrims certitude because it is reliable;

---

definition of truth by the Church, the canonical boundaries are enlarged and Holy Scripture is materially extended« (*ibid.*, p. 389) misreads the thrust of the texts cited from Gerson's later works. For a thorough discussion of this point, see below, 6.A.3.

[42] See below, 6.A.3.

[43] On this point, Gerson's position seems to qualify Courtenay's lucid discussion of »the dialectic of the two powers of God,« a distinction he argues which »is deceptive for the modern reader because it seems to be talking about possibilities and avenues for divine action when in fact it is making a statement about the non-necessity of the created order. Both parts of the dialectic, which must be taken together to be meaningful, face in the direction of creation, not God .... The distinction, therefore, was a statement about the created order, not the divine nature.« »Nominalism and Late Medieval Religion,« pp. 39, 42. His argument is generally convincing, though it now appears that Gerson utilized the »two powers« distinction, in a manner apparently uncharacteristic among nominalist theologians, to make a statement not only about creation and the contingent pacts within the created order but about the divine nature itself.

God will not and indeed *cannot* deny these promises, Gerson argues, since this would be tantamount to denying himself — which God cannot do. With forceful rhetoric Gerson's Volucer instructs his despairing interlocutor to hold God accountable to the ordained promises: »Say to God, ›Rise up, Lord God, in the precept which you have commanded‹ (Ps. 7.7); ›I throw myself upon you at your command. You are not cruel or deceptive so as to reject me, especially where your manifold promises are involved. By them you have promised those hoping in you that you would free them, snatch them away, save and glorify them. . . . You cannot deny yourself.‹ In this way address yourself in these matters to God.«[44] The ordained covenants of scripture, therefore, give to *viatores* a language of dialogue with God: scripture becomes the covenantal meeting ground by which God approaches us with promises and we approach God with confidence on the basis of those promises.

Scripture as the language of God's *commercium* with humanity[45] thus expresses only part of this sufficiency, since this biblical language functions at the same time as the means by which *viatores* approach God with certitude. This rationale explains why it is that Gerson collapses together, almost without distinction of purpose, *scriptura sacra* and *theologia*, and in so doing embraces the nominalist suspicion of any metaphysical construct or theological enterprise which would move beyond the revealed language of the biblical text. But this suspicion is only one side of his hermeneutic: the other side is the affirmation of scriptural language as both contingent and reliable, since God cannot deny the covenants which God established *de potentia sua ordinata*. That is, God »binds« or »limits« himself in the covenantal language of scripture, a language which is sufficient not only as revelation but as the means of the human approach to God. In short, scripture becomes the dialogue between God and humanity. This emphasis upon the dependability of God represents a central concern of late-medieval nominalism in general; Ockhamist theologians during the later fourteenth and early fifteenth centuries distinguished the »two powers of God« — viz. *potentia ordinata* and *potentia absoluta* — as an explanation of the divine freedom vis-à-vis the created order and of the consequent contingency of creation, while stressing with increasing emphasis *potentia ordinata* as operative within the arena of human history.[46] This is certainly true for Gerson's

---

[44] G 9, p. 199.

[45] This phrase is to be found in *De consolatione theologiae*, G 9, p. 199. As we have earlier suggested the phrase may represent an allusion to Boethius' description of prayer as *inter homines deumque commercium*; cf. *Consolatio philosophiae* V pr. 3, *CCSL* 94: 94.

[46] Ozment has accentuated this development in particularly clear and convincing language, arguing that »nominalism reveals itself as a science of the *potentia Dei ordinata* — a study of historical covenants, of God's will as expressed in Scripture and tradition, of the raison d'être of penultimate churches, priests, and sacraments, of order instituted and maintained. Nominalists perceived an unsettling ›extra‹ dimension in the system itself; but they discovered that it was a verbal relation . . . . Nominalism is a scholastic science of the

thought, and this preference established the basis for his insistence that scripture was sufficient for salvation. In other words, Gerson accepts the argument regarding the absolute reliability of scripture as an uncontroverted point. His primary concern with the *potentia Dei ordinata* by which God binds himself irrevocably thus reflects theological convictions which carry pastoral implications.

In illustration of this point, Gerson returns to the theme of the inviolability of the divine covenants later in this treatise, arguing once again that within the bounds of scripture at least God is no longer free. In describing the supernatural certitude (*certitudo supernaturalis*) of faith which rests »not upon the evidence of reason« but upon »divine authority,« Gerson argues that this certitude is »of such a character that through no power, and not even the absolute power of God, is it able to deceive us; for otherwise God would be able to deny himself,«[47] a premise which Gerson refuses to admit. Pastoral concerns win out here over all others, yet they derive from the deeper foundation of Gerson's theological conviction that God cannot deny the divine promises conveyed in scripture since to do so would be self-denial. Indeed, it would appear that Gerson carries this Ockhamist emphasis upon the reliability of God's ordained power – which he interprets to safeguard the reliability of scripture – to a point which distinguished him among nominalist theologians: Gerson explicitly states that God cannot contradict himself, either *de potentia sua ordinata* or *de potentia sua absoluta*; he turns the dialectic of the two powers back toward God, as it were, in order to hold God accountable to the established covenants. But why this emphasis, and what lies behind this argument against philosophy? Apparently, Gerson is here countering a philosophical skepticism which threatened to erode the confidence of faith, based as it is upon what he calls *certitudo supernaturalis*. As he contends, faith based upon this certitude has moved beyond philosophy: »hanc philosophorum schola non vidit.« Against those who would interpret faith according to the »power of logic« or the »evidence of reason« alone, Gerson insisted upon a peculiar logic and a singular evidence. And, as we have seen, for Gerson scripture becomes as a consequence a reliable source of this certitude since it remains inviolable even for God.

On the basis of this correlation between the reliability of God and the reliability of *scriptura revelata*, therefore, Gerson establishes scripture as the trustworthy foundation not only for faith but for a »certitude of action.«

---

potentia Dei ordinata.« See »Mysticism, Nominalism, and Dissent,« pp. 80–81. Hamm offers an intriguing explanation for this emphasis, speaking of »der Verweis auf die freie Selbstbindung Gottes [i. e., *potentia Dei ordinata*] als Gegengewicht zur schwindenden Bedeutung des Gnadenhabitus,« an argument he attributes above all to Ockham and Biel. See *Promissio, Pactum, Ordinatio. Freiheit und Selbstbindung Gottes in der scholastischen Gnadenlehre* (Tübingen, 1977), pp. 360 ff.

[47] G 9, p. 231.

Throughout this treatise he utilizes scripture to establish not merely a theoretical point of method, but the concrete means by which scripture is sufficient to »teach,« »counsel,« and »admonish,« and he consistently refuses to qualify this affirmation. This is for Gerson a matter of theological propriety, the humility by which nominalist theologians in general argued against unwarranted metaphysical speculation, and by which Gerson in particular hones the edge of his argument *contra curiositatem vanam*, applying Paul's warning as a rule governing the theological task: »Non plus sapere quam oportet, sed sapere ad sobrietatem« (Rom. 12.3). Just as Volucer advises that we should speak to God *cum pio et humili affectu*,[48] so the manner by which *theologia* guides the reader toward God remains within the discrete limits of biblical language. This is a matter of theological method, but it is at a deeper level a matter of the proper theological posture: the humility of the theologian binds him to what God has revealed in scripture, and what is hence both »reliable« and »useful« for theological discourse (i. e., *per scripturam revelatam*). Thus, Gerson places the question of the sufficiency of scripture in the first instance not over against an encroaching tradition but as an explication of the boundaries for *theologiae traditio*. The related issue of how tradition itself functions as the formal guide in interpreting the scriptures is, according to Gerson, not a question of the »matter« of revelation but of the »form« through which that revelation reaches us. For this reason he places this question, which so occupied theologians of a later epoch in terms of the doctrine of revelation, under the rubric of ecclesiology; we shall hence return to this theme in the sixth chapter of this study.

4. Biblical hermeneutics and ecclesiology

The question of scripture's sufficiency in functional terms, according to Gerson in this treatise, must be raised on two levels. Thus far our discussion has explored the first of these: namely, the matter of the biblical text as the vehicle of God's speech — i. e., as revelation — which underscores this sufficiency. While Ockham and theologians succeeding him, including Gerson, would have insisted on a broader horizon of revelation,[49] Gerson raises the qualifying

---

[48] G 9, p. 194. Brown addresses this theme by speaking of an »anti–intellectual« strain of Gerson's thought; see *Pastor and Laity*, p. 161. This is a misreading of his intention, however, since in actuality this is a conclusion rather than a premise of his argument, a conviction Gerson himself reached on the basis of his grasp of revelation and the limitations this doctrine placed on human inquiry. In this he drew upon a long tradition of polemic aimed against »vain curiosity,« a theme which emerged with particular force in the epistemology of nominalist theology, with its rigorous restraint against metaphysical speculation.

[49] Ockham discusses, *alongside* the view that these truths included »*only* those things

question of sufficiency and in this regard points to scripture and *only* to scripture as reliable and necessary for the faith to be held by the *whole* church.[50] But these texts do not come to us, with or without interpretation, outside the bounds of the church, and they do usually come to us in interpreted form

---

which were asserted explicitly or implicitly in the biblical canon,« a broader interpretation, by which one could discern five »grades« of »catholic truth«; cf. *Dialogus*, I lib. 2, c. 1 and c. 5, and, for an overview of this tradition, Lang, »Das Verhältnis von Schrift, Tradition und kirchlichem Lehramt,« esp. pp. 223–28; and *idem, Die theologische Prinzipienlehre der mittelalterlichen Scholastik* (Freiburg i. B., 1964), pp. 210–22. Lang's discussion is generally accurate, though in the latter work he misreads Gerson and consequently places him (incorrectly) within the trajectory of Ockham's »opinio secunda« from the *Dialogus*, which accepted as authoritative scripture and extra-scriptural revelation. Oberman also reaches this conclusion in *Harvest*, pp. 385–93, identifying Gerson as an advocate of this position which he distinguishes as »Tradition II« — viz. a view of a plurality of authoritative sources of revelation. We shall correct this misreading of Gerson in the following discussion; see below, 6.A.3.

[50] Thus in his *Quae veritates sint de necessitate salutis credendae*, composed during the Council of Constance (1416) and hence before *De consolatione theologiae*, he placed the »entire canon of scripture, and all particular things it asserts in its literal sense« as the »first degree« among such truths. These truths are, in this carefully circumscribed sense, to be believed *always* and *by all* persons. In the second degree are those truths taught by the church and carried through apostolic succession, but Gerson is quick to point out — and the events of his day made this an unavoidable conclusion to reach — that not everything publicly taught or tolerated was necessarily to be believed. Indeed, he extends by deliberate inversion Augustine's well-known and often used maxim — which, as Oberman has noted in *Harvest* (pp. 384, 385 n. 71), d'Ailly was also fond of using — that »evangelio non crederem nisi me auctoritas ecclesiae compelleret,« to affirm that »ecclesiae non crederem si non auctoritas sacrae scripturae impelleret.« Scripture, in other words, becomes the determining norm, or *norma normata*, over what the church as the *norma normans* teaches as »necessary« for salvation; this is the same affirmation which Johann Adam Möhler would later distinguish through his distinction of the language of »matter« (scripture) and »form« (tradition), as we have earlier noted. The third grade — those truths which are specially revealed to particular persons — Gerson insists are to be believed, but they are »necessary« *only* for those to whom they were made. Thus, Gerson safeguards the singularity of scripture's unqualified »sufficiency,« even though he does expand the realm of truths which under particular conditions *might* be necessary for salvation — but not for *all* Christians, he is quick to add. In this regard his discussion in *Quae veritates* is much more cautious, and more deliberately and carefully qualified, than Ockham's (see preceding note), and it is probably not accidental that Gerson speaks simply of »truths« necessary to be believed rather than Ockham's more encompassing reference to »catholic truths.« On this basis we must correct the conclusions reached by Lang and Oberman, both of whom in pointing to these texts are correct in identifying Gerson's insistence on the church's role in establishing these truths, but incorrect in failing to recognize Gerson's point that the scriptures *alone* provide these truths »sufficiently« and for the *entire* church. Gerson's approach in these later texts is thus closer to what Oberman has called »Tradition I,« a point which brings his hermeneutical method closer to Hus, though only in terms of the »material« sufficiency of revelation as I have earlier pointed out. In a later discussion (see below, 6.A.3), I return to this point to establish how it is that Gerson invokes his view of tradition in terms of how scripture itself is to be interpreted — viz. within the church as historical community. Here

within the church: as he elsewhere affirmed with Augustine, »evangelio non crederem nisi me auctoritas ecclesiae compelleret.«[51]

The problem now confronting us must be to determine how Gerson held the sufficiency of scripture in this first sense as revelation which must be believed generally within the church, while qualifying this sufficiency by pointing to the church's necessary role in identifying these truths from scripture − viz. »evangelio non crederem nisi me auctoritas ecclesiae compelleret.« We must therefore inquire with careful precision whether − and, if so, in what manner − Gerson raised the matter of biblical sufficiency as a hermeneutical issue involving tradition, such that both text and context functioned together in establishing scripture's sufficiency.[52] Yet here we are on the different grounds, as Gerson himself admitted, of interpretation − or of the »form« by which the »matter« of revelation reaches us, rather than the substance of extra-scriptural revelation itself. By annexing the question of the text's sufficiency not with a dual source of revelation but within the broader problem of the necessary *context* of interpretation, Gerson interprets the hermeneutical task in ecclesiological terms.

This is evident, as earlier suggested, in his reluctant consultation of »doctrinam . . . quam theologica tradit schola« precisely in matters in which the »literal« sense of a biblical text either is not unambiguous or is in apparent contradiction with another text. In such circumstances Gerson resorts to

---

the full force of his anti-Hussite polemic becomes clear: scripture cannot be read in a manner which either ignores or refutes the interpretation of the literal sense *as determined by the church.* Cf. Gerson's *De sensu litterali sacrae scripturae*, and particularly the seventh and eighth theses: »Sensus litteralis si, et dum, expugnatur temporibus nostris in his quaesunt jam aperte per ecclesiam determinata ac recepta . . .« etc.; and, »sensus litteralis sacrae scripturae si reperitur determinatus et decisus in decretis et decretalibus et codicibus conciliorum . . .« etc. G 3, p. 335 f.

[51] See below, Ch. 6, n. 43.

[52] On this point, Lang has characterized the hermeneutic of Oyta in similar fashion. Even though Oyta extended the scope of truths which the faithful were necessarily to believe beyond the substance of scripture, he insists that such truths do not contradict the sufficiency of scripture but actually ratify it by bringing extra-scriptural truths to bear which »zur Sicherung der wirksamen Offenbarungsverkündigung notwendig sind und deshalb zum Gebiet der kirchlichen Lehraufgabe gehören und infolgedessen auch in den Bereich des Glaubens fallen.« See »Das Verhältnis von Schrift, Tradition und kirchlichem Lehramt,« pp. 222. In this regard he cites Oyta's claim that »multae [veritates] sunt determinatae per ecclesiam, quae nec explicite continentur in biblia nec ex contentis in ea formaliter inferri possunt« (*Quaestiones Sententiarum*, q. 1 a. 2 cor. 1); see also *Quaestio de sacra scriptura et de veritatibus catholicis*, in *Opuscula et Textus*, ed. Albert Lang (Münster, 1953), q. 2, a. 3. conc. 5 (p. 69). On the other hand, when faced with the question of the relation of scripture and tradition, Oyta established the scope of truths to be believed as *veritates catholicae* by emphasizing biblical revelation in a manner similar to Gerson here: »An istae veritates solae reputandae sint catholicae et de necessitate salutis credendae, quae vel explicite in canone bibliae asseruntur vel ex eis in consequentia necessaria et formali inferri possunt.« *Ibid.*, q. 2, a. 3, (p. 61).

tradition, not as another source of revelation which somehow extends the canonical boundaries but as the necessary guide in resolving exegetical difficulties.[53] Gerson also suggests that although the scriptures themselves offer instruction (*doctrina* or, variously, *eruditio*) to us *in via*, it is still necessary for »most« persons that the biblical texts be interpreted – in other words, *inferiores* in the ecclesiastical hierarchy are to look to *superiores* for an interpretation of the text (i. e., what he calls *intelligentia scripturarum*). This qualification does not extend the domain of what is in itself sufficient as *eruditio*, but rather concedes that an interpreting or teaching tradition is necessary in order that the majority

---

[53] Once again, Oberman's discussion of this point is correct when he argues that »in the apostolic succession [according to Gerson], it is not the separate truths which are handed down but the proper interpretation of Holy Scripture« (*Harvest*, p. 388), but too hasty in concluding that »through the ongoing definition of truth by the Church, the canonical boundaries *are enlarged* and Holy Scripture is *materially extended*«; ibid., p. 389 (my emphasis). The interpretive definitions of the church do not *add* to the material of revelation, but simply explicate its literal sense in order to clarify its intent. This is particularly clear in his *De sensu litterali*, cited above (see n. 50). In the sixth thesis of this treatise Gerson marks out the progression by which revelation is received and understood in its »literal sense« within the church: »first the literal sense of scripture was revealed by Christ and the apostles, elucidated by miracles, and thereafter confirmed by the martyrs' blood; subsequently the holy doctors drew out [*elicuerunt*] this sense through their diligent reasoning against heretics and set forth the conclusions which followed from this more clearly and laudably. After this came the determinations of the holy councils so that those doctrinal matters discussed by the doctors might be defined by the church in the form of ›sentences.‹« G 3, p. 335. The point should be quite clear: the later interpretation of scripture in its literal sense does not add to the original revelation, but rather »draws it out« (*elicere*) and »defines« it through conciliar decree. The emphasis here falls not upon the »sufficiency« of the text but the necessity of its interpretation, faced as he was with those who disputed the manner in which this sense was »determined and decided in the decrees, decretals, and conciliar transactions« by suggesting that this interpretive process was »grounded only in human or positive law« (G 3, p. 336, »propositio octava«). This analysis, which we shall return to in the final chapter of this study (see below, 6.A.3), should call into question Oberman's characterization of Gerson as holding »Tradition II«; this is a position which Gerson allowed for in accepting the possibility of extra-scriptural revelation, a concession reflecting his devotion to *theologia mystica* (on this general question, see Ozment, »Mysticism, Nominalism and Dissent,« pp. 80 ff.). But Gerson's qualified application of »Tradition II« parallels his cautious and limited acceptance of miracles and mystical revelations in exceptional cases; normally, and for the church as a whole, God's revelation *per scripturam* was sufficient and necessarily to be affirmed, and this was done through the church's established channels. Throughout this argument we must recall the historical horizon in which these later treatises were written: this argument was not aimed at those who wanted to *extend* the scope of revelation, but rather against those such as Jean Petit who disputed the traditional exegesis of biblical texts, as well as the reductivists such as Hus and his circle who resisted the binding authority of canon law and any other vehicles of interpretation which were disjoined from scripture; on the former, see Froehlich, »Fifteenth-Century Hermeneutics,« pp. 27 ff, and on the latter, Tavard, *Holy Writ*, pp. 48–51.

of persons might understand or at least accept what the few — whom he calls *perfecti* and *spirituales* — grasp *propter claram suae complexionis harmoniam.*[54] This functional characterization of the church's order reflects the dominant influence upon Gerson's thought, which we shall subsequently explore in further detail,[55] of the Dionysian view of the ecclesiastical order as a hierarchical reality by which »subordinates have to be led back to God through their superiors.«[56]

Yet Gerson goes even further than this in *De consolatione theologiae,* clarifying his insistence that scripture's sufficiency functions within the context of the church as the authoritative voice of interpretation. In the penultimate prose section of this treatise he describes »good« and »evil« persons, emphasizing that the latter »impudently force the sacred writings to serve their own corrupt habits and desires, distorting their meaning [*sensus*] as handed down by the holy fathers.«[57] This is a critical passage for ascertaining Gerson's understanding of how scripture should be used, since his insistence on what we shall subsequently characterize as a »hermeneutic of tradition« accentuates his conviction that perspective — in this case, the tradition of interpretation mediated by the church — determines how one should read scripture. Gerson insists that the tradition establishes what he calls the »sense« of the text, a level of meaning by which we are prevented from manipulating the text to justify our own »habits and desires.« This is an even stronger position than what we discerned in his argument that »many« must be instructed by the understanding of »others« or must simply obey what others teach in order to grasp the *eruditio sacrae scripturae,* since here Gerson recognizes that moral corruption can distort this reading: in such cases one disregards the »sense«

---

[54] G 9, p. 236. This echoes Aquinas's argument that »we stand in need of being instructed by divine revelation, even in religious matters the human reason is able to investigate; for the rational truth about God would be reached only by few, and even so after a long time and mixed with many mistakes, whereas on knowing this depends our whole welfare, which is in God.« *Summa theologiae* Ia q. 1 a. 1, resp. The teaching order of the church, and here Gerson is in essential agreement with Aquinas, is intended to overcome any elitism of knowledge, since »on knowing this depends our whole welfare«; it is, in this sense of conveying such knowledge, an edificatory instrument.

[55] See below, 6.A.1.

[56] G 9, p. 222; this is the same text which Aquinas applies in his discussion of the »hierarchy« of faith within the church, by which those who teach are obligated to have a greater »explicit« faith than those whom they are to teach; cf. *Summa theologiae* IIaIIae q. 2 a. 6, resp. The striking difference which Gerson's application of this Dionysian principle, in contrast to Aquinas's, is his insistence that even those lower in the ecclesiastical hierarchy were obliged to have *fides explicita*; in other words, both affirmed that an order existed within the church by which some had the task of teaching others, but Gerson insisted that the *idiotae* or *simplices,* while arriving at little more than *fides simplex,* nonetheless were to have an »engaged« (»formed«) and fully articulate (»explicit«) faith (i. e., *fides formata* and *fides explicita*). Cf. also above, n. 31.

[57] G 9, p. 237; see also below, 6.A.3.

conveyed by the church's tradition in order to legitimize one's own desires.[58] Hence, although Gerson has not called into question the material sufficiency of scripture as *eruditio*, he has qualified its proper use within the church, exposing presumably in reaction to the Hussite position the practical inadequacy of any *scriptura sola* principle. Scripture, in other words, is of itself sufficient for offering instruction and counsel, but it actually functions in a sufficient manner principally, usually, and for most people within the interpretive context of the church's magisterial tradition.

B. From philosophy to theology: methodological premises and pastoral implications

In the opening section of the previous chapter we considered the dialectical nature of *consolatio*, and in so doing raised the fundamental issue of how theology functions as *paideia*. Theology forms *viatores* through the virtues it alone conveys, directing them by faith, sustaining them through hope, and enlivening them by charity as they make their way through life's trials *ad Deum*. As such the treatise serves as an enchiridion, a manual of conversion by which theology seeks to root *viatores* in a »true« consolation, or what he calls »the firm and and solid hope« in God. Yet *De consolatione theologiae* is not only a handbook with exclusively practical intentions, though as we have already demonstrated Gerson certainly applies himself to the pastoral implications of doctrinal themes he here raises. Or, to put this another way, his conceptualization of the Christian life as *vita ambidextra*, a notion itself rooted in the classical model of the philosophical life which Gerson here introduces by citing Cicero's definition of the philosopher,[59] meant that *theologia* would be a discipline at once practical and theoretical.[60] In this section we shall devote our

---

[58] Gerson also expressed this conviction in this treatise and elsewhere under the general rubric of *discretio*; cf. for example Gerson's lengthy discussion of discretion as the »second sign of the legitimate spiritual coin« in a much earlier treatise, *De distinctione verarum visionum a falsis* (1401); G 3, pp. 42 ff. In this discussion, in fact, Gerson calls the life of discretion the *via regia*, emphasizing that one who walks in this way »media quodam tenore regulas vivendi sequitur a patribus institutas, nec transgreditur fines quos patres sui posuerunt.« *Ibid.*, p. 42.

[59] Cf. G 9, p. 237. Jaeger explores this thesis in terms of its impact upon the early Christian fathers in *Early Christianity and Greek Paideia*, pp. 73 ff. In a familiar passage from Gregory Nazianzus' »Panegyric on St. Basil,« which Jaeger does not cite, we find a striking early formulation of this theme: »For those who are successful in either life or learning only, but deficient in one or the other, do not differ at all in my opinion from one-eyed men, whose disadvantage is even greater when they look at others or are regarded by them. But those who excell in both and are, as it were, ambidextrous are in a state of perfection and live lives of heavenly happiness.« *In Laudem Basilii Magni*, PG 36: 510.

[60] On this point, Gerson distances himself from Boethius and the monastic tradition

attention to the *theoria* he here articulates, focusing first upon Gerson's precise explication of the relation of philosophy, theology, and law.

1. Philosophy, theology, and the divine law

On the level of literary genre the very decision to write a *theological* consolation already expresses Gerson's conviction about the limited usefulness of philosophy when compared to theology. Yet this arrangement is a conclusion first of all, and not the premise of his argument; we must look elsewhere if we would discern how it is that Gerson conceived of this relationship. We find an important clue to this question in his carefully crafted view of the divine law, the matrix of Gerson's epistemology of revelation throughout his writings. In pointing to this facet of his thought we perceive the continuity established by *lex divina* as well as the progressive dimension of this law by which theology stands as the final stage in God's historical self-disclosure.

   In the opening pages of the treatise Gerson explains the relation of philosophy and theology in terms of two vivid metaphors: the image of a chain, which he attributed to Plato, and that of Jacob's ladder. Each of these metaphors, he argued, exemplified in its interconnectedness »the divine law and order« (*lex divinitatis et ordo*). For the moment what is of interest to us is not the metaphoric detail of this argument but his attribution of these images to the divine law. A proper grasp of the relationship of philosophy and theology must first recognize the divine law which governs and orders all reality. In this instance he conceives of this order in terms of a hierarchy of knowledge, by which philosophy leads to but is finally superseded by theology. He also interprets this sequential dimension — by which philosophy and theology are bound as if in a chain or ladder — in historical terms. Here again the continuum undergirding his dynamic model of this relationship is that of *lex divina*: the

---

which interpreted his text. Boethius describes the dress of »Lady Philosophy« as follows: »Her dress was made of very fine, imperishable thread, of delicate workmanship: she herself wove it, as I learned later, for she told me. Its form was shrouded by a kind of darkness of forgotten years, like a smoke-blackened family statue in the atrium. On its lower border was woven the Greek letter Π and on the upper ϑ, and between the two letters steps were marked like a ladder, by which one might climb from the lower letter to the higher.« *Consolatio philosophiae* I pr. 1; *CCSL* 94: 2. This reference points to the first letters of the Greek words for »theoretical« and »practical,« the two divisions of classical philosophy. He confirmed this perspective, which viewed the theoretical as the highest form of philosophy, later in the same treatise: »If . . . a mind fully aware of its own nature, loosed from its earthly prison, is free to seek its heavenly home, will it not despise all earthly affairs, and in the joy of heaven rejoice to be freed from earthly things?« *Ibid.*, II pr. 7; *CCSL* 94: 34. Elsewhere, he stated that »philosophy is a genus of which there are two species, one of which is called theoretical, the other practical, that is, speculative and active.« Cited by Richard Green, *The Consolation of Philosophy*, p. 4, n. 1.

faith which »in the time of grace« (*tempore gratiae*) is fully manifest becomes progressively »less explicit,« as he puts it, as one regresses historically — i. e., first in »the prophets« who had the »written« law of the old covenant, and before that among »philosophers and other gentiles« who had only the law of nature, an order which mirrors Augustine's concept of history's »three ages. «[61] Within the arena of history, as Gerson understands it in Augustinian fashion, the divine law serves a linear and ordered dynamic by which it progressively »unfolds«: namely, as *lex naturae*, *lex antiqua*, and finally *lex nova* or *lex evangelica*, becoming in this process increasingly accessible or »explicit. « The reason for this progression, as he argues in one of the later poems from this treatise, is that *lex naturae* which God had impressed on our hearts *per indelebile lumen* had been darkened by »the night of sin«; this »cloud of disgrace« led to God's act of inscribing this natural law — the »ten commandments of nature« — upon »stone tablets, « though even then »stubborn habit« overcame this law, prompting God to »illumine« us *per fidem* and to »command« us again »by signs and miracles« so that this law might be a »vigil« for us.[62]

These various dispensations of *lex divina*, therefore, are occasioned by human resistance, by sin in its habitual and actual forms. And, as Gerson makes clear early in this treatise, because of the declining human condition this law acquires a progressive dynamic: God has »added« theological perception to our *ratiocinatio naturalis*, which is the form of cognition accessible to »the philosophers and other gentiles« as they labored under the *lex naturae*, in a form he refers to as *theologia supernaturaliter infusa*. Theology, therefore, is a divine supply »infused« to meet a human need, bringing to our recognition »those necessary and saving truths to which philosophy is not able to rise, «[63] and thus disclosing the *lex divina* to us through *fides explicita*.[64] It is for this reason that we begin to discern why Gerson insists so vigorously that *all* Christians — and not only those who are to teach — are to have *fides explicita*; anything less than this

---

[61] G 9, pp. 196—97. In his *Enchiridion*, Augustine had explained this conception in a schema which became widely used in medieval theology: »Itarum quattuor differentiarum prima est ante legem, secunda sub lege, tertia sub gratia. . . . Nam fuit primitus ante legem, secundo sub lege quae data est per Moysem, deinde sub gratia quae revelata est per primum mediatoris adventum. « *CCSL* 46: 112—13. See also *idem*, *De Trinitate*, *CCSL* 50: 169—70 (4.4.7).

[62] G 9, pp. 196—98.

[63] G 9, p. 189.

[64] Elsewhere Gerson returns to this theme, arguing that God »repeats« the laws a »third« time *per fidei traditionem in evangelio*, the same »principles of morality« which God originally imprinted on us »by nature« and subsequently wrote again upon »tables of stone. « G 9, p. 237. Gerson comes back to this theme one final time in the following poem (IV m. 3; G 4, pp. 3 f.), where he describes how Jesus »lifts the ten [commandments] on high, « thereby strengthening those commandments which were self-evident (*per se nota praecepta*) but which people had rejected in favor of »their own ways and rules of living. «

would be a retreat to what he calls the »dim awareness« of God held by those under the *lex naturae,* and hence would fail to discern fully how this law should instruct us. Such a faith would not yet attain to man's final and »supernatural« end.[65] The theme of *lex divina,* therefore, plays a central role in Gerson's thought, not in establishing any quantitative hierarchy of truth[66] but in identifying the qualitative continuum of this law: he thereby accentuates the identity of the divine law which God progressively revealed because of human need.[67] but in identifying the qualitative continuum of revelation. Gerson

---

[65] G 9, p. 189: »... sicut humanus supernaturalis est finis.« Posthumus Meyjes recognizes this point already in Gerson's early lectures on Mark 1, *De vita spirituali animae:* »Avec cette définition Gerson ouvre son étude de la teneur et de la signification de la loi divine. Il explique en détail le définition, par laquelle il insiste fortement sur la fin surnaturelle de la loi de Dieu, c'est-à-dire sur la *beatitudo* de la créature rationelle. Cette finalité est la caractéristique la plus important de la loi divine; son rapport exclusif avec le surnaturel la distingue aussi bien de la loi naturelle que de la loi humaine.« *Jean Gerson et l'Assemblée de Vincennes,* p. 94. The only difference in *De consolatione theologiae,* and it does appear to be a point evident by omission, is that Gerson here mentions neither the »human« (positive) law nor ecclesiastical (canon) law.

[66] That is, although the clarity of this law increased progressively from the time of the prophets to the apostolic age (cf. I pr. 4; G 9, pp. 196–97), it was merely a deepening of the same knowledge. The »substance of the articles of faith,« as Aquinas had earlier phrased it, had not increased in any quantitative sense, though the quality with which these were perceived became progressively »more explicit.« This is a theme which Gregory had also addressed in his sermons on Ezekiel, a text which Gerson favored (cf. especially *Hom. xvi in Ezech.*); a clearer anticipation of this notion, which may well stand as a source given the thematic parallels along with close verbal similarities, is Aquinas (cf. *Summa theologiae* IIaIIae q. 1 a. 7, *sed contra*), who also cites Gregory along with a critical reference to the gloss on Rom. 8.23: »Now the apostles were most fully instructed about the mysteries, for ›they received them more fully than others. . . .‹«

[67] Although Oberman does not mention Gerson in his helpful and penetrating chapter on »Natural Law as Divine Order« (see *Harvest,* Ch. 4), he apparently groups Gerson together with those theologians of his day who identified »natural« and »eternal« law; indeed, it does appear that Gerson held this position even more emphatically, if also more simply, than we find in Biel's later discussion. This tendency in Gerson's later works may not be without polemic significance: that is, because »theology« reveals this law in its »most explicit« form, and provides at the same time the formal means — i. e., the theological virtues of faith, hope, and love — by which we might live under this law, Gerson ennobles theology not only over philosophy, but over both society's »positive« (civil) law and the church's canon law. This is a suggestion which gains credence from a passage later in *De consolatione theologiae,* where Gerson returns to a theme he had earlier articulated: namely, his conclusion that theology deserved a higher ranking than canon law in the church. In his sermon *Dominus his opus habet* (G 5, pp. 223–27, dated April, 1410) as in his earlier *Pax vobis* (G 5, p. 439, dated April, 1407), Gerson had articulated a strident attack upon the presumption of canon lawyers to elevate their status over that of theologians; he here suggests that theologians of the pre-Constantinian church functioned at the same time as jurists, and the advent of canon law as a separate discipline occurred only because of the rising disorder within church and society after the official endorsement of Christianity during the fourth century. In these sermons he reminds students training in canon law that

hereby accentuates the identity of the divine law which God progressively revealed because of human need. The rationale Gerson thus gives for the »supernatural infusion« of theology has to do with the progressive unfolding of *lex divina*, and the need for it to be »strengthened« or made »more explicit« because human sin had obscured it from view. This law, in other words, becomes the context in which Gerson describes the relationship of philosophy and theology since theology »unfolds« *lex divina* in time: this dynamic is based on his anatomy of the postlapsarian human condition, since sin had dimmed the *ratiocinatio naturalis* and thus necessitated a clearer dispensation (revelation) of the divine law through *theologia*.

2. Philosophical prolegomenon to an epistemology of revelation

In the first book of this treatise Gerson devotes considerable attention to the nature of philosophical knowledge, and how it serves as prolegomenon to the theological task proper. This stands as a matter of fundamental importance to Gerson, and one which has decisive implications for his pastoral strategy: epistemological considerations establish the theoretical foundation for a cluster of practical questions relating to *cura animarum*, as we shall see in the following section.

One of the key problems which occupied Gerson's attention throughout his life, and particularly after his return to Paris during the first decade of the fifteenth century, involved the limitation of speculation – either philosophical or theological, as we shall later note – into metaphysical questions. This is, of course, no peculiarity with Gerson's thought, but rather represents a theme characteristic of Ockhamist theologians for whom theology represented »the science of the *potentia Dei ordinata*.«[68] Already in his early lectures *Contra*

---

theirs was thus an ancillary, derivative function within the church; the leading authority still belonged to theologians. In *De consolatione theologiae* Gerson returns to this theme, arguing here that those who exercise the true »ambidextrous life« (*vita ambidextra*) – i. e., those who »with zealous circumspection are versed in both [the active and contemplative lives] « – thereby become »perfect« and deserve the name of both »jurist« and »theologian, « or what he calls simply »theologian-cum-jurist.« Such persons, he here concludes, are to be compared with »the early doctors [of the church] from whose teaching the decretals and decrees were composed.« G 9, p. 239. That is, by identifying *lex divina* with the role originally fulfilled by *theology*, and not canon law, Gerson contends that the theologian's task has to do fundamentally with the divine law. On this point see further Burger, *Aedificatio*, pp. 51 ff., 94–95; Pascoe, *Jean Gerson*, pp. 93–94.

[68] Thus, Ozment, »Mysticism, Nominalism, and Dissent, « pp. 77, 80. One might well vary this language to say, more simply, that so-called »nominalist« epistemology articulates an empirical »science of the actual« (i. e., *de potentia Dei ordinata*) in contrast to a speculative »science of the possible« (i. e., *de potentia Dei absoluta*).

curiositatem studentium (1402) Gerson addressed this problem, identifying in *superbia* the source of two stumbling blocks facing the schoolmen (*scholastici*): *curiositas* and *singularitas*. These elicit his wrath particularly because they turn us from »the more useful things« to the pursuit of »the less useful« which are »both unattainable and harmful« for us; together they detract from the church as a whole, since persons distracted by such matters neglect the necessary work of *aedificatio* and attend rather to the knowledge which »puffs up« with pride. For this reason Gerson here consigns philosophical investigation (*philosophica perscrutatio*) within »certain limitations,« since »when it tries to go beyond those boundaries with prideful curiosity . . . it tumbles down, blindly dashes itself upon the stone of error and, persisting in its efforts, bashes itself to death.«[69] He returns to this theme in *De consolatione theologiae*: echoing the Pauline argument − or, at least the thesis which medieval theologians had often gleaned from Rom. 1.20 − for »natural theology« which held that philosophy can »ascend« to the recognition of God's »eternal power and divinity« (Rom. 1.20),[70] he limits this knowledge to a »dim awareness« of God's nature and judgments. With equally forceful language here as in this earlier treatise, Gerson concludes that those »philosophers or poets« who attempt to press beyond these limits »sink into the oblivion of their own thoughts, having no other power than that of fabricating incredible errors, and are only able to conduct themselves in dissension.«[71] Philosophy, based as it is upon empirical reasoning (*philosophica ratiocinatio*), functions by »lifting itself« from »the inferior and better known [causes] to those which are superior and concealed«;[72] such a form of perception remains untrustworthy, he argues, and must finally mislead us precisely because of the fundamental »mutability of things below,« the »variability of the human condition which never remains in the same state.« There is an irony at work here, and one that is probably not without an intentional polemic edge, since Gerson's portrait of these »certain limits« applies the *Boethian* skepticism toward the mutable, »lower« world to the philosophical enterprise itself − i. e., as Boethius apparently failed to do himself.[73] Hence, not only does Gerson

---

[69] G 3, pp. 230−31; translation taken from *Selections*, ed. Ozment, p. 31. For a perceptive discussion of this treatise, see Burger, *Aedificatio*, pp. 110 ff.

[70] G 9, 188−89; cf. also *Contra curiositatem studentium*, G 3, p. 231.

[71] G 9, p. 189.

[72] Cf. G 9, p. 205.

[73] That is, Boethius ridiculed those who trusted in the »sufficiency« and »stability« of the »lower« world of human acts throughout the early books of his *Consolation*, and he even argued explicitly that »the lower [power of comprehension] in no way [*nullo modo*] rises to the higher«; cf. *De consolatione philosophiae* V pr. 4; CCSL 94: 97. But this did not prevent Boethius from advocating, in a subsequent passage, what appears as a direct contradiction to this epistemological principle: he counsels us to »submit to the divine mind« and »be raised up . . . to the height of that highest intelligence.« *Ibid.*, V pr. 5; CCSL 94: 100. In other words, Boethius admonished his reader to accomplish in practice what he had previously dismissed as an epistemological impossibility.

limit philosophy by narrowing the scope of its knowledge to the observed world, he goes even further in questioning its reliability because of the flux within the lower world of human experience. A refrain which we find expressed throughout this treatise underscores this limitation: *philosophia non cognovit* or, variously, *philosophia non attingit.*

Yet he does not overlook altogether the useful role which philosophy plays as prolegomenon to the theological enterprise. His approach to philosophy in *De consolatione theologiae* is if anything less polemical and more constructive than in his earlier university lectures. He speaks of *philosophiae fundamenta* as the necessary foundations with which theology undergirds itself, a claim he bolsters by borrowing the Thomistic parallelism of philosophy and nature, theology and grace: »Just as grace exceeds nature ... so also does theology surpass philosophy – not by rejecting it, but by taking it into servitude.«[74] In other words, he takes Boethius at his word when »Lady Philosophy« concluded that »a great necessity is laid upon you, if you wish not to deceive yourself, when you act in the presence of an all-seeing judge.«[75] Philosophy recognizes this necessity, but because of its limitations it is unable to suggest how we should meet such judgment: herein lies the crux of his dispute with Boethius, if not also with philosophers contemporary to him. But he goes even further than this, arguing – curiously again in concert with Thomas Aquinas[76] – that God has revealed scriptural truths *non irrationabiliter,* in a manner not accessible to reason but not on that account opposed to it. This is an intriguing admission, because Gerson hereby accentuates the limited but useful role played by philosophy as prolegomenon to theology. Philosophy causes us to recognize our need for theology, since it steers us toward a destination beyond us but without discerning either the goal itself or the exact path we must follow to attain that end. In this sense it has a limited and even necessary role to play. Yet Gerson emphasizes side by side with this limiting argument the constructive role it is to serve as the foundation (prolegomenon) upon which theology builds: *theologia* begins its work »at that summit where philosophy terminated its consolation.«[77] As he had argued, theology does indeed surpass

---

[74] G 9, p. 188. Elsewhere Gerson argues, in a similar vein, that we must bring »the entire intellect« into submission to faith, a variation upon the Pauline language of 2 Cor. 10.5 (»et in captivitatem redigentes omnem intellectum in obsequium Christi«); cf. G 9, p. 191. The parallel to Aquinas's basic axiom that »grace does not scrap nature, but perfects it« (*Summa theologiae* Ia q. 1, a. 8, ad 2) is striking; Gerson's use of this Thomistic theme guides in broad terms his interpretation of the relationship of philosophy and theology, reason and revelation.

[75] G 9, p. 188; the citation, of course, is to the closing lines of Boethius' *De consolatione philosophiae* V, pr. 6; *CCSL* 94: 105.

[76] Cf. *Summa theologiae* IIaIIae q. 2 a. 5, *sed contra.*

[77] G 9, p. 188.

philosophy — not, however, by rejecting it but by surpassing it and yet bringing it into the service of its own designs.[78]

3. *Ad finem aeternae beatitudinis*: theology as pastoral tool

Having established the limited utility of philosophy and its role as prolegomenon to the theological task, Gerson delineates the foundation of theology in concrete functional terms. The theoretical questions of epistemology give way, and this at a fairly early juncture of the treatise, to a consideration of pastoral implications. Theology as he conceives it is not after all a strictly academic enterprise, serving the professional guild alone, but is rather a vocation intended for the edification of the entire church. With this clarification, we have come to one of the deepest strata of Gerson's thought, discerning the foundation of his passions as both churchman and theologian.

It is in this regard that Gerson contrasts theology and philosophy in teleological terms. The *viator* through strictly »natural« knowledge (i. e., *philosophica ratiocinatio*) can indeed come to a »dim awareness« of God's *virtus et divinitas* (Rom. 1.20), but this is to discern life's goal in a clouded and confused manner and to do so without conveying »the virtues or formal operations by which this state might be reached.«[79] What is needed is a clearer and more penetrating grasp first of this goal and second of the means of attaining it, since as he argued in the early pages of this treatise »man's end is itself supernatural.«[80] Theology, which as revealed in scripture is »added« to this philosophical knowledge by being »supernaturally infused,« accomplishes this

---

[78] This restates Gerson's earlier conceptualization of theology as »architect« for the entire edifice of knowledge: »Quamobrem decernere de legibus omnibus manifestum est spectare principaliter ad theologiam velut ad scientiam superiorem architectonicam. ...« Gerson also pointed to the dire consequences of either »ignoring, neglecting, or spurning« this: ». . . ideo turbationes in politiis et conscientiis saepius oriri compertum est.« *De vita spirituali animae*; G 3, p. 161. Moreover, in *Collatio de angelis* he explores the question of the relationship of theology to philosophy, rhetoric, and poetry; citing Paul, Augustine, and Jerome as his authorities, he portrayed this relationship in similar terms: »Modus attamen habendus est fateor ut illae scientiae non dominae, sed ancillae, ministraeque sint; sic quod Theologiae praecipuus honor, summa auctoritas, et frequentius studium a theologis semper impendatur.« On the basis of this and other texts from his early writings, Combes concluded that we must recognize in Gerson an »humanisme impénitent«; this is true, as far as it goes, though only if one defines »humanism« in Augustinian terms, to recall his sympathetic approach to »pagan« letters which he endorsed through his famous exegesis of »Egyptian gold and silver.« See *De doctrina christiana*, 2.40.60, CCSL 32: 73—74; also, Combes, »Gerson et la naissance de l'humanisme,« pp. 281 ff., and, on the same theme, Burger, *Aedificatio*, pp. 51 ff.

[79] G 9, p. 189.

[80] *Ibid.*

through directing us *ad finem aeternae beatitudinis*, or, as he elsewhere says, *ad certam beatitudinis expectationem*.[81] Indeed, this function identifies a fundamental aspect of theology: *theologia* is to lead us beyond the trials and tribulations of this unstable life toward »a certain expectation of beatitude,« a journey which finally leads toward God, »the refuge of the human pilgrimage.«[82] The essential function of theology is to lead *viatores* on the human pilgrimage beyond »the mutable, transient things here below«[83] — in a word, *in Deum*. As *cognitio Dei* it is not a speculative undertaking but rather a guide for living »added« to what we can know naturally, in order that we might discern and move toward the goal for which we were created and toward which we were fashioned. Theology alone — and, pace Boethius, not philosophy — can »lift« us beyond this world and show us our ultimate destination »in God.«

This theme discloses what one might call the eschatological frame of Gerson's thought by defining the end toward which theology leads us. Yet he deliberately underscores the point that theology is not itself this goal but directs us *toward* this end. Thus, while he contrasts the limited vision of philosophy with faith, which »enlightens our darkness« by securing us in »that excellent light« of revelation,[84] he insists vigorously and repeatedly that *in via* even *theologia* is an »interim« knowledge: although faith has its source at »the fount of light,« it nonetheless »carries darkness [*aenigma*] along with it.«[85] As a tool to lead the *viator* toward God, theology does not cause us to dissolve into union with God,[86] and here Gerson's abiding reticence toward an essentialist mysticism is once again clear. Rather, theology is the guide steering us toward the »end of *eternal* beatitude,« mediating what he elsewhere calls *altior felicitas* and granting to us »a legitimate consolation.«[87]

Yet this is not Gerson's last word on how theology plays an instrumental role in leading *viatores* to God as *humanae peregrinationis refugium*, and in recognizing this we must correct the suggestion that this treatise is in no sense about mystical theology.[88] Such a conclusion ignores the dynamic structure of

---

[81] G 9, pp. 214, 196.

[82] G 9, p. 196: »Est autem humani cordis desiderium et pondus in Deum sicut in locum suum et centrum ferri; est supremum post quod non relinquitur aliud humanae peregrinationis refugium.«

[83] G 9, p. 226.

[84] This language echoes Ps. 17.29; see G 9, p. 206.

[85] G 4, pp. 3–4.

[86] This is a familiar theme in Gerson's earlier writings; for a detailed discussion of this, with particular regard to *De mystica theologia speculativa*, see Burger, *Aedificatio*, pp. 139–43. Burger concludes that »das In-Gott-Sein der mens in der unio sieht [Gerson] als Aufgehen in Gott geschildert . . . . Gerson liegt daran, zu betonen, daß die Seele (nicht etwa nur ihr höchster Teil) in der unio ihr eigenes Sein nicht etwa verliert.« *Ibid.*, p. 141.

[87] Cf. G 9, pp. 191, 226. The force of the comparative Gerson here intends as a contrast with philosophy and its inadequate consolation.

[88] This is the conclusion which Combes reached; cf. *La théologie mystique*, 2: 306, where

Gerson's argument in this text, a literary movement by which he introduces *theologia* as the guide, finally, toward an imperfect mystical experience of God. Although Gerson's Monicus does suggest that *theologia mystica* must remain the subject of conversation elsewhere,[89] his Volucer breaks this silence in a critical and revealing passage of *De consolatione theologiae*, describing the »status« toward which *theologia* »persuades« *viatores* to aspire as that of the contemplative life. The end of theology is to lead *viatores per contemplationem* to that state when

> the mind through contemplation arrives at an understanding pure and simple of the [divine] form, without motion or activity; this understanding, though very imperfect, contemplates by the simplicity of the divine understanding and in a single intuition what is present, past, and future.[90]

This mystical state, as he describes it, leads the *viator* to the point of heightened experience of God — here described in Boethian terms as apprehending »the intelligible center« which, »remaining itself fixed, grants movement to all else[91] such that simple and unchanging, one looks upon and grasps all that is subject to motion.«[92] He concludes this description of *vita contemplativa* by noting that the identity of *theologia* itself is the force moving *viatores* toward the mystical state in which they enter, however »imperfectly« or »darkly,« into the »eternal present« of God. This is no »essential« union with God, but rather serves as a glimpse of the peace for which pilgrims yearn *in via*, the *pax Dei* toward which the treatise points and with which it closes.

At first glance this passage (II pr. 4) appears to stand as an isolated theme, the single text from this treatise in which Gerson discusses *theologia mystica*. But this is to ignore the momentum which he here ascribes to *theologia* itself — i. e., in persuading *viatores* to aspire to this mystical state. Furthermore, upon closer scrutiny of the language of this passage we find that Gerson has taken over a key phrase of Boethius: the neoplatonic vision of God as *stabilis manens das cuncta moveri*. In other words, Gerson broadens the attraction of the mystical life by describing it as the ultimate status which theology persuades *all* viatores to seek. The *peregrinatio ad Deum* becomes nothing more nor less than an approach, *per contemplationem*, to the divine life itself as Boethius had described it. As an instrument fashioned to lead us toward this status, and ultimately *ad*

---

he argues that the dialogue has no bearing upon *theologia mystica*, and is rather an essentially »rational« work on the Christian life: »Le *De consolatione theologiae* est un œuvre rationnelle, et même, dirais-je volontiers, puissamment rationnelle.«

[89] G 9, p. 193: »Sed super his [i. e., ›theologia mystica‹], altera fortassis die sermo fiet.« Combes calls this »le réfus gersonien«; *La théologie mystique*, 2: 314, 315.

[90] G 9, p. 211 f. See also above, 3.A.5.

[91] Gerson borrows, verbatim, Boethius' phrase, »stabilis manens das cuncta moveri«; see *De consolatione philosophiae* III m. 9, *CCSL* 94: 51, and G 9, p. 212.

[92] *Ibid.*

finem aeternae beatitudinis as the denouement of the mystical life and indeed —
lest we miss the full weight of his point — of life itself, theology serves us *in via*
by guiding us toward the divine stillness which is God. It leads us toward
eternal beatitude, an unattainable goal in this life though one which we glimpse
in speculo et in aenigmate.[93] With this theme Gerson establishes theology in its
functional role not only as *paideia* in terms of character formation, but as
delineating the eschatological framework by which all *viatores* — monks as well
as lay persons — journey in faith toward the divine »stillness,« the »refuge of
the human pilgrimage« and the »end of eternal beatitude« which is God
himself.

C. On the integration of *theoria* and *praxis*

In our analysis early in this chapter of Gerson's formulation of a *theologia biblica*
and the consideration of how he moves from philosophy and theology, we
have again and again skirted an issue which attracted Gerson's attention
throughout his academic career, and which must now occupy our attention: the
matter of the necessary integration of *theoria* and *praxis*, and the nature of the
theologian as one who engages knowledge (*eruditio*) with piety, or what he calls
»an erudition of the heart« which leads to the performance of good works.
Here it is the balance of thought and piety which is of utmost concern to
Gerson, the constructive side of his criticism of a theologizing which led to
sterile, abstract, or »unuseful« speculation. He defines the theologian in terms
radical for his day as the person — whether learned or simple, ordained or lay —
who manifests an erudition of the heart: »non quidem eruditione solius
intellectus, sed multo magis affectus.« Against the pretensions of the
professional theology of the university masters, Gerson here suggests that »the

---

[93] G 9, p. 231. This is, of course, an echo of 1 Cor. 13.12. Already in his early treatise, *De
comparatione vitae contemplativae ad activam* (ca. 1401), Gerson had articulated this theme in
explicit terms: »Unde ... quando licite potest utraque vita exercerit speculativa scilicet et
activa, speculativa eligibilior est et dignior et statui gloriae seu innocentiae conformior .... .
Et conformiter, licet magis elevate, ponunt theologi beatitudinem in fruitione et cognitione
Dei.« G 3, pp. 63 ff. Gerson's early articulation of this theme, and in a work specifically
devoted to considering the relationship of the active and contemplative lives, strengthens
the argument for continuity from this early juncture to his later writings (e. g., *De
consolatione theologiae*). Gerson does — pace Combes — consider *theologia mystica*, ascribing
to it the highest theological role; the treatise does not, of course, devote extended attention
to this theme as in earlier works, and his discussion here suggests that mysticism is not a
special calling reserved for the few but the status toward which theology leads all *viatores*.
Here the issue under discussion is not that of vocational perfection, a theme which had
earlier absorbed his attention; rather, he is speaking about the end of human life, the goal
not only of monks but of laity as well. With regard to this earlier theme, cf. Burger,
Aedificatio, pp. 183–87.

spirit of catholic judgment« (*animus catholicae sententiae*) might well reside »more fruitfully« among pious lay persons than among learned masters who demonstrate only an »erudition of the mind.«[94]

We also find Gerson here advancing a theme uncharacteristic of his earlier writings: he defends the solitary life and calls for a new appreciation of the »active« work effected by those living the cloistered life. This represents a change of perspective for Gerson who had earlier defended the secular clergy as the true representatives of the *vita ambidextra*,[95] or the »balanced« life, since priests actually embodied the »contemplative« precisely — and unexpectedly, for modern readers — in exercising the *cura animarum* (e. g., preaching, administration of the sacraments, etc.). Thus, during the years leading up to the Council of Constance, Gerson had confronted this issue with pressing urgency against the attacks of mendicant critics upon the hierarchical status and dignity of secular clerics.[96] In *De consolatione theologiae*, however, we find Gerson defending the cloistered life as the most effective means of bringing about reform within the church.

Finally, we shall examine in explicit terms an issue which has already appeared several times along the margins of this study: the question of the broadened nature of the theological task as Gerson perceived it, and whether speaking of his democratization of that task in this treatise requires us to reconsider the shape of his ecclesiology. With these questions before us, we shall inquire whether the later Gerson has altered his perception of church order; this discussion will thus introduce themes explored more fully in the sixth chapter of this study which is devoted specifically to ecclesiology.

---

[94] G 9, p. 238.

[95] Elsewhere he refers to this as *vita mixta ex utraque* as well; cf. G 3, p. 71, and a discussion of this theme in Burger, *Aedificatio*, pp. 183 ff. See also Pascoe, *Jean Gerson*, pp. 157–64.

[96] In an early treatise, *De consiliis evangelicis et statu perfectionis* (ca. 1400), written as Abramowski has convincingly argued against members of the Dominican order, and in a later tract *Contra conclusiones Matthaei Graben*, written in the same year as *De consolatione theologiae* (1418), Gerson expressed his conviction that secular clerics because of their execution of the three-fold pastoral duties of »purging,« »illumining,« and »perfecting,« stood higher than monks: *status curatorum perfectior est statu religiosorum*. The critical distinction by which he advanced this aim was not to imply that »religious« could not attain perfection themselves, but that they »acquired« this status rather than the higher calling of the secular clerics who actually »exercised« it: »status curatorum est status perfectionis exercendae, religionis vero status magis est acquirendae. Secundum praedicta autem status perfectionis exercendae perfectior est statu perfectionis acquirendae.« Cf. Abramowski, »Jean Gerson, ›De consiliis evangelicis et statu perfectionis,‹« pp. 63–65, 73 ff.; see also Burger, *Aedificatio*, pp. 178 ff. Finally, for a discussion of the broader trajectory of this theme, since this was a long-standing debate during the Middle Ages, see Giles Constable, »The Popularity of Twelfth-Century Spiritual Writers in the Late Middle Ages,« in »*Renaissance Studies in Honor of Hans Baron*, ed. A. Molno, J. A. Tedeschi (Dekalb, IL, 1971), pp. 39 ff.

1. The theologian and the »erudition of the heart«

On initial examination this treatise appears to demonstrate a deliberate continuity of theme in this most characteristic of Gersonian concerns: namely, the union of knowledge and piety. Just as the chancellor had earlier defined *cognitio Dei* as a matter not of intellectual investigation but of the affects,[97] so does he return to this theme in this treatise, insisting that what one learns *per theologiam* must be »transmitted« (*traducat*) through »constant rumination« to the heart and to the performance of (good) deeds (*in affectum cordis, et executionem operis*).[98] Theological knowledge must lead to an engaged or vital piety, one which is not only a matter of the heart — though it is first of all this, according to Gerson — but which also flowers in works of charity, or what medieval theologians referred to as »formed faith.« And yet Gerson here advances an argument that would have been heard as radical in his day: he defines the theologian, and not merely the Christian, as a person whose erudition is rooted not in thought alone but in life itself. In a world which identified the theologian as an academic professional — if not as a professional academic, to recall Gerson's earlier criticism in *Contra curiositatem studentium* of university theologians — Gerson makes the radical suggestion that the identity of *theologus* has little to do with formal training and everything to do with a knowledge which is engaged in piety and charity. For the professional this meant exemplifying *vita ambidextra*, an adeptness in the intellectual dimension of faith (*theologia speculativa*) which was integrated in the inner life (*vita contemplativa*) and formed by good works (*vita activa*). For the lay person (*idiota*) this meant an embodiment of »simple faith,« »certain hope,« and »sweet charity.«[99]

In the latter pages of the treatise Gerson approaches this theme again and from a different angle, here shifting his concern from those whose erudition was not yet formed in the pious and active life to those seeking after mystical experiences *not* rooted in knowledge or without proper understanding (*non secundum scientiam*) — i.e., the pursuit of spiritual experience to the neglect of knowledge. Addressing the question of those desirous of »the sweetness of the

[97] Cf. *De mystica theologia speculative conscripta*; G 3, p. 273, and Combes 70, 6–8: »Cognitio Dei quae est per theologiam mysticam melius acquiritur per poenitentem affectum quam per investigantem intellectum.«
[98] G 9, p. 237. We should note that whereas Gerson had earlier defined mystical theology in terms of an affective knowledge which exceeded the intellect, he here defines not mystical theology but simply theology in these terms. As we have already suggested, and shall subsequently argue regarding other themes, Gerson seems to interpret *theologia* in this treatise in terms which he had elsewhere reserved solely for *theologia mystica*. That is, even while he does not address the subject of mystical theology explicitly, he has projected such concerns more broadly upon the domain of theology itself.
[99] G 9, pp. 237–38.

Lord« (*dulcedo Dei*), Gerson's Volucer warns that many who seek or desire this mystical sentiment »too much« (*nimia sentimentorum hujusmodi*) — and he goes on to cite, explicitly, the Beghards and Turlupins[100] — fall into deception.[101] In abandoning an integration of knowledge and piety for an exclusive preoccupation with the *vita mystica*, by which such persons desired to attain »scientiam mysticam de Deo ... per unionem apicis mentalis cum Spiritu sancto,« Gerson insists that these persons »went astray« by exchanging the »sentiments of God« for »the delusions of their hearts.« »Mystical knowledge« alone, he here argues, can become just as distorted as an arid knowledge rooted only in the intellect. But this is no retreat from mysticism, nor is this a new theme in Gerson's writings; it expresses once again his deeply rooted pastoral conviction that one must strike a proper balance not only between the active and contemplative lives (i. e., *vita mixta ex utraque*), but between the religious feelings (*devotio* or *affectus*) and intellectual understanding (*scientia* or *intellectus*).[102]

In emphasizing an engaged piety which integrates knowledge, spiritual experience, and acts of charity, Gerson faces and finally rejects the two extremes of either an essentialist mysticism, on the one hand, which by seeking an absorption in God neglected »acts of voluntary love,«[103] or, on the other,

---

[100] This is by no means Gerson's first criticism of these groups; cf. his letter to Guillaume Minaudi, *De religionis perfectione et moderamine* (G 2, pp. 232 ff.), *De mystica theologia speculative* (G 3, p. 285 ff.), etc. This subject has been adequately treated by Combes in *La théologie mystique*, 2: 179, 347—48; Brown also touches upon it in *Pastor and Laity*, pp. 202 ff. See also Pascoe, *Jean Gerson*, p. 121.

[101] G 9, p. 234.

[102] Ozment pointed to this theme with regard to Gerson's earlier writings, and in particular his *De mystica theologia speculativa conscripta*, when he concluded that »the mutually supporting relation between *devotio* and *scientia* ... reflects one of the strongest, clearest, most common sensical, and *yet most overlooked* motifs in Gerson's mystical theology, viz., the naturally correlative and reciprocal character and operation of the affective and intellective powers. Gerson is convinced that the only *devotio* worthy of the Christian is that which is *secundum scientiam*, and the only *scientia* worthy of the Christian that which is *secundum devotionem*.« *Homo Spiritualis*, p. 53 (my emphasis). This conviction is ably articulated in *De consolatione theologiae*, a continuity of theme which suggests that we consider this treatise in line with Gerson's abiding interest in mystical theology (pace Combes).

[103] G 9, pp. 234—35. After characterizing four methods in which *scientia mystica* could deceive *viatores* by being sought »in excess« — including acting with *devotio* which was *non secundum scientiam*; attempting to live without any passion whatsoever; seeking God in complete passivity; and, desiring a union of the mind's summit with the Holy Spirit — Gerson concludes by wondering whether the mystical life should lead us beyond love: »Sed ab istis et a prioribus inquiritur ubi meritum erit, si dilectionis voluntariae nullus habeatur actus.« This concern echoes what he had earlier expressed in *De theologia mystica*: »Cognitio Dei quae est per theologiam mysticam melius acquiritur per poenitentem affectum quam per investigantem intellectum. Ipsa quoque, ceteris paribus, eligibilior est et perfectior quam theologia symbolica vel propria de qua est contemplatio; sicut dilectio perfectior est

arid speculative knowledge divorced from the affective and active dimensions
of life. The force which establishes this balance is *theologia* itself which Gerson
here introduces without qualification as the integration of both *scientia* and
devotio, the vehicle of *peregrinatio ad Deum* which finally »persuades« us to aspire
to the contemplative life. Similarly, in an earlier passage Gerson had identified
theologia as the guide directing us along what he calls »the straight way of the
divine mandates, by which one proceeds to the life which is the state perfected
by the addition of every good.«[104] Hence, although Gerson does not introduce
any considerable discussion of mystical theology in this treatise, theology
includes within its own functions what Gerson elsewhere attributed to *scientia
mystica*.

2. A call to the cloistered life?

In approaching *De consolatione theologiae* on the basis of Gerson's earlier
treatises, we might expect to find here an explication of *theologia* integrated into
the concrete dimensions of life. Gerson had earlier introduced the contrast

---

cognitione et voluntas intellectu, et caritas fide« (G 3, p. 273). His insistence that »love is
more perfect than (mere) knowledge« is another expression of his long-standing and
deeply-rooted conviction that *aedificatio* is the final measure of all acts. It is intriguing to
note Gerson's proximity to Lorenzo Valla in this regard, since his counterpart also would
argue that goodness must be willed voluntarily, and for this reason insisted that voluntary
piety was superior to external constraints imposed by monasticism. In *De professione
religiosorum* Valla argued that »goodness springs from the free impulses of a will which is
internally well directed and not from outward obedience to obligations externally
imposed.« Cited by Hanna Gray, »Valla's *Encomium of St. Thomas Aquinas* and the
Humanist Conception of Christian Antiquity,« *Essays in History and Literature Presented to
Stanley Pargellis* (Chicago, 1965), pp. 48 ff. More to the point is the fact that here Gerson
parts company with Aquinas whose thoughts he may have had in mind judging from the
proximity of theme and verbal parallels; Gerson refused to elevate the contemplative over
the active life as did Aquinas (cf. *Summa theologiae* IIaIIae q. 182 a. 2). This is perhaps a subtle
point, since Aquinas also advocated the »mixed life« in this passage; but he did so, unlike
Gerson, by distinguishing a hierarchy of merit by which *vita contemplativa* occupied the
nobler position. Gerson's view approximates more closely that expressed by Gregory the
Great, when he wrote (*Homiliae in Hiezechihelem Prophetam* I.3.10; *CCSL* 142:38):
»Without the contemplative life it is possible to enter the heavenly kingdom, provided one
omit not the good actions we are able to do; but we cannot enter therein without the active
life, if we neglect to do the good we can do.« This conviction permeates this treatise, and
this may suggest why it is that Gerson deemphasizes *theologia mystica* here, since he is
writing an enchiridion not for mystics — those whom he calls »the highest theologians,«
who concern themselves with mystical theology (G 9, p. 239) — but for all *viatores*.

[104] G 9, p. 189. In this passage Gerson is contrasting theology with philosophy, though
he does not qualify the nature of theology which leads us toward this *status perfectionis*, the
very term he had earlier applied to the office of the secular clergy in his debate on the
hierarchy of offices within the church.

between *vita activa* and *vita contemplativa* as a contrast between an active engagement of the former »in the world« and the isolated retreat of the latter »out of the world,« but in terms that probably strike the modern reader as peculiar: the »active life« entailed the »physical works of mercy« which all Christians shouldered while the »contemplative« involved those dealing with »spiritual goods« (*bona spiritualia*), among which Gerson identified, alongside prayer, preaching and the administration of the sacraments.[105] Against monastic voices who saw their calling as »more perfect« than that of the secular clergy, Gerson identified the contemplative life in what we would consider as active terms, a tendency toward a spiritualizing action which has been traced well back into twelfth-century debates.[106] The *status perfectionis*, following this controversial view, fell within the purview of the secular rather than regular clergy since even minor prelates were under obligation to fulfill all three of these duties for others. They held these responsibilities, Gerson argued at this earlier stage of his career, in addition to their participation »in septem operibus misericordiae exterioribus, sicut Martha providebat corpori Christi.«[107] In a word, such secular clergy occupied the highest office in the ecclesiastical hierarchy, as they were called upon to exemplify through their vocation the *vita mixta ex utraque*, the active and contemplative life.

We might well expect to find continuity of this theme in Gerson's later works, and particularly in *De consolatione theologiae* given the literary structure of the treatise which sets forth a dialogue between a hermit (Monicus) and one who appears to be a secular prelate (Volucer). And yet an examination of this dialogue, as we have earlier noted, reveals a startling, even radical revision of this characteristic Gersonian theme: Gerson here retreats from his earlier defense of the secular clergy to pose what appears to be a call to the cloistered life — and with poignant irony he advances this defense of »the solitary life« not, as we might expect, through the voice of Monicus, the hermit, but through the contribution which Volucer makes. Having discussed in the third book of this treatise the frustrations and difficulties facing those who exercise public authority, both in the civil and ecclesiastical domains, Gerson's Volucer concludes that »I am forced to call blessed [*beatos*] those content with their solitude,« a claim he defends by pointing to the example of Gregory the Great who desired to be »absolved from the chains of public rule.«[108] In the sub-

---

[105] Cf. *De comparatione vitae contemplativae ad activam*; G 3, p. 71.

[106] For an elaboration of this »a spirituality of action,« as it developed from the twelfth through fifteenth centuries, see Constable, »Twelfth-Century Spirituality,« pp. 40 ff.

[107] *De comparatione vitae contemplativae ad activam*; G 3, p. 71. What is quite striking in this use of the Mary/Martha story is not what Gerson attributes to Martha, but what he identifies in peculiar fashion as falling to Mary as representative of the contemplative life — viz. alongside prayer, preaching and the administration of the sacraments.

[108] G 9, p. 219.

sequent poem, in fact, Volucer continues »to sing the praises« of those living the eremitic life (*solitarii*), contrasting them favorably with those bound to the *vita publica*. This encomium on the cloistered life ends with language we would have expected to hear not from Gerson himself but from one of his earlier critics among the mendicants:

> Is it not better to close the windows of death
> Than use the lower senses?
> To see celestial spheres with a decent mind,
> Where the tormenting and fierce cares
> Of the people do not disturb?
> Death, untamed, becomes its entrance into life;
> Jesus is his hope, he lives in him:
> Recalling the saints' merits
> Which are honored, he places trust in prayer.[109]

This irony of literary voice continues in the following prose section (III pr. 3) in which Monicus chides his counterpart for bringing potential harm to the state through a too excessive praise of the cloistered life, concluding that »the state would surely perish without rulers.« Yet this counter-argument, which carries strains of the humanist concern for civic life, has a feeble ring to it, appearing as a necessary but not entirely convincing argument of one bound by public office but frustrated by the immense effort required for even minimal reform within the public sphere.

This call to the cloistered life, delivered in this dialogue not by the hermit (Monicus) but by the priest (Volucer), registers a note of frustration not usually detected in Gerson's writings. Indeed, the substance and mood of the poem as a whole (III m. 2) reflect Gerson's discontent in finding himself exiled from France; he writes this treatise during a dark period of political exile, in the turbulent wake of Constance and in the vivid shadow of Boethius. In any event this poem conveys a strong note of resignation in his wistful portrayal of Gregory as the »sighing« pope (*suspiravit*). As if to assure the reader that this is no isolated caveat, Gerson returns to this theme later in the same book where he offers a lengthy apologia of the cloistered life. Once again, Gerson's choice of literary voice carries a poignant irony, since it is Monicus who prompts this discussion through his skeptical assault upon the utility of the *solitarius*. In strains unfamiliar to us from Gerson's earlier writings, this rejoinder even includes a direct qualification of public speaking – presumably including preaching – as an instrument capable of effecting reform: Volucer's answer to the solitary's cynical question resonates with a resignation foreign to Gerson's earlier-held convictions when he poses the rhetorical question, »Who is there, then, who does not know that vices are conquered more effectively by prayer [*oratio*] than by speech [*peroratio*]?« Is this a defense of quietism? We should not

---

[109] G 4, p. 133.

draw this conclusion too hastily, since Gerson speaks of the prayers of those who are otherwise »absent and silent« in terms of direct efforts at reform within the public sphere. Prayer itself stands as the most effective way of reforming the church — public reform from the private cloister, as it were. Although not yet an invitation to quietism with its resignation from any manner of participation in worldly affairs, this call to the cloistered life does appear to stand at odds with his otherwise consistent emphasis of the *vita mixta ex utraque*, the balanced life of action and contemplation which the secular clergy exercised.

Upon closer scrutiny, however, this theme may suggest no abrupt thematic change of course from his characteristic defense of the *vita ambidextra*, though he does favor an alternate approach to how this life was to be conceived: Gerson here advocates not the direct intervention of pastoral work but a hidden reform effected by prayer. With this defense of the utility of prayer in effecting reform he has not yet lapsed into quietism but has simply modulated the nature of how that »mixed« life should be realized: the *solitarius* who is cloistered *from* the world nonetheless applies his prayer both to the accomplishment of reform *within* the world and to the support of those actively engaged in the pastoral offices of »preaching,« »admonishing,« and »correcting.«[110] Gerson still conceives the work of prayer undertaken by *solitarii* as set within the social matrix of the church, and *aedificatio* remains the norm governing life within the cloistered state. Is this meant as a polemic rejoinder to those secluded in religious communities, reminding them of their broader social responsibilities for the church as a whole? This is plausible. He now enobles »the way of Mary,« recalling the classic biblical story by which medieval theologians discussed the relationship of the active and contemplative lives; Mary escaped the labor which rendered Martha »anxious and troubled about many things.«[111] Hence, it would appear that even those cloistered, although living

---

[110] Cf. G 9, p. 224.

[111] Gerson's exegesis of this passage (i. e., Lk. 10.38—42) represents a departure of emphasis rather than substance over his earlier treatment of this pericope. In *De comparatione vitae contemplativae ad activam*, for example, he identified Martha with the *vita activa* and Mary with the *vita contemplativa*, here following the typology popularized for later medieval theologians by Gregory the Great (see *On Morals in Job*, VII.37; *PL* 75: 764; and, *Hom. iii, in Hiez..*; *PL* 76: 809). Yet as we have earlier noted his analysis of *vita contemplativa* departs from Gregory's straightforward interpretation, since Gerson included in addition to prayer both preaching and the administration of the sacraments as the duties properly falling to those pursuing the *contemplative* life; secular clergy thus stood for him as representatives of *both* the active and contemplative. In this sense, Gerson's exegesis of this Lukan passage in *De consolatione theologiae* represents a modulation back toward Gregory's interpretation, since Gerson's portrait of Mary as a type of the contemplative life here represents those cloistered from the world; his *solitarius* rather than the secular clergy now comes to embody the *vita mixta ex utraque*, since he applies prayer as an edifying tool within the church. It is

out the *vita contemplativa* in intentional isolation from the world, yet embody something of the »mixed life«: even hermits must offer a »worldly« ministry of intercession. Gerson's apparent yearning – along with Pope Gregory – to be released from the »chains of public office« to pursue the solitary life does suggest his frustration, above all in terms of his fresh memories at this juncture of his efforts to bring about *reformatio ecclesiae* at Constance. But this must not be read as a frustrated retreat to quietism.[112] His pastoral commitment to the substance of the *vita mixta ex utraque* remains intact, even while he varies the shape of that model and alters the emphasis he had earlier placed on the worldly duties falling to secular clerics by advocating the effectiveness of a hidden reform of prayer. One might still discern his emphasis upon a »spirituality of action« in this late treatise, but Gerson appears to be equally concerned to speak of an »active spirituality« in which those living the cloistered life intercede to effect reform within the public church.[113] Both of these concerns reflect his conviction that every vocation within the church had a useful social responsibility: namely, the duty of *aedificatio*, the upbuilding of the church. It is this ecclesiological conviction, therefore, which remains intact as a foundational theme in his early and later writings, even while the particular emphases by which he supports this conviction do vary.

3. Mysticism and the »democratization« of theology

Earlier in this study we addressed the question of Gerson's anti–elitism, particularly in terms of his resistance to the professionalizing of theology. In this treatise he carries earlier convictions about the usefulness of theology into a higher key, arguing that theology itself must accommodate all within the church, an argument which counterbalances his adherence otherwise to the hierarchical ecclesiology of Dionysian provenance. In this regard we have noted his argument that the rhetoric of scripture, with its metaphoric character, is *paideia* for all *viatores*, the *idiotae* alongside the theological *periti*. We have also discussed Gerson's aggressive suggestion in this treatise that the establishment

---

in this particular sense a worldly ministry of intercession, albeit of a different scope than his earlier portrait of what the *vita contemplativa* entailed.

[112] In this regard see G 9, pp. 229 f., where Monicus advocates quietism because of the »scruples« and »doubts« surrounding human acts and the »uncertainties« of all human affairs. Yet faced with such an attitude Gerson's Volucer offers bold encouragement to act: »One will dare [to act] if certain from sacred teaching [*ex doctrina sacra*], because his efforts are founded in the righteousness of faith [*in justitia fidei*].«

[113] That is, just as Gerson had earlier identified »preaching« and »administering sacraments« as part of the *contemplative* life, thereby identifying active duties of minor prelates as part of the contemplative life, so he here inverts this approach in order to suggest that the cloistered life has its own kind of activity, albeit via the »hidden« action of prayer.

of »the spirit of catholic judgment« occurs »more fruitfully« (*fructuosius*) among the simple (*apud idiotas*) than among the learned (*apud repletos litteris*), a theme which from the voice of a university chancellor would not have been understood without a biting measure of irony.[114] And, finally, we have observed his insistence that all the faithful (*omnes fideles*) are to have explicit faith (*fides explicita*) not only in terms of the »twelve articles« of the creed (*articuli fidei*), following a well established theological precedent, but with regard to »the whole of scripture« as well.[115] Each of these themes suggests that Gerson's idea of reform sought to broaden the scope and audience of theology, and thus to reconstitute theology not by clarifying its doctrinal emphases with technical precision but by translating it into broader social terms within the church as a whole. Against the tendency of the schools to accent often subtle doctrinal differences as well as the rancor of theological disputation which had brought increasing divisiveness upon the church of his day, Gerson argued for unity and simplicity of expression, a concentration upon useful matters which were »necessary for salvation.« As an advocate of a populist approach to theology (*theologia vulgata*), Gerson's principal concern at this late juncture was not the reform needed to reinstate the purity of theological argument in academic discourse. Rather, he argued for the faithful use of theology in reforming the human person and the church. In short, theology was for the church and not the church for theology; it was to be the »companion« who accompanied all *viatores* upon the human pilgrimage. It is in this sense that we have spoken of this treatise as offering in programmatic terms a »democratization« of theology.

In the preceding chapters we also noted that Gerson has here projected thematic concerns which he earlier attributed more narrowly to *scientia mystica* or *theologia mystica* into the broader and unqualified terms of *theologia* itself, albeit first of all by »persuading« us to aspire to the contemplative state. But what can this mean for our grasp of Gerson's commitment to mystical theology at this late juncture of his life? Has he altered his conception of theology, and of mystical theology, because of a change of mind or under force of external events? Or do the thematic continuities we have identified suggest that it is simply »business as usual« for Gerson in terms of his theological perspective, even if the accidental expression of it has changed to accommodate the literary form he here adopts? To answer these questions we must retreat some distance from the detail of these arguments, inquiring more generally

---

[114] G 9, p. 238. This theme also suggests that we should not interpret Gerson's ecclesiology — at least, not in terms of his later writings post-dating Constance — as one recent study has done: viz. as a church »made up of ordered ranks of clergy only, with the laity as outsiders, inferiors to be helped towards their spiritual end by the church, but not true members of it.« Brown, *Pastor and Laity*, p. 39; cf. also Pascoe, *Jean Gerson*, p. 32.

[115] *Ibid.*, p. 231.

how the various themes articulated in *De consolatione theologiae* function in relation to the broader purposes of the treatise.

It might at first appear that Gerson's close identification of *theologia mystica* with *theologia* in this treatise signals a more diffuse understanding of mysticism − or, variously, a more specific view of the identity and function of theology. Yet this hypothesis overlooks the various passages in this treatise where Gerson continues to speak of mystical knowledge with the metaphor *dulcedo Dei*, »the sweetness of God,« formal terminology of the affective tradition of medieval mysticism which echoed the language of the Song of Songs and of the Psalms.[116] This »sweetness« is as he subsequently notes *manna reconditum* or *sapientia abscondita*, the »hidden manna« or »hidden wisdom,« since »the one who has it cannot transfer it to another, nor can it be seized by one who does not have it.« This »hidden sweetness« is the proper subject of *theologia mystica*, he concludes, and is not the principal concern of the present dialogue. This admission notwithstanding, Gerson returns to this theme several times in the dialogue, arguing that the quest for this experience reflects the highest nature of theology itself but that this quest »in excess« is an aberrant form of mystical theology. Hence, it would appear incorrect to assume that Gerson simply intends in this treatise to collapse theology and mysticism into the same mold, nor should we assume that he has abandoned *theologia mystica* altogether.

But thematic continuities do remain, such that *theologia* itself and without any more precise qualification fulfills many of the functions Gerson had elsewhere attributed to *theologia mystica*. On this basis alone we find ourselves forced to part paths with Combes's interpretation of this treatise, since his thesis that *De consolatione theologiae* is a rational argument with no regard for mystical theology finally misreads this text. This should not prevent us, however, from noting that Combes's thesis conveys an accurate perception, viewing this treatise against Gerson's broad oeuvre: it is correct to note that Gerson has here significantly altered the approach he had earlier taken toward *theologia mystica*. With this interpretive problem before us, we are now in a position to consider more carefully the question of Gerson's approach to consolation as the task properly falling to theology and what this implies for his grasp of mysticism.

By raising this question once again at this juncture of our study, and by posing it as a more general inquiry into Gerson's oeuvre as a whole, this matter has acquired a different shape and import. It is no longer sufficient to conclude, as we earlier pointed out, that consolation is the inherent purpose of scriptural language; rather, we must now inquire about the nature of consolation and its relation to theology in terms of Gerson's strategic portrayal of *scientia mystica*.

---

[116] For example, cf. Ps. 30.19−21 (LXX): »... muta fiant labia dolosa quae loquuntur adversus iustum iniquitatem in superbia et in abusione, quam magna multitudo dulcedinis tuae domine: quam abscondisti timentibus te.«

Here the related questions of audience and authorial intent once again suggest themselves, since his deliberate approach to a wider readership – namely, all *viatores* – appears to be the natural consequence of his broadened view of how *theologia* functions in the church. Admittedly, we are here speaking of audience in a somewhat unusual sense, since our concern lies not with the technical question of who read – or *could* have read – this treatise, but upon the subjective question of the audience for whom *theologia* offered its consolation, according to Gerson's exposition. We now recognize that Gerson intended *De consolatione theologiae* as a comprehensive statement of the nature and purpose of theology, and of its broad purpose for the church at large. He wrote this treatise for *viatores*, and included teaching and counsel for people of every status within the church: for lay people and for those in religious vows; for priests and for monks; for the young and old, the doubting and the confident; for beginners and for those trained in theological knowledge. For all of these theology functioned as a guide toward God who stood as »the refuge of the human pilgrimage,« a pilgrimage which would finally lead *viatores* into the divine presence itself.

The point Gerson's democratization of theology accentuates is that this journey is itself the matrix of theology, and theology is consequently to be understood as consolatory for *all* persons by leading them beyond despair toward the »highest hope« in God. Theology leads not toward the academy but toward God. And, although Gerson does not project the goal of the human pilgrimage *ad Deum* as a present reality, nor does he conclude that *viatores* are all to attain the summit of mystical experience, he insists that theology is to persuade all *viatores* to »aspire« to this state. In this sense there remains an eschatological reticence in Gerson's thought, a dimension which the less bridled apocalypticism of his day ignored: in teleological terms theology reminds us that in the journey toward God we see only *per speculum in aenigmate*, and that certitude *in via* is not direct vision but rather that »dim« recognition »which faith possesses and which prevails in the hearts of the faithful.«[117] As a »democratized« instrument for the edification of the entire church, theology has a broader pastoral mission than the goal attained or even sought by the mystics, one which is comprehensive and useful in terms of its scope: it is present as »companion« to assist in the formation of each *viator* en route *ad Deum*, the *refugium humanae peregrinationis*. But it does not lead *viatores* beyond the life of this human journey.

In this sense, theology moves every wayfarer forward on this pilgrimage *ad Deum*, but because it must move *every* wayfarer even the most expert mystics

---

[117] G 9, p. 231; the reference, of course, is to 1 Cor. 13.12. The contrast to the highest level of certitude, or »natural« certitude, is unexpected given the terminology: »natural« certitude is that possessed by the *beati* in heaven, for whom alone the *visio Dei* is *facie ad faciem*, or based on what he calls »clear and intuitive evidence.«

are not permitted to isolate themselves from others. The key for them, as for all others, is *aedificatio ecclesiae*, the duty of upbuilding the entire church, the *idiotae* alongside the *periti*. Again we feel the force of Gerson's conviction that *vita mixta ex utraque* stood as guiding norm of every vocation within the church. As he points out in a poignant passage late in this treatise, the very nature of *scientia mystica* requires even those »highest theologians« (*elevati theologi*) who have attained union with God, and »cleave to the Lord [as] one spirit with him, «[118] to »descend« once again to mundane affairs (*ad inferiora*) when necessary.[119] Such persons alone are worthy of being called perfect, since they have attained a harmonious balance of the contemplative with the active. Gerson insists, in other words, that theology may lead to mystical knowledge and the experience of »the sweetness of God,« but never in a manner which obliterates its social responsibilities, a requirement which sustains Gerson's conviction that the *vita ambidextra* itself and not the mystical experience is the means by which *viatores* finally attain perfection in this life.[120] In this sense if *theologia* leads mystical theologians to God and »persuades« others that they ought to aspire to the *vita contemplativa*, it never eclipses its »useful« character which required assisting others on that journey.

Now we are in a position to appreciate why it is that this treatise, though not explicitly devoted to mystical theology, nonetheless does not represent a departure from Gerson's earlier approach to the issue. Here as elsewhere *theologia mystica* is the natural apogee of the Christian life, the integration of the intellect and the heart in the pursuit of God. Here, too, Gerson identifies the essential outline of mystical perception or experience, and integrates its themes within the broader texture of *theologia*. Furthermore, he emphasizes in this treatise the »useful« character of the *scientia mystica*, since such knowledge does not distance *viator* from the church; for the mystical theologian, as for *theologus* more generally, *vita ambidextra* is the way in which one »begins,« »progresses,« and is »perfected« in this life. Raising the question of audience thus clarifies

---

[118] The allusion is to 1 Cor. 6.17, which Gerson applies in terms of the mystical experience; here, as elsewhere in his writings, Gerson is intent on opposing any notion of an »essentialist mysticism,« since he held that the »duplex« nature of the *vita ambidextra* applied also to mystical theologians.

[119] G 9, p. 239. Gerson goes on to cite Rachel and Leah, Sarah and Hagar, typological allusions to the *vita contemplativa* and *vita activa*, respectively, which were a commonplace in later medieval theology and exegesis, particularly on account of the precedent set by Gregory the Great and as utilized again by Aquinas. These Old Testament figures represent, alongside Mary and Martha, types of the active and contemplative life for medieval theologians. Cf. Gregory, *On Morals in Job* vi. 37, 59–61 (*PL* 75:763 ff.) and Aquinas, *Summa theologiae* IIaIIae q. 182 a. 1; also, see Gerson, *La montaigne*; G 7, p. 26, for an earlier reference to this theme in the setting of one of his most popular vernacular treatises on mysticism.

[120] The parallel in the later thought of Gabriel Biel is once again striking; see Oberman, *Harvest*, pp. 342–43.

why it is that themes which Gerson here attributes to *theologia* more generally he elsewhere had articulated in narrower terms of *scientia mystica*. *De consolatione theologiae* represents no dramatic shift of theme regarding the high purpose of mystical theology, but this treatise does reflect Gerson's altered strategy in conceptualizing the audience for this knowledge. Here his overriding concern is to present theology as a useful vehicle for assisting every *viator* on the journey toward God, and as such *theologia* already anticipates in functional terms what *theologia mystica* manifests: namely, a concern for the upbuilding of the entire church as it sojourns toward its identity as the heavenly city, the »new Jerusalem.« The treatise functions, to return to a theme explored in an earlier chapter, as an enchiridion for all wayfarers, such that its very comprehensiveness requires Gerson to introduce *theologia* and *theologia mystica* not in contrast but in continuity with one another, as steps on an ascending ladder *in Deum*. In so doing Gerson consolidates the diverse spectrum of themes and problems which had earlier engaged his thought in a single treatise, introducing theology in a »de-professionalized« form accessible to all seekers of God.

Chapter V

Via Media et Regia:
Toward a Mediating Soteriology

Our examination of Gerson's *De consolatione theologiae* thus far has suggested that a revision of the current perception of his thought is in order. In the opening chapters of this study we have pointed to a variety of distinct theological developments in his thought, shifts which suggest that the period of the Council of Constance coincides with a modulation of his perspective on a broad range of issues. Most of these themes, set within the broader scope of Gerson's work, point not to a radical disjunction in his later thought but rather to developments of a more nuanced character. Indeed, this revisionist interpretation has often proceeded by pointing to texts omitted, or hastily interpreted, by earlier studies which have blazed exploratory paths through Gerson's wide-ranging oeuvre. This is particularly true, as we have argued in the preceding chapter, with regard to two foundational themes in his work: his modified discussion of mysticism in his later work by which he integrates *theologia mystica* within the broader structure of *theologia*, and his argument for the »sufficiency« of scripture for the theological task, two themes which have been of particular prominence in recent historical discussion. As a consequence of this, the revised view we have offered of Gerson's contribution to these issues is of an interest which transcends the narrower realm of Gerson studies. As the »mirror« of his age, to call once again upon a metaphor aptly applied to Gerson's thought, the images we have found reflected in his later writings are of considerable interest also to those working more broadly in the field of late-medieval theology.

Yet our earlier focus upon the foundational themes of method has not yet touched the most significant change in Gerson's theological perspective: namely, his apparently revised approach to soteriology, one of the fundamental theological themes which dominates scholastic discussion during the later Middle Ages.[1] We have already suggested, in however tentative a manner in

---

[1] For a recent survey of this question, see Oakley, *The Western Church*, pp. 133–48. Oakley here provides both a clear and penetrating insight into the scholarly debate on this matter over the past several decades and a balanced and original interpretation of the

the opening chapters of this study, that *De consolatione theologiae* represents a significant departure from Gerson's earlier understanding of this theme. Indeed, this work reveals nothing short of a groundshift in his basic theological approach. As a consequence, the reappraisal of his thought which we offer in this chapter suggests that the current alignment of Gerson, within the broad spectrum of late-medieval nominalism, as belonging to a »main stream« Ockhamist »school« (Oberman) now calls for critical revision.

Recent studies of nominalism have warned against an undifferentiated use of this term, or have abandoned it altogether as a meaningful rubric in describing the horizon of late scholasticism. In the context of this development these studies have broadened our appreciation of the *via moderna* as a *theological* development, pointing not only to its reticence toward metaphysical speculation and the restrictive force this exerted upon its epistemology but to other characteristic themes as well: e. g., the distinction of the »two powers« of God; the articulation of an epistemology of revelation, and the corresponding emphasis of faith over reason as the source of theological knowledge; a positive anthropology based upon the doctrine of merit; and, above all, an approach to soteriology which underscored human cooperation in the process of salvation. Soteriology became for theologians of the late-fourteenth and early-fifteenth centuries the focus of considerable discussion since it was under this rubric that they discussed the crucial question of *merita*, an issue which they delineated under the umbrella of the divine covenant *de potentia Dei ordinata*. Within this arena of discourse Ockhamists of the mediating school drew upon the »old

---

problem based upon a representative sampling of the primary literature. He does not, however, provide any insight into Gerson's position on the question. Oberman's early work on Gabriel Biel does include a discussion of Gerson's theology, though our analysis of the chancellor's later works – and, particularly, *De consolatione theologiae*, which Oberman only occasionally cites – suggests that his interpretation does not yet account for the shifting contours of Gerson's mature work. Cf. *Harvest*, pp. 185 ff. Other recent contributions which have clarified in general terms the current state of the question and which must be acknowledged include three essays by Courtenay, already referred to earlier in this study: his study entitled »Nominalism and Late Medieval Religion,« »Nominalism and Late Medieval Thought: A Bibliographical Essay,« and »Late Medieval Nominalism Revisited, 1972–1982« (the latter two are both reprinted in *Covenant and Causality in Medieval Thought* [London, 1984], pp. 159–64, 716–34). Studies of a more general nature which offer pertinent discussions of soteriology within the late-medieval scene include Hamm, *Promissio,* pp. 355–90 and Alister E. McGrath, *Iustitia Dei. A History of the Christian Doctrine of Justification*, Vol. 1: *From the Beginnings to 1500* (Cambridge, 1986). Hamm's work provides an excellent general orientation to this question, particularly in the section entitled »Zwischen Johannes Duns Scotus und Martin Luther,« pp. 355–90, though he does not devote any considerable attention to Gerson. McGrath's work, despite the breadth of his survey and the detailed nature of his analysis in general, is largely unoriginal and occasionally eccentric in approaching the late-medieval discussions of justification and soteriology. Neither of these works, therefore, offers more than a general orientation to this question vis-à-vis the late-medieval scene, and both ignore Gerson almost entirely.

Franciscan« *facere quod in se est* doctrine in order to provide theological mooring for merit language. This theme above all, which seems to have dominated the soteriological undergirding of late-medieval *cura animarum*, integrates theological premises with an optimistic anthropological model, such that both the substance and passion of scholastic debate moved insistently beyond an abstract approach to soteriology to address concrete pastoral issues raised by this doctrine.

It is something of a surprise, therefore, to suggest at this fairly advanced juncture of Gerson studies that we must revise our estimate of Gerson's place within the broad spectrum of Ockham's progeny. Yet such a revision appears to be in order as we shall suggest in this chapter, since the peculiar shape of Gerson's theological perspective in *De consolatione theologiae* departs from the soteriology characteristic of Ockhamism, considered by some as the »main current« of late-medieval nominalism.[2] Indeed, the thematic *via media et regia*[3] which Gerson announces in this treatise carves out a new soteriological model, a mediating approach for which the Ockhamist emphases of his own earlier works had not prepared us. The terminology at least is not new for Gerson and suggests that he had for some time considered the true task of theology – and, in more concrete terms, the academic responsibilities which were his as university chancellor – as that of articulating a mediating voice in the midst of divisive school debates. He had introduced this as a programmatic concern as early as his university lectures *Contra curiositatem studentium*,[4] and in addressing

---

[2] This terminology was first suggested by Oberman, though the characterization has been criticized from a number of perspectives in recent years. See above, pp. 2–6, and especially nn. 4, 5. In utilizing such language we must remember that while many theologians of the later fourteenth and early fifteenth centuries did stand quite deliberately within the shadow of Ockham's theological accomplishments, the eclecticism of these thinkers (including Gerson) should caution against applying the Ockhamist label to what is a quite heterogeneous theological tradition. Those belonging to the *via moderna*, broadly understood, were heirs of the Venerable Inceptor, but they often blended this influence with a deliberate eclecticism drawing upon a wide-ranging and varied theological legacy as well.

[3] G 9, p. 200. This phrase appears in a discussion early in the treatise of two positions – one of which, explicitly cited as Cicero's, rejected divine providence, while the other, which he refers to an unnamed »other,« perhaps Gregory of Rimini, projected a thorough-going divine determinism even of sinful acts – to which Gerson adds: »Porro viam mediam et regiam tradit theologia revelata fide subnixa, qua gradiendum est, etiam ubi ratiocinationis contrariae dissolutio plena non pateret.« Cf. Burger, »Der Augustinschüler gegen die modernen Pelagianer. Das ›auxilium speciale dei‹ in der Gnadenlehre Gregors von Rimini,« in *Gregor von Rimini. Werk und Wirkung bis zur Reformation*, ed. H. Oberman (Berlin, 1981), pp. 195–240. On this question, cf. also Bradwardine, *De causa Dei contra Pelagium*, ed. H. Savile (London, 1618), especially I.34, pp. 294–307: »Si, et quomodo Deus vult, et non vult, peccatum.« See also Gordon Leff, *Bradwardine and the Pelagians. A Study of His* De causa Dei *and Its Opponents* (Cambridge, 1957), pp. 140–64.

[4] Cf. G 3, p. 240, »quinta consideratio«: »Signum curiositatis et singularitatis poenitentiam atque credulitatem impedientis apud scholasticos est gaudere potius in im-

the problem of distinguishing true from false revelations in the preceding year
had similarly advised that theologians should heed Ovid's advice by pursuing
a »middle« way.[5] Hence, the theme he strikes again in this later treatise of the
via media et regia is familiar to us already as the basic posture of his earlier
theological approach, but it acquires both a new foundation and a different
shape in this treatise. Building upon the textual precedent of Boethius' *De
consolatione philosophiae*, Gerson establishes a theological middle course
between the two extremes the earlier philosopher had outlined: namely, an
approach which emphasized human freedom as a condition excluding divine
providence altogether, at one extreme, and, at the other, a severe view of
providence which embraced a thorough determinism of human acts. This is a
via media, in other words, by setting a mediating course similar in broad outline
to Boethius' argument; it is a *via regia* as a theological version of this
philosophical argument, following his overarching rule that *theologia
philosophiam exsuperat.*[6]

In exploring the contours of this *via media et regia*, specifically in terms of
Gerson's soteriology, we find that the theological perspective of his later
thought aligns him not with the »main current« of nominalism — the broad
trajectory of moderate *via moderna* theologians from Ockham to Biel — but
rather with what has been termed »right-wing nominalism,« the theological
reaction to this current which articulated a more severe Augustinian position.[7]

---

pugnatione doctorum aut in defensione unius pertinaci quam ad eorum dicta concor-
danda operam dare.«

   [5] G 3, p. 39: »... scio certissimum esse quod apud Nasonem scribitur: Medio tutissimus
ibis.« Later in the same treatise he identifies the *via regia* as the sign of discretion, a
»willingness to accept counsel« which is »the true daughter of humility.« *Ibid.*, p. 42. This
theme also figures prominently in *De consolatione theologiae*, as we shall subsequently note;
see below, 6.B.1.

   [6] G 9, p. 188.

   [7] To speak of »Augustinianism« in the later Middle Ages is, of course, to broach a
delicate and complex question. Jaroslav Pelikan has rightly argued that because of the
universal sway of Augustine's authority throughout the Middle Ages it could be said that
his authority, though interpreted along quite diverse lines, was universally acknowledged
and affirmed; indeed, he concludes that in some sense »everyone was an ›Augustinian‹«
during the Middle Ages. See *Reformation,* p. 17. In an earlier volume he concludes,
paraphrasing Whitehead's famous aphorism about Plato and western philosophy, that »it is
possible to view the medieval development [of many of the doctrinal controversies] as ›a
series of footnotes‹ to Augustine.« *The Christian Tradition. A History of the Development of
Doctrine,* Vol. 3: *The Growth of Medieval Theology (600—1300)* (Chicago, 1978), p. 3. I am
here speaking of »Augustinian« in a more restricted sense, applying the epithet to those
theologians such as Thomas Bradwardine and Gregory of Rimini who »sought to reaffirm
the distinctive teaching of the ›doctor of grace‹ against what they believed to be the virulent
Pelagianism and Semi-Pelagianism of their own time.« Pelikan, *Reformation,* pp. 17—18.
Oberman goes further than this to identify Gregory of Rimini as representative of a »right-
wing nominalist« tradition. He argues, furthermore, that Gerson along with Biel stood
outside this camp, since »they prove to be unable to absorb the remarkably tenacious late-

To be more specific, Gerson's later theology appears to be more faithfully re-presented as »an eclectic nominalist mediating theology,« to borrow a phrase applied to Henry Totting of Oyta, a moderating synthesis of diverse themes drawn from Augustinian, Thomist, and Scotist traditions.[8] What is also now evident is the fact that Gerson owes more to Oyta than earlier studies recognized. Our discussion of his soteriology will delineate exactly what this mediating model implies for our grasp of Gerson's theology as a whole, and how it is that he constructs a »theology of seeking« as the fulcrum of his *via media et regia*: namely, as a view of salvation in which the pivotal themes of human freedom and divine providence intersect in terms of the *viator*'s search for God. On this basis our study sketches a revised appreciation not only of Gerson's doctrine of salvation but of his theology in more comprehensive terms, discerning in this late-medieval *enchiridion* a middle course between the Scylla of a radical Augustinian approach to election which would obviate any human contribution to salvation, and the Charybdis of an Ockhamist position which relied upon the language of merit to accentuate the human contribution to salvation. As we shall suggest, Gerson articulates a mediating theology through emphasizing the covenant of Heb. 11.6, that God promises »to reward those who seek him«; such an approach to soteriology ensures both the priority of divine election (*ante praevisa merita*) and the human responsibility under this covenant — not through works of merit, but by seeking the grace of God and the God of grace.

A. Beginning with the Fall: An Augustinian anthropology

Earlier in this study we sketched the problem facing the human wayfarer as Gerson perceived it, the spiral of despair into which *viatores* inevitably fall through the *tentationes* facing them and their inability to surmount the ensuing

---

medieval Augustinian tradition«; my analysis of *De consolatione theologiae* suggests otherwise, since in this late treatise Gerson rejects themes which Oberman characterized as belonging to »the main current of late-medieval nominalism,« among them the *facere quod in se est* doctrine and predestination *post praevisa merita*.

[8] In his study of Oyta's later writings, Lang coined the phrase »eklektisch-nominalistische Vermittlungstheologie« because he noted an attempt to develop the material of his earlier Augustinianism within a Thomist theological form. This characterization appears ably suited to describe Gerson's later theology as well, since like Oyta his eclectic and mediating theological perspective blends Augustinian themes within a Thomist framework. Indeed, this parallel may be anything but circumstantial, since Gerson himself often testified to the esteem in which he held Oyta and I have earlier pointed to significant areas in which Gerson borrows from his predecessor at Paris; see Lang, *Heinrich Totting von Oyta: Ein Beitrag zur Entstehungsgeschichte der ersten deutschen Universitäten und zur Problemgeschichte der Spätscholastik* (Münster i. W., 1937), pp. 161, 177.

desolation by their own effort. Absent in this treatise is the introspective self-scrutiny by which one measured the worthiness of one's »natural« acts of merit (*merita de congruo*), the preoccupation with »the internal forum« by which a penitent might seek an effective cure against despair through the ordained channel of the sacraments. In its place Gerson mounts a driving indictment of all human effort, including of course the familiar Ockhamist *facere quod in se est* doctrine: »desperes volo,« he concludes, »sed de te et in te.« By establishing the point of reference for *consolatio* as the context of human desperation, a thematic emphasis which Gerson articulated not via theological abstractions but rather in terms of the vivid language of human experience, he established what we have called a paideutic approach to theology as an answer to this problem. Gerson also developed this theme in broader terms, however, interpreting the *tentationes* which established the experiential basis for human despair on a personal level within the broader historical framework of the Fall. In so doing Gerson aligns his anthropology not with the Ockhamists but with the more severe tradition of late-medieval Augustinianism with its unqualified pessimism regarding the »natural« human condition.[9]

1. Adam as *praevaricator* and the *mortis damnatio*

In his earlier vernacular sermons Gerson repeatedly addresses the admittedly speculative question of the nature of Adam before the Fall.[10] There he argues, in a mood which is distinctively Augustinian, that Adam in accord with his natural capacities had »original justice« in his prelapsarian state, but that he

---

[9] Oberman infers on the basis of thematic parallels that such a position reflects the perspective of a »Parisian syncretistic school,« one which aligns Gregory of Rimini with the young Henry Totting of Oyta, Hugolin of Orvieto, et al. See *Harvest*, pp. 204–205, n. 50. He also criticizes Zumkeller's conclusion that the thematic emphasis upon the insufficiency of human works was broadly heard in the preaching of the later Middle Ages; on this point cf. Zumkeller, »Das Ungenügen der menschlichen Werke bei den deutschen Predigern des Spätmittelalters,« pp. 265 ff., and Oberman's critical review in *Harvest*, pp. 181–82, n. 112. Bouwsma offers an explanation for this phenomenon which he also observes in agreement with Zumkeller, identifying the ascendance of Augustinianism during this period as an adequate response to the »terrible anxieties of a life in which the familiar conventions of a close and traditional human community had given way to a relentless struggle for survival in a totally unpredictable and threatening world.« See »Two Faces of Humanism,« p. 17. On the basis of *De consolatione theologiae*, we should now recognize that Gerson's mature thought aligns him with this Augustinian tradition, viewed in soteriological terms; indeed, Bouwsma's analysis that the uncertainties of the later Middle Ages produced a climate hospitable to a severe Augustinian response would help explain this shift in Gerson's thought. For a more detailed explanation of this point, see also below, 6.B.

[10] For a similar conclusion see Brown, *Pastor and Laity*, p. 96.

forfeited that condition because of original sin. And this act of forfeiture became an inheritance by which humankind as a whole — i. e., *pour toute leur ligne* — became enslaved to *tribulacion* and *desolacion* and fell »from riches into poverty, from nobility into meanness, from life into mortality ... and, in short, from all good into all adversity.«[11] This observation regarding *tentationes* or *tribulacions*, a theme central to his preaching by which he delineates the precarious nature of the human condition, is not then merely the result of his long experiences as an astute pastor engaged in the care of souls. This is true, as far as it goes, but such a conclusion views the matter only in terms of present experience. In a deeper sense, and one which Gerson considered not merely theological but indeed historical, these *tentationes* are the consequence of Adam's Fall; this »original sin« bequeaths these to all *viatores* as the inevitable condition of life.[12] The trials and tribulations of life are therefore a sign of the fall and the inescapable lot of every *viator*.

In *De consolatione theologiae* Gerson does not deviate from this path, though his emphasis of the effects of the Fall in this later treatise determines in a more pessimistic (Augustinian) vein the broader shape of his soteriology. He defines Adam with Pauline terminology which he had not used earlier, describing him as *praevaricator* who has handed all *viatores* over »to the condemnation of death.«[13] This language, which recalls Paul's formulation in Rom. 5.12 ff. in

---

[11] *La mendicité spirituelle*; G 7, p. 221: »Trop male fut l'eure quant le premier pere commit envers Dieu, le souverain roy, tele traison, tel crime de lese maiesté que tout nostre heritage fut fourfait et osté, et que du lieu de plaisance, de joye et d'excellence fumes dechassiés en ce lieu de pleur, de tribulacion d'angoisses et de desolacion, de richesse en povreté, de noblesse en vilté, de vie en mortalité, de lieu seur en lieu hors de toute seurté, et a brief dire de tout bien en toute maleurté.« In a later context Gerson addressed this theme in similar terms: »Vray est que nos premiers parens, Adam et Eue, qui a ceste fin d'auoir paradix furent noblement crees, cloirent par leur pechiez de desobeyssance l'antrée de paradis a tout l'umain lignage car ilz pardirent et forfirent comme traitres le don lequel ilz avoyent receu par maniere de heritage pour eulx et pour toute leur lignié, lequel don se nommoit justice originele, qui estoit une grace par laquelle s'elle n'eust esté pardue nous eussions esté sans quielconquez payne ou misere en ce monde.« See also his *Le miroir de l'âme*; G 7, p. 194.

[12] For this reason we cannot accept Brown's dismissive interpretation of these *tribulacions* as »largely metaphor,« since this underestimates the significance these played in Gerson's soteriology more generally. His anatomy of the Fall interprets all human experience not merely in metaphoric terms, nor as a »mood« of »sombre melancholy,« to recall Huizinga's portrait of the age. Rather Gerson viewed *tribulationes* with theological precision as the inevitable effect of the *traison* committed against God by *le premier père*. On this point see Brown, *Pastor and Laity*, p. 97. These are, in other words, the »signs« of the Fall and hence the marks which remind us of our incapacity to overcome this condition *ex puris naturalibus*; or, as he later remarks in *De consolatione theologiae*, our salvation depends upon moving *supra vires et merita*, since these cannot lead us to God. Gerson in this late treatise goes so far as to interpret *tentationes* as »willed« by God to drive *viatores* from confidence in their own abilities: »Vult [i. e., Deus] autem viatores homines tribulationibus multis exerceri«; G 9, p. 205.

[13] G 9, p. 190. The phrase he here uses, *mortis damnatio*, apparently signifies more than

its Vulgate rendering, repeats what he had earlier affirmed: that Adam's sin of disobedience destroyed »original justice« for the »entire human lineage,« forfeiting this heritage of goodness for »all manner of misery.«[14] But here he demonstrates in contrast to his earlier writings a reluctance to press this question in a more optimistic direction, avoiding altogether the question whether *viatores* still have a natural inclination to virtue. Gerson now speaks not of the human ability to accomplish works of congruous merit, but of our complete incapacity to loose ourselves from sin; describing our condition as »like that of a serpent weakened or debilitated by paralysis,« he here characterizes our natural efforts in exceedingly bleak terms as »dragged down« by »the heavy weight of the original tinder [*gravi fomitis originalis*], the heavier weight of actual sin [*graviori peccati actualis*], and the heaviest weight of persistent habit [*gravissimo inveteratae consuetudinis*].«[15] The effect of Adam's sin (*fomes originalis*) and its consequence (*mortis damnatio*) dismantles the human incapacity to do any meritorious works; in this weakened condition salvation depends upon »God's only-begotten Son,« »the sacrament of reconciliation« which is *supra naturae vires et merita*. Gerson has retreated, apparently, from the more optimistic Ockhamist soteriology with its doctrine of merit (i. e., *facere quod in se est*), setting forth in its place an argument more consistent with an Augustinian view of the human condition, perhaps as mediated by Thomas Aquinas's reserved approach to this question.[16] All *viatores* are handed over by

---

the mortality of the human condition, since Gerson is here relying upon the Pauline language of Rom. 5.12−21. Rather, this death signifies the complete condemnation of humanity *per unum* (i. e., Adam), which is only to be overcome *per unius obeditionem* (i. e., of Jesus Christ, whom Gerson here calls *sacramentum reconciliationis*). This is an important parallelism in his thought, as we shall later see, since he delineates this Pauline emphasis upon the »first« Adam (the fall) and the »second« Adam (reconciliation) in terms of the restoration of *obedience*. See also below, 5.D.2.

[14] Alongside this theme it is interesting to note that here as in his earlier writing (cf. *De vita spirituali animae*, G 3, pp. 116 f.) we still see vestiges of the Thomistic theme of »diminution,« applied in terms of epistemology but *not* soteriology − i. e., Gerson is reluctant to concede that *viatores* have completely lost not the natural knowledge of God but the natural desire for that knowledge which carried over from their prelapsarian condition. That is, we note that Gerson again echoes Aquinas in describing the fallen human condition as one of »weakened« vision, even to the point of borrowing his (Aristotelian) metaphor of the »owl« whose »weak and darkened eyes« cause it to sink in »thicker darkness . . . before the brilliant light of the sun.« G 9, p. 206; cf. also Aquinas, *Summa theologiae* Ia q. 1, a. 5, ad 2, and a related use of the light/dark imagery in Boethius, *De consolatione philosophiae* V pr. 2, *CCSL* 94:90. Gerson speaks of our quest, like that of the owl's, *ad nitidissimam solis lucem*; Aquinas simply says *ad lumen solis*, but the verbal parallels are otherwise striking.

[15] Gerson's use of the phrase *fomes originalis* is a variation of the more familiar *fomes peccati*, the »tinder of sin« which is the punishment (*poena*) imposed by God because of original sin.

[16] Cf. *Summa theologiae* IaIIae q. 85 aa. 2−4. As Aquinas here argued, »as a result of original justice, the reason had perfect hold over the lower parts of the soul, while reason

Adam to the *mortis damnatio*, and in this act they forfeit »original justice« and their natural »strengths« and »merits« are rendered ineffective; they were part of the *massa peccati*, and consequently stand condemned to death with all other *viatores*.[17] This is an anthropological model, therefore, which moves away from that of the Ockhamist appropriation of the Franciscan *facere quod in se est* doctrine, shaped rather by the skepticism of a traditional Augustinian soteriology.[18]

---

itself was perfected by God and was subject to him. Now this same original justice was forfeited through the sin of our first parent . . . so that all the powers of the soul are left, as it were, destitute of their proper order, whereby they are naturally directed to virtue, which destitution is called a wounding of nature.« For Aquinas as for Gerson in this later treatise, the wound runs so deep that one cannot do any meritious acts *ex puris naturalibus*. Later in the *Summa theologiae* Aquinas returns to this theme, arguing that the *facere quod in se est* teaching must be understood as identifying the human ability to do what is in one's power »according as one is moved by God.« *Summa theologiae* IaIIae, q. 109, a. 6, resp., ad 2. Gerson agrees with this Thomist (and Augustinian) emphasis, which affirms the necessity of grace preceding any meritorious act, yet without denying that *viatores* can accomplish acts which are morally good; Gerson did not go to this extreme, as had Gregory of Rimini before him. But he did insist in good Augustinian style, and in striking agreement with Aquinas, that whatever good one had done could not be attributed as a meritorious human achievement, but was rather something one had necessarily received »freely from God«: »Quod si voluerit gloriari de bonis suis, mendax est si non habet; si habet, illa gratis accepit a Deo.« G 9, p. 198. This is the single instance in this treatise where Gerson utilizes language which approaches the *acceptatio Dei* argument, a thematic emphasis which dominated the Franciscan theological tradition; in *De consolatione theologiae*, however, Gerson does not use this argument as had Duns Scotus, since he insists unlike Scotus that acts could be good without ever becoming meritorious. This argument thus appears to stand as a criticism of the more extreme Augustinian position advocated by Gregory of Rimini et al.

[17] G 9, pp. 198−99. As he here concludes, *viatores* are »ex eadem peccati massa . . . , quales venerat salvare Deus.« *Ibid.*, p. 199.

[18] Here we must acknowledge once again that epithets such as »Augustinian« become during this period elusive and perhaps finally too diffuse to suggest more than a general theological orientation. Recognizing this difficulty, it appears that Gerson's *via media* steers between the two extreme uses of Augustine during the later Middle Ages: the search for »an Augustine who could once more inspire and legitimate a synthesis of Christianity with classical thought,« on the one side, and a severe application of the Augustinian doctrine of grace by theologians seeking to counteract »what they believed to be the virulent Pelagianism . . . of their own time,« at the other (Pelikan, *Reformation*, pp. 17−20). It is within the scope of this »middle ground,« with its eclectic use of Augustine, that we speak of Gerson's »Augustinianism«: on the one hand, he draws upon the Augustinian view of grace in crafting a soteriology which accents human dependence in the absence of meritorious acts upon divine grace; on the other, he insists − with echoes to the terminology of Aquinas − that grace is not hostile to but rather »perfects« nature, that there is a »legitimate synthesis« of reason and revelation. Thus, while one might justifiably say that the later Gerson leans toward the »right« side of the theological spectrum of those drawing upon Augustine, particularly by invoking an Augustinian view of sin and grace, he should not be placed within an Augustinian »school«; even in his later treatises, including *De consolatione theologiae*, he rejected the extremes to which he viewed Gregory of Rimini

2. *Ab horto voluptatis*: the limits of human nature

But is this Thomistic qualification of the *viator*'s potential *coram Deo* — this retreat from the *facere quod in se est* — the last word Gerson offers on the subject? At least in his earlier works he had mitigated this view to avoid an extreme Augustinianism, not only in order to carve out a legitimate role for good works which benefit others but in terms of the Ockhamist view of meritorious works accomplished by »doing our best« (i. e., *facere quod in se est*) — the »natural« merit (*meritum de congruo*) on the basis of which one receives an infusion of justifying grace (*meritum de condigno*). Previous studies of Gerson, drawing upon the chancellor's earlier university writings, have characterized his thought in these terms, positioning him within the Ockhamist tradition as a theologian at the midpoint of a trajectory from Ockham to Gabriel Biel.[19] On the basis of his earlier treatises this remains an accurate assessment.[20] Gerson had concluded, for example, that it was »impossible« for a person to work his salvation solely by natural acts, since such a proposition would be sheer Pelagianism; nonetheless, he »did not wish to deny that the human spirit is able

---

as having fallen. McGrath has recently identified a *schola Augustiniana moderna* during this period, in contrast to the older *schola Aegidiana*; he associates Gregory of Rimini, Hugolin of Orvieto, and, eventually, Martin Luther with the former. Cf. *Iustitia Dei*, pp. 174—79. Our analysis of Gerson suggests that the chancellor at least leans heavily toward this tradition in his later works, and thus might be called Augustinian in terms of broad emphases; he certainly did not see himself, nor should we portray him, as part of a narrower Augustinian »school.« Yet we might well speak of his »mediating« soteriology as bearing distinctively Augustinian tendencies, in the sense in which McGrath has used this term: viz., to refer to those who retained »the *dogmatic content*, if not the *conceptual forms*, of Augustine's theology.« *Ibid.*, p. 175.

[19] Thus, for example, Oberman, in *Harvest*, pp. 206—207; distinguishing Gerson from »the defenders of Augustine's understanding of predestination,« Oberman describes »his *main* theme« as »the call for repentance and genuine love for God with the encouragement that God has committed himself to infuse his grace in those who do their very best,« here citing a cluster of early treatises which do indeed articulate this theme in straightforward fashion. In his study devoted primarily to Gerson's university career leading up to Constance, Burger also follows this lead, citing a similar textual base for his conclusion that, although Gerson considers the effects of Adam's sin, »er hält es für unbedenklich, dem Menschen zuzutrauen, sich durch Handlungen moralischer Qualität auf den Empfang der Gnade vorzubereiten«; *Aedificatio*, p. 59. Brown argues in a similar vein, again in terms of the same early texts, that Gerson »follows Occam's assertion that men, by doing their natural moral best, without the infusion of grace can merit *de congruo*, not salvation, but the grace necessary for salvation«; *Pastor and Laity*, p. 101.

[20] Thus, for example, Gerson addressed this theme with persistence and penetration in *De vita spirituali, aegritudine et morte animae* (G 3, pp. 113 f., 117—18), concluding in this early work (ca. 1402) that good acts, while not meriting us eternal life in themselves, nonetheless are morally good and elicit temporal merit, and are consequently »ad gratiam de congruo praeparatorii quia per eos homo facit quod in se est; nam facere quod in se est hoc intelligo facere quod homo potest secundum vires quas actualiter habet.«

of its own natural life to do morally good acts — viz., by doing what lies within us [*facere quod in se est*] and thus disposing ourselves to the life of grace. «[21] This passage from *De vita spirituali* is one of the significant instances in which Gerson speaks directly and forcefully to this theme. Yet all of these occur in his writings predating Constance, and it is worth noting that recent interpreters locating Gerson within the Ockhamist tradition have based this conclusion on these early texts.[22] This Ockhamist doctrine (i. e., *facere quod in se est*) thus served the younger Gerson as the functional basis of his soteriology. It is worth noting that historians following Auer's lead have repeatedly ascribed the use of this doctrine, which sanctioned natural acts as meritorious, as evidence of a *pastoral* concern: i. e., this thematic emphasis underscores what it is that *viatores* can do of their own nature (*ex puris naturalibus*) in accomplishing the first steps of their justification before God.[23] This is certainly an accurate portrayal, if by »pastoral« one understands a message which underscores the role of human responsibility and thus affords *viatores* a role in initiating their own justification, a synergistic approach to soteriology which lends itself to preaching in the hortatory voice.[24]

---

[21] *Ibid.*

[22] Thus, Oberman, *Harvest*, p. 206, n. 52; apparently, Oberman has in mind Gerson's admission that while he did not wish to articulate a Pelagian position in which the *viator* accomplished his own salvation (*operari salutem suam*) through purely natural acts, he also did not wish to negate altogether the worthiness of human acts, at least as »preparations« for the infusion of grace: »Nolo tamen negare quin anima possit ex sua vita naturali bene moraliter agere et, faciendo quod in se est, se ad vitam gratiae disponere.« Burger cites the same text (*Aedificatio*, p. 57, n. 85), correctly observing however that here »die Lehre des Pelagius ist vergröbernd unterschätzt« (*ibid.*, p. 57); Burger also astutely draws attention to the polemic argument this perspective levelled against the austere soteriology of Gregory of Rimini. Finally, see Brown, *Pastor and Laity*, p. 101, for a similar use of the same Gerson text.

[23] These views have echoed, with varying emphases, Johann Auer's conclusion that this nominalist soteriology was prompted by pastoral concerns: »Es war das religiöse und vielleicht seelsorgliche Bedürfnis, aus der Güte Gottes die Möglichkeit einer wirksamen Vorbereitung auf die Gnade zu erweisen.« *Die Entwicklung der Gnadenlehre in der Hochscholastik*, Vol. 2: *Das Wirken der Gnade* (Freiburg i. B., 1951), p. 85. For more recent expressions of this thesis, see also Oberman, »Wir sein pettler. Hoc est verum: Bund und Gnade in der Theologie des Mittelalters und Reformation,« *Zeitschrift für Kirchengeschichte* 78 (1967), pp. 256–57 and *idem*, »Duns Scotus, Nominalism, and the Council of Trent,« in *John Duns Scotus, 1265–1965*, ed. J. K. Ryan, B. M. Bonansea (Washington, DC, 1965), pp. 323 f., reprinted in *Dawn*, pp. 212–13; Douglass, *Justification in Late Medieval Preaching*, p. 161; and, most recently, Brown, *Pastor and Laity*, p. 101.

[24] On this interpretation, see Oberman, »The Shape of Late Medieval Thought: The Birthpangs of the Modern Era,« reprinted in *Dawn*, p. 29: »Nominalism did call traditional truths and answers into question in order to replace them with a new vision of the relationship between the sacred and the secular by presenting coordination as an alternative to subordination and partnership of persons instead of the hierarchy of being.« In her study of Geiler, Douglass speaks of his »sense of pastoral responsibility for his hearers,« a

But this does not represent the »whole« Gerson. In his later writings, and
above all in *De consolatione theologiae*, we find no trace of this theme, an
omission which he reinforces through his vigorous assertation that God not
only allows but actually wills *tentationes* in order to bring *viatores* to the point of
desperation.[25] This theological shift requires at the very least that we now
revise our estimate of Gerson's soteriology. More than this, such a dramatic
change calls for a reassessment of our understanding of the pastoral logic of his
approach: Gerson's abandonment of the *facere quod in se est* doctrine, based on a
fundamentally different soteriology, is the result of a quite altered understanding of the human predicament itself. As such his pastoral concern expresses
itself with cadences which stand in contrast to his earlier Ockhamist approach:
Gerson here opposed the legitimacy of any meritorious accomplishments
which would dispose us for grace or prepare us for consolation, basing the hope
of salvation not on human acts but on »God alone« as known in Christ, the
»sacrament of reconciliation.« It would appear, then, that we have identified
something more than a shift of emphasis in the later Gerson. Here we come
upon a thoroughly revised soteriology of Augustinian character, one which
leads him to articulate a pastoral strategy of fundamentally altered structure and
mood from that based upon his earlier Ockhamist convictions.

This suggestion of a deliberate soteriological shift — with an attendant shift
in pastoral strategy — in Gerson's later thought is strengthened by a revealing
passage late in this treatise where Gerson returns to the subject which occupied
his attention in the early chapters of the work: namely, the *tentationes*. »You are
subjected to tribulation and trial, but this is the common lot of every living
person,« he warns, adding a string of biblical laments which affirm that
»human beings are born to labor« and that »the present life is by no means [*nullo
pacto*] without tribulation, because it is warfare« (cf. Job 5.7, 7.1). Thus far we
hear nothing more than a repetition of themes presented earlier in the treatise,
themes which link Gerson with a broad tradition in the later Middle Ages of
rhetoric which emphasized human unworthiness in the presence of the divine
iustitia.[26] But at this point Gerson shifts his perspective away from experience
toward the broader theological horizon, recounting what he interprets as the
biblical rationale for such matters: »Believe me,« he concludes, »God did not
eject humankind from the garden of delight [*ab horto voluptatis*] in order that we
might build for ourselves a new one here, but so that we might live in labor

---

commitment which »leads [Geiler] back to an emphasis on man's own responsibility to do
what is in his power before he can expect God to help him.« *Justification in Late Medieval
Preaching*, p. 161.

[25] See, for example, G 9, p. 205.

[26] Zumkeller notes this persistent use of Job by German preaching of this period; see his
»Das Ungenügen der menschlichen Werke,« esp. pp. 265—68, 301 ff. Douglass questions
Zumkeller's thesis by noting that such rhetoric is not unique but is part of »a common
medieval teaching«; *Justification in Late Medieval Preaching*, p. 177.

and hardship.«[27] Not only does he view Adam as *praevaricator* through whom death has entered the human race, but he insists that our ejection from »the garden« means that there is no shortcut back to the state of original bliss, nor should *viatores* expect to move toward God — or, as he phrases it here in graphic terms, to »build for ourselves a new garden« here — through any form of human acts, least of all meritorious works which would bolster our confidence. Tribulation serves as a warning and constant reminder not to rely upon our own effort, showing *viatores* that the way to peace is »through the affliction of the world.«[28] »Whom should we beseech?« he asks, responding forcefully, »Deus unicus!« God alone: Gerson insists here upon a severely limited approach to the human potential *coram judice Deo* since all we can do amid life's tribulations is despair in ourselves, a conclusion which renders more faithfully an authentic Augustinianism than the synergism of the Ockhamist position. No recourse remains for returning »to the garden,« or for a retrieval of the optimistic language of human merit expressed in terms of »doing one's best« (i. e., *facere quod in se est*). On the contrary, it would appear that Gerson has abandoned these themes altogether, turning away from what has often been described as the pastorally motivated soteriology of late-medieval Ockhamism.

But has Gerson abandoned a »pastoral« approach in favor of what has been called a »confessional« theology which devoted its attention almost entirely to the radical implications of divine grace vis-à-vis human acts?[29] We have already suggested that such a characterization does not hold in terms of Gerson's later thought; he refuses to choose between a confessional and a pastoral theology. Let us pose the question from another angle: How are we to evaluate the pastoral intentions of Gerson in the midst of this soteriological shift in his thought, particularly since this shift signifies a deliberately critical revision of the human involvement in justification? It appears, though firm conclusions must await the more detailed analysis provided later in this chapter, that the manner in which Gerson here understands his pastoral office has changed at this later juncture of his life, not as an attempt to follow the *schola Augustiniana moderna* in order to accentuate a vigorously anti-Pelagian position. In fact this doctrinal shift does set forth the basic shape of Gerson's mediating soteriology, but doctrinal concerns do not apparently establish the cause for this revision in the first instance; he remains conspicuously silent regarding the termi-

---

[27] G 9, p. 227. Here I intentionally translate *homines* as »humankind,« yet utilize pronoun references in the first person plural form, since this carries the direct force of Gerson's language and intent.

[28] *Ibid.*

[29] This is the terminology introduced by Oberman, *Forerunners of the Reformation: The Shape of Late-Medieval Thought Illustrated by Key Documents* (Philadelphia, 1966), pp. 128–29, and subsequently used by Oakley, *The Western Church*, pp. 135–37.

nologically precise scholastic debates on points of doctrine.[30] This shift seems
rather to reflect Gerson's revised estimate of the human predicament, a view
which he probably fashioned in direct response to the general turbulence of his
day and, more specifically, the challenge which Hus's anthropology of the
»elect« had brought to bear on his own earlier thought. In other words, Gerson's preference for a more thorough-going Augustinianism may reflect what
Bouwsma has identified as a broad phenomenon during this period, a development of one of the »faces« of humanism which provided a suitable response to
the »terrible anxieties« of the age, »the relentless struggle for survival in a totally unpredictable and threatening world.«[31] This concrete historical context,
in quite specific detail, would explain Gerson's thorough-going reluctance in
the face of *tentationes* to place any confidence in human effort, a pessimistic
stance which approximates d'Ailly's critical response during the trial to Hus's
attitude toward human virtue. Citing 1 Jn. 1.8 in attacking Hus's ecclesiology
− »If we say that we have no sin, we deceive ourselves« − d'Ailly added his
own severe interpretation of the text by asserting that »thus we must ever act
wickedly.«[32] In a similar mood Gerson addressed *viator* by insisting that »I
want you to despair in yourself,« adding in support of this stark claim the
words of Jeremiah: »For cursed is the one who confides in himself.«[33] It would
appear, then, that the concrete circumstances emerging from the Hussite
threat, rather than any abstract doctrinal considerations pointed against an encroaching Pelagianism, provoked Gerson's shift in soteriology and pastoral
strategy at this juncture.

Throughout *De consolatione theologiae*, as we earlier suggested, Gerson has
pressed beyond the late-medieval sacramental system and has abandoned the

---

[30] Even in the midst of his most optimistic affirmations of the human role in »disposing«
ourselves (i. e., *faciendo quod in se est*) to receive the »life of grace,« Gerson insisted that this
was only a preparation for grace and not its achievement (»ad gratiam de congruo
praeparatorii quia per eos homo facit quod in se est«; G 3, p. 117); he further qualified this
claim by noting that one could not »naturally« work one's own salvation, since asserting
the opposite of this was »the Pelagian error« (*ibid.*, p. 116). In other words, Gerson at least
felt that his affirmation of human acts by which we are »disposed« to grace was not liable
of Pelagianizing tendencies; if he had changed his mind on so fundamental an issue it seems
likely that he would have noted this explicitly.

[31] Cf. »The Two Faces of Humanism,« p. 17. On the matter of Hus's position, cf. his *De
ecclesia*, ch. 21, which Peter Mladoňovice includes in his account of the trial at Constance
(thesis 22); cf. *Hus at the Council*, pp. 197 f. It is quite suggestive that d'Ailly's response to
Hus's view, which we shall examine in considerable detail later in this study, anticipates
Gerson's view here in its basic outline: d'Ailly also emphasized, against Hus's insistence that
virtue should delineate who the elect were, that all *viatores* sin. D'Ailly insisted that one
could not delineate the church, against Hus's presumption, as the »pure.« See also Spinka,
John Hus, pp. 265 f.

[32] *Ibid.*

[33] G 9, p. 199.

corresponding Ockhamist theme of the »congruous« merit of human acts (i. e., *merita de congruo*), and this for two reasons. First, he contends that meritorious works cannot free *viatores* of the deep anxiety over their soul, and that the persistent and inevitable *tentationes* lead to a spiral of despair. And, second, he insists that as a consequence »true« consolation depends upon becoming more rather than less scrupulous in condemning one's own effort in this regard. Gerson does not conclude that *viatores* must therefore simply resign themselves to an ignorant and desperate resignation in which one hoped for some miraculous intervention of God. But not so obvious is how his restructured soteriology might yet support a pastoral strategy, particularly in the absence of the Ockhamist *facere quod in se est* doctrine. At this juncture we can only raise this as an issue requiring our attention, since we must first penetrate more deeply into Gerson's soteriological model from the »other« side as it were: namely, from the perspective of God's role in salvation. In other words, we must here consider, borrowing Oberman's useful terminology once again, what this shift away from »coordination« – at least as defined and applied by Ockhamist theologians of this period – implies for Gerson's soteriology, and whether Gerson has rejected altogether or merely reconstituted the nominalist »partnership of persons« by which *viatores* meet God as »contractual partners« in the context of the covenant of grace.[34]

B. Divine election *ab aeterno* as the foundation of soteriology

The foundation for Gerson's doctrine of salvation in *De consolatione theologiae*, and at the same time the theological basis upon which he grounds his anthropology, is his advocacy of divine election *ab aeterno*. This is an important connection to be made, since the shift we have seen in his anthropology by which he severely limits the effectiveness of human achievements *ex puris naturalibus* is part of a broader development, if not transformation, of his soteriology. The doctrine of election emerges here as the focal point of his pastoral argument, replacing the *facere quod in se est* doctrine together with its covenantal model juxtaposing »congruous« merits and divine »acceptation.« In its place he now emphasizes God's unmerited election »from eternity.« In a decidedly different vein than in his earlier writings, he here builds his soteriology in conjunction with an Augustinian anthropology, concluding that »God has predestined and elected from eternity some out of pure generosity and grace [*pura liberalitate et gratia*].«[35] Indeed, he goes so far as to argue that »of

---

[34] See Oberman, »The Shape of Late Medieval Thought: The Birthpangs of the Modern Era,« in *Dawn*, pp. 27, 29.

[35] G 9, p. 196.

all Paul's arguments, his consideration of divine predestination and fore-knowledge functions as *the central and supreme hinge.*«[36]

But what does Gerson understand to be Paul's view of predestination, and how does he interpret this as a »hinge« argument? A statement of such deliberate force demands a closer and more precise examination, particularly since this theme provides the fulcrum for Gerson's soteriological *via media*; his emphasis upon election *ab aeterno* as the hinge of his own soteriology reorients Gerson's pastoral message in this treatise along a new axis altogether. He here replaces his admonition in earlier treatises − i. e., to »do one's best,« trusting that God would answer persons thus disposed by infusing »first grace« − with a message of an altogether different shape: he now consoles *viatores* by instructing them not to »do« anything, but rather to despair in their own efforts in order that theology might lead them »per summam desperationem de homine . . . ad summam de Deo spem.« Indeed, he accentuates this theme by insisting that God wills *viatores* to despair through »many tribulations,« since such true desperation *de homine* provides the foundation for true hope *de Deo.*[37] This is more than a change in mood; it represents nothing less than a fundamental groundshift for Gerson's soteriology, both in terms of the doctrinal framework of his thought and in terms of the manner in which he applies that structure to address pastoral concerns.

1. *Praedestinatio ante praevisa merita*: a shift to the »right«

In our introductory remarks to this chapter we noted that Gerson constructs his soteriology upon an Augustinian foundation, though it would be more precise to say that he like Augustine roots this doctrine in the Pauline language of justification − above all by blending the Psalmist's emphasis upon God's *iustitia* with Paul's insistence on our utter dependence upon God. In a lengthy discussion of election *ab aeterno* in the opening book (I pr. 2−3), Gerson gathers together a catena of such citations, including Paul's metaphoric account of the potter and the clay (Rom. 9.20−21) − which he now interprets, against his own earlier Ockhamist perspective, in the style of Bradwardine and the »right-wing nominalism« of a more radical Augustinianism.[38] By abandoning his

---

[36] G 9, p. 191 (my emphasis).

[37] G 9, p. 205.

[38] Once again I borrow this terminology from Oberman (cf. *Harvest*, pp. 204−205), though qualifying Gerson's position as a »tendency« rather than strict allegiance to a school tradition; as we have earlier noted, Gerson resisted the severe formulations of Gregory of Rimini who has been characterized as an extreme representative of this tradition. As here noted we find Gerson using Paul's metaphor of the potter and clay as had Bradwardine before him − i. e., without the qualifying gloss which Holcot had added. This text poses a revealing test case because it emerges consistently in the discussion of divine election and

earlier reliance upon the nominalist doctrine of congruous merits, in other words, Gerson also relinquishes his earlier view of election for which the divine covenant with *viatores* called for a view of predestination *post praevisa merita*. Such confidence in a »contract« of works as *merita de congruo* disappears altogether from Gerson's theological vocabulary, and he now leans toward what has been called a »confessional« theology with its emphasis upon God's unconditional or unmerited grace.[39] In short, Gerson here reverses the soteriological approach he had earlier followed, embracing an Augustinian view of predestination *ante praevisa merita*.[40]

---

human merit, having been vigorously and variously interpreted by both »right-wing« and »left-wing« nominalists to argue diametrically opposing points of view. Bradwardine used it in a fairly straightforward manner, interpreting it in order to lay down one of the foundational planks in his anti-Pelagian platform (cf. *The Cause of God against the Pelagians*, in *Forerunners*, ed. Oberman, p. 162; *De causa Dei*, ed. H. Savile, I.47, p. 440–41); Holcot, on the contrary, cites the passage in its Old Testament form (cf. Jer. 18.6) but glosses it quite painstakingly to make the opposite point: in contrast to Bradwardine, he disputes its force as a valid analogy by arguing that no covenant existed between potter and clay such as binds *viatores* to God. Hence, according to Holcot's exegesis this text was incapable of negating the question whether God was »required to give grace to one who prepares for its reception,« since »although we are like clay in comparison to God, one cannot by any means apply the analogy in every respect to man.« »Nor is the analogy totally correct,« Holcot continues, »because there is no covenant between the potter and the clay; and even assuming that there could be such a covenant, the potter could very well break it without abrogating the covenant law. But God cannot break his pact with man without the covenant being destroyed.« Cf. Holcot's *Lectures on the Wisdom of Solomon*, in *Forerunners*, ed. Oberman, pp. 148 ff. It is clear that Gerson here follows Bradwardine's »right-wing nominalist« use of this text, in the process turning against the Ockhamist qualifications imposed by Holcot and »left-wing nominalism«; this provides a striking instance of Gerson's preference for a soteriology which tended toward a more severe Augustinianism.

[39] This terminology of »confessional« theology, useful in signifying the overall emphasis of a particular doctrinal perspective, is borrowed from Oberman, *Forerunners*, pp. 128 ff. We shall qualify the rigid contrast he here suggests, however, since his discussion sets a »confessional« over against a »pastoral« theology as contrasting paradigms; in Gerson's »mediating« theology, at least, we come upon an effort to combine the two, a feat he accomplishes by pointing not to a covenant of meritorious works but to the covenant of those who seek God (i. e., as based on Heb. 11.6). This new model of a covenant of »seeking« safeguards the divine priority of election (or, God's freedom vis-à-vis the contingent order of creation) *and* human freedom, though it divorces that freedom from a concern with moral works or »congruous« merit. This particular development of Gerson's thought qualifies the otherwise suggestive analysis of Brown: although she notices Gerson's altered approach to predestination in the later works, she does not recognize the critical point that Gerson has retreated from any confidence in »moral efforts« without sacrificing an emphasis upon the *viator*'s free will. Cf. Brown, *Pastor and Laity*, p. 115; see also below, 5.C.

[40] In Oberman's analysis of Gerson in *Harvest*, he had assumed apparently on the basis of the chancellor's earlier works that Gerson advocated *predestinatio post praevisa merita*; *ibid.*, pp. 204–205. This is no small point of interpretation, since it is one of the key themes upon which Oberman builds his view of a moderate nominalist »school« in the later Middle Ages

This thematic shift signals Gerson's realignment of his theology not only within the general horizon of an Augustinian perspective, but within the more specific parameters of the Scotist approach to predestination. This development, which lies at the very heart of Gerson's theological approach in this treatise, thus suggests a decisive revision of his earlier Ockhamist soteriology.[41] In the Scotist vein he argues, varying the doctrinal accents found

---

as a tradition which refused to follow an Augustinian lead and chose rather to articulate a »moral or pastoral« theology with its emphasis upon human merit. This is also the doctrine prompting Oberman's characterization of Ockhamist theology (which he characterizes as the »main current« of nominalism) as at least semi-Pelagian; see *Harvest*, p. 426. In other words, Gerson in his later works retreated from the supposedly semi-Pelagian Ockhamist tradition in his approach to justification. Nor should we assume that Gerson would have been content any longer with an emphasis upon »the dignity of man«; his later variation of the nominalist anthropology in terms of a more severe or pessimistic Augustinian model moved away from this position. As we have earlier suggested, this shift may be the doctrinal basis for his opposition to the Hussite perspective, and as such represent a further outgrowth of his consistent identification of pride as the greatest human vice. This context might finally be the determining factor which led to his formulation of this mediating soteriology, particularly in terms of his opposition to any positive evaluation of human effort. As we shall subsequently point out in greater detail, Gerson's mediating contribution to the ongoing consideration of justification attempted to bridge the abyss which divided theological discussion during the early fifteenth century, a chasm which polarized a predominantly »confessional« theology (right-wing nominalism) which emphasized God's unmerited act of election from what has been called a »pastoral« theology (left-wing nominalism) with its positive accent upon the human contribution in justification.

[41] In his early study devoted to *Die Prädestinationslehre des Duns Skotus im Zusammenhang der scholastischen Lehrentwicklung* (Göttingen, 1954), Wolfhart Pannenberg recognized the fact that both d'Ailly and his »student« Gerson followed the Scotist doctrine of predestination; *ibid.*, pp. 145 ff. Curiously, this interpretation does not emerge in recent studies of nominalism or of Gerson's thought (e. g., those of Oberman, Ozment, Burger, and, most recently, Brown; Hamm in his *Promissio* acknowledges Pannenberg's work, and follows it quite closely in his discussion of the nominalist trajectory, but he remains silent on Gerson). Pannenberg's interpretation of Gerson, as suggestive as it is in broad terms, is not fully correct in detail; for instance, he mistakenly concludes – pointing, interestingly enough, to a text from *De consolatione theologiae* (I pr. 3; G 9, p. 194) – that Gerson articulated this doctrine with a »deterministic« accent, and hence distanced himself from Duns Scotus' doctrinal formulation of predestination: »Johannes Gerson, der Schüler Aillys, scheint ebenfalls die skotische Lehre vertreten zu haben, wenn auch mit deterministischen Akzent.« Pannenberg, *Die Prädestinationslehre*, p. 147. Yet he rightly concludes, apparently recognizing that this »accent« does not run deep in Gerson's thought, that »im Sinne Gregors [von Rimini] scheint mir Gerson nicht gedeutet werden zu dürfen, weil er in starker Betonung des freien Willens jeden Determinismus ablehnt, der jenen gefährden könnte.« *Ibid.*, p. 147, n. 32. This is an astute observation, even if it stands as an unsubstantiated and finally mistaken interpretation of the *later* Gerson. In other words, Pannenberg fails – and in this has the company of most modern readers of Gerson – to recognize the soteriology which Gerson developed after Constance as a deliberate *via media*, a »mediating« approach which harmonizes the freedom of the human will with God's sovereignty. This is a critical point for our appreciation of the broader context in which

in his earlier writings, that God's act of electing is an »uncaused« and »eternal« decision, since God »is debtor to no one« and »the eternal will of God has no prior cause.«[42] Predestination, in other words, cannot be caused in any sense; on the contrary, God »has from eternity predestined and elected some [for beatitude], out of pure generosity and grace.«[43] Indeed, he cleverly inverts the

---

Gerson articulates this »Vermittlungstheologie«: his position follows in structure at least that of Scotus, about whom Pannenberg rightly concludes that »Erst wenn man das Dilemma zwischen Determinismus [i. e., seines Gottesbegriffs] und Synergismus als *innerhalb der scholastischen Diskussion des Prädestinationsproblems* unentrinnbar erkennt, wird man die Größe der geistigen Leistung des Duns Skotus darin würdigen können, dass er sich diesem Zwang nicht unterworfen hat« (*ibid.*, pp. 118 f.). In *De consolatione theologiae* Gerson follows this interpretation of Scotus quite closely. Furthermore, Pannenberg is certainly correct in noting this as an »inescapable« dilemma faced by late-medieval theologians, particularly given their stubborn tendency to interpret the doctrine of justification as a corrolate to predestination, and hence to place it within the doctrine of God rather than the doctrine of grace. But is this dilemma »eine vollständige Disjunktion,« as Pannenberg argues, or might we also see in Gerson's peculiar soteriology a more successful attempt at maintaining the tension of this dilemma though within a quite different approach to the human side of the equation than Scotus had offered? It is this question which apparently drives Gerson's thought in this treatise, and this problematic which identifies the larger systematic significance of his soteriology. For as we shall here suggest Gerson attempts to maintain the necessary tension of this theological dilemma but without interpreting this as a disjunction; he accomplishes this feat, unlike the *doctor subtilis*, by abandoning the categories of created grace and sacramental habit. In this manner his soteriology is neither fully »deterministic« nor is it »synergistic,« and even while he joined Scotus in opposing both of these doctrinal solutions, he did this by constructing a »Vermittlungstheologie,« a mediating »theology of seeking« which brought together both divine sovereignty and human initiative on the basis of the divine covenant of Heb. 11.6.

[42] G 9, pp. 193–94. This theme of the uncaused nature of God's acts, which has been rightly identified as one of the qualifying theses of Ockham's soteriology, underscores the unconditional nature of God's freedom and power in its absolute potential (i. e., *de potentia Dei absoluta*). Theologians following Ockham's lead offered this argument – viz. *Deus nulli debitor est* – as a soteriological safeguard *de potentia Dei absoluta* against the suspicion of Pelagianizing tendencies; normally, however, they admitted that God *de potentia sua ordinata* did bind himself to a covenant of grace. The positive side of this assertion was the theme of the *acceptatio Dei*: that is, God chooses to establish and honor his covenantal promises according to his ordained power, and this »acceptation« is finally what assures *viatores* that their good works are indeed also meritorious works. On Scotus' position see Otto Pesch and Albrecht Peters, *Einführung in die Lehre von Gnade und Rechtfertigung* (Darmstadt, 1981), p. 112 ff. Pesch argues here that Scotus' foundational argument that *nihil creatum formaliter est a Deo acceptandum* – which anticipates Ockham's *Deus nulli debitor est* and apparently influenced Gerson's claim here – elicits the »controlling characteristic« of the late-scholastic doctrine of God: namely, the divine freedom. *Ibid.*, p. 113. Gerson follows Scotus quite carefully on this point, though his position stood over against the Ockhamist conceptualization of predestination as foreknowledge; this contrast reminds us that the Scotist emphasis upon God's freedom could be quite variously applied in terms of the doctrine of the *acceptatio Dei*, depending upon how theologians related this »acceptance« to human merit – i. e., either as *ante* or as *post praevisa merita*.

[43] G 9, p. 196: »jungit quod ad illam pura liberalitate et gratia Deus ab aeterno quosdam

Pauline claim regarding election — »if by grace, then not by works« (Rom.
11.6) — to argue that not only is election unrelated to our own works, but it is
not dependent upon »the merits and works of those whom God has predestined
from all eternity, because if it were because of works, [salvation] would not be
by grace.«[44] Salvation by grace and not by works: the parallel to Scotus'
vigorous outcry against any synergism which would bind God in an absolute
sense, either through our own (congruous) merits or through the intercession
of the saints' merits, is unmistakable.[45] Yet in this opposition we must note that
Gerson refuses to follow Scotus in interpreting human acts as in any sense
meritorious, here approaching justification not following scholastic teaching as
a protracted process involving habits or acts of merit but in terms of the
mystics' awareness of »a personal encounter of the individual with God.«[46]
Does this formulation betray the lingering influence of his view of *theologia
mystica*, with its apprehension of an immediate encounter with God? This
seems a likely suggestion, though it must remain an hypothesis at this juncture.
It is at least now clear, however, that Gerson's revised Scotist doctrine of
predestination provides the basis for his eclectic and apparently unprecedented
view of justification, posing yet another solution to what has been aptly called
»a general disquiet« concerning the theological foundations of created grace.[47]

---

praedestinat et eligit. « This is a peculiarly eclectic argument, since Gerson here draws upon
the nominalist argument regarding God's *liberalitas*, which was characteristically applied to
the *acceptatio Dei* of meritorious acts, but aligns this rather with God's »acceptation« in
election — i. e., *ab aeterno* and hence in terms of *praedestinatio ante praevisa merita*. With this
alteration, therefore, he moves beyond even Scotus' soteriological formulation, as we shall
later consider in more careful detail, since Gerson left no room for meritorious human acts.
Concerning the doctrine of grace, one might say that Gerson adds a more severe
Augustinian accent to his soteriology than had Scotus.

[44] G 9, p. 194; later in this passage Gerson adds that »no one will be condemned without
fault, just as no one will be saved without grace,« an argument meant to counter a view of
»double election« (contra Gregory of Rimini) which Gerson did not embrace.

[45] As suggested above (see n. 42) Scotus had argued that »nihil creatum est a deo
acceptandum,« a theme which would later become an almost programmatic facet of
Ockham's thought: e. g., he argued that »nullum temporale est causa alicuius aeterni« (I
Sent. d. 41, q. 1 [L]), and in a similar vein »Deus nihil agit ad extra ex necessitate« (*Quod.* VI,
q. 2; IV, q. 32); these texts are cited in Hamm, *Promissio*, p. 376, and in E. Hochstetter,
»*Viator mundi*: Einige Bemerkungen zur Situation des Menschen bei Wilhelm von
Ockham,« *Franziskanische Studien*, 32 (1950), p. 19. In Gregory of Rimini's thought we see
this same principle used for a very different purpose: namely, to support his thorough-
going determinism; see Werner Dettloff, *Die Entwicklung der Akzeptations- und
Verdienstlehre*, pp. 318—19; Hamm, *Promissio*, p. 358; Pannenberg, *Die Prädestinationslehre*,
p. 143.

[46] See McGrath, *Justification*, pp. 153—54. It is this theme which represents a broadened
interpretation of mysticism, if we might still call it that, in Gerson's thought, since *viatores*
are justified *coram judice Deo* by a »translation« or imputation of the *iustitia Dei*; see below,
5.C.3—4.

[47] *Ibid.*, p. 154; see also Hamm, *Promissio*, p. 360 ff., for a discussion of the gradual

2. Behind Scotus:
A theological variant of Boethius' view of providence

As we examine Gerson's doctrine of providence in this treatise, we find that although his view approximates Scotus' position outlined above, its deeper grounding is to be located in terms of Boethius' general formulation in *De consolatione philosophiae*. Gerson's emphasis upon divine freedom, unlike Scotus', did not rest upon an *acceptatio* doctrine, at least not in the developed form which the Subtle Doctor had fashioned in order to »neutralize« any potential Pelagianism or safeguard what might otherwise appear as an at least semi-Pelagian synergism.[48] And, as we have already suggested, while Gerson's formulation follows Scotus in opposing both a bare determinism and an undifferentiated synergism, he offers his *via media* for apparently differing reasons. Demonstrating less concern than had the Subtle Doctor with the doctrinal difficulties raised by a synergistic formulation,[49] Gerson's view of providence shows a more vigorous and self-conscious concern to displace the pastoral argument of nominalist teaching which Scotus also maintained: the admonition to »do one's best« in order that *viatores* might dispose themselves in anticipation of either an infusion of »first« grace (following Holcot and so-called »left-wing nominalists«) or the divine acceptation (Scotus). Hence,

---

disappearance of the language of the »habit« of grace during the later Middle Ages. McGrath suggests that the central thrust of later medieval theories of justification moved away from created grace toward »the uncreated grace of the Holy Spirit« (see *Iustitia Dei*, pp. 145–54); it appears, however, that while Gerson's thought reflects this general movement, he is not willing to ascribe uncreated grace to the Holy Spirit in specific, as had Peter Lombard before him, but attributes it more generally to the direct encounter of God and man as witnessed in the biblical promises of hope. *Iustitia*, as we shall later see, presents according to Gerson the pivotal focus of justification in Christological rather than sacramental terms.

[48] Cf. Oberman, *Forerunners*, p. 130. In Hamm's analysis of the nominalism of Ockham and Biel he emphasizes more strongly than had Oberman the force exerted by the Scotist theme of *acceptatio Dei*: »Doch erst dort, wo die ontologische Relevanz des Gnadenhabitus zurücktritt, rückt die freie Selbstbindung Gottes *in das Zentrum* der Lehre von Rechtfertigung und Erlösung. Sie ist die Klammer, die Freiheit Gottes und Freiheit des Menschen zusammenhält und so vor einem beziehungslosen Nebeneinander bewahrt.« *Promissio*, p. 367 (my emphasis). With this conclusion Hamm follows Pannenberg's thesis, portraying Scotus' approach in contrast to that of Anselm before him as moving »aus einer Dimension metaphysischer Gesetzmäßigkeiten in die Dimension personaler Entscheidung.« Cf. Pannenberg, *Die Prädestinationslehre*, p. 137, and Hamm, *Promissio*, p. 359.

[49] For Scotus, the *acceptatio* theme functioned as the safeguard against a blatant synergism, and thus served as a defense against the accusation of Pelagianism; Hamm thus speaks of »die antipelagianische Spitze der Prädestinationslehre« (see *Promissio*, p. 358), while Oberman talks about Scotus' *acceptatio* doctrine, the mainspring of his teaching on predestination, as »the insuperable wall of defense against the inroads of Pelagianism« (see *Harvest*, p. 213).

Gerson argued that salvation could not be by works — not even by works of congruous merit — and was necessarily by grace alone,[50] leaving no room for synergism of the nominalist variety by which salvation (*de potentia Dei ordinata*) would be both »by grace« and »by works.«[51] Gerson's articulation of a Scotist perspective on predestination *ante praevisa merita* yet parts paths with *doctor subtilis* by refusing to maintain a positive evaluation of human effort in soteriology. He has here abandoned altogether a covenant of human works *and* divine grace beneath the canopy of *praedestinatio post praevisa merita*.

Neither does Gerson collapse *praedestinatio* into *praescientia*, and thereby minimize the force of election, in the manner of both Ockhamists and so-called »left-wing« nominalists.[52] He does speak of God's »foreknowledge« of every link in the chain of causation, since »nothing is done in the world which God has not foreseen from eternity [*ab aeterno praeviderit*],« and he even prefaces his earlier discussion of election by referring to it as »a reflection on divine predestination or foreknowledge.«[53] But Gerson's use of this language reflects Paul's conviction that »quos praescivit, et praedestinavit« (Rom. 8.29), echoing and probably directly borrowing the terminological equation from the *Liber soliloquiorum animae ad Deum*.[54] With Boethius before him, and in a manner and

---

[50] Thus, he argued early in this treatise that »absque gratia salvabitur nullus,« an argument which admittedly of itself was an entirely uncontroverted doctrinal claim; this would have been accepted as a general truth by both the accused and accusers in the late-medieval debate on Pelagianism. But Gerson appends to this affirmation his view of human acts as worthy only of desperation, and hence as in no sense consolatory as meritorious *de congruo*. Cf. G 9, p. 194.

[51] Cf. Oberman's description of Biel's doctrine of justification, which he assumes stands in line with Gerson; he contends that nominalists such as Biel held a »remarkable« doctrine of justification, because when »seen from different vantage points, justification is [for Biel] at once *sola gratia* and *solis operibus*!« *Harvest*, p. 176. His emphasis upon Biel's synergism is well intended, though Biel himself would not have agreed with the emphasis of »by works *alone*«; such a formulation ignores Biel's concern to counter a view of justification which would conceive of these as falling outside what has been called the »dome« of grace according to God's ordained power. In other words, while Biel (along with the younger Gerson) insisted that such works were free and unassisted by grace, they were meritorious only under the covenant which God freely established within time (i. e., *de potentia ordinata*; *ibid.*, pp. 186, 214). At this late juncture of his thought, Gerson turns away from his earlier Ockhamist position, here refuting *any* efficacy of works in the process of justification; the force of his advocacy of *praedestinatio ante praevisa merita*, in other words, preempted any role for human works, even those occurring under the »dome« of God's covenantal relationship with *viatores*.

[52] Oberman has rightly pointed to this tendency, by which »predestination« is preserved as a doctrinal emphasis while diluting its function by interpreting it as foreknowledge; see *Dawn*, p. 107; *Harvest*, pp. 189 ff.

[53] Cf. G 9, pp. 212, 194. In this particular passage, however, Gerson is contrasting divine and human knowledge, and not attempting to define predestination itself.

[54] In this treatise, now attributed to Ps.-Augustine, we find a chapter entitled »De praedestinationis ac praescientiae Dei mysterio,« a passage which appears for circumstantial

mood distinct from Scotus, Gerson's discussion of election carefully contrasts *providentia* and *praevidentia*: while God certainly »foreknew . . . the entire series of causes, even the smallest,« predestination represents a more ambitious intervention, since God »predestined« and »chose« »out of pure generosity and grace« and not simply by foreknowing the outcome of human acts.[55] The *praedestinatio* of the »elect« was a fact accomplished by God *ab aeterno*, and hence entirely unconditioned by meritorious works or created (sacramental) habits of grace. In this manner Gerson approaches the basic logic of Scotus' position on predestination (*ante praevisa merita*) yet without mimicing the exact structure of the Scotist soteriology, perhaps because his view of providence actually owes more to the overarching Boethian argument than to Scotus directly.[56] In order to consider this issue more carefully, we must inquire about the broader theological framework which Gerson builds upon this foundational theme of predestination.

In examining this point we must ask whether Gerson advocates election *ab aeterno* in such a manner that predestination brings with it a rigid determinism of human acts. Does he, in other words, follow the severe Augustinian line of Gregory of Rimini which by emphasizing the priority of God's election largely dismantles the meritorious significance of free human acts? That this is not the case should come as no surprise to us, since the integrity of Gerson's soteriological *via media* depended upon avoiding not only Cicero's denial of providence in order to establish human liberty, but the extreme view of a theologian identified only as »another« (Gregory of Rimini?) who »so wished to establish divine providence that he imposed necessity upon our power of choice. «[57] In short, Gerson here steers a mediating course in theological terms

---

reasons to represent a likely influence upon this argument of Gerson's: this text anticipates the general shape and mood of Gerson's argument on this point, and it is one which he cites explicitly earlier in this treatise. On this last point see G 9, pp. 199–200; the text in question is to be found in PL 40: 884 (c. 25).

[55] G 9, p. 196. At the same time, we must note that Gerson steered clear of any doctrine of »double« predestination such as Gregory of Rimini had proposed; with Scotus he argues here that God »predestined« only the elect, while the reprobate he »foreknew«: »Recogitat ne supremum Judicem Deum homines ex massa peccatrice praedestinasse quidem hos ab aeterno sempiternae beatitudinis fore participes; alios vero praescitos et reprobatos, ad supplicium perpetuum. « G 9, p. 193. On Rimini's position see Oberman, *Harvest*, p. 205; Leff, *Gregory of Rimini* (Manchester, 1961), pp. 196–204.

[56] The proximity of Gerson's soteriology with Scotus' should not lead us to call him a »Scotist« in any significant sense, since he remained consistently hostile throughout his career to those whom he disparagingly called *formalizantes*. On this point, see Kaluza, *Le querelles doctrinales*, pp. 35 ff., 61–65. The parallels of Gerson's approach to *praedestinatio* with that of Scotus finally suggest a coincidental proximity, not a philosophical or metaphysical »conversion. «

[57] G 9, p. 200. This allusion may refer to Seneca, as expounded by Augustine in *De civitate Dei* V.8, a reference brought to my attention by Prof. Lee Miller. This suggestion gains credibility in that Gerson cites this position alongside the single reference to Cicero

much as Boethius had done in *De consolatione philosophiae* in terms of the philosophical spectrum: i. e., a *via media* which would avoid any view (such as Cicero's) which discounted divine providence, at one extreme, while also resisting, at the other, a fatalism which left no integrity for free human acts. Gerson's *via media et regia* is, therefore, best understood as a theological expression of the Boethian view, a moderating position which harmonized providence and human freedom and in this important sense moves beyond — or we might more aptly say »behind« — Duns Scotus' unresolved attempt to find a »unified solution« to the dilemma of determinism and synergism.[58] It is not unimportant that at this juncture of his argument Gerson admits that his *via media* will not resolve all difficulties of the argument, but ought to be followed »even where the full solution of a contrary argument is not yet clear.«[59]

3. *Via media* as a synthesis of »confessional« and »pastoral« concerns

With this said, we begin to sense that labelling Gerson as an Ockhamist does not yet account for the distinct theological shift in his later thought. Indeed, this ascription simply fails to provide an accurate account of the soteriology which Gerson articulates in the wake of Constance, one which he establishes in proximity to the Scotist doctrine of predestination. Neither is he a Scotist in any pure sense, as we have argued, since Gerson leaves no room for human works of merit, or a »created habit,« in the process of justification, as had the Subtle Doctor.[60] That is, his theological *via media*, based in its essential

---

in the text, and he might well be considering further parallels from classical sources. Yet it may at the same time refer to (or, at least, echo) the more recent position argued by Gregory of Rimini, which included a defense of »double predestination,« particularly since his concern here settles upon the theological rather than philosophical argument; for a discussion of Gregory's position, see Oberman, *Harvest*, pp. 196 ff.

[58] This is the language by which Pannenberg describes the »breakthrough« he perceives in Scotus' predestination doctrine; see *Die Prädestinationslehre*, p. 118. In an apt survey of the theological world which succeeded Scotus, Pannenberg concludes that »die Spaltung der nominalistischen Schule des 14. Jahrhunderts über der Prädestinationsfrage muß als ein Zurückfallen hinter den bei Duns Skotus schon erreichten Grad der Klärung dieses Problems angesehen werden. Die von Skotus als falsch erkannte Antithese zwischen Determinismus und Synergismus trat wieder hervor.« Yet as we have suggested — and now argue with detailed reference to Gerson's thought in *De consolatione theologiae* — this conclusion simply does not hold for the later Gerson, even though Pannenberg is certainly correct in citing both d'Ailly and Gerson — at least, in his later writings — as theologians adhering to the Scotist doctrine of predestination. *Ibid.*, pp. 144–45; see also above, n. 41.

[59] G 9, p. 200.

[60] Duns Scotus had, of course, introduced this dimension under the »dome,« to recall Oberman's language, of the divine ordination; it functioned within the context of what McGrath has usefully called »the concept of covenantal causality« on which the created habit of the *viator* was not to be understood as necessary in any autonomous sense, but

structure upon Boethius' overarching approach to providence and human freedom, limits the human contribution to salvation through espousing a view reminiscent of the Scotist doctrine of predestination. This is the »confessional« side of his soteriology, an apologetic defense for the priority of God's act in saving the elect.[61] But Gerson's argument does not drive this point so hard that it excluded any contribution of the *viator* to the process of salvation, even though he did avoid emphasizing human acts of merit.[62] What, then, was this contribution, and how did Gerson thereby restructure his soteriology by means of a »covenantal causality,« a contractual arrangement (*de potentia Dei ordinata*) by which he varied the Ockhamist reliance upon meritorious acts (*de congruo*)? What, in other words, is the pastoral strategy Gerson here pursues in the absence of the *facere quod in se est* doctrine?

This is the point where Gerson proves himself not merely an eclectic thinker, which is only to say the obvious without penetrating the complexity of his thought, but a constructive theologian of the first rank. By articulating an Augustinian emphasis of election *ab aeterno*, but without referring to congruous works of merit, Gerson accomplishes what had eluded Scotus and had generally appeared to nominalist theologians of the later fourteenth and early fifteenth centuries as a logical contradiction: he adapted the Scotistic emphasis upon the freedom and priority of God's election to a reconstructed version of the Ockhamist view of the human participation in salvation, while dismissing altogether the language of human merit.[63] No longer does Gerson speak of the

---

functioned in a thoroughly contingent« manner in a »secondary and derivative role« in justification. See McGrath, *Iustitia Dei*, pp. 148–49; see also above, n. 56.

[61] This terminology derives, as earlier noted, from Oberman's discussion of »justification«; cf. *Forerunners*, pp. 128ff., where he speaks of a »confessional theology« in contrast to a »moral or pastoral theology« with a distinctively »missionary« emphasis.

[62] In this movement of thought, we see that Gerson strikes out in exactly the opposite direction later followed by Biel: whereas Biel rejected Scotus' doctrine of predestination while emphasizing his doctrine of merit *de congruo* (see Oberman, *Forerunners*, p. 130), Gerson here maintains Scotus' doctrine of predestination while dismissing his emphasis upon human merit. This distinction places their soteriologies in categorically different horizons.

[63] That is, he has taken over the bare structure of the Ockhamist synergism, while refuting entirely the moral dimension of the *facere quod in se est* doctrine. In this particular sense Gerson transcends the dichotomy posed by Oberman between Scotistic and nominalistic doctrines of justification; cf. *Dawn*, p. 107: »The independence of the nominalistic theologians vis-à-vis Duns Scotus and his disciples comes through most clearly in their rejection of the scotistic doctrine of the *praedestinatio ante praevisa merita*, according to which the predestination of the elect in God's eternal council precedes the foreseen good works of the elect. This doctrine is rejected by the nominalists – with the notable exception of Gregory of Rimini – and transformed into a doctrine of *praescientia*, the doctrine of the foreknowledge of God of the future behavior of both the elect and the damned.« On the basis of *De consolatione theologiae*, we must now revise this sweeping thesis, as helpful as it is in providing a general orientation to other nominalists – including the younger Gerson – of this period. Gerson stands quite surprisingly with Gregory of

facere quod in se est doctrine, as he had in his earlier writings. In its place we find him relying upon a biblical covenant which holds in careful balance the strictly theological and pastoral arguments he here advances, a covenant by which he merges what otherwise would appear as either sheer determinism (a severe Augustinian approach to predestination) or synergism (a synergistic semi-Pelagian emphasis upon meritorious acts wrought *ex puris naturalibus*): namely, the biblical argument of Heb. 11.6, that »God rewards those who seek him. «[64]

This peculiar covenantal affirmation establishes the fulcrum of Gerson's soteriology, serving as the pivotal theme by which he articulates his *via media* in order to mediate supposedly discrete »confessional« and »pastoral« emphases.[65] In so doing Gerson constructs a covenantal soteriology which is sui generis, clearly moving beyond the Ockhamist construct that emphasized the moral acts of the *viator*'s preparation for infused grace, while maintaining at least the functional structure of this synergism in terms of a »disposition« for grace. The key point by which Gerson advanced the discussion has to do with how he conceived of this disposition: not as human acts of achievement which earn *merita de congruo* but as the posture of seeking God in the midst of moral failure and consequent despair. This is the newly conceived pastoral dimension of Gerson's soteriology, and this establishes the structural dynamic of his covenantal *via media*. As a mediating soteriology, his emphasis upon the divine reward given »to the one seeking« (*inquirentibus*) rather than »to the one doing« (*facientibus*) established a pastoral theology in a new key, one which complemented his emphasis upon *desperatio*: nothing we »do« could make us worthy of God's acceptance, but the very act of abandoning all presumption in human

---

Rimini in arguing for a Scotist doctrine of predestination. But it is important to note that Gerson moves beyond Scotus in terms of the doctrine of merit and its corollary doctrine of *acceptatio Dei*, on the one hand, and transcends Gregory's determinism on the other. He steers this *via media* on the basis of what he conceived as the biblical covenant of Heb. 11.6, with its definition of the covenant of seeking by which God »rewards those who seek him.« In this manner he nonetheless follows Scotus in attempting to reconcile the generally antagonistic positions of determinism and synergism within the doctrine of soteriology. See also above, n. 57.

[64] This theme Gerson introduces early in the treatise (I pr. 2), and he repeats it at key points later in the first book (e. g., I pr. 4); this is not an accidental placing, since this opening section deals with the theme of the consolation offered by theology through contemplation of the divine judgment: *coram judice Deo* we are only able to »seek« God rather than to attempt to »do« morally good acts of congruous merit.

[65] For a general discussion of these varying theological approaches, see Oakley, *The Western Church*, pp. 136–37. What is striking about Gerson's mediating formulation of the doctrine of soteriology is that he accentuated what Oakley has here called »the providential role of divine grace« (i. e., the leading theme of »confessional« theologies of the period) through his doctrine of predestination, without obliterating human freedom and responsibility (the central thrust of the »pastoral« theology as advanced by »left-wing« nominalists).

achievement and seeking God carries the promise of hope via the assurance of divine reward. As we have suggested, this promise is the »inner« side of a biblical covenant which functions for Gerson as the unifying bridge between the apparent polarities of divine sovereignty and human freedom. We shall return to this crucial theme in the following section of this chapter as we turn to examine the »outer« side of this covenant: namely, the initiative of seeking God (Heb. 11.6) by which *viatores* themselves steer a middle road between the pride of accomplishment and the despair of resignation.

C. Pastoral theology in a new key:
The *viator's* role as seeker

Gerson's *via media* presents, as we have seen, a mediating position between the soteriologies of what have been called »left-« and »right-wing« nominalists. His peculiar covenantal model balances an emphasis upon divine predestination without reference to moral acts (i. e., *ante praevisa merita*) with an incentive for human initiative rooted in the biblical covenant of seeking which he discerned in Heb. 11.6. By articulating a theology − at once »pastoral« and »confessional« − not dependent upon meritious acts but rather upon a mystical quest for God, Gerson advances a moderating soteriology which steers between an unbridled determinism at one extreme and a synergism based upon moral effort at the other. Both, he suggests, would lead to intractable desperation: the former by dismantling all human initiative *coram Deo* (»Could any effort be effective?«) and the latter by promoting a devastating scrupulosity (»Could any effort be enough?«). And, as we have suggested, this mediating soteriology merges what has been characterized as a »confessional« theology with its Scotist emphasis upon God's unprecedented and unsolicited act of election *ab aeterno*[66] together with a variation of the *facientibus quod in se est*

---

[66] In the process Gerson demonstrates a vigorous effort to bolster the priority and unconditional nature of divine predestination, arguing once again with Scotus for a doctrine of single predestination *ab aeterno* whereby God had predestined the elect while the reprobate − contra Gregory of Rimini − were only »foreknown« as such. Cf. G 9, p. 193: »Recogitat ne supremum judicem Deum homines ex massa peccatrice praedestinasse quidem hos ab aeterno sempiternae beatitudinis fore participes, alios vero praescotis et reprobatos, ad supplicium perpetuum?« To this question, posed by the skeptical voice of Monicus, Volucer responds, »Recogitat, Monice, et id sane frequenter.« And, at a pivotal juncture of his discussion Gerson explicitly cites Ockham's variation upon this Scotist theme, guarding not against Pelagianism − or, at least, not explicitly − but against »any blasphemy toward God«: »God . . . is debtor to no one,« he concludes with the Venerable Inceptor. He adds to this claim that God »shows no partiality« in election, a reference to Rom. 2.11 which Ockham had used in the same passage; cf. I *Sent.* d. 41, q. 1 (H). Hochstetter also cites the central force of this passage; cf. »Nominalismus?«, *Franciscan Studies* 9 (1949), p. 17.

doctrine (i. e., *inquirentibus . . .*). His soteriology thus mediates between the extremes of both »right-« and »left-wing« nominalism, yet his *via media* also offers a revisionist version of what has been called the pastoral basis of Ockhamism.

In this regard we must again pose the question raised earlier in this chapter. Is Gerson's theology based upon a strict doctrine of justification *sola gratia*, or does it with the Ockhamist soteriology also carve out room for works — albeit the work not of moral initiative but that of seeking God under the »dome« (Oberman) or »canopy« (Oakley) of God's ordained order? »Nulla tibi superest fiducia de propriis operibus«: Gerson quite deliberately opposes any form of trust in one's own accomplishments; salvation is »not by works,« since these inevitably lead to desperation in one's abilities *coram judice Deo*.[67] But the broader structure of the Ockhamist soteriology apparently remains intact: that is, what Gerson takes away through his suspicion of moral works he replaces with a covenant of seeking. Hence, the shift in the pastoral basis of Gerson's soteriology from *facientibus* to *inquirentibus* is extremely significant, since this conceptualization of the biblical covenant by which *viatores* become contractual partners with God[68] both avoids absolute resignation while also preempting the pride falling upon those who trust in their own works as effecting salvation. Justification is »by grace alone« and not strictly speaking by works, though the biblical covenant of Heb. 11.6 calls *viatores* to the »work« of seeking God and trusting in divine rather than human *iustitia*. That is, while Gerson's soteriology does in nominalist fashion identify God as the »covenant God,«[69] we here find a quite distinctive »theology of seeking« rather than one which emphasized the »doing« of works leading to congruous merit. In coordination with his negative emphasis upon the despair into which human effort casts us (i. e., through *tribulationes* and *tentationes*), the act of seeking God becomes the positive fulcrum on which his mediating theology finally swings. This constructive model of the covenant, therefore, establishes the »middle way« between an emphasis upon sheer determinism and unaided human freedom.[70]

---

[67] G 9, p. 199. We should also note that here Gerson moves decisively beyond Boethius, since although he had criticized *philosophia* in this treatise as being unable to discern God's judgments and thereby direct us to act properly *coram judice Deo*, our salvation finally has nothing whatsoever to do with human acts, since these lead only to an ineradicable despair.

[68] Again, cf. Oberman, »The Shape of Late Medieval Thought,« in *Dawn*, p. 29: »In the nominalist view man has become the appointed representative and partner of God responsible for his own life, society and world, on the basis and within the limits of the treaty or ›pactum‹ stipulated by God.«

[69] On this point, see *ibid.*; cf. also Hamm, *Promissio*, p. 375 ff.

[70] Elsewhere in this treatise Gerson offers an explicit argument in favor of *liberum arbitrium*, one which qualifies freedom as human acts initiated within the realm of divine grace: »Neque tamen ita sunt accipienda, quae dicta sunt, quasi tollatur libertas arbitrii; fortificatur siquidem magis et instituitur, sed in Deo vivificante per gratiam, quae est velut

It now remains for us to explore how Gerson conceives the human predicament in terms of the initiative by which *viatores* seek God, and how he envisioned this peculiar contract which we have called a »theology of seeking« — in short, how he conceptualized »pastoral theology« in a new key.

1. Incorporation in Christ *per fidem*

In a striking passage early in *De consolatione theologiae* Gerson establishes faith as the operative concept — or what has been called the »Klammer,« or brackets[71] — by which divine and human freedom are held together, thereby distancing his soteriology from the *acceptatio Dei* doctrine which for Scotus had served this purpose. This distinctive emphasis demands a more detailed analysis, since Gerson utilizes it to link Christology not to the outward structure of divine acceptation but to the *viator*'s subjective response to Christ *per fidem*. Gerson held that the faith by which *viatores* seek God is not simply dependent upon the abstract nature of the divine covenant as revealed in scripture, even though it is also certainly this. Rather, this faith has Christ as its object, and Christ according to Gerson — and not the *viator*'s faith itself — is the vehicle of »sufficient« grace, the mediator between God and humanity (i. e., *mediator Dei et hominum*). His Christology thus serves as the doctrinal context within which *viatores* seek after God; Christology functions as the specific doctrinal safeguard protecting human seeking from becoming itself a meritorious work.

The passage to which we have referred occurs within Gerson's discussion of »the divine judgments,« and more specifically in a passage earlier examined in which he discusses in detail the theme of election (i. e., I pr. 4). Having argued that predestination and election occur »from eternity« and according to the »pure generosity and grace« of God, an argument which renders the essential components of the Scotist emphasis upon the *acceptatio Dei*, Gerson bends this theme in an eccentric direction. He argues that although God has ordained »fitting means without number« (*media convenientia variis modis sine numero*) for acquiring the »beatitude« that God's acceptance promises, »principal among these means is grace« itself:

This grace, however, is given and will be given to no one, except by means of the mediator between God and man [i. e., Jesus Christ], since [Christ] has merited this grace in

---

anima quaedam vitam habens in potentia ad vitam secundam, ad meritoriam videlicet operationem.« G 9, p. 200. This is one of the few passages in this treatise in which Gerson broaches the subject of merit, yet even here he clearly brackets any concept of merit within the arena of works »vivified« by grace — much in the manner of Aquinas, as earlier suggested. Human freedom is not so much inoperative as ineffective outside this realm; within it, however, *liberum arbitrium* is »strengthened the more« and »established,« an argument which bears the marks of an anti-Pelagian safeguard.

[71] See Hamm, *Promissio*, p. 367.

sufficient measure for all; but this [grace] is not efficacious unless one is incorporated in Christ through habitual faith [*per fidem habitualem*], as in the case of children, or through both habitual and actual faith which through works of love acts with perseverance.[72]

In other words, Gerson avoids any discussion of the sacraments and created habits of grace, that doctrinal complex which has aptly been described as »the natural setting of justification«;[73] rather he chooses to speak of Christ (»the means [*medium*] of the mediator«) as the »sufficient« and faith as the »effective« cause of salvation. Turning first to his Christological emphasis, we find that the resonance with Aquinas's formulation is striking: it is in this theological context that we must read Gerson's deliberate explanation of the significance of Christ's mediation as the »sufficient« cause of grace.[74]

Yet he makes one crucial modification of Aquinas's explanation of the »twofold« nature of efficient grace, an alteration which brings us to the second operational definition in this passage of how God mediates grace. On this point Gerson discloses the functional logic of his eclectic soteriology: he here contrasts the »various modes« — apparently referring to the sacraments[75] — by

---

[72] G 9, pp. 196–97; the first biblical allusion in this passage — viz. *per medium mediatoris Dei et hominum* — probably echoes 1 Tim. 2.5. The second reference, »per fidem ... vel actualem et habitualem quae per dilectionem perseveranter operatur« (a close variant of Gal. 5.6, »fides quae per charitatem operatur«), is of greater interest to this discussion. This assertion suggests that by »actual« faith Gerson is here referring to the medieval concept of *fides formata*, or faith which is formed by works of love. Cf. for example Lombard, *Collectanea*, PL 191: 1367C, as cited in Froehlich, »Justification Language in the Middle Ages,« in *Justification by Faith. Lutherans and Catholics in Dialogue VII*, ed. H. G. Anderson, T. A. Murphy, J. A. Burgess (Minneapolis, 1985), p. 152. See also Aquinas, *Summa theologiae* IIaIIae q. 4 a. 3. It was a doctrinal commonplace that the traditional Augustinian emphasis upon perseverance should occur at this juncture, an argument which both Lombard and Aquinas — and, on their authority, a broad group of later medieval theologians — also utilized.

[73] Oberman, *Harvest*, p. 189. This is another instance of a trend during this period which McGrath has characterized as »a general disquiet concerning the theological foundations of created grace«; see *Iustitia Dei*, p. 154, and above, p. 231, n. 39.

[74] Cf. for example, *Summa theologiae* IIIa q. 61 a. 1: »We must say ... that an efficient cause is twofold, principal and instrumental. The principal cause works by the power of its form, to which form the effect is likened; just as fire by its own heat makes something hot. In this way none but God can cause grace . . .. But the instrumental cause works not by the power of its form, but only by the motion whereby it is moved by the principal agent, so that the effect is not likened to the instrument but to the principal agent.« And, later in the same question, Aquinas continues: »Now an instrument is twofold; the one, separate, as a stick, for instance; the other, united, as a hand. Moreover, the separate instrument is moved by means of the united instrument, as a stick by the hand. Now the principal efficient cause of grace is God himself, in comparison with whom Christ's humanity is as a united instrument, whereas the sacrament is as a separate instrument.« *Ibid.*, a. 5.

[75] We should note that Gerson is not intent on speaking only of the sacraments, since he speaks of these *media* as *sine numero*; to make sense of this reference at a period when the »means« of grace were already established in terms of the seven sacraments, we must apparently understand this reference as pointing to the sacraments, of course, but also to

which *viatores* attain beatitude with the »principal means« (grace), thereby restating the Thomist view of the instrumental character of the sacraments which convey grace deriving from Christ. But he goes further than this, identifying not the sacraments as the instrumental cause of grace by means of which we are »incorporated« with Christ, but rather *faith* itself: »per fidem . . . actualem et habitualem« is this grace »efficacious« for us. This is an important variation of the Ockhamist doctrine of justification, both because Gerson avoids reference to the sacraments and because he replaces an emphasis upon meritorious works with an emphasis upon faith. By faith *viatores* seek God, and not by works; by faith *viatores* fulfill the biblical mandate of Heb. 11.6 to seek God, and yet it is Christ rather than faith itself which is the »sufficient« cause of the grace promised in this covenant. Gerson thus circumscribes the means of approach to God within a Christological matrix; in this sense his »theology of seeking« depends fundamentally upon grace given *per Christum*, grace which we appropriate instrumentally *per fidem*. This formulation leaves intact Gerson's emphasis upon *desperatio* as a discouragement to resort to a covenant of works, even the »work« of faith. And, as an added safeguard against any Pelagianizing claim of »natural« access to grace, he echoes the Augustinian insistence that even the knowledge of whom *viatores* must implore in order to receive such grace is *donum Dei*.[76] In this sense, although Gerson points to the covenantal language of Heb. 11.6 with particular force, he places his understanding of seeking God underneath the canopy of predestination once again, since we are able to seek God only on the basis of the divine gift (i. e., *de potentia Dei ordinata*). The initiative, in other words, lies first of all not on the side of the *viator* but with God. Yet while this qualifies it does not abrogate his emphasis upon human initiative: the seeker's response to Christ *per fidem* is itself a divine gift.[77]

---

those »innumerable« means by which we could possibly receive grace, depending upon the exercise of God's absolute power. The sacraments in general, and the eucharist in particular, functioned as an example through which Ockham and later nominalists identified the »absolute power« of God. Gerson articulates this theme with similar emphasis in this treatise; see G 9, p. 205.

[76] G 9, p. 200. Cf. for example, Augustine, *De praedest. sanct.* 3.7 (*PL* 44:964). To look to more immediate instances of this argument, we might also cite Gregory of Rimini's doctrine of *auxilium speciale* as well as Aquinas's discussion of the *initium fidei*, particularly as articulated in *Summa theologiae* (e. g., IIaIIae q. 6, a. 1) and his later writings. Thus, Aquinas concludes that »Per hoc autem excluditur error Pelagianorum, qui dicebant quod initium fidei in nobis non erat a Deo, sed a nobis.« See *Summa contra Gentiles* III, c.152 ed. C. Pera, D. Marc, D. Caramello (Rome, 1961), 2:227. For a clear summary of this theme in its medieval development, see Froehlich, »Justification Language,« pp. 150–53. Also, with regard to Gregory of Rimini, see C. Burger, »Der Augustinschüler gegen die modernen Pelagianer. Das ›auxilium speciale dei‹ in der Gnadenlehre Gregors von Rimini,« in *Gregor von Rimini. Werk und Wirkung bis zur Reformation*, ed. H. Oberman (Berlin, 1981), pp. 195–240.

[77] In this formulation we find something of the paradox earlier expressed on this theme

It is significant that Gerson here avoids both an excessively introspective (subjective) grasp of faith as well as one which would interpret the reception of grace principally in (objective) terms of the church's sacramental life. Christ stands as the »mediator« of grace, while faith in Christ is the means or instrumental cause of that grace. That is, the *viator* is incorporated *per fidem* not in the church but *in Christ himself*, a theme bearing overtones to his *theologia mystica*; Gerson thus anchors his doctrine of justification not in an ecclesiological setting via the doctrine of the sacraments, but in Christology.[78] This emphasis buttresses his identification of faith rather than works as the means of access to grace. His covenant of seeking as we have called it finds its focus not in terms of the subjective act of believing nor in terms of the objective reception of the sacraments, but in terms of Christ as the *medium* of grace. Thus, for example, he points out in specific terms that the means of acquiring »such rewards« as God offers »to those seeking him« (i. e., Heb. 11.6) is not through human works, nor even the »work« of faith; rather, this is »per mysterium ... incarnationis filii Dei.« Furthermore, Gerson utilizes this Christological focus to avoid placing any confidence — even under the dome of God's ordained power — in meritorious acts (i. e., *de congruo*). As he argues early in the treatise, *viatores* who had been handed over to »the condemnation of death« by Adam's sin were able to evade God's just judgment only »through the sacrament of reconciliation [accomplished] by God's only-begotten son,« and this *per fidem* and hence »beyond the strength and merits of nature.«[79] In a similar vein he contends that hope, like faith, must be anchored not in »the fragile and fluid sands of human effort« but rather upon »the firm rock, which is Christ.« This is dialectic theology at its sharpest: desperation and hope meet ultimately, according to Gerson, in the mediating presence of Christ; it is in this context that the spiral of self-despair is finally overcome. With this Christology Gerson constructs his positive evaluation of how *tentationes* function, driving us from any trust in ourselves (i. e., *fiducia de propriis operibus*) to faith in the »mediator between God and man,« Jesus Christ.

---

by Aquinas, for whom human freedom could only be understood within the context of God's activity: thus, for example, »man's turning to God is by free choice; and thus man is bidden to turn himself to God, but free choice can be turned to God only when God turns it. ...« *Summa theologiae* IaIIae q. 109 a. 6.

[78] On this point we note, once again, the complete absence of references to the sacraments in this treatise, those *media* which have been properly called »the natural setting of justification« (cf. Oberman, *Harvest*, p. 189); in this Gerson deviates from medieval theologians in general, and moves away from the later Ockhamism of Gabriel Biel for whom »the doctrine of justification, connected intimately with the sacrament of penance, gravitates not toward Christology but toward ecclesiology« (*ibid.*, p. 121). This is an important point of emphasis, accentuated by Gerson's tendency to speak of salvation »by faith« rather than in terms of the church's sacraments.

[79] G 9, p. 190.

In Gerson's Christology, therefore, we find the theological grounding for the pastoral shape of his consolatory argument. This language of Christ as the singular *sacramentum reconciliationis* establishes the context for his understanding of justification: Christological language deflects attention from an ecclesiological interpretation of justification — by which medieval theologians before and after Gerson emphasized the effective instrumental role of the sacraments in mediating our salvation — toward an immediate (mystical?) linkage of faith with Christ.[80] But if Gerson's approach not only to the content but to the *context* of justification moves beyond a consideration of the sacraments, principally by substituting the discussion of faith in their place, his position should not be misconstrued as *anti*-sacramental.[81] Against this development, however, we must recall that Gerson's soteriology, although theologically progressive in moving beyond accepted formulations concerning the »regular« channels of grace via the church, has a decidedly conservative ecclesiological mooring. In this regard, while his thought does reflect the broad tendency during this era to substitute a »spiritual« for a »sacramental« criterion of Christian discipleship[82] — and here we discern his abiding concern for the themes of *theologia mystica* — we should be wary of suggesting that this alteration of criteria represents a proto-Lutheran position. In other words, for Gerson, unlike those he perceived as more reckless critics of the church of his day who lacked »discretion,« soteriology did not lead to a denial of the church's sacramental or institutional foundations; rather, we find here a shift of emphasis, an attempt to bring »the source and nature of spiritual power« not »away from its institutional forms,« which has been identified as the broad trend of this period, but in altered yet still compatible relationship to those forms.[83] It is in this sense that we must interpret Gerson's move away from an

---

[80] Indeed, in his essay on »Justification Language,« Froehlich points to this theme in general terms, suggesting that those late-medieval theologians who »followed Scotus in his strong emphasis on predestination [i. e., *ante praevisa merita*] as the necessary safeguard of God's sovereignty over the ordained order of salvation . . . were immediately drawn into a consideration of the place of Christ in this contingent plan and thus in the justification process.« *Ibid.*, p. 161.

[81] This is a striking thematic development in his thought. Should we interpret this omission in Gerson, which stands in line with broader developments during this tumultuous period of schism and official and populist calls for church reform, in terms of a preference for »a spiritual« rather than »a merely sacramental criterion of Christian discipleship«? This conclusion, persuasively articulated by Gordon Leff as leading toward »a new theological conception of the church which was to come with the Reformation,« yet fails to characterize Gerson who as I here argue remained consistently conservative in terms of his ecclesiology. Cf. Leff, *The Dissolution of the Medieval Outlook*, p. 119.

[82] *Ibid.* Hamm has also pointed to the progressive disappearance during the later Middle Ages of the doctrine of the »habit« of grace; see *Promissio*, pp. 360 ff.

[83] Once again, Leff portrays this theme as a more extreme and sweeping trend in the later Middle Ages, one which created a »new« spirituality by taking »an apocalyptic or directly antisacerdotal form«; *Dissolution*, p. 144. His perception may indeed be correct as a general

emphasis upon the sacraments and the corresponding language of
»preparation,« from the human side, and the »infusion of grace« which this
entailed, on the divine side, as a consequence of his view of justification within
a Christological context — i. e., as the *viator*'s immediate »incorporation« in
Christ *per fidem*. Thus, too, it is only natural, to return to an earlier theme
considered in this study, that we find Gerson broadening his notion of the faith
— both implicit and explicit, habitual and actual — exercised by all Christians,
both university theologians and *idiotae*. Faith is not a »deposit« within the
hierarchical church to be held vicariously by the theological *periti* for the
simplices; it is rather the direct means by which all *viatores* find access to divine
grace by becoming incorporated in Christ. The priest's role has not become
obsolete for Gerson, though salvation depends not upon a priestly mediation
but upon a direct encounter of *viatores* with Christ *per fidem*. Christ has merited
grace in sufficient measure for all, but this grace is efficacious only if one is
»incorporated in Christ through . . . faith.«[84]

2. *Per desperationem ad spem*: a linear dialectic toward hope

Earlier in this chapter we suggested that *De consolatione theologiae* announces a
distinctive shift in Gerson's soteriology, a deliberate variation of doctrine in
contrast to his earlier writings by which he restructures the essential shape of
his pastoral theology. Consolation here takes on a decidedly different shape and
arises within a different theological framework than had been the case in his
writings predating Constance. This development has to do above all with his
conceptualization of God's covenant in Heb. 11.6: *viatores* are to approach God
not through moral effort but through the act of seeking God *per fidem*. »For
those who seek« (*inquirentibus*) rather than »for those who do what lies within
them« (*facientibus quod in se est*), God promises a reward, and this seeking itself
transpires through the faith which *viatores* have as a gift of God. But here again
we must ask whether Gerson's soteriology moves beyond the fear prompted
by the manifold *tentationes* of life, the unavoidable trials which lead *viatores* to an
utter despair in themselves. Does Gerson's approach offer consolation, or does
his pastoral strategy here actually »create the disease he sought to cure,« as one

---

portrait of the age, but this makes Gerson's contribution all the more fascinating, since we
might understand his viewpoint — theological and pastoral — as an attempt to take the
energy of this criticism but to set it within a framework which was compatible with the
institutional church. In this sense, he also develops an ecclesiology which is deliberately
anti-apocalyptic. I suggest in the final chapter of this study that Gerson does not allow for
any outright »exclusion of the hierarchy from the dialogue between the individual believer
and Christ,« though he does emphasize Christ's role (i. e., as *mediator Dei et hominum*) rather
than »the sacramental power of the church, as mediator.« *Ibid.*
[84] G 9, pp. 196—97.

recent study has concluded?[85] He admonishes the reader to hope, and promises consolation. But does he offer any coherent pastoral logic – particularly in the conspicuous absence of sacramental references – by which one might attain that desired goal, or is his theology finally nothing more than an »oscillation between ›mercy‹ and ›justice,‹«[86] an unsteady and finally precarious predicament by which the *viator* is »driven simultaneously by hope and fear«?[87]

These are critical questions to raise at this juncture, since our inquiry has exposed but not yet fully explored the dynamic nexus where divine and human initiative meet in Gerson's soteriological schema. And, as we find, these are not questions thrust upon the treatise from outside its range of interests, but are themselves part of a careful debate which Gerson himself fashions early in this dialogue. Already in the second prose section Monicus contends, here playing devil's advocate, that fear of divine judgment – or, as Gerson suggests, of God's execution of justice – overwhelms the *viator* and preempts any possibility of genuine consolation: »Nor is one ever free of this fear while he lives, for no human being knows his end, whether he is worthy of love or hate.«[88] These are not fabricated criticisms, but rather claims emerging from the biblical legacy – in this case, Eccl. 9.1, 12 – in which Gerson found both the constructive voice of *theologia* as well as a vivid portrait of human life at its point of desperate need.[89] Such a driving scriptural indictment grasps something of the pessimism of this historical period, though the dialectic movement of this theme identifies this as the more general problematic facing *viatores*. For Gerson the *viator* was not »driven simultaneously by hope and fear,« but utilized fear as the occasion for finding »firmer« hope in Christ. Fear becomes the necessary occasion driving *viatores* toward God, a linear dialectic rather than an oscillating journey, led above all by *theologia* with its accompanying virtues of faith, hope, and love.

Here, then, the inner movement of the dialogue itself becomes the key to grasping Gerson's careful pedagogical intent, and a random citation from the treatise cannot capture the linearity of his argument. It is the structure of the dialogue itself which conceives of the Christian life as a progressive movement

---

[85] Brown, *Pastor and Laity*, p. 170.
[86] Oberman uses this phrase to describe Biel's doctrine of justification, which he also aligns with the earlier thought of Gerson. Cf. *Harvest*, pp. 181 ff.
[87] *Ibid.*, p. 183.
[88] G 9, p. 189.
[89] None of Gerson's editors, early or late, recognized the specific biblical source of this citation, even though this phrase is often to be heard in this context in late-scholastic treatises. Thus, for example, we find this reference in the works of Gabriel Biel and Geiler of Keisersberg; on this point, see Oberman, *Harvest*, p. 183, n. 115, and Douglass, *Justification in Late Medieval Preaching*, pp. 176, n. 2. It is important to note that Gerson here poses the question of certitude vis-à-vis election not first with recourse to psychological analysis but with direct reference to the cadences of biblical language.

from fear to hope, a thematic movement expressive of a careful pedagogical strategy by which theology itself re-forms the character of the *viator* — precisely in the midst of *tentationes* leading one *ad Deum*, but by way of what we have called the spiral of despair. Monicus' skeptical and even brooding question about the inevitability and inescapability of fear only superficially bolsters the popular stereotype of the late Middle Ages as a darkening time of insufferable melancholy and *angst*, a view articulated so vividly in Huizinga's study of the period. Our analysis of this particular treatise would not dispute this as a general perception, since the point of departure for Gerson's theological consolation is precisely this emphasis on fear and its attendant melancholy. Yet we must also recognize that for Gerson this is only the initial problematic which theology confronts, not its final character. As Volucer argues, against this exact point, »Your judgment would be correct, Monicus, if faithful theology did not progress through that fear to things lying beyond [*ad ulteriora*],« compelling us »to flee to that hope which does not disappoint us.«[90] Theology itself together with the theological virtues moves us *beyond* fear, even though *tentationes* remain as the unavoidable texture of the human »pilgrimage« *ad Deum*.

How, then, did Gerson conceive what we have called this linear dialectic from fear to hope, and how is it that *theologia* facilitates this movement? Such an inquiry drives to the very heart of Gerson's soteriology, exposing the foundation of his *via media* where doctrinal and pastoral considerations coalesce: namely, his understanding of how faith and righteousness intersect, following the Pauline formulation *credere ad iustitiam* (Rom. 10.10). Indeed, this theme establishes the biblical rationale for Gerson's newly conceived pastoral theology by which he argues for a »certitude« of salvation, since *viatores* who »believe unto righteousness« do so by moving from despair in themselves and their own *iustitia* to hope in God and a trust in the divine *iustitia*. As he expresses this dialectic with rhetorical efficiency, theology leads *viatores* »per desperationem ad spem,«[91] a journey toward God which he elsewhere describes as *per desolationem*, adding that the purpose of theology itself is »to lead us upward to a sure consolation.«[92] His is a theology of hope precisely in anchoring hope in Christ, »the rock,« and in the divine rather than human achievement — whether by achieving congruous merit or by attaining satisfaction through the sacraments. *Viatores* must seek hope and consolation *extra nos*, much in the style of the union mysticism of the later Middle Ages, in this case by being incorporated *per fidem* in the Christ whom Gerson calls *sacramentum reconciliationis*.

---

[90] G 9, pp. 189—90. The biblical allusion, of course, refers to Rom. 5.5: »... spes autem non confundit.«

[91] G 9, p. 234.

[92] G 9, p. 198: »... sursum ducere ad solidam consolationem.«

3. Humility and hope: *Deus salvat damnantes se*

But how does Gerson envision this linear dialectic by which *viatores* move beyond fear toward this »firm consolation« and hope? To answer this question we must examine Gerson's basic approach in this treatise to justification, that doctrine which has aptly been characterized as »the touchstone of soteriological speculation« during the later Middle Ages.[93] While Gerson does not utilize the word *justificatio* in *De consolatione theologiae*, he addresses the central concerns of justification − namely, the forensic context of judgment; the transformation of human existence expressed in terms of »formed faith«; the non-imputation of sin and the imputation of God's *iustitia* − throughout the treatise, and particularly in the opening book. Indeed, the treatise as a whole sets forth in non-technical language an invitation to justification *per fidem*, calling *viatores* to order their lives *coram judice Deo* through justifying faith rather than works. »God is the giver of rewards to those who seek him,« he insists on the basis of the covenant found in Heb. 11.6, and that reward is a life justified through the divine *iustitia*. In order to grasp this aspect of Gerson's thought, therefore, we must begin by looking at the forensic dimensions of the work, since his persistent discussion of judgment orients the reader to an *ordo salutis* or what he here calls the *ordo judiciorum*, a carefully crafted »order of judgment« that delineates how mercy and justice are to be juxtaposed.

Gerson grounds his treatise in the structure of Boethius' *De consolatione philosophiae*, yet this is anything but a merely formal literary parallel. The closing paragraph of his predecessor's treatise, with its language of the human predicament *ante oculos iudicis* (V pr. 6, ll. 174−6), affords Gerson an organizing matrix for his own discussion of theological consolation. Like Boethius before him, Gerson locates *viatores* »before God the judge,«[94] and this language of judgment and justice which is characteristic of the broader scholastic discussion of justification permeates the dialogue throughout. Gerson introduces this theme by speaking of the *ordo judiciorum* in the opening pages of the treatise and again in the final book, describing it in both places with metaphoric language as a »triple throne« or three-fold tribunal: »God resides in the first tribunal and throne by tenderly granting grace, in the second by correcting with mercy, and in the third by judging with justice, about which the apostle has said that ›It is a fearful thing to fall into the hands of the living God.‹«[95] Moreover, he formulates the so-called »order of judgment« with deliberate care: the judgment facing us comes first in the form of grace, next as mercy, and only in the final instance as justice; he adds to this that the first two tribunals − i. e.,

---

[93] See Froehlich, »Justification Language,« p. 161.

[94] G 9, p. 190; Gerson utilizes a similar phrase later in the treatise, speaking of this predicament as »coram tremendo tribunali districti judicii Dei«; G 9, p. 232.

[95] G 9, p. 190. Cf. Heb. 10.31.

those of grace and mercy — are established »through the sacrament of reconciliation of God's only-begotten son,« such that Christology becomes the soteriological bridge between God and man (i. e., *mediator Dei et hominum*) and this »beyond the strength and merits of [human] nature.«[96] And finally, as a scriptural defense of this ordered metaphor, he draws upon the biblical claim that *superexaltat autem misericordia judicium*, adding the Pauline assertion that »where sin abounded, grace may abound even more« (Rom. 5.20). The thrust of this peculiar pastoral argument should now be clear: Gerson's intent is precisely not that of advocating an avoidance of sin; in stark contrast to any reliance upon what he calls *naturae vires et merita* he here emphasizes the *necessary* role of sin which is to expose human weakness and thereby evoke in the *viator* the proper posture for the reception of divine mercy.[97]

This *ordo judiciorum* functions as a theological and biblical rationale for Gerson's retreat from the language of merit, and in the process he follows the lead offered by Thomas Aquinas in defining *iustitia* in terms of *misericordia*, rather than vice versa.[98] Yet Gerson goes further than Aquinas, adding to what had become by this juncture a broadly diffused scholastic emphasis upon the priority of divine *misericordia* an eccentric pastoral application. In the second reference to this metaphor of the »thrones« of justice found late in the treatise (IV, pr. 2), Gerson builds a curious argument by combining scriptural references with a passage from Gregory the Great which he had often invoked earlier in his career.[99] Gerson here cites Prov. 18.17, which asserted that »the just man is first accuser of himself,« along with Gregory's dictum that »it is characteristic of good minds to acknowledge guilt [*culpa*] where there is none,« constructing a forensic case which would initially appear to contradict his

---

[96] *Ibid.*

[97] Here again we see the contrast of Gerson's grasp of justification from that which, following Oberman's analysis at least, is later found in Gabriel Biel's writings. Cf. *Harvest*, pp. 182: »But hand in hand with God's mercy goes God's righteousness, which is clearly understood [by Biel] as punishing righteousness.« Unlike Biel, apparently, Gerson here understood *iustitia Dei* in terms of *misericordia*, and not vice versa, such that even *iustitia Dei* comes to be understood not primarily as »punishing« righteousness but as the grace which tenderly cares for us (*indulgens gratia*) and the mercy which corrects us. Only then does Gerson speak of *damnans iustitia*, a reference which he reserves apparently for the reprobate alone, for whom the »sufficient« merit of Christ — whom he here aligns with the first two tribunals of grace and mercy — had no »efficient« cause. This is a crucial point, since it is the single reference in the work to God's »punishing« righteousness, and even here its application seems reserved only for the »foreknown« who were not predestined to be among the elect.

[98] Cf. *Summa theologiae* Ia q. 22 a. 3 ad 2: »Mercy does not destroy justice, but in a sense is the fulness thereof«; and, *ibid.*, a. 4, resp: »Now the work of divine justice always presupposes the work of mercy, and is founded thereupon.« The development of the notion of *iustitia* during the Middle Ages receives concise treatment in Froehlich, »Justification Language,« pp. 154 ff.

[99] On this point see Burger, *Aedificatio*, p. 103.

stated purpose of offering »instruction for a serene conscience.«[100] But this is precisely Gerson's point, and he hereby builds upon his earlier insistence that »desperes volo, sed de te et in te«: his intention is to provide a more circumspect and directly biblical rationale for this endorsement of self-despair, arguing again with a scriptural precedent that »if we judged [*dijudicaremus*] ourselves, we should not thus be judged [*judicaremur*].«[101] At least with regard to our past acts, we are to reject what he elsewhere calls »the timid, uncertain dwelling place of one's own achievements,«[102] learning from them that our own merits (*merita propria*) are empty (*vana*). Furthermore, Gerson constructs his forensic argument on two levels: first he insists that *viatores* who stand *coram judice Deo* receive mercy and grace *per sacramentum reconciliationis*, a gift which they apprehend *per fidem* and not on account of any works of merit; and, second, he argues that *viator* must accept a deliberately self-critical role, standing as »prosecutor, witness, and judge against himself, exaggerating [the guilt] as much as he is able« and thereby raising his scruples, since God »saves those who condemn themselves, conferring absolution upon them with opportune help.«[103] In both cases he affirms the biblical principle *misericordia superexaltat judicium* as if in answer to the brooding words of Ecclesiastes, also cited in both passages, that »one cannot know whether he is worthy of love or hatred« since »we cannot know to what end our acts . . . will come« (cf. Eccl. 9.1, 9.11). In other words, Gerson assumes that *desperatio* is not only unavoidable but is to be encouraged: by raising the accusation against oneself and giving in »through the highest desperation regarding man,« *viatores* are to be led by theology up to »highest hope in God,« from »an inestimable and intolerable desolation to a

---

[100] G 9, p. 232; the controlling motif of the final book, which had been introduced in the short preface to the treatise, proposed *per doctrinam in conscientiae serenatione*. Regarding the citation from Gregory, and as we have earlier noted, however, Gerson is also here willing to revise this maxim for pastoral reasons, since he refused to create what he calls an »erroneous« conscience wracked by scrupulosity regarding *future* acts. Cf. G 9, p. 235: »Primum vero respectu eorum quae futura sunt, de praeteritis quippe jam diximus, sic observare convenit: *ut non reputetur culpa ubi culpa non est*; alioquin causatur erronea conscientia contra quam si quidlibet attentetur fieri, jam culpa est si fluctuet animus« (my emphasis). For the further uses of this biblical text (Prov. 18.17), cf. also Cyril, *In Ioaninis Evangelium* 2.9, *PG* 73:394; and, finally, Bernard of Clairvaux, *Sermones super Cantica Canticorum*, II.1.2, in *S. Bernardi opera*, ed. J. Leclercq et al. (Rome, 1957), I:56.

[101] *Ibid.* His exegesis of this passage is quite irregular, of course, since he here applies this biblical passage (1 Cor. 11.31) in a manner which tears Paul's message out of its specific context; our principal concern here, however, has to do not with Gerson's exegetical accuracy but with the manner in which he applies this biblical theme to his theological argument.

[102] *Ibid.*, p. 195: ». . . industriarum propriarum quae timida est et incerta.«

[103] *Ibid.*, pp. 232–33. This is the single instance where Gerson mentions the priest's role in penance but with deliberate reference to God's direct intervention in this role. Here, too, he avoids reference to the sacrament, a point which supports our suggestion that Gerson's avoidance of sacramental language is not accidental.

solid consolation.«[104] This is a linear dialectic by which theology leads us through tribulation and despair in ourselves toward hope in God. And, as if to clinch this argument, he affirms that *Deus salvat damnantes se*: this is certainly not the language we have come to expect from Gerson the Ockhamist, suggesting from another angle that in his sojourn after Constance he began a reconstruction of his soteriology by shaping it according to an altogether different theological orientation than we find in his earlier writings.

This dialectic suggests that Gerson conceived of justification in forensic terms: the *viator* becomes righteous through faith in Christ, and this depends not upon the attainment of a meritorious state but upon despairing in oneself and consequently trusting in God's mercy and grace and being incorporated in Christ *per fidem*. The inner dynamic of his »pastoral« theology depends upon a humility toward oneself − »humiliet se homo quantum potuerit, sibi vilescat, se dejiciat«[105] − and, at the same time, a trust and hope in God: »quo fit ut damnandus in curia justitiae habeat aditum cum fiducia ad thronum gratiae eius, quae [Deus] salvat damnantes se, absolutionem conferens in auxilio oportuno.«[106] This does not directly render the content of Luther's later formulation *simul iustus et peccator*, but the soteriological context of this theme as well as its broad theological structure certainly anticipates the function of this Reformation insight.[107] Gerson approaches this theme with the conviction that the *viator* is to be »at once overcome with humility in oneself, and filled with hope in God.« He had earlier expressed this conviction in similar terms: »to whatever extent one is assailed by many trials and to whatever extent that one is overcome by them . . ., the more frequently, certainly, and forcefully because more humbly does he cast himself upon God and place his hope and trust in God. And thus he places no trust in himself to resist vices or to acquire virtues or salvation.«[108] Finally, expressing this theme in a tidy formula, Gerson affirms with sweeping programmatic language that »theology wishes to raise us up from highest desperation in man to highest hope in God,« a transforming journey which occurs *per medium mediatoris Dei et hominum*.[109] In the course of this linear dialectic, humility stands for Gerson not as one of the several virtues structuring Christian experience, but as the foundation of that life. If his is a theology of hope, as we have suggested, it is necessarily also a theology of

---

[104] *Ibid.*, p. 198.

[105] *Ibid.*, p. 233.

[106] *Ibid.*

[107] On this point, Gerson's approach contradicts Werbeck's conclusion that »es fehle [in Gerson's thought] das Hinüberspringen (*transilire*) von meiner Sünde zur Gerechtigkeit Christi . . .«; »Scrupulositas im Spätmittelalter,« p. 350. For a more detailed explication of this facet of Gerson's thought, see also below, 5.D.1.

[108] G 9, p. 195.

[109] *Ibid.*, p. 196.

humility,[110] a humility embodying his conviction that »Deus salvat damnantes se.« Humility is the interior condition of the human quest for God, a seeking through faith in Christ which grants consoling hope by fulfilling from the human side the divine covenant of Heb. 11.6.

4. *In Deum se projicit:* a mystical doctrine of justification

Earlier in this chapter we have illustrated Gerson's retreat from the language of human merit, and his calculated avoidance of the Ockhamist *facere quod in se est* doctrine. Thus he contrasts *iustitia Dei* and *iustitia mea*, arguing that God accepts us on account of his rather than our righteousness. Constructing the foundation of his argument by relying upon the biblical language of prayer, Gerson cites the psalmist's cry that »it is good for me to cling to God, to place my hope in the Lord God« (Ps. 72.28), and glosses another passage, » ›Free me in your righteousness [*in tua iustitia*],‹ (Ps. 30.2) *and clearly not in my own.*«[111] Drawing

---

[110] This is not an original description of Gerson's theology; in his essay »Gabriel Biel and Late Medieval Mysticism«, Oberman concluded that »we are not surprised to find that humility is for Gerson the central value, not only on the first stage of purgation but as the abiding context within which alone the mystical experience can be attained«; *ibid.*, p. 265. He returned to this phrase in his later Tübingen inaugural address, »›Wir sein pettler. Hoc est verum.‹ Bund und Gnade in der Theologie des Mittelalters und Reformation,« *Zeitschrift für Kirchengeschichte* 78 (1967): 232–52. The phrase has an even earlier origin, which establishes the polemic context of Oberman's use of it, having been used by Ernst Bizer to describe Luther's early theology; cf. *Fides ex auditu* (Neukirchen, 1958). Yet despite Oberman's largely revisionist disagreements with Bizer vis-à-vis Luther and the various stages of his so-called »Humilitastheologie,« he remains uncritical of Bizer's suggestion that the medieval tradition of *humilitas* derived principally within the monastic context. Furthermore, in his discussion of later medieval modulations of the nominalist doctrine of *facientibus quod in se est*, Oberman locates the shift to a conception of *humilibus Deus dat gratiam* first in the theological efforts of Luther's opponent, Kaspar Schatzgeyer (cf. *De perfecta atque contemplativa vita*, 1501), and marks this shift as a sign of the true »Vorabend« of the Reformation; cf. »Bund und Gnade,« p. 245. Yet this premise and subsequent conclusion miss the mark on two points: first, Gerson's theological posture is essentially compatible on this point with broader trends in lay devotion during the period, including movements in the Low Countries known as *devotio moderna*; this realization should discourage us from isolating »Humilitastheologie« as a strictly monastic legacy. And, second, already in Gerson's later works we find the shift toward *humilitas* as the characterization of the biblical covenant, in this case described by Gerson with the language of seeking God by first despairing in oneself. Indeed, in *De consolatione theologiae* Gerson extends the applicability of this theme (*humilitas*) to encompass not only mystics but all seekers of God; or, to put this another way, all seekers of God strive to attain this posture as *viatores*, and this regardless of their vocational status. Hence, our allusion to Gerson's thought under the rubric of »Humilitastheologie,« or »theology of humility,« is no insignificant or isolated claim; it remains to be seen how Gerson's persistent use of this particular theme influenced readers of his works later in the fifteenth century.

[111] G 9, p. 195; my emphasis of his gloss.

upon the proverb which held that »even the just one falls [into sin] seven times each day« (Prov. 24.16), Gerson again adds a gloss to a text from the Psalms, this time claiming that »that one is blessed to whom the Lord has not imputed [*non imputavit*] sin« and concludes from this that the blessed is thus »not one who has not sinned.«[112] Again, the force of this rejoinder might well reflect Gerson's anti-Hussite polemic, particularly since his repeated insistence upon the inescapability of sin recalls quite directly Cardinal d'Ailly's sharp rejoinder to Hus's highly moralistic view of the virtuous life.[113] Indeed, Gerson's argument which echoes d'Ailly's questioning of Hus at Constance bears a strong anti-Pelagian edge, a polemic which was not without significant ecclesiological consequences: namely, as a view of the church not as the bride »without spot or wrinkle,« but as the community of those elected *ab aeterno* and predestined *ante praevisa merita*. Yet there is another constructive side to Gerson's argument. With this view of justification as God's non-imputation of sin rather than as the consequence of our avoidance of sin, he carries this theme beyond a merely negative qualification: speaking as a seasoned veteran of the *cura animarum*, Gerson's message of consolation rests upon the conviction that it is not possible nor even desirable to avoid sin altogether, since such an effort inevitably leads to a self-absorbed scrupulosity.[114] Indeed, his intention runs in quite the opposite direction, as he here calls upon the Pauline dictum in support of what appears as a much more deliberately constructive emphasis on sin: *ubi abundavit delictum, superabundet et gratia* (Rom. 5.20).[115] His pastoral intent thus couples the non-imputation of sin with the imputation of *iustitia Dei* in the place of our own righteousness. *Viatores* should not trust in themselves and in their own *iustitia* but rather in God (*fiducia de Deo*), subjecting themselves »all the more to God's *iustitia*.«[116] His grasp of justification establishes the deepest stratum of his theology of humility.

---

[112] *Ibid.*

[113] See, for example, Peter of Mladoňovice, *An Account of the Trial and Condemnation of Master John Hus in Constance,* in *John Hus at the Council*, ed. M. Spinka (New York and London, 1965), p. 197.

[114] Here we must revise the assessment of Brown's study, focusing as it does primarily upon the earlier vernacular treatises, when she concludes that »Gerson's sermons and tracts for the laity certainly stress, if not over-stress, sin.« *Pastor and Laity*, p. 170. This does seem to be an apt characterization, as she argues, for his earlier writings. But in *De consolatione theologiae* as in other treatises written after Constance, Gerson distances himself from rhetoric aimed at avoiding sin. In this treatise, in fact, he concedes that such efforts are useless if not also impossible, choosing instead to speak of justification as the non-imputation of sin: »Beatus cui non imputavit Dominus peccatum,« a theme corresponding to his twice used metaphor of the tribunal of God before which *viatores* stand.

[115] G 9, p. 190; as he goes on to argue in this regard, this insight is something which »philosophy has not recognized,« and one might add as he does not that he himself had earlier taken a different and more traditional approach for this period by advocating the avoidance of sin. On this theme, cf. Brown, *Pastor and Laity*, pp. 116–70.

[116] The language he here uses offers the technically precise terminology to be heard in

The pivotal function of God's *iustitia*, therefore, fills as an »alien righteousness« − a technical term from a later discussion which Gerson did not use, but which aptly expresses his intent − the void created by the utter rejection of the *iustitia* proper to *viatores*, the effect of human works accomplished *ex puris naturalibus*. Yet Gerson does not leave the matter here. As if to clarify his meaning in terms of the mystical tradition, he goes on to restate this theme in a quite remarkable reference to »the writings of the devout,« here apparently drawing upon the rich medieval tradition of commentaries on the Song of Songs: »These authors speak of the entrance of the bride into the bridegroom's chambers, of her kiss of his mouth after having kissed his hands and feet, and of the dwelling place in the help of the most high,« continuing, in order to strike a contrast, »not in an empty dwelling place of future punishments, nor in the timid, uncertain dwelling place of one's own achievements.«[117] Gerson has taken one of the most fervent expressions of *theologia mystica*, the sensuous imagery of bridal union based upon the Song of Songs, to interpret justification. By recasting this doctrine in terms of the mystical tradition − and, specifically, by speaking of it in language usually reserved to describe mystical union with God − he has added an experiential depth to the scholastic language regarding justification. This tactic also broadens the appeal of mystical theology. In this manner Gerson aligns his thought with the tradition of affective mysticism, an approach to the mystical life which recognized that »there is something higher than all virtues, a ›righteousness‹ which surpasses all human works and all that can be achieved in the realm of the creature, a supernatural, a perfect righteousness« which consists of »man's becoming nothing and God's becoming all in man.«[118] This is precisely the theological dynamic that Gerson applies to his view of justification. Thus his abrupt reference to the mystical understanding of union with God, language offering yet another variant on his insistence that *per fidem* we are »incorporated« in Christ, functions in his soteriology in the manner otherwise assumed by the technical scholastic language of justification, though

---

medieval discussions of justification: »apud vere humilem quanto minus est in se spei, minus in ope aliena fiduciae, minus denique vult constituere iustitiam suam, tanto plus spei, plus fiduciae de Deo concipit, plus quoque iustitiae Dei sit subjectus. ...« G 9, p. 195.

[117] *Ibid.*, p. 195.

[118] Bengt Hägglund, *The Background of Luther's Doctrine of Justification in Late Medieval Theology* (Philadelphia, 1971), p. 10. Hägglund also points out that for Tauler and *Theologia Deutsch* this language functions to describe how justification occurs »although the word justification is rarely used in this connection«; *ibid.*, pp. 9−10. We have found this to be true also in Gerson, and it may be that this trait has to do with his propensity to describe doctrine such as this in experiential rather than technical terms; this also suggests, as we earlier pointed out, that Gerson's approach in this treatise advocates a democratization of mysticism (see 4.C.2). Froehlich also points to this characteristic, though without reference to Gerson's work, in »Justification Language,« p. 156.

with one critical difference: Gerson moves away from the Ockhamist propensity to speak of righteousness as a virtue and justification as the reward (i. e., via *acceptatio Dei*) for congruous merit,[119] approaching more closely to a mystical view of justification which portrayed the divine *iustitia* as both *extra nos* and *in nobis*.[120] And, as we have already suggested, he characterizes the vicarious role of *iustitia Dei* in justifying *viatores* in terms of our unqualified seeking for God: only when the *viator* has abandoned all trust in self is he in a proper position to »cast himself upon God, hoping and confiding in God.«[121]

In Deum se projicit: this emphasis on the dependence of *viatores* upon God, which he elsewhere calls *fiducia de Deo*, may also provide a crucial clue which explains Gerson's movement away from the *facere quod in se est* doctrine. Not only is this shift a reaction to the Hussite position, as we have earlier suggested, but Gerson interprets this development within a specific tradition of mysticism which resisted the legitimacy of any language of human merit. Justification as expressed in such mystical terms was a matter of stark dialectic, a »coincidence of opposites« in terms of *iustitia* by which the *viator* contributes only a contrite and seeking spirit which God rewards with his own *iustitia*. Such a formulation calls for a significant revision of Combes's conclusion that Gerson has here abandoned mystical theology entirely; in point of fact, we must now affirm the very opposite, since Gerson's soteriology as expressed in *De consolatione theologiae* articulates explicitly and with evocative language a mystical doctrine of justification.

The suggestion that Gerson's use of the language of *iustitia* offers his own approach to justification in the style of a particular tradition of mysticism finds further support in the concluding book of this treatise. Gerson begins the

---

[119] For a summary of the Ockhamist doctrine of justification, here referring above all to the work of Gabriel Biel, see Hägglund, *Luther's Doctrine of Justification*, pp. 33–34.

[120] Froehlich has pointed to this facet of mysticism in the late medieval horizon: »Late medieval mystics added a strong sense of paradox [to the earlier tradition represented by Bernard of Clairvaux]: mine, yet not mine; it understood the righteousness of God reaching human beings as an utterly divine reality, superior to anything the human virtue of justice may mean. Here the two dimensions of ›outside of us‹ (*extra nos*) and ›in us‹ (*in nobis*) become fused.« »Justification Language,« p. 156. This observation is peculiarly appropriate to the later Gerson, for we find in *De consolatione theologiae* a sustained effort to distinguish divine from human *iustitia*, understood both as »righteousness« (a personal attribute) and as »justice« (an external, or forensic matter). In the discussion following we examine the former in considerable detail; regarding the latter, Gerson remarks in the context of his second use of the »throne« metaphor, having first described the graciousness of God's judgment through which *misericordia superexaltat judicium*, that »quo contra fit in humanis judiciis, quoniam confitenti crimen mors infertur: apud Deum vero apud quem est misericordia et copiosa redemptio, misericordia hic dum vivimus superexaltat judicium, quo fit ut damnandus in curia justitiae habeat aditum cum fiducia ad thronum gratiae eius. …« That is, the human *curia iustitiae* has a more severe and merciless justice when contrasted with the judgments *ad thronum gratiae*.

[121] G 9, p. 195.

dialogue aimed at providing »instruction for serenity of conscience« by resuming his discussion of *iustitia Dei*, a topic he had first explored in the opening book. Once again he first accentuates the terror facing *viatores* who stand *coram judice Deo*, a peculiar strategy at first glance for a consolatory argument. But this is the necessary starting point since this is the arena of human experience: *viatores* find it impossible to justify themselves and salvage their innocence *sub judiciis Dei terribilis*. To bolster the argument from experience Gerson here cites a catena of biblical passages — above all from Job and the Psalms — to accentuate the spiral of despair by which *viatores* recognize the complete travesty of their own *iustitia* in the presence of the judging God. But this argument of despair, as in his first exploration of this theme (cf. I pr. 3), serves as the necessary preface to a deeper theological argument. Within this context he now introduces a biblical text from Isaiah which declared that »all our righteousness [*omnes iustitiae nostrae*] is as a menstrual rag,« a passage which emerges at the heart of Ps.-Augustine's discussion of »the mystery of predestination or foreknowledge«[122] and which was a commonplace in the works of Bernard of Clairvaux and mystical theologians — including Gerson — influenced by him.[123] In citing this text in *De consolatione theologiae* Gerson adds his own gloss in the form of a driving rhetorical question: »For who would show his righteousness [*iustitias suas*] to God as if he were exulting any more than a wife would show her husband the rag of her blushing [*pannum confusionis*]?«[124] The graphic language of this biblical metaphor, apparently

---

[122] We must note again that this biblical text (Isa. 64.6) also serves a similar function in the argument »On the Mystery of God's Predestination and Foreknowledge« found in *Liber soliloquiorum animae ad Deum*, a treatise which circulated during Gerson's lifetime under the name of Augustine and which he elsewhere cites *in extenso* in this treatise; cf. *PL* 40: 826 and above, n. 54. Gerson also cites this biblical text in a lengthy letter (see G 9, 199) to his brother Jean, prior of the Celestine house in Lyons, which is really a short treatise offering instruction on prayer; in this treatise he asks: »Tu quis es qui oras? Si ad propria merita respexeris, incertus es an amore vel odio dignus sis; incertus es idcirco an tremenda cadat super te illa sententia: cum is qui displicet, inquit beatus Gregorius, intercedendum mittitur, irati animus ad deteriora provocatur. Porro certus dicere poteris cum Isaia: omnes iustitiae nostrae quasi pannus menstruatae. . . .« G 2, p. 170. It is also worth noting that the same passage appears in the preaching of Geiler, who was deeply influenced by Gerson; cf. Douglass, *Justification Language in Late Medieval Preaching*, p. 168. Finally, we find reference to this biblical text in the second book of Biel's *Sentences*, just where one might expect to find it (i. e., d. 27); Oberman notes this occurrence (cf. *Harvest*, p. 181, n. 111), but points out that for Biel this emphasis leads to what he calls »the remarkable oscillation . . . between these two attributes of God« (viz., *misericordia* and *iustitia*). Gerson's theological argument in *De consolatione theologiae* is thus distinctively different from Biel's, since in place of an oscillation we find here what we have called a linear dialectic from despair to hope and from justice to mercy.

[123] See here Zumkeller, »Das Ungenügen der menschlichen Werke,« pp. 265, 302; also, for a representative citation from Bernard of Clairvaux, see *PL* 183: 357 ff.

[124] G 9, p. 228.

serving as a stock citation in the tradition of affective mysticism following
Bernard, drives home his point that *viatores* have nothing meritorious to show
coram judice Deo, and should be not only fearful but ashamed in God's presence.
Once again we are reminded of his claim in the opening book (I pr. 4),
»desperes volo, sed de te et in te.« And, in similar style to the Ps.-Augustine
text which Gerson had apparently consulted in writing this treatise, this
contrast undergirds his emphasis upon *praedestinatio ante praevisa merita*: God's
election could take no account of human worthiness, a variation of his earlier
use of the Ockhamist argument that »Deus nulli debitor est.« The interweaving
of these themes of the unworthiness of human *iustitia* and the unmerited mercy
of the divine *iustitia* provides the overarching thematic structure for Gerson's
mystical doctrine of justification in this treatise. Thus, it is not without
significance that Gerson's emphasis of this contrast between the two, as well as
the vicarious role of the latter in justifying wayfarers already »while we are
living« and not merely at the final judgment,[125] occurs both in his opening
discussion of the consolation offered by theology »through hope in contemplating the divine judgments« and in the final book devoted to »instruction
for serenity of conscience.«

De consolatione theologiae as a whole stands as an extended meditation upon
the theme of *iustitia*, and as a »manual of conversion« it is this theme above all
others which provides the functional mechanism of consolation: beset with
tentationes, the *viator*'s flawed righteousness is itself the force driving him into a
spiral of despair while at the same time inviting him to trust vicariously in
God's *iustitia*. And, as we have earlier noted, this is a form of justice which
Gerson interprets in terms of the »tribunals« of grace and mercy — *per fidem* on
the subjective side and *per Christum* (or *per medium mediatoris Dei et hominum*) on
the objective side of his soteriological schema. It is this dynamic which sets
forth what we have called »the new key« of Gerson's pastoral theology, since
his treatment of *iustitia* defines the role of *viatores* as that of seeking God in the
midst of self-despair; in humility *viatores* are to »cast« themselves more
completely upon God's mercy and trust in the divine righteousness. Thus, the
human initiative as Gerson here conceived it, in accord with his emphasis upon
the covenantal obligation to seek God (Heb. 11.6), approaches not a strictly
monastic but a mystical accent on humility before God,[126] though he prefers to

---

[125] In this sense Gerson's argument is again strikingly different than that of Biel (cf.
Oberman, *Harvest*, pp. 182—83); Gerson does not resort to the theme of the last judgment
in order to set forth an understanding of *iustitia Dei*, but concludes that »God's mercy
exceeds his judgment *already while we are living* [*dum vivimus*].« G 9, p. 233 (my emphasis).

[126] Again, Hägglund's terse discussion of this mystical theme, offered in explanation of
Tauler's soteriology, affords a suggestive parallel to Gerson's approach: »The renunciation
of all his own works on the part of man and stress on man's inability to prepare himself for
the reception of grace stand in clear contrast to the *facere quod in se est* of scholasticism. God's

speak of this — here blending Cistercian piety within the framework of Bonaventure's paradigm of the Christian life as a journey *ad Deum*[127] — by describing life as a pilgrimage of the soul by which the *viator* »thrusts himself in God« (*in Deum se projicit*).

D. Beyond resignation:
The construction of a voluntarist soteriology

The early decades of the fifteenth century were a period of considerable confusion if not dissolution in the external affairs of the church. This was an era described in a recent study as a time of »decomposition and disintegration,« a gradual breakdown of the external structures and internal forms of assent by which European society — and, in particular, the fragile bonds of the western church during a period of both internal schism and the rising swell of nationalism — had earlier maintained at least the outward vestiges of stability.[128] Yet this is to speak of this age only in terms of its negative side. In a positive sense this was also a period witnessing a new birth of religious sensibility, a flowering of mysticism and of the arts, and an aggressive and often violent transformation of the social and political horizon of European society. Above all it was a period marked by a resuscitation of voluntarism, here broadly defined as an emphasis upon the will — both the divine will within the order of creation and the free and consequently responsible role of the human will in sustaining the vitality of the religious life.

In order to situate Gerson's thought within this horizon, we must inquire beyond this broad portrait of life in the quattrocento about the specific theological background of the voluntarist tradition. Here we are only able to offer a terse summary of this development, and we do so primarily in terms of those specific traditions which exert an influence upon Gerson's later writings. Earlier in this chapter we noted the presence in *De consolatione theologiae* of

---

sole operation in the work of redemption is given decided prominence in Tauler's work. The fact that resignation or humility is viewed as a necessary preparation does not contradict this.« Hägglund, *Luther's Doctrine of Justification*, p. 13. As we shall subsequently suggest, however, Gerson does not allow for the possibility of resignation or passivity before God; in this, perhaps, we might still see vestiges of the *facere quod in se est*, defined in the quite different categories of the seeking of God through *conformitas voluntatis* (see below, 5.D.2).

[127] Gerson had on several occasions recommended Bonaventure's *Itinerarium mentis ad Deum*, speaking of it on one occasion as »totum miro et compendiosissimo artificio complexus est«; see Combes, »Études gersoniennes,« 2: 292.

[128] See, for example, Walter Ullmann, *Medieval Foundations of Renaissance Humanism* (London, 1977), p. 195; Bouwsma, »The Two Faces of Humanism,« pp. 16–17; Oakley, *The Western Church*, pp. 15 ff.; and, finally, Leff, *Dissolution*, pp. 118–44.

dominant elements of a Scotist soteriology, above all the view of predestination
with its uncompromising accent upon God's freedom and omnipotence.
Broadly speaking, this emphasis upon the sovereignty of the divine will
permeated the fourteenth and fifteenth centuries, such that advocates of
soteriologies of quite different stripes — such as Robert Holcot of one school,
and Gregory of Rimini of another — could nonetheless join in affirming the
Ockhamist themes of the »unity, freedom, and omnipotence of God. «[129] Thus,
within this broad voluntarist spectrum one is able to delineate a »right-wing«
voluntarism with its extreme Augustinian statement of the divine freedom and
initiative in salvation over against a »left-wing« voluntarism with its
heightened emphasis upon the human initiative (i. e., *facere quod in se est*) under
the canopy of the divinely ordained covenant of salvation. Within the broad
scope of this spectrum we are now in a position to locate the later Gerson of *De
consolatione theologiae*, against a near consensus in recent historical studies,
among the former: his soteriology in *De consolatione theologiae* offers no simple
identity with nominalists on the »right,« but it does signal a shift in his
theological perspective *away* from Ockhamism and *toward* a more severe
Augustinianism as represented by Bradwardine and Gregory of Rimini.[130]

But this is only part of this story, albeit the theological context of most
immediate proximity to Gerson. Behind this immediate horizon of scholastic
influence we must again point back to Boethius, an unexpected source of
voluntarism perhaps but an authority for Gerson whose influence is reflected in
his admission in this treatise that he had studied *De consolatione philosophiae*
»diligently from his youth.« Indeed, this influence finds explicit form when he
concludes at the opening of the second book of this treatise, devoted to
»revealing through scripture the form of the world's government,« that
»according to Boethius *philosophia* posited and salvaged both the freedom of
God and the freedom of any nature having the use of reason.«[131] In point of fact
this is the essential framework within which Gerson crafts his soteriological *via
media*, since he varies Boethius' view only by delineating *per theologiam
revelatam* the manner in which divine and human freedom coinhere.[132] It is to

---

[129] Oakley, *The Political Thought of Pierre d'Ailly*, p. 22. Also, see Pelikan, *Reformation*,
pp. 23 ff.

[130] On Bradwardine, see Oberman, *Archbishop Thomas Bradwardine: A Fourteenth Century
Augustinian. A Study of His Theology in Its Historical Context* (Utrecht, 1957), pp. 65 ff.; on
Gregory of Rimini, see Burger, »Die Augustinschüler gegen die modernen Pelagianer,«
pp. 195ff, and Leff, *Gregory of Rimini*.

[131] G 9, p. 207.

[132] He sets Boethius, in fact, apart from »the philosophers« of classical (pagan) antiquity,
since as he concedes »Boethius himself was established in a higher light and could see in a
way that neither Platonists nor Stoics saw, established as they were only in the light of
prophecy.« As we have earlier argued, this analysis depends upon his view of the
progressive revelation of *lex divina* by which the knowledge of God (*cognitio Dei*) became

this coinherence and to the voluntarist logic by which Gerson explains it that we now turn our attention; here we shall examine Gerson's theological construction of a voluntarism which is itself a *via media*, a mediating position between those on the »right« and »left« who emphasized in their doctrine of salvation either the divine or the human will respectively.

1. The Christological basis for voluntarism

Earlier we have examined Gerson's insistence on identifying grace as the »principal medium« ordained by God to bring *viatores* to final beatitude. Our consideration of this passage (I pr. 4) sketched in some detail his preference to speak of Christ as the »mediator between God and man« rather than the »various other modes« by which wayfarers were to be brought to the »refuge of the human pilgrimage. « We suggested in that context that in Gerson's later writings, and particularly *De consolatione theologiae*, a tendency emerges which is characteristic of this period: namely, a movement away from an emphasis upon the church's mediatorial role vis-à-vis the sacraments, recently described as an »unraveling« of »the Augustinian synthesis« which had held during the early and high Middle Ages, and toward a more dominant Christology functioning in an unmediated soteriological role. With the dissolution of this Augustinian synthesis, a distinct doctrinal bifurcation of two traditional emphases of Augustine's thought can be perceived in late-scholastic theology: namely, the anti-Pelagian doctrine of the sovereignty of grace and an anti-Donatist doctrine of the objectivity of sacramental grace.[133] This is a provocative thesis, and one which offers a fascinating insight into broader developments during this period. It might also help clarify the apparent anomaly that Gerson seems to retreat from a pastoral advocacy of the sacraments as the source of grace and the means by which *viatores* receive consolation. His concern with the sovereignty of grace − articulated most forcefully in his insistence that *viatores* receive Christ's »sufficient« grace through the instrumentality of faith − apparently prevents him from emphasizing the sacraments as »security« *coram Deo*. With this emphasis, as we

---

»more explicit« as that law unfolded: first in nature, then in the law »written on stone« (i. e., the ten commandments revealed to Moses), and finally in the »time of grace« when it became »fully« explicit. See also above, 4.B.1, especially n. 61.

[133] Pelikan, *Reformation*, p. 19; also, see Leff, *Dissolution*, pp. 143−44, and Ullmann, *Medieval Foundations*, pp. 189 ff. Gerson's writings after Constance would suggest that he has moved even more decisively away from the anti-Donatist position: in contrast to other nominalists Gerson does not emphasize »the arbitrary decree of God rather than . . . grace inherent in the sacraments themselves« (*ibid.*); on the contrary, he avoids any reference to the sacraments whatsoever, and shifts the emphasis from a trust in the sacraments as mediators of grace to a trust in Christ *per fidem*. See also above, 5.C.1, and 4.B.2, especially n. 47.

have earlier noted, he devises a pastoral strategy of fundamentally different shape than his earlier Ockhamist approach allowed. But this observation focuses primarily upon the general soteriological function Gerson assigns to his Christology. We must now consider his approach to this doctrine not in its theological foundation but in terms of the more subtle and quite intriguing psychological basis by which Gerson orients his voluntarist soteriology.

This consideration brings us at the very outset to an interpretive difficulty which has surrounded those, like Gerson, who addressed this doctrine as *imitatio Christi*. Historians of the later Middle Ages are easily persuaded to interpret this theme in terms of the classic argument between Anselm and Abelard in an earlier age, yet such an approach distorts this theme in its later medieval manifestations.[134] The matter was not so clearly or unambivalently set forth in the writings of this period, nor were the emphases – doctrinal and devotional – so discretely distinguished as Aulén and others have suggested with their magisterial typologies. On the contrary, despite the broadly diffused tendency during this period to speak of an *imitatio* Christology – and on this point we find a strange chorus of quite diverse voices, including Wyclif, Tauler, Thomas à Kempis, Hus, and Gerson[135] – the human Christ as moral example functioned within the broader context of the divine Christ who effects our salvation through his atoning death. Thus, Gerson speaks with a pastor's voice in his sermons, vernacular and Latin, of Christ and the saints as *exempla* to be imitated, emphasizing gospel pericopes which conveyed distinctive themes to be applied to the Christian life; yet he placed such themes directly alongside a confessional portrait of Christ as divine savior, the »mediator« whose death was »a satisfaction to justice« and »who was made by God for us both righteousness and redemption.«[136] In Gerson's Christology as often in

---

[134] For an overview of this debate, cf. Gustaf Aulén, *Christus Victor. An Historical Study of the Three Main Types of the Idea of Atonement*, trans. A. G. Hebert (New York, 1969), esp. pp. 81 ff. See also Oberman, *Harvest*, pp. 268–70, »Imitation of the *Christus Victor.*«

[135] Cf. for example Hägglund, *Luther's Doctrine of Justification*, pp. 14–15; Pelikan, *Reformation*, pp. 24, 36–37. The latter describes Wyclif's Christology in language which seems peculiarly close to Gerson's approach as well, concluding that »frequently, but by no means consistently, such statements about the primacy of the imitation of Christ as the means for attaining salvation had as their context a more comprehensive summary of the saving work of Christ: imitation stood as the middle member of three such means, the first being the memory of the passion of Christ as the divine-human satisfaction for sin and the third being the veneration of Christ or the resistance of future temptation.« *Ibid.*, p. 36.

[136] Cf. for example G 5, pp. 17–18, 64–65; G 7, pp. 960, 965. In *Pastor and Laity*, Brown also notes this ambivalence, yet without considering the differing purposes each of these emphases conveyed. As she concludes: »... above all in his sermons there is Christ, seen on the one hand as the human Jesus, ›humble, gentle, compassionate, and kind‹, our brother to be emulated. On the other hand, Christ is portrayed as the risen Saviour, ushering in the age of grace and mercy, revealing the love of God and making possible our salvation.« *Ibid.*, p. 170. Geiler later articulates a Christology of similar ambivalence; see Douglass, *Justification Language in Late Medieval Preaching*, pp. 157–60, 179–89, and esp. p. 157, n. 2.

later medieval treatments of this theme the old antagonism of an »imitation« (Abelard) and »atonement« (Anselm) model is overcome in a mediating approach which holds the two together.

When we turn to *De consolatione theologiae*, we find a Christology which draws upon both models and thus integrates ethical and soteriological themes. Thus, Gerson designates Jesus as an *exemplum* for *viatores* – »imitandus est Jesus« – utilizing the familiar Johannine language to contend that »God has given us an example« in Christ; at the same time he insists that Jesus »has merited grace sufficiently for all persons,« serving as the *sacramentum reconciliationis*, as »mediator between God and man.«[137] Yet his argument moves beyond this general model, offering a Christology of more complex psychological dimensions than we find in the twelfth-century discussions. This appears to represent another area in which Thomas Aquinas' thought influenced Gerson, since Gerson expounds his view by utilizing language strikingly similar to the elaborate psychological approach by which Aquinas had discerned Christ's »unity of will.«[138] Of course, Gerson's use of Thomas is original, introducing this psychological Christology within the arena of his soteriology: here we find an intriguing discussion of the inner life of Jesus, a consideration of Christ's *obedientia activa*[139] discussed in terms of his properly ordered wills, which serves as the mainspring of Gerson's voluntarism. That is, Jesus represents the »mediator between God and man« not only in terms of his expiatory death, but in terms of the inner psychological dimension of his personality. On this basis Gerson's portrayal of Jesus as the »second Adam,« whose obedience overcame the effects of the »first« Adam's »prevarication,« is much more than a model for moral imitation: this »restoration« establishes the anthropological rationale of his voluntarism precisely because it is through Christ's obedience that the devastating effects of original sin are overcome. His articulation of a psychological Christology, though similar in basic structure to the Angelic Doctor's analysis, moves beyond Aquinas in linking Christology and soteriology not in terms of a sacramentology but in the general realm of ethics itself: the theme of Christ's »restoration of obedience« finally overflows into a pastoral application which he offers according to the theme of *conformitas voluntatis*.

Gerson thus roots his *imitatio* Christology in a careful psychological dis-

---

[137] For a similar use of Jn. 13.15 in one of his Latin sermons, see G 5, pp. 17–18.

[138] Cf. *Summa theologiae* IIIa q. 18 aa. 1–6.

[139] This is a technical term in the later debates of Protestant scholastic orthodoxy, though it portrays Gerson's intent in this discussion by emphasizing the voluntarism of Jesus' obedience; cf. Heinrich Heppe, *Die Dogmatik der evangelisch-reformierten Kirche*, ed. E. Bizer (Neukirchen, 1935), p. 358. Gerson speaks only of »obedience,« applying this in a critical discussion which contrasts the fall of humankind *per unum* with the salvation effected *per unius obeditionem*, or through the obedience of Christ, the »second Adam«; cf. G 9, p. 190.

cussion of Jesus' inner person, representing Jesus as the archetypal *viator*[140] seeking beatitude who attains this goal through a proper ordering of what he calls »the three-fold will.«[141] According to this psychological model, Gerson envisions the will as a complex, three-tiered structure. Of the two highest levels, which pertain to human beings but not to animals, the highest is engrafted into »higher reason,« and is thereby oriented toward »the eternal law«; this is the will found, first of all, in those already beatified (*in beatis spiritibus*) for whom the will is »immovably conjoined with God's will . . . so that in them there is but a single willing and not willing,« as with God. It is also found, second, in »good wayfarers« (*in viatoribus bonis*) though here in a changeable manner (*licet mobiliter*) and hence differently than in God and the saints. This second level of the will, annexed with »lower reason,« is joined to »inferior laws or realities« and becomes »darkened« and »weakened« in this entanglement; it is also called »sensual appetite,« yet although it is »inferior« to the first it is nonetheless »free through participation« in the higher will. Finally, the third level of will encompasses appetites not joined to reason, but ordered by God in such a way that »he allows« them to perform their proper activities«; we would call this appetite instinct, since it is found in animals whose »sensual

---

[140] See G 9, p. 208: »Nos itaque Jesum secundum hanc voluntatem debemus imitari. . . . Secus in Christo, sicut in beatis, quia secundum hanc portionem beatus fuit in via Christus. . . . Exemplum igitur nobis dedit Deus, ut quemadmodum juxta hanc duplicem voluntatem fecit secundum quam erat viator, ita et nos faciamus.«

[141] While Gerson follows Aquinas in his description of Jesus' psychological makeup, he apparently follows Scotus in evaluating what might be appropriately called the »divine« psychology; he argues, against those who »either denied or were not aware of the reason for this,« that »God did not will things outside himself [*ad extra*] because they are good . . .; on the contrary, things outside him are good because God wills them to be so. . . . For God's will has done everything for its own sake [*propter se fecit omnia*], and existed for itself [*propter se erat*] before all things were made.« G 9, p. 204. This position stands in stark contrast to Aquinas's approach, for whom *bonitas* functions as the principle governing divine acts; on this point cf. *Summa theologiae* IaIIae q. 93 a. 1, and a clear summarizing discussion in Steinmetz, *Misericordia Dei. The Theology of Johannes von Staupitz in Its Late Medieval Setting* (Leiden, 1968), pp. 47–50. Gerson interpreted such a view, following both Scotus' and Ockham's lead, as an unwarranted limitation upon God's nature. For him God's freedom was without limits, not even the limitation of *res bonae*: »Deus quippe non vult res ad extra fieri ideo quia bonae sunt, quemadmodum movetur humana voluntas ex objectione boni veri vel apparentis; est e contra potius quod ideo res ad extra bonae sunt quia Deus vult eas tales esse, adeo quod si vellet eas vel non esse vel aliter esse, id quoque jam bonum esset.« G 9, pp. 204–205. Yet he went even further than this here, arguing that God might act – *de potentia Dei absoluta* at least – not only *libere*, but *contradictorie*; this picks up once again a theme he had earlier articulated in his lectures *Contra curiositatem studentium*, where he argued that »philosophical reason« might discover the premise that God was »first mover,« but could not penetrate more deeply into the divine will to recognize with theology that »God possesses the freedom to act in a contradictory way« (»non invenit tamen quod agat libere libertate contradictionis«); G 3, pp. 232–33. Both a philosophical »necessity of goodness« as well as the limitation of »non-contradiction,« according to Gerson, introduced an unacceptable determinism into the doctrine of God.

activities are without fault.«[142] On the basis of this threefold model of the will, therefore, Gerson articulates the pastoral thrust of his voluntarism, concluding that the »rectitude of our hearts« consists in »the conformity and application of the will« in its complex character to »higher reason,« since this level of reason mediates »the single eternal law of God,« or what he later calls »the first and unwavering rule of the divine will.«[143]

It is within this context, then, that Gerson offers a concise analysis of Christ's psychological nature, delineating the inner character of the *obedientia activa* demonstrated by his properly ordered will. In this particular sense Christology itself, considered in terms of this psychological model, provides for the integration of the themes of *imitatio Christi* and Christ as *sacramentum reconciliationis*: Jesus is the archetypal *viator* who as such is both model and mediator of the obedient life. Thus, when he here concludes that »one should imitate Jesus who became for us the wisdom of God, and who took up and showed in his own life what we should do,« we understand this exhortation in quite specific terms as a call to order one's own will in accordance with Jesus', but also within the more comprehensive confessional framework of Christ as »mediator between God and man«:

In Christ, beside the divine will — for he was himself God — the threefold will ... is to be found. According to the first [will] Christ wished continually [*assidue*] whatsoever God willed, praising and approving the order of divine wisdom, goodness, and justice in whatever God willed and accomplished: in heaven regarding [our] salvation, in the abyss of condemnation, and on land and sea regarding the various activities of those to be saved and those damned. Therefore we ought to imitate Jesus according to this will, even if we are not in everything able while we live to reach equality [with Christ], both because we have not yet been confirmed [in grace] and because through the second of these wills the higher will within us is able to be distracted and disturbed.[144]

Christ willed *assidue* that which God wills: this theme of the conformity of Christ's human will with God's eternal law or will establishes a psychological paradigm which orients Gerson's voluntarism. He did not apparently offer any more specific integration of this psychological Christology within the more comprehensive contours of the doctrine of atonement; the two remain side by side in this treatise as in his earlier homiletical works. This is a point worthy of mention, however, since the accent must be placed not upon imitation but upon Christ: that is, the imitation of *Christ* who provided an example for us insofar as he properly ordered his wills »... and accordingly was a *viator*.«[145]

---

[142] G 9, pp. 206–207.

[143] *Ibid.*, p. 206.

[144] *Ibid.*, p. 208. This passage refutes any tendency toward Nestorianism; see further Oberman, *Harvest*, pp. 255–58, for a discussion of Biel on this point.

[145] G 9, p. 208: »Exemplum igitur nobis dedit Deus, ut quemadmodum juxta hanc duplicem voluntatem fecit secundum quam erat viator, ita et nos faciamus. ...« For

The fact that Christ represents the paradigm of a properly ordered inner life – and as such is *viator* par excellence – is by no means incidental to Gerson's soteriology, since Christ is both *exemplum* and *mediator*. This is not to say that Gerson has moved ahead of his time by casting this doctrine as the determinative matrix of justification.[146] We look in vain for any explicit linkage between *iustitia Dei* and *iustitia Christi* in this treatise. But he does interpret Christ, whom he characterizes as »mediator between God and man,« as the *sufficient* cause of salvation, and goes further to identify not the sacraments as in later medieval theology generally but *faith* itself as the *efficient* or *instrumental* cause by means of which *viatores* are incorporated in Christ.[147] In this sense, pastoral and confessional arguments meet in the immediacy of Gerson's Christology, the doctrine which joins his anthropology and his soteriology on the basis of a voluntarist model. It is significant for Gerson that the psychological paradigm be offered by Christ, the perfect *viator*. Christology becomes, therefore, the basis for his pastoral admonition: *viatores* are »to imitate Jesus« by conforming their wills to God's.

2. *Conformitas voluntatis:* the intersection of divine and human freedom

Throughout this chapter we have explored from various angles Gerson's theological *via media*, a mediating soteriology which sought to safeguard both divine and human freedom. In an earlier section we considered the careful manner in which he emphasized the doctrine of predestination *ante praevisa merita*, here following in general outline the Scotist position; we also examined how Gerson moved beyond Scotus, apparently under the influence of Boethius, to deny the meritorious capability of human acts and thereby eclipse almost entirely medieval virtue theory. We have also suggested that Gerson constructed a pastoral theology of seeking, based specifically on the promise offered *inquirentibus*, in place of the nominalist *facientibus quod in se est*: in the presence of the judging God *viatores* are only able to despair, but this is no invitation to resignation since we are to apply ourselves to the biblical covenant that God »rewards those who seek him« (Heb. 11.6). How, then, does Gerson coordinate this pastoral theme, if at all, with his elaborate discussion of the

Gerson, as later for Biel as Oberman has convincingly argued, the focus falls on Christ's *life* rather than death; see *Harvest*, p. 266 f.

[146] Cf. for example Pesch and Peters, *Gnade und Rechtfertigung*, pp. 110 ff. As Pesch correctly argues, the development characteristic of the later Middle Ages brought the doctrine of justification into the context of the doctrine of God, and particularly the understanding of election as *acceptatio Dei*. Gerson adheres to this general tendency, as we have earlier noted.

[147] This approach stands in marked contrast to the sacramental views held later by Biel and Geiler; on this point see Douglass, *Justification in Late Medieval Preaching*, p. 183.

obligation placed upon *viatores* to order their will in imitation of Christ? In short, is his theology of seeking, rooted as it is in a mystical doctrine of justification, compatible with the voluntarist emphases of his soteriology, and particularly with his admonition that *viatores* are to conform their wills to God's?

This would appear not to be the case, at least upon first consideration. But as we probe more carefully into the proper and distinct contexts of these respective themes the deliberate balance by which Gerson orders his mediating soteriology becomes evident. To review the first of these in brief form: Gerson's approach to election, and more specifically his Scotist understanding of predestination, disputed any suggestion that human acts might place a »necessary« force upon God's will. »Deus nulli debitor est,« as he had concluded in an Ockhamist vein, or, with cadences reminiscent of the more severe formulations of Scotus, »sed neque priorem aeterna Dei voluntas causam habet.« With such claims Gerson located himself within the main current of late-scholastic debate, since such themes established what has been properly described as »the governing feature of the Scotist and of the late-medieval doctrine of God more generally: namely, divine freedom.«[148] In terms of the doctrine of election, Gerson placed the emphasis solidly upon the side of God's freedom and initiative, and not that of *viatores*; consequently, the question of justification falls entirely under the canopy of God's free »acceptation« of us,[149] regardless of our meritorious achievements as well as any »habit« of grace conferred by the sacraments. Within this context at least there can be no room for any discussion of human initiative; all depends upon God's free act of electing (i. e., *ab aeterno*), and upon God's institution *de potentia sua ordinata* of the biblical covenants, in this case the »covenant of seeking« as expressed in Heb. 11.6. Yet even on the basis of this covenant Gerson is unwilling to apply such biblical promises as guarantees of election, concluding in more muted tones that even those *viatores* who are seekers of God must resign themselves to »whatever future [God] has ordained.« This conclusion is nothing less than the consequence of the Pauline view he consistently expresses

---

[148] Pesch, *Gnade und Rechtfertigung*, p. 113.

[149] As we earlier suggested, Gerson does not use this specific language though he does allude to the more general Scotist phrase regarding God's freedom of election vis-à-vis *acceptatio personae*; cf. here I pr. 3, and Dettloff's extensive discussion of this theme in Scotus in *Die Lehre von der acceptatio divina bei Johannes Duns Scotus mit besonderer Berücksichtigung der Rechtfertigungslehre* (Werl, 1954), pp. 163–69. And yet even in the context of this covenant – and this even more sharply for the later Gerson than for Scotus before him, since he unlike his predecessor allowed no place for the habits of grace in justification – *viatores* can only hope that they belong to the elect, since no one can finally know how she stands before God's final acceptation. See especially G 9, p. 194, where he concludes: »quicquid postremo de me futurum ordinaverit voluntas tua, corde credo et ore profiteor quoniam nulla est iniquitas apud te qui sanctus es in omnibus operibus tuis.« See also above, p. 183.

in this treatise that salvation is *sola gratia*, and as such one cannot know
»whether he is worthy of [God's] love or hate.«[150]

Justification depends finally upon God's act of electing *ab aeterno*, and even
the structure of the covenant places no necessary or binding force upon this
divine *acceptatio*. This theme appears to stand at odds, therefore, with his
emphasis upon the initiative placed upon *viatores* to order their wills in
conformity with God's will. But here we must emphasize the quite different
context of this instruction: Gerson's discussion of the will is entirely devoid of
the language of *iustitia* which we had found in passages treating the theme of the
viator's justification *coram judice Deo*. That is, he evaluates our psychological
orientation not in soteriological but in moral terms, with the result that any
conformity of our will with God's he speaks of as *rectitudo cordis nostri*.[151] Yet he
goes even further than this. After admonishing *viatores* to order their wills in
imitation of Christ's *obedientia activa*, Gerson's Monicus raises the doubting
message conveyed by Paul's deliberately skeptical anthropology, citing his
admission that despite our best efforts we are nonetheless »sold into the power
of sin« (Rom. 7.14) and find »another law in [our] members warring against the
law of [our] mind and making [us] prisoner to sin« (Rom. 7.23).[152] At the level
of human achievement, therefore, the exhortation to an unaided *imitatio Christi*
falls flat, since as *viatores* we find ourselves burdened by »the heavy weight of
original sin, the even heavier weight of actual sin, the heaviest weight of
engrained habit.« Moral obligation does not become a condition of salvation;
imitation alone brings *viatores* once again to the brink of despair, because the
fundamental and irreversible condition of the soul is that it »slips back when it
attempts to rise.«[153] At precisely this juncture of his argument, therefore,

---

[150] See above, n. 88.

[151] G 9, p. 206.

[152] *Ibid.*, pp. 208–209.

[153] One detects in this skeptical admission a frontal assault upon Boethius' admonition,
on the strength of philosophy alone, to »lift up your spirit to right hopes« (*De consolatione
philosophiae* V pr. 6; *CCSL* 94: 105). Gerson has a much less optimistic evaluation of what
moral exhortation alone can accomplish, as we see here, another index of his retreat after
Constance from an earlier adherence to the *facere quod in se est* doctrine. At the same time,
however, his comments on the nature of the will approximate Boethius' discussion, even to
the detail about the »threefold will«: »Human souls must indeed be more free when they
preserve themselves in the contemplation of the divine mind; less free, however, when they
slip down to the corporeal, and still less free when they are bound into earthly limbs. But
their ultimate servitude is when, given over to vice, they have lapsed from the possession of
the reason proper to them. For when from the light of the highest truth they have lowered
their eyes to inferior, darkling things, at once they are befogged by the cloud of
unknowing, they are disturbed by destructive affections, by giving in and by consenting to
which they strengthen that servitude which they have brought upon themselves, and are in
a way made captive by their freedom.« *De consolatione philosophiae* V pr. 2; *CCSL* 94: 90.
Cf. *De consolatione theologiae* I pr. 2, G 9, p. 207.

Volucer raises the issue from the moral to the soteriological plane, reiterating in the voice of prayer the biblical language of despair as the starting point of the human pilgrimage *ad Deum*: »Let us cry out with the apostle, ›Unhappy man that I am! Who will deliver me from this body of death?‹ And thereupon let us answer, ›The grace of God through Jesus Christ our Lord‹ (Rom. 7.24); let us say to him, ›Let it be done to us, O Lord, according to the judgment and desire not of [our] lower reason but of [your] higher reason and will. ...‹«[154] Ultimately, the conformity of the human and divine wills depends upon divine grace, as mediated *per Jesum Christum*, such that Gerson places the discussion of *imitatio Christi* within the broader soteriological framework of *Christus victor*.

Is the human will, then, truly free *coram Deo*, and does Gerson allow any language of the free conformity of the will from the human side? Apparently his *via media* does allow for this, though without giving up any ground on the question of election. And with this he falls back upon the language of paradox, offering an argument strikingly similar to Aquinas's explanation that »man's turning to God is by free choice, and thus man is bidden to turn himself to God; but free choice can be turned to God only when God turns it.«[155] Gerson echoes this Thomist theme in essential structure and logic, though varying the language to suit his purposes: he prefers to speak of the human will not as free in an unqualified sense, but as »free by participation« in God's higher will;[156] the human will must be »freed« by participation in the divine will, since the *libertas arbitrii* is ultimately »fortified« and »established« insofar as the human will is »vivified in God through grace.«[157] In other words, the human will must be »confirmed in grace« in order to overcome its native »variability,« the consequence of sin in its various manifestations (i. e., original, actual, habitual). Thus, whatever freedom the *viator* could experience was of a strictly derivative character, but in this way the human will escapes resignation precisely by »conforming« itself to the utterly free divine will.[158] What had begun as a

---

[154] *Ibid.*

[155] *Summa theologiae* IaIIae q. 109 a. 6, ad 1. This argument opposed a view of »preparation« by which *viatores* could prepare themselves for the infusion of divine grace.

[156] G 9, p. 207.

[157] G 9, p. 200.

[158] Cf. G 9, p. 204: »Vehemens prorsus haec est divinae libertatis in omni actione concurrentis expressio; cui voluntati nostra ut conformetur oportet.« Oberman correctly identifies this theme of *conformitas voluntatis* as the juncture where nominalism and mysticism of Gerson's type coincide; cf. *Harvest*, pp. 330 ff. See also Burger, *Aedificatio*, pp. 140–41. As we have earlier suggested, Gerson here concludes that *viatores* reach the apogee of that freedom not *per amorosam voluntatis conformitatem*, as he had argued in an earlier treatise on mystical theology (cf. *De mystica theologia speculativa*, cons. 40.4 ff. [Combes p. 104, ll. 22 ff.]) but rather *per contemplationem*, because »the closer one is to [this state] the steadier [*stabilior*] and freer [*liberior*] is the will which commands and enjoins the sensual will as if from on high. « In this sense Gerson appears to be influenced principally — and in quite different form than in his earlier mystical treatises — by Boethius' argument:

discussion of *imitatio Christi* moves full circle back to the nominalist emphasis upon divine freedom: for those *viatores* divesting themselves of any trust in their own works and indeed despairing in their *iustitia*, the path of salvation lay in emulating Christ by subjecting themselves to Christ in obedience to the divine will. Only in this »seeking« and »submitting« might the *viator* be »incorporated« in Christ *per fidem*, a union with God which occurs »per medium mediatoris Dei et hominum« but one which *viatores* experience as a *conformitas voluntatis* of their wills with God.[159]

3. *De providentia* as the »co-operation« of God and *viatores*

A discussion of Gerson's soteriological argument in this treatise would not be complete without raising the theme which had so exercised Boethius in *De consolatione philosophiae*: namely, divine providence. In this, of course, we might expect to find that his intentions do not deviate from the basic contours of Boethius' argument, just as he intended to build a theological argument upon the foundation of philosophy.[160] Our expectations are not disappointed. In the shadow of Boethius, Gerson steers a mediating course between those at one extreme like Cicero who denied providence altogether in their defense of human freedom, as well as those at the other such as Gregory of Rimini who embraced a determinism which at least seemed to threaten human responsibility.[161] Hence, we must finally inquire about the parallel of his

»... human reason should submit itself to the divine mind, such that we should be raised up, if we can, to the height of that highest intelligence; for there reason will see that which it cannot look at in itself ..., viz. in the simplicity, shut in by no bounds, of the highest knowledge.« The close proximity of this argument to Gerson's suggests that the parallel shapes the peculiar character of Gerson's argument, particularly when we recognize the departure this represents from the view expressed in his earlier writings; cf. *De consolatione philosophiae* V pr. 5; *CCSL* 94: 100, and G 9, pp. 211 f.

[159] See also *De mystica theologia speculativa*, cons. 39, ed. Combes, p. 104.

[160] More specifically, of course, his argument builds upon Boethius' discussion of these themes in *De consolatione philosophiae*, a correlation which Gerson grounds upon the Thomistic thesis that »theology exceeds philosophy, not by scrapping it but by submitting it in obedience« to its purposes. G 9, p. 188: »... theologia philosophiam exsuperat, quam non abjicit, sed in obsequium sumit.« See also above, 4.B. 1–2.

[161] See G. 9, p. 200. Oberman has rightly argued with reference to Bradwardine that this appears to be the case, and that Bradwardine balanced his extreme view of predestination with a doctrine of »coefficiency«: »God and man are *similiter causa efficiens* of every act of will: ›Quod omnem actum voluntatis creatae totum efficit voluntas creata et totum similiter increata.‹ ... Neither man alone – autonomy – nor God alone – heteronomy – finally decides the movement of the will.« *Archbishop Thomas Bradwardine*, p. 81. For Bradwardine's argument, see *De Causa Dei*, ed. H. Saviles, I.27, 30, 32, and II.18; he argues that »omnia a providentia divina eveniunt,« and »omnia proveniant a Dei providentia actualiter disponente, non solummodo permittente,« and yet »contra quosdam dicentes actum Liberi Arbitrii nihil esse.«

theological argument to Boethius' philosophical statement of this paradoxical conjunction, since Gerson quite self-consciously constructs his mediating soteriology as a union of providence and human freedom.

Beyond the basic arrangement by which Gerson, like Boethius, united divine providence with human freedom as a *via media et regia*, a voluntarism which safeguarded the initiative both of the human and divine actors in history, Gerson once again demonstrates the eclectic character of his broadly ranging mind. In developing his argument *de providentia*, he blends together Boethian with Thomist themes and emphases, as we have earlier noted. Borrowing the explicit neo-Platonic terminology Boethius had used, Gerson conceives *providentia* on the basis of »a simple divine understanding [which] in a single intuition comprehends present, past, and future at once,« an »intelligible center which, remaining stable, makes all else move.«[162] But at this point he imprints a distinctively Thomist character upon the argument. With Aquinas he relies quite deliberately and at a critical juncture of his consoling argument — i. e., II pr. 4, devoted to revealing »through scripture . . . the governance of the world« — upon the Aristotelian argument from causality. This »governance,« he argues, is a matter of divine foreknowledge, such that »nothing is done in the world which God has not foreseen from eternity [*ab aeterno praeviderit*], with the entire series of causes down to the smallest,« a governance »built into the order of causes which God set up from the beginning [*ab initio*].«[163] This is not merely an argument intent on avoiding the metaphysical or logical problem of infinite regress, such that the first cause would have to be inextricably but distantly related to later secondary causes; Gerson explicitly dismisses such an argument with its too tidy solution to this paradox, denying that God is to be conceived as some sort of »clockmaker« (*artifex horologium*) who merely sets the world in motion and retreats to observe its movement »without concern for individual things.«[164] Rather, he explains divine providence as a »universal cause« which »concurs principally and directly in every effect,« such that for God »nothing is fortuitous, nothing merely casual, nothing due either to some necessity external to him or to fate.«[165] Gerson thus defines foreknowledge

---

[162] G 9, pp. 211−12; for the Boethian texts, cf. *De consolatione philosophiae* III m. 9, *CCSL* 94:51 and V pr. 6, *CCSL* 94:102. See also above, 3.A.5, and 4.B.3.

[163] G 9, pp. 212, 213.

[164] The parallel of this argument, of course, provides a marvelous anticipation of the later deist position; Gerson's criticism of this view was that it was a flat and ultimately lifeless perspective, only a short step above a sheer fatalism and an approach that ignored the obvious vitality of the created order.

[165] G 9, p. 212. This argument reproduces in considerable faithfulness Aquinas's argument in *Summa theologiae* Ia q. 22 aa. 2−4; the proximity of Gerson's argument extends all the way to Aquinas's conviction that »all particular causes are included under the universal cause,« and are hence not »predestined« or »determined« but rather »foreseen« (cf. *ibid.*, a. 2, ad 1).

(*praescientia*) in causal terms, contending that God's will can be detected as a participatory cause »in every effect.« Still echoing Aquinas, apparently, he further states that God's providence is a matter of a »cooperating« causation which allows for »certain intermediaries«; Gerson introduces the language of cooperation (*coagere*), arguing with a Thomist accent that human freedom is not obliterated by divine providence, and that even though providence establishes a necessary contingency it fixes no absolute *necessity* upon human acts. Human freedom is rather a vital reflection of *viator*'s rational nature, the human characteristic par excellence by which God confers upon *viatores* what Aquinas called »the dignity of causality« and what Gerson similarly describes as cooperation.

It is this Thomist conceptualization of providence as the »co-acting« of God with *viatores* which secured the *via media* of Gerson's voluntarist soteriology, even though for its general outline he depends upon Boethius. As a mediating soteriology, in other words, this approach safeguarded God's freedom by accentuating the contingency of »the entire series of causes,« while at the same time preserving the integrity of human acts. These he conceives as part of the fabric of what he calls *ministratio Dei*: *viatores* serve as partners in God's providence, and thereby act with a freedom which confers upon them what Thomas had called »the dignity of causality.« God's *ministratio* does not stand over against, but encompasses free human acts in the broad spectrum of causation; yet these require »beyond nature« the »gratuitous governance of the spiritual« in order to attain »to the goal of eternal beatitude« (*ad finem aeternae beatitudinis*), an eschatological qualification which again brackets the scope of human freedom in teleological terms.[166]

This conception of *ministratio Dei*, which unites divine and human freedom in a process of cooperation, overcomes any tendency toward determinism in Gerson's soteriology. And, against a synergism of human acts, he conceives of the theological virtues of faith, hope, and love along with »the prayer linked to them« as the means by which the *viator* freely chooses to »participate« in the divine will. In this manner *viatores* direct themselves »through their affections and intentions in the way of peace and salvation,« and thus conform themselves to the divine will; this is *ministratio Dei* viewed from the human perspective, as it were.[167] The freedom of choice exercised by *viatores*, therefore, acquires its highest character as obedience, a posture which he bases upon *conformitas voluntatis*; this is only one part, and a necessarily contingent one at that, of the *ministratio Dei*. But it is nonetheless a crucial aspect of this voluntarist conceptualization of providence, since by it Gerson marks out his soteriological *via media* by underscoring his opposition to both divine determinism at one extreme and human resignation at the other.

[166] G 9, p. 214.
[167] G 9, p. 212.

Throughout this soteriological schema, as we have argued in this chapter, we find a careful integration of confessional and pastoral arguments by which Gerson explains and defends his *via media*. Yet this mediating argument casts its influence upon the conservative ecclesiological framework of the chancellor's thought, the theme which ultimately establishes the governing context of Gerson's thought. It is to this theme that we must finally turn our attention.

Chapter VI

The Church *in Via*:
Ecclesiology as the Shaping Matrix of Theological Theory and Practice

During the past several decades historical analysis of the late-medieval church has included a number of significant studies of Gerson's ecclesiology.[1] This should not surprise us, since Gerson devoted much of his professional energies and personal attention to addressing ecclesiological issues, questions related to the problems posed by the papal schism and the legitimation of a moderate conciliarism.[2] Indeed, given the church-political context of Gerson's work and his almost constant involvement in matters impinging upon ecclesiological issues, this development seems to be peculiarly late in coming. As such it offers an important and broadened interest in Gerson, one which extends both chronologically beyond the narrower analysis of his university career and thematically beyond the parameter of mysticism by which Combes dissected Gerson's writings in a series of magisterial studies. This development has illumined from various perspectives the practical motivations found throughout Gerson's oeuvre, on the one hand, as well as alerting us to the mystical or spiritual concerns he applied to problems of church order, discipline, or canon law, on the other. Ecclesiology was not, for Gerson, a

---

[1] Here the work of Pascoe deserves first mention, both his various essays on the subject and his major work, *Jean Gerson. Principles of Church Reform* (Leiden, 1973). See also the earlier study by Posthumus Meyjes, *Jean Gerson. Zijn Kerkpolitiek en Ecclesiologie* (s'Gravenhage, 1963), and his recent essay, »Jean Gerson,« *Mittelalter II*, ed. Martin Greschat (Stuttgart, 1983). This development is explicable, in part at least, because of the favorable ecclesiastical circumstances brought about by the Second Vatican Council and by the impact of an ecumenical – or, at least, less polemical – approach to the historical study of the Middle Ages more generally. Within such a horizon it is not surprising that the past several decades have witnessed such a resurgence of scholarly interest in Gerson's work, among both Protestant and Roman Catholic historians.

[2] Oakley's description of the conciliar position taken by d'Ailly, Gerson et al. is as concise as it is accurate when he notes that this position, particularly when set within the more radical shadows cast by earlier theorists such as Marsilius of Padua, represented »an essentially moderate doctrine of ecclesiastical constitutionalism, with unimpeachably orthodox foundations in the cozy respectabilities of the pre-Marsilian era.« See Oakley, *The Western Church*, p. 169.

strictly practical discipline, nor did he address theoretical concerns without considering ecclesiological premises and ramifications. As a theologian committed to upholding the model of the *vita ambidextra*, Gerson himself seemed relentlessly concerned to blend *theoria* and *praxis*: theology might raise one to the height of mystical contemplation, but the theologian must remain involved in the church's practical life, just as »practice« to be faithful needed proper theological grounding and interpretation.

It cannot be our intention in this study to address the question of Gerson's ecclesiology in a comprehensive fashion. This has already been accomplished in good form by others who have devoted their entire attention to this question.[3] Nor should an exhaustive analysis of Gerson's ecclesiology here occupy our attention, and this for two reasons. First, the general subject has already received competent and thorough treatment by others, and aside from several disagreements of detail the comprehensive shape of Gerson's ecclesiology remains constant in his writings post-dating Constance. Second, the treatise which dominates the focus of our study, *De consolatione theologiae*, does not concern itself in any systematic fashion with this theme, despite its comprehensive breadth. Ecclesiology provides the stage upon which this dialogue transpires and not the script for the conversation. Admittedly, this should not surprise us given the particular circumstances under which Gerson wrote the piece: viz., in the wake of the Council of Constance, which had at the very least resolved the looming ecclesiological crisis of the papal schism. The conciliar position to which Gerson ascribed, in other words, was successful in its goal of restoring order to the papacy. We might conclude on this basis that the outer argument of the text discourages an extended discussion of this theme, and that ecclesiology might well require only a passing reference alongside the theological analysis of themes and problems already introduced.

Despite such disclaimers, ecclesiology does merit our attention in this study, but not because this is a theme which Gerson belabors in this treatise; as we have suggested, it intrudes only occasionally as an explicit topic in this con-

---

[3] In addition to the contributions of Pascoe and Posthumus Meyjes, mentioned above (n. 1), we must note that other studies have also made significant contributions to this theme. An early work on this subject, Connolly's *John Gerson,* is useful as a general orientation, but his perspective is ultimately distorted by his efforts – understandable, perhaps, given the ecclesial mood which prevailed during his day within the Roman Church – to rescue Gerson's reputation from the supposed heterodoxy of nominalism, on the one hand, and the threat of an unacceptable association with Luther, on the other. More recently, Ozment offered a penetrating essay on Gerson's approach to reform, arguing that the key to his reform program was the role he attributed to the Holy Spirit; see »The University and the Church. Patterns of Reform in John Gerson,« pp. 111–26. Finally, and most importantly, Pascoe's monograph, *Jean Gerson,* explores the general theme of ecclesiology in terms of what he identifies as »the ideological pattern of reform at work« in Gerson's writings; see especially pp. 1, 17–48.

solatory dialogue. Yet, there is a pressing rationale for such a chapter, and reason enough to locate this discussion as the fitting conclusion of our study: although an admittedly ancillary theme in this dialogue, ecclesiology establishes the orienting foundation or governing context for many of the theological problems and pastoral questions which Gerson here raises. It functions as what one might call the »shaping matrix« of his thought, the context within which Gerson interprets controversial topics as they emerged in the concrete circumstances of his day. The question we must now consider is whether previous studies devoted to his ecclesiology — which concentrate primarily on his pre-conciliar writings — have properly grasped how it is that this theme shaped Gerson's theological perspective in the wake of the Council of Constance. If reform is »the ideological pattern« structuring Gerson's work in general, as one historian has argued, what will his ecclesiology look like after the council? In our study thus far we have suggested that *De consolatione theologiae* discloses a significant theological shift in Gerson's thought, above all in terms of soteriology; we must now consider how such developments relate to his ecclesiology, particularly since this appears to remain consistent with the basic approach he articulated earlier in his university career.

As we shall argue in this chapter, Gerson develops the theoretical components of his ecclesiology in constant reference to the concrete horizon of church life.[4] We shall also note a close proximity between his understanding of the human actor as *viator* and his conceptualization of the church itself as *in via*, a parallel which is indicative of his cautious, conservative temperament. Gerson stabilizes his ecclesiology, and within this matrix his theology more generally, through the influence of both a hierarchical (Dionysian) model of the church and a restrained eschatology of Augustinian provenance. It is this conservatism, finally, which rivets his attention not to the ideal church[5] but to the admittedly problem-ridden *ecclesia visibilis*: with the empirical church squarely in view he criticizes both an unbridled desire for mystical communion with God which might lead to passivity, on the one hand, and what he per-

---

[4] In general terms, it would appear that he moves here beyond the (neo-Platonic) Boethian hierarchy of *theoria* over *praxis*. Yet upon closer inspection this hierarchy is still to be found, notably in his insistence that even the »highest« (i. e., mystical) theologians must »descend« to involve themselves in the public affairs of the church. On this question see above, 4.C, and below, 6.B.3. Gerson cannot, therefore, be accused of quietism, a theme he had consistently attacked in terms of mystics who advocated a union leading to passivity. On this point cf. Brown, *Pastor and Laity*, pp. 203–204.

[5] Gordon Leff has argued that the »ideal of an apostolic church was ... the great new ecclesiological fact of the later Middle Ages,« and suggests that this trend — brought about by diverse persons including Marsilius, Dante, John of Paris, Ockham, Dietrich of Niem, Wyclif, and Hus — sought »to return the church to its primitive apostolic state as preached by Christ and his disciples.« See »The Apostolic Ideal in Later Medieval Ecclesiology,« *Journal of Theological Studies*, n. s. 18 (1967), pp. 71–81.

ceived as a mistakenly zealous reform lacking in *discretio*, on the other. Once we have examined Gerson's ecclesiology on the basis of the treatise before us, an effort which must often proceed with recourse to the specific context of the council and the difficulties which he confronted during his years at Constance (1415–1418), we find that this theme is absolutely central to his arguments, theological and pastoral. His ecclesiology serves again and again as the comprehensive and finally determinative horizon of his thought, the matrix within which he attempts to interpret his various concerns regarding *theoria* and *praxis*. Thus, Gerson's concern for *reformatio ecclesiae Dei*[6] becomes a program for comprehensive reform, reaching far beyond the question of the papal schism (i. e., *reformatio . . . in capite*); rather, reform as he conceived it extended throughout every stratum of the hierarchical church (*reformatio . . . in membris*). And, as we shall suggest, his concern for reform is at once conservative and progressive: conservative in seeking to preserve the hierarchical reality of the church during a period of rising criticism; and, progressive in conceiving of that hierarchy in dynamic terms, as a »pilgrim« church in which »ad suprema reducantur infima per media.«[7] His ecclesiology is at the deepest point – the point where conservative and progressive dimensions finally converge – an ecclesiology of pilgrimage, of the *viator*'s journey *ad Deum* in and through the church. Hence, the question presses upon us: Is *De consolatione theologiae* intended merely as a consolatory manual, or should we not rather interpret it as a treatise meant to instruct *viatores* as part of a more ambitious and comprehensive reform? This is the question which undergirds the work of this chapter.

---

[6] This phrase emerges in the conciliar decree commonly known as *Sacrosancta*, from the fifth session at Constance; he gives this decree in full within a sermon preached on the feastday of St. Anthony, 1417; see G 5, p. 384. This decree, which is indicative of what Oakley has called »a constitutional revolution in the church,« stated the conviction that the synod derived its power »immediately from Christ« and required obedience in all matters leading to »generalem reformationem ecclesiae Dei in capite et in membris.« See Oakley, *The Western Church*, p. 223.

[7] This is a fundamental theme by which he explains the logic of his ecclesiology; he articulates this theme, which he calls a »divine law,« in a letter to his brother Jean dated September 7, 1416 (G 2, p. 171), as also in *De consolatione theologiae* (G 9, p. 222). This matter receives further discussion below; see 6.A.1. See also Pascoe, *Jean Gerson*, p. 207 f. Gerson stood against this crescendo of criticism, and sought to conserve not the supposed ideal apostolic church of antiquity but the actual apostolic church as it had developed historically. On this point, see below, nn. 9, 11.

A. From the garden to the church:
Ecclesiology as social hierarchy

The theme of hierarchy dominates Gerson's vision of the church, early and late, an emphasis owing much to his dependence upon Ps.-Dionysius as he himself acknowledged with staccato-like regularity in his writings.[8] This then is no new formulation in *De consolatione theologiae*, but the reappearance of a characteristic Gersonian theme. Indeed, his explanation of the *ordo hierarchicus* as the means by which »the lower [in the church's hierarchy] have been led to God through the higher,« as he expresses it in this treatise, appears in many of the chancellor's earlier, pre-conciliar writings. We need not rehearse this point, since the character of this influence has received sufficient attention in recent Gerson studies.[9] What is not yet clear, however, is: first, the relationship of this theme to the quite distinctive theological and soteriological approach Gerson follows in this late treatise; and, second, the manner in which his application of this theme to specific problems raised in this treatise grounds his anti-Hussite polemic.

In raising this theme at this final juncture of our study we now see that Gerson relates his hierarchical ecclesiology to one of the foundational themes of his soteriology: namely, his insistence that God »did not eject man from ›the garden of delight‹ [*ab horto voluptatis*] in order that he might build for himself a new one here,« a theme which forms the theological rationale by which Gerson understands and defends his conservative reform.[10] Reform neither sanctions nor requires a restitution or reconstruction of an apostolic ideal; rather, it calls

---

[8] This dependence is to be measured less in points of detail than in the dynamic, hierarchical logic of his ecclesiology. As he concludes in a letter written during the Council of Constance, cited in the preceding note, ». . . recte pronuntiavit Dyonisius hanc esse legem divinitatis ut ad suprema reducantur infima per media.« G 2, p. 171. For a discussion of this point in terms of Gerson's earlier writings, see Pascoe, *Jean Gerson*, pp. 35–39, and esp. p. 39, n. 75.

[9] See, e. g., Pascoe's chapter entitled »The Church: Order, Hierarchy, and Reform,« in *Jean Gerson*, pp. 17–48, especially pp. 32 ff.; see further Combes, *La théologie mystique*, 1: 83 ff., 98–108, and 2: 401 ff., 449 ff., 663 ff.; Burger, *Aedificatio*, pp. 76 f., 147 f.; and, most recently, Brown, *Pastor and Laity*, pp. 36–48.

[10] G 9, p. 227. The theme of Gerson's conservatism has been ably addressed by Hübener with particular attention to his philosophical contribution; see »Der theologisch-philosophische Konservatismus des Jean Gerson,« pp. 171–200. My use of this description has less to do with the epistemological conservatism Gerson advocated, the theme which dominates Hübener's study, and more to do with his ecclesiological conservatism. In his broad survey of Gerson's life and thought, Burger rightly recognized this dimension of his thought when he spoke of »die Grundgedanken seiner konservativen Reform«; see *Aedificatio*, p. 148. Brown also notes this in her final chapter, concluding that Gerson was »in favour of reform in church and state but never in the direction of undermining hierarchy«; *Pastor and Laity*, p. 253.

for renewal from within and demands respect for the divinely ordered hierarchy in effecting this end. This image of »the garden« as an ideal unattainable because of the irreversible effects of Adam's fall expresses a more skeptical tone than his earlier use of this metaphor: in *De auferibilitate sponsi ab ecclesia* (1409) he had characterized the church in developmental terms as *seminarium*, a »garden« in which the seeds planted may develop to their full potential with the passing of time, but not in a manner exceeding their original potential.[11] In the later passage from *De consolatione theologiae* he speaks quite deliberately not of *seminarium* but of *hortus voluptatis*, and his intent seems less descriptive than polemic: in this passage he opposes any reform interpreted as retrieval of an apostolic or primitive ideal, a return to the original paradise. His commitment to reform resisted such radicalism, remaining self-consciously conservative in terms of the *present* church; indeed, he probably intended this specific use of the garden image as a rebuttal of Hus's criticism of the Roman church. It is within the historical circumstances of these opposing views of reform, and amid the precarious mood which still prevailed in the wake of Hus's trial and execution at Constance, that we must interpret Gerson's ecclesiology in this treatise – and, more specifically, his deliberate program of reform as expounded here.

A proper interpretation of Gerson's *De consolatione theologiae*, therefore, depends upon recognizing the influence of his reform-minded ecclesiology. And yet his commitment to a conservative reform, particularly as expressed after Constance, was not in the first place reactionary: he had long opposed any assault upon the church's hierarchical order – *viatores* were not to attempt to build a »new garden« for themselves – because of his conviction of long standing that the church's identity was »virtually contained« in its hierarchical structure. Gerson's firm commitment to the hierarchically ordered nature of the church thus stood as the conservative parameter for his progressive view both of the church's historical development and of his dynamic program of reform within her hierarchical structure.[12] In short, his conservative ecclesiology reflects his realization that the church *in via* could not simply

---

[11] See G 3, p. 294 f. In his study of Gerson's »principles of reform,« Pascoe points to this text to argue that Gerson did have a developmental ecclesiology, yet not one in which development meant any change of essential identity; cf. *Jean Gerson*, p. 27. Gerson even utilized a developmental metaphor which would come again to peculiar prominence in nineteenth-century discussions of doctrinal development, namely the image of the »nut« and the »tree«: »et nux arbor in nuce virtualiter continetur; has vocant philosophi inchoationes formarum in materia.« *Propositio facta coram anglicis*; G 6, p. 133.

[12] His view of ecclesiastical history did allow for development, as we have argued above; thus, for example, he interpreted the rise of canon law as a necessary development, a kind of necessary reaction – supplied to meet a particular need – because of the increasingly secularized character of the Constantinian church. Cf. for example, *Dominus his opus habet*; G 5, pp. 223 ff. Burger discusses this theme under the rubric »Das Kirchenrecht als Gottes Notordnung«; see *Aedificatio*, pp. 92–95.

return to »the garden«; progress would need to conserve the hierarchical order, not abandon or reconstruct it. Thus, he envisions reform within the context of what he calls in this treatise a »law and order« view, a reference of course to the *divine* law and order already found within the church. Within the scope of these basic themes, then, we shall not belabor his basic defense of ecclesiastical hierarchy; he here offers little that moves beyond his earlier treatment of this theme. Our focus in this chapter falls rather upon the manner in which Gerson applied this principle to specific pastoral issues and problems of his day. In the process we shall discover that his ecclesiology, structured by a dynamic but conservative approach to reform, provides the broad framework within which he views the church as itself *in via*, a »pilgrim church« by means of which *viatores* are led *ad Deum*.

1. *Lex divinitatis et ordo*: a Dionysian vision of the church

Much has been said in earlier studies of Gerson concerning the influence which Pseudo-Dionysius exerted upon his ecclesiology. We shall not here dispute this influence, at least not in a general sense. But a further level of precision does appear in order regarding the precise derivation of this influence, a correction which while not altering the structure of this theme nonetheless affects our apprehension of how Gerson applied it. To be more specific, it appears to be the case in *De consolatione theologiae*, if not also in earlier treatises, that Gerson's use of a Dionysian model of the church – one which portrays the church as a »hierarchical order« in which those of lower status (*idiotae*) are led back to God by those of higher rank[13] – may in fact be mediated through another source: namely, the writings of Thomas Aquinas, and above all his treatment of this capsulary expression in the *Summa theologiae*. This mediation does not dispute the underlying Dionysian thought, though the context in which Aquinas had cited this theme – and Gerson's critical revision in this treatise of that argument – sheds further light upon the altered theological perspective he here articulates.

The suggestion that Gerson derives this fundamental Dionysian theme from Aquinas is a premise supported in the first instance by circumstantial evidence. We know from a comment Gerson made in one of the sermons he delivered at Constance that his reading was severely restricted while at the council: here he admits that he had read »nothing except Bonaventure and Thomas« during this period.[14] This would be a weak argument and difficult to apply to any concrete

---

[13] This phrase occurs in several pivotal arguments in *De consolatione theologiae*; see for example, G 9, p. 222: »ordinem hierarchicum quo inferiores reduci habent ad Deum per superiores.«

[14] See *Sermon nuptiae factae sunt*; G 5, pp. 385 ff.: »Vidi nuper sanctum Thomam et

example, at least if it stood alone. But it does not, and the additional evidence is of a more decisive nature. When we examine how Gerson utilizes this Dionysian theme, we find that his approach borrows the thesis directly from Aquinas: already in a sermon delivered in 1415, shortly after having journeyed from Paris to Constance, Gerson had noted Dionysius' claim but cited it with specific reference to the use Aquinas had made of it. On this public occasion he even quotes Thomas directly, and the written manuscript adds the exact textual reference. Gerson agrees with Aquinas – here explicating a Dionysian theme – that »it is necessary that *matters of faith* come to those of lower degree through those of higher degree,« adding that »Thomas had proved this on the authority of Dionysius, concluding that it is necessary [for those of higher degree] *to have fuller knowledge of the things to be believed*, and *to believe them more explicitly* [*magis explicite*].«[15] Thus, when Gerson returns to this theme in *De consolatione theologiae* several years later, we find that he applies the Dionysian theme in a manner now quite critical of Aquinas's application of it. At this juncture it would appear that Gerson still has the Thomistic version rather than the original Dionysian theme in mind: The language Gerson now uses – expressed not as a direct citation but as a summary of this position – echoes not the more elaborate Dionysian speculations but the simpler expression of Aquinas. With the latter Gerson argues that it is »the hierarchical order ... by which those of lower status have to be led back to God through those of higher rank.«[16] But he now utilizes this citation in striking contrast to its earlier use by the Angelic Doctor: he is here speaking no longer of the mediation of *faith* through the church, since he now disputes Aquinas's point and insists that even the laity are to have a »formed« faith, at once »implicit« and »explicit«; rather he now applies this hierarchical theme strictly to matters of church discipline. Furthermore, his focus upon the Thomistic mediation of this theme offers a clue to questions raised by several recent studies of Gerson: namely, why he cites Dionysius without the elaborate cosmological framework of his writings,

---

Bonaventuram; hic reliquorum libros non habeo .... Nullum legi praeter Bonaventuram et Thomam.« This is not, of course, meant to suggest that Gerson showed any skepticism toward Dionysius' authority; indeed, in this same sermon we find him citing *De mystica theologia* in a positive vein (*ibid.*, p. 388), and he honors Dionysius in a letter written during this period by noting that he pronounced »the divine law« concerning ecclesiology. On this point see also above, nn. 8–9.

[15] The reference here is to *Summa theologiae* IIaIIae q. 2 a. 6. Cf. *De protestatione circa materiam fidei*; G 6, pp. 159 f.: »Explicatio, inquit, fidei ad inferiores homines oportet quod veniat per majores, quod probat auctoritate Dionysii; concludens quod oportet eos pleniorem habere notitiam de credendis, et magis explicite credere.« This is a direct and exact recitation, suggesting that Gerson did not simply reconstruct this text from memory: he apparently had access to a copy of the *Summa theologiae* during his stay in Constance, and perhaps utilized it to cite this passage (see n. 14).

[16] G 9, p. 222; see also above, n. 12.

and why his formulation of what is clearly a Dionysian assertion yet bears no close resemblance to the actual texts of the Areopagite.[17] Apparently, then, Gerson's use in *De consolatione theologiae* of the Dionysian text has a narrower application than he had earlier held; he now disputes Aquinas's application of this text to delineate a hierarchical mediation of faith in the church, confining his use of hierarchy to speak of the character of discipline and, more specifically, to defend the legitimacy of *correctio judicaria*. Within this framework he defines the *ordo hierarchicus* as the visible manifestation of the *lex divinitatis et ordo*, the »divine law and order« which structured both church and society.[18] Indeed, that order was essentially and not accidentally hierarchical, a dynamic structure by which *viatores* through disciplined obedience are to find their way *ad Deum*.

Hence, we must here locate Gerson's vision of the hierarchical church not only within the Dionysian horizon, but within the more specific context of Aquinas's mediation of that tradition – and, as we have suggested, of Gerson's

---

[17] Thus, any reference to the celestial hierarchy and above all the angels as the mediators of divine »revelations« and »power« is missing. Dionysius introduces this model of celestial mediation in both of his treatises on the hierarchies; cf. *The Celestial Hierarchy*, Chs. 4, 7; and, *The Ecclesiastical Hierarchy*, Ch. 1; in *Pseudo-Dionysius: The Complete Works*, pp. 156 ff., 161 ff., 195 ff.; *PG* 3: 182 ff., 214 ff., 370 ff. In Brown's *Pastor and Laity*, one finds a terse acknowledgement that Gerson has »departed in some respects from his mentor« (i. e., Dionysius); *ibid.*, p. 41. This is true enough as far as it goes, but it does not go far since Brown avoids discussing the thorny problem of transmission. Pascoe also wonders about the difference in the language Gerson uses, concluding by identifying »the principle behind the phrase« as »definitely Dionysian«; *Jean Gerson*, p. 35, n. 75. Combes is more specific and ambitious in his reconstruction of textual dependencies. He identifies Gerson's early use of Dionysian themes, above all in matters related to *theologia mystica*, as derivative from either Hugh of Balma or Thomas Gallus, theologians whom he calls »spiritual Dionysians.« These men, according to Combes's analysis of the pertinent Gerson texts, stand as the sources for his use of Pseudo-Dionysius. See *La théologie mystique*, 1: 83–108; and, from the same work, 2: 401 ff., 449 ff., 663 ff., etc. His insights are undoubtedly correct in terms of the various Gerson texts he cites. But he has not considered treatises written during and immediately after the Council of Constance. In terms of these texts – which, admittedly, did not occupy Combes's attention because he did not interpret them as concerned with mystical theology – the identification of Aquinas as the source behind Gerson's modified use of this Dionysian theme is simpler and more convincing, particularly given the evidence cited above. At this later juncture in his life, he draws upon the Dionysian theme of hierarchy with a narrow interest in church discipline, and indeed disputes explicitly the use Aquinas had made of the same material to refer to the mediation of faith within the church's hierarchy.

[18] G 9, p. 188. This conviction was a commonplace in medieval thought; what is striking in this instance is that Gerson felt it necessary to articulate this point, a reflection of the turbulence of the age and more specifically of the recent disorder at Constance which had erupted over matters of *doctrina* and *disciplina*. The controversies and debates during the trial of Hus stand as the background for much of the dialogue in the third book of *De consolatione theologiae* in which Gerson explored the themes of »patience« and »the moderation of zeal«; see below, 6.A.2 and 6.B.1–2.

critical reception of that position. The clarification of this critical departure from Aquinas should remind us that Gerson is no Thomist; indeed, his departure in *De consolatione theologiae* from Thomas's view, which he had accepted without criticism only several years earlier, suggests that this theme might prove important in delineating the circumstances surrounding Gerson's shifting theological perspective at this juncture. As we have suggested, he continues to cite this Dionysian argument, but now directs it to matters of church discipline: it is the Hussite threat to church order and what he interpreted as their opposition to discipline which provokes him to apply the hierarchical theme as he does in this treatise. We shall explore this point more fully in a later section of this chapter. Here we must return to the topic at hand: namely, the coherent order to be found in Gerson's social and hierarchical vision of the church, a theme which provides an unusual insight not only into Gerson's epistemology of faith with its encumbent pastoral ramifications, as we have earlier established, but into his approach to the problem of church discipline as well.

With regard to the image of the church as a hierarchy, we must note once again that Gerson views not only the church but indeed »the entire human community . . . as one body.« On the basis of this metaphor, which he does not derive from the Pauline text of 1 Corinthians 12.12 ff. as we might expect but from the Psalms, Gerson moves from theory to practice to argue that the actions of any member of that body bear responsibilities toward others: just as one member »debilitates« the entire body through harmful acts, so also do virtues resound throughout society as a whole.[19] With this text before us it is again difficult to appreciate the criticism directed against Gerson which suggests that he identified the church primarily in terms of the clergy (*superiores*), and was consequently »paternalistic« toward the laity.[20] Judging

---

[19] G 9, p. 224.

[20] Brown, *Pastor and Laity*, p. 36. Pascoe reaches a similar conclusion, suggesting that »for Gerson . . . the whole of Christianity has its foundation in the order of Prelates. « *Jean Gerson*, p. 32. Brown reaches the obvious conclusion that Gerson »conceived of the church as essentially hierarchical in nature« and goes further to argue that »from one point of view, he can be said to have seen the church as made up of ordered ranks of clerics only, with the laity as outsiders, inferiors to be helped toward their spiritual end by the church but not true members of it.« *Pastor and Laity*, pp. 38–39. This is an anachronistic reading, at the very least, one which ignores Gerson's intentional and, for his day, controversial support of lay movements such as the Brethren of the Common Life. And, as we here see, Gerson's hierarchical ecclesiology did ennoble the clergy's role while insisting that their pastoral role was to lead the *inferiores* to God. But the laity are anything but »outsiders.« This is not to deny that Gerson distinguished persons within the church according to a ranking of authority; he certainly did this, though in this he was only articulating the ecclesial realities of his day. Yet in *De consolatione theologiae* he demonstrated a remarkably progressive view toward lay responsibility and the service which *idiotae* offered for the church: that is, he here suggests that »the spirit of catholic judgment« resides among the laity rather than the

his ecclesiology from the medieval rather than modern context, we can only acknowledge his thought in general to demonstrate a decidedly progressive evaluation of the laity's role.[21] And, as we have noted earlier in this study, Gerson makes remarkable strides in *De consolatione theologiae* toward acknowledging the laity not only as *ecclesia audiens* but as the very bearers of »the spirit of catholic judgment,«[22] heirs of the theological tradition which, as he here argues, might well reside »more fruitfully« with »the simple folk« in whom one finds »a simple faith, a sure hope, and a sweet love« and who are at the same time »concerned about their salvation« (*apud idiotas sollicitos de salute sua*) than with those merely »filled with learning« (*apud repletos litteris*).[23] The

---

»learned.« See G 9, p. 238; also, see above, 4.C.1. Burger offers a more cautious criticism, interpreting Gerson more faithfully within the historical context of the fifteenth-century church by rightly noting that the chancellor's quite positive approach to the *simplices* yet did not dismiss the hierarchical ecclesiology, according to which Gerson insisted upon the superiority of theologians to the »simple Christians«; cf. *Aedificatio*, pp. 191—93. Regarding the early Gerson this perspective is certainly accurate; Burger's conclusion appears well-founded when he notes that »solange Gott nicht etwa *de potentia absoluta* neue Ordnungen schafft, müssen die hierarchischen Grade der Kirche unbedingt erhalten bleiben«; *ibid.*, p. 191.

[21] See above, 4.C.1,3.

[22] G 9, p. 238. I here follow the Glorieux reading, viz. *in animo catholicae sententiae*, though as usual this edition provides no clues to manuscript variations or the rationale for the choices made; Du Pin renders this *in animo theologicae sententiae* (cf. *Opera omnia* I, 177C). Both readings, however, are startling given the specific application Gerson is driving at, and while each has its own slightly different flavor, the force of the phrase in either case is similar.

[23] G 9, p. 238. This is not an isolated text. Indeed, in the *Tractatus primus speculativus* of his early lectures on mystical theology, *De mystica theologia* (i. e., *De mystica theologia speculative conscripta*), first written in 1402/3, but revised in 1422/3 and again shortly before his death in 1429, he arrived at a position less ambitious but equally illuminating in this regard: »Sicut multis, qui clerici vel litterati sunt aut sapientes vel phylosophi aut theologi nominantur, occultandus est sermo de mistica theologia, sic plurimis illitteratis et simplicibus, fidelibus tamen, tradi potest.« This particular passage, according to Combes's careful textual analysis, derives largely from the 1422/3 recension. Cf. *De mystica theologia*, cons. 31.1, ed. Combes, 80.3—6. Finally, in another late treatise, *De elucidatione scolastica theologiae mysticae* (1424), Gerson returns to this theme, again displaying an openly critical view of the *theologi litterati* whose learning was often accompanied by moral corruption; these he contrasts here to the *simplices illiterati* who despite the deficiency of their learning had genuine faith: »Coniecturemus ex ista similtudine quod philosophi vel theologi litterati vigent in visu et auditu spiritualibus, sed evenit multis quod tribus aliis carent sensibus vel impeditos et obtusos prorsus habent. Provenit e contra de simplicibus illiteratis quod velut ceci et surdi sunt ad philosophie scolastice perceptionem, qui ceteris sensibus vigent in spiritualium olfactu, gustu et tactu. Nullus ergo mirabitur ista considerans, si simplices et illiterati, ceci et surdi nisi quantum fides insonat, oblectantur in Deo, quem desiderando et amando olfaciunt, gustant et amplexando tangunt, habentes per vite puritatem et simplicitatem sensus istos purgatos atque reformatos, dum in aliis male viventibus penitus stupidi sunt nec percipiunt ea, que de divinis suaviter redolent, sapiunt et mulcent, quamvis videant et audiant.« Cf. *ibid.*, 232.42 ff. and G 8, p. 160. Although Gerson's contrast of the

church, as Gerson conceived it, was a social body in which *viatores* of every status — lay and clerical — shouldered the same obligation: namely, the call to return *ad Deum*, and to assist others (*inferiores*, a comparative rather than pejorative term) on that same journey. In this sense, the theme of universal obligation to »the common good« tempers any individualism and mitigates against an elitism of rank, since Gerson's view of the church »as one body« placed the duty of service upon all *viatores* without distinction of person or office.

This ambitious portrait of the role fulfilled by *idiotae* reflects Gerson's long-held skepticism toward academic theology — or, to be more precise, toward academic theologians whose efforts he felt were not fully devoted to the »useful« and »edifying« tasks of their pastoral office. His program of reform as set forth in *De consolatione theologiae*, therefore, was in the first instance a reform not of theology but of the *theologus*; as he argues in this and subsequent treatises,[24] that theologian responsible for articulating the *theologiae traditio* might more likely come from among the *idiotae* than from the ranks of the university professionals. This theme conveys a message of quite different intent and tone — more critical, if not also cynical — when compared with the letters and public addresses of 1400/1401 in which he set forth a program for theological reform.[25] Perhaps this abrupt difference in tone and approach suggests a loss of patience as well as trust in those occupying professional teaching offices in the university, theologians whose first duty involved not the speculative dimensions of their academic office but the more mundane pastoral responsibilities that he here identifies as »preaching,« »admonishing,« and »correcting.« Yet such comments about the *simplices illiterati* should be interpreted with care: Gerson may intend these not primarily as an ennoblement of the laity but rather as a strong exhortation to the clergy first of all. By defining *theologus* as he does in moral rather than intellectual terms,

---

»learned but immoral theologian« with the »uneducated but good simpleton« appears to be offered in these passages primarily as incentive for a moral and religious reform of the clergy, the sentiment nonetheless approaches in principle the famous assertion of Ockham's: viz. that the church resides in the faithful, even in a single member of the laity and even in a woman. The point of which both Ockham and Gerson were convinced is that learning or clerical status alone is no guarantee of fidelity; Gerson's point arises, admittedly, from different concerns than Ockham's, since his concern here has less to do with epistemological questions than with the moral implications raised by his social ecclesiology. For the citation from Ockham, see *Dialogus* 2.25, 6.12; a detailed discussion of this theme, with particular focus upon Ockham's contribution, is to be found in George de Lagarde, *La naissance de l'ésprit laique au declin du moyen âge* (Paris, 1963), 5: 30–52.

[24] See above, n. 23.

[25] See e. g., his letter to Pierre d'Ailly, dated April 1, 1400, to which he appended a list of projected reforms; G 2, pp. 23–28. He elaborates on themes expressed in this letter, upon returning from Bruges to Paris, in his important lectures *Contra curiositatem studentium*; see G 3, pp. 229 ff. For further discussion of these lectures, cf. Burger, *Aedificatio*, pp. 110–25.

Gerson appears to be admonishing those »filled with the learning which brings forth a knowledge which ›puffs up,‹ as the Apostle says. «[26] Perhaps, in other words, this message is meant to evoke reform among professional theologians through humiliation!

In any case, his concern to reform the church must be interpreted in terms of the social model of his ecclesiology, since Gerson was convinced that the diverse parts of the church — the various offices — were divisions of service, not of hierarchical privilege. At the same time they did constitute distinctive strata of the ecclesiastical hierarchy, and as such each had a function within the »body« of society: i. e., to return *ad Deum* and at the same time to lead others of »lower« rank (*inferiores*) on this journey. His approach to the hierarchical order of the church is set within a dynamic ecclesiology, one that envisioned the church as itself *in via*. Gerson thus understood the church as indeed the »entire human community« in social terms as a cohesive body, and in dynamic terms as a body on pilgrimage to God.[27] Those clergy who had abrogated their responsibilities within and for the church disrupted this purpose and brought »deterioration« upon the entire corpus; their failure to exercise their edifying or pastoral duties toward the *simplices*, like an omission of virtuous acts, weakened the body as a whole. Throughout this discussion it is this social context which dominates Gerson's ecclesiology, an approach which modifies any trace of elitism in his hierarchical model by emphasizing the obligation of mutuality placed upon all *viatores*, the *inferiores* as well as *superiores*.

2. *Correctio judicaria*: the priority of *communitas* over *libertas*

Gerson's ecclesiology establishes the framework, as we might well expect, in which he addresses himself to matters of church discipline. That this theme should emerge in a treatise written on the immediate heels of the Council of Constance should not surprise us; what is unexpected, however, is the manner in which Gerson approaches this issue: he here addresses himself not so much to answering particular theological criticisms, but to defending the necessary role of discipline within the coherent structure of his ecclesiology. Even in the one apparent exception to this — the extended exegetical argument which

---

[26] G 9, p. 238; see also above, 4.C.1. The biblical reference is to 1 Cor. 8.1.

[27] Elsewhere in this treatise he augments the »body« image by describing the church by means of the aggressive biblical metaphor *acies ordinata*, one which he takes apparently from the Song of Songs 6.3: »ego dilecto meo et dilectus meus mihi qui pascitur inter lilia pulchra es amica mea suavis et decora sicut Hierusalem terribilis ut castorum *acies ordinata.*« Pascoe has pointed to Gerson's use of this metaphor in earlier contexts, one of which includes his address delivered to the English delegation en route to the Council of Pisa (G 6, p. 133); *Jean Gerson*, pp. 23, 26.

apparently stands as a direct response to the Hussite attack upon simony within the church[28] — it is ultimately his ecclesiology, through which he viewed the church as an interrelated (social) body, which undergirds his defense. Throughout the treatise, therefore, the centrality of his ecclesiology holds forth, since this finally functions as the determinative matrix of his approach to diverse theological and pastoral questions.

This is particularly apparent in his theoretical analysis of church discipline, a problem he raises in this treatise not in any systematic manner but as an implicate of his comprehensive ecclesiology. And, as we have earlier suggested, he applies the Dionysian argument for hierarchy precisely at this juncture of the dialogue: namely, as a description of the communal context within which discipline functions as the mechanism to conserve »the divine law and order.« In III pr. 3 Gerson's Volucer interrupts his own explanation of the necessary moderation of zeal with an excursus of sorts in which he expounds a careful terminological distinction between *correctio fraterna* and *correctio judicaria*. The former is fairly straightforward in scope: within the social framework of his ecclesiology Gerson identifies »fraternal correction,« in striking proximity to Thomas Aquinas, not as a punitive category of judicial restraint but as a »work of spiritual almsgiving« (*opus eleemosynae spiritualis*), an »affirmative precept« governed by Jesus' instruction given in Mt. 18.15: »If your brother sins against you ...« etc.[29] Yet Gerson probably intended this argument as a direct if posthumous response to Hus's insistence in the final session of his trial that under no condition was the church able to punish a person »by corporeal death.« Indeed, in his argument Hus had utilized the same biblical basis, citing Mt. 18.15 ff. along with Jn. 8.11, »Neither do I condemn you. ...«[30] Thus,

---

[28] See above, 4.A.1. Gerson bases his defense, as I have earlier suggested, on his insistence that the benefice system was not »simoniac« if priests receiving such stipends provided someone to discharge the requisite pastoral care. Brown also addresses this theme, primarily with reference to Gerson's vernacular homilies, under the rubric of the »decent status rule«; see *Pastor and Laity*, p. 167.

[29] G 9, p. 222. Cf. *Summa theologiae* IIaIIae q. 33 a. 1: »To correct the wrongdoer is a spiritual almsdeed.« This is an admission which occupies a pivotal function in his answer to the question »whether fraternal correction is an act of charity?« Van Engen notes that »fraternal correction,« which was similar to the monastic »chapter of faults,« was a prominent practice among the Brothers and Sisters of the Common Life; See *Devotio moderna*, pp. 17–18.

[30] Cf. *Summa theologiae* IIaIIae q. 33 a. 1, *resp.* The term *epikeia* was frequently heard during Gerson's life, and often emerges in his own thought, particularly with regard to discussions on the legitimacy of conciliarism. Gerson often invoked *epikeia* to suggest that the »end« of the law sometimes did justify an otherwise unlawful means; this was so because the general principles of law could not account for every case. In this regard, *epikeia* was an important consideration not only for lawyers, ecclesiastical or civil, but for pastors as well who often had to consider the projected outcome that an application of general principles to specific cases might entail. Aristotle, whom Gerson frequently cites as the authority on this point, set forth the classic statement of the principle of *epikeia* (or *aequitas*)

Gerson's distinction of *correctio fraterna* from *correctio judicaria* accepts Hus's
contention in terms of errors or sins which have ramifications *only* for the one
committing them; if the implications of such acts have a wider effect on the civil
or ecclesiastical community, however, Gerson insists that a different sort of
correction is in order, one that would safeguard not individual liberties but the
»common good« of the body politic. This is, therefore, much more than an
accidental use of a biblical text: it seems to stand as a quite specific response to
Hus, and perhaps to those sympathetic to his cause who viewed his execution
as a martyrdom rather than an act meant to preserve the faith and order of the
church.

In making this distinction between *correctio fraterna* and *correctio judicaria*,
Gerson does qualify the former through recourse to *epikeia*, admitting with
distinct echoes to Aquinas's position that even this form of discipline should be
suspended if such correction might either be without effect or lead to the
»deterioration« of the one corrected.[31] But it is the latter form which interests
us here, particularly because Gerson's approach to *correctio judicaria* offers a
penetrating insight into the controversial side of his ecclesiology. This theme
also appears to be of greater interest to Gerson himself, since he prefaces what
was a disputed topic at Constance − a controversy, we might assume, which
Hus's trial and execution would only have exacerbated − through the
introduction of an uncontested theme: namely, his treatment of *correctio
fraterna*, which follows Aquinas's discussion in straightforward fashion. Both
forms of correction Gerson interprets not in theoretical or abstract terms but
with an eye to concrete pastoral circumstances, qualifying the general rule in
each case to embrace individual instances in which this rule should be bent (i. e.,
epikeia) and thus interpreting these themes not as ends in themselves but as
means to a greater end. That end, as we shall see, is shaped according to the
social structure of his ecclesiology. But his treatment of the former seems to

---

for medieval theology: »Equity, though just, is not legal justice, but a rectification of legal
justice. The reason for this is that law is always a general statement, yet there are cases
which it is not possible to cover in a general statement. . . . When, therefore, the law lays
down a general rule, and thereafter a case arises which is an exception to the rule, it is then
right, where the lawgiver's pronouncement because of its absoluteness is defective and
erroneous, to rectify the defect by deciding as the lawgiver would himself decide if he were
present on the occasion, and would have enacted if he had been cognizant of the case in
question. Hence, while the equitable is just, and is superior to one form of justice, it is not
superior to absolute justice, but only to the error due to its absolute statement. This is the
essential nature of the equitable: it is a rectification of law where law is defective because of
its generality.« *Nicomachean Ethics* 5.10.3, trans. H. Rackham (Cambridge, Mass., 1926),
pp. 315−17. Gerson's use of this phrase has received substantial treatment elsewhere, and
need not be rehearsed here; see e. g., Pascoe, *Jean Gerson*, pp. 66 ff.; Burger, *Aedificatio*,
pp. 87 ff. and 90 ff.

[31] See Mladoňovice, »Account,« in *Hus at the Council*, ed Spinka, pp. 193−94.

function primarily as a polemic foil against which he delineates the more severe
form of discipline, »judicial correction.«

Gerson insists that *correctio judicaria*, which he applies to matters transcending
one's own salvation and infringing upon that of the *communitas* or »the entire
population« (*salus ... totius reipublicae*), is a markedly different matter than
correctio fraterna.[32] At the outset of his discussion he interprets this kind of
correction also with a certain degree of latitude, once again applying the
principle of *epikeia* out of pastoral concern to avoid unnecessary or ineffective
forms of punishment. Here circumstance and intention provide the qualifying
norms governing his reticence: for example, he admits that one should not
correct children with severity on account of their »innate weakness« (*ratio
fragilitatis propriae*), nor should one discipline those who merely hold the
opinions of others since such convictions are often neither easily relinquished
nor lightly corrected.[33] Yet, once such exceptional cases have been considered,
the rule of *epikeia* is no longer serviceable; this is particularly true in cases
involving sins which »taint publicly the teachings of the Christian religion
[*doctrina christianae religionis*], bringing offense to the weak [*cum scandalo
pusillorum*].« In such matters, judicial responsibility cannot countenance silence
or passivity since one has to consider not the individual but society: in cases
which infringe upon »the body politic,« one has an obligation to judge not with
respect to the individual liberties of a heretic or criminal but in terms of the
possible consequences of heretical or criminal acts within the wider
community. Once again it is the *social* structure of Gerson's ecclesiology which
shapes his specific approach to judicial discipline. Within this context he insists
that matters infringing upon the common good — among which he identifies
the violation or deliberate disregard of the church's teaching — require severe
judgment in order to preserve the social fabric of the human community,
whether civil or ecclesiastical, which functions »as one body.« Can there be any
doubt that Gerson is here fashioning a careful defense of the church's recent
judicial proceedings at Constance, and particularly the council's condemnation
of Hus?

Gerson's first concern in this regard is not to defend *libertas*; issues of doctrine
and discipline were not subjects for a free and open forum of theological debate.
This might have been possible »in the garden,« where an original righteousness
prevailed as Augustine also had suggested, but he insists that the Fall had
inaugurated a different social arrangement, one in which coercive authority

---

[32] On Gerson's discussion of the latter and its relationship to his exegesis of Mt. 18.15,
see Pascoe, *Jean Gerson*, p. 121.

[33] G 9, p. 222. In point of fact Gerson expends a great deal of energy discussing the
various times when »judicial correction« should be qualified in the manner of *epikeia*; this
would have been welcome advice to lower clergy faced on a regular basis with matters of
dispute brought before their jurisdiction.

— and, particularly, the application of *correctio judicaria* — had become a necessary condition of human life, a safeguard applied for the common good of the wider social community.[34] This theme has a distinctive voluntarist bent, corresponding to the character of his theology more generally. In this sense it is clear that Gerson was no advocate of an unlimited freedom of the will even in the private sphere, but spoke rather of *an ordered freedom* which depended upon obedience exercised already within the hierarchy of wills (i. e., *conformitas voluntatis*). As he argued elsewhere in this treatise, God's will is the *prima voluntas liberrima*, and our freedom consists entirely in conforming ours to that »first and most free will. «[35] In a similar and related sense, Gerson arrives at his »law and order« approach to discipline not only because of the social model of his ecclesiology but because he conceived of the *doctrina christianae religionis* as the fullest — or, as he puts it in this treatise, »most explicit« — expression of *lex divina*. It is for this reason, and not simply because of a capricious effort to defend the ecclesiastical status quo, that Gerson remained adamant in his defense of *doctrina* as an instance in which the *correctio judicaria* might be justifiably applied. Christian doctrine is itself, according to Gerson, an outward expression of the divine law, and consequently *viatores* were to be obedient toward that law and the institutional structures which supported it. Conformity of doctrine, in other words, stands as one concrete instance in which Gerson applies the voluntarist principle of *conformitas voluntatis*, a theme by which once again the obligation of the *viator* to the community of faith takes precedence over any notion of individual freedom. Throughout his treatment of these themes, therefore, we find resonances to the Pauline insistence that »omnia mihi licent, sed non omnia aedificant« (1 Cor. 10.23). The sociality of the church — the church as *communitas* — finally establishes an absolute limitation upon human freedom. To state this thesis as Gerson does in a positive sense: *communitas* takes priority over *libertas*, obligating *viatores* in accordance with the *lex divinitatis et ordo* to engage in the edifying work of »judicial correction,« discipline exercised within the hierarchical order against those who impede the church as she returns *ad Deum*.

3. *Sensus a sanctis patribus traditus:*
Exegesis within the church as historical community

Similar reasoning shapes Gerson's understanding of how exegesis should proceed within the church, since the social dimensions of his ecclesiology qualify how he understands the task of biblical exegesis. This conviction

---

[34] See also *De vita spirituali*, where he defines the jurisdiction by which the church exercises the *potestas coercitiva*; G 3, p. 144.

[35] G 9, p. 215.

reflects, of course, the general anthropological principle he had earlier applied, a principle which shapes his ecclesiology throughout this treatise: echoing Aristotle's view of the human condition, Gerson held that »man is by nature a social animal«[36] and thus cannot live faithfully in isolation from others. Individualism finds no place in his theological vocabulary nor within the social structure of his ecclesiology. This general conviction led him repeatedly to condemn the defiant attitude by which *viatores* refused to accept advice from others. In his early treatise *De distinctione verarum revelationum a falsis* (1401) Gerson had interpreted such defiance as *discretionis defectus*, a defect which he identified as the cause of the many misfortunes — including the papal schism — facing the church. He buttressed this conviction with a colorful reference to John Climacus, who in his *De scala perfectionis* had argued that »the arrogant person who makes himself his own guide needs no devil to tempt him since he has become his own devil already.«[37] Gerson returns to this theme in *De consolatione theologiae*, although this time setting it within a quite different framework: here he notes that the »strong passions« (*passio vehemens*) distort human reason and persuade *viatores* — against reason — not to seek the advice of others; he even goes so far as to gloss the Psalm which held that »your justifications are my counsel« (Ps. 118.24) by insisting that this claim should in no way dissuade us from seeking *human* counsel since this is »divine« if one seeks it »correctly, humbly, with devotion, and obediently.«[38] In short, this general emphasis upon discretion and the necessity of seeking advice, which derives from Gerson's anthropology and structures his ecclesiology, is at the same time the general framework in which we must interpret his approach to exegesis.

This analysis sketches Gerson's perspective in only the most general terms, preparing us in a quite preliminary way for the more specific and demanding question of how the exegetical task is to be conceived. Beyond this general context, and in a more comprehensive sense, Gerson understands the rules governing exegesis within the social dimension of *communitas*, which he interprets primarily in *historical* terms. This approach is not different in broad strokes from his insistence that one must generally seek advice within the present hierarchy of the church: he demonstrates no tolerance for an individualism which defies hierarchical authority, just as he also rejects any individual reading of the biblical text since the scriptures are inextricably lodged within the church as a social community. *De potentia Dei ordinata* these scriptures offer God's speech, the »revealed theology« which conveys to *viatores* the divine commands and promises; as the expression of an »ordained« covenant, the Bible itself shapes the church as a »gathering of the faithful«

---

[36] Gerson cites this approach, for example, in *De vita spirituali animae*; G 3, p. 135.
[37] G 3, pp. 43–44; the reference from Climacus is to his *De scala perfectionis*; PG 88: 970.
[38] G 9, p. 239.

(*congregatio fidelium*). But the intention of this governing rule is decidedly different in origin and scope, and here again we must note the expansive influence of Gerson's close alliance of *scriptura* and *theologia*: not unlike his defense of *doctrina* within the body politic, biblical interpretation as the horizon of theological work requires the individual exegete to submit to the church's authority. In this thesis two of Gerson's ecclesiological convictions coalesce: first, the church as *social* community stands as both the product of the scriptures and the horizon within which they are to be read; and, second, the church as *historical* community represents the tradition by which one grasps the »sense« of the text. This latter affirmation demands closer attention, since this brings us to one of the most elusive and recently disputed facets of Gerson's exegetical theory. It is to this question which we must now turn our attention.

From the twelfth century onward theologians devoted increasing attention to the *sensus litteralis* of scripture, a development which historians of medieval exegesis have noted in particular vis-à-vis the early Victorine school.[39] In the adroit hands of Thomas Aquinas, the literal sense again stands at the center of exegetical — and, for that matter, theological — work. As he argues at the outset of the *Summa theologiae*, »all meanings« gleaned from a biblical passage »are based on one, namely the literal sense.«[40] But when we inquire what this »literal sense« represented for Aquinas it becomes clear that he has moved decisively beyond earlier exegetes: he defines this »literal sense« in terms of its *author* and *authorial intent* rather than an »objective« content. Furthermore, since he assumes that the author is none other than God who »comprehends everything all at once in his understanding,« he concludes that this »intended« (literal) meaning encompasses several of the »senses« by which the biblical text had earlier been interpreted.[41] This did not, however, eliminate the practical confusion surrounding the exegetical task primarily because one critical problem remained, a difficulty which Gerson recognized with particular clarity: despite the clue Thomas had provided regarding authorial intention, or perhaps we must rather say precisely *because* of this assertion, exegetes still had to cross the perilous bridge of discerning that intention and thereby identifying the (intended) literal meaning. Gerson approached this question by also affirming the priority of the *sensus litteralis* in exegetical study and theological argument. But he no longer shares Aquinas's confidence that this literal sense is accessible in an undisputed manner; indeed, the controversies of the early

---

[39] On this development, see Smalley, *The Study of the Bible*, and her later essay, »The Bible in the Middle Ages,« *The Church's Use of the Bible, Past and Present*, ed. D. Nineham (London, 1963), especially pp. 59 ff.

[40] *Summa theologiae* Ia q. 1 a. 10, *resp.*

[41] That is, Aquinas expands the horizon of the literal sense to include history, etiology, analogy, and what he calls »the parabolic sense« (*sensus parabolicus*). See *Summa theologiae* Ia, q. 1 a. 10, ad 1–2. On this question, see also Froehlich, »Fifteenth-Century Hermeneutics,« pp. 34 f.

fifteenth century – and here we might mention Matthew Grabow's assault upon the Brethren of the Common Life, Jean Petit's defense of tyrannicide, the Hussite insistence on communion »in both kinds« – which confronted Gerson consistently involved exegesis, and often converged on the question of properly interpreting scripture precisely in its literal sense. For Gerson as for theologians of the early fifteenth century generally, the problematic of biblical exegesis collapsed into a perspectival issue rather than remaining a question of identifying in an objective fashion the literal sense of the text. As Aquinas himself had earlier suggested, offering a directive which unwittingly conveys the difficulty at the heart of ensuing debates, »the duty of every good interpreter is to contemplate not the words, but the sense of the words.«[42] *Non considerare verba sed sensum*: the search to respond faithfully to this claim lies at the center of theological debates during the later Middle Ages, disputes that were often exegetical conflicts over what exactly constituted the literal sense.

Gerson is no stranger to this debate. During the years of the Council of Constance (1414–1418) we find him responding to this question in letters, sermons, and academic treatises both polemical and didactic. Often he frames his arguments in the heat of debate, and almost always his response returns to the question of exegetical method as he defends an »ecclesial« reading of scripture – that is, an interpretation of scripture anchored within the church's historical witness. Indeed, Gerson's response to the various challenges he faced during this period led him not to assert a simple defense of ecclesiastical prerogative but to articulate what might be called a »hermeneutic of tradition,« a defense of the historical church as the authoritative, normative guide for rendering an authentic interpretation of the *sensus litteralis*. He thus answered Aquinas's admonition to ascertain »the sense of the words« by reading scripture within an *ecclesial* framework: the literal sense of the text must be discerned within the church as historical community, and thus he resolves the hermeneutical question not as a *textual* but as a *contextual* problem. The question of exegesis, in other words, has become subsumed within his ecclesiology: the reception and interpretation of scripture – i. e., *doctrina* – were to transpire in harmony with the church's historical tradition.

But what is this tradition as Gerson understood it – or, to press this question to a deeper level, what is the *church* which receives and interprets scripture in an »authentic« fashion? Recent studies of Gerson in specific and of late-medieval exegesis in general have concluded with differing accents that Gerson identified the *present* church, guided by the spirit, with this tradition.[43] As a *perspectival*

---

[42] *In Matth.* XXVII. 1, n. 2321, ed. R. Cai (Turin, Rome, 1951), p. 358. This text is cited in Joseph Cardinal Ratzinger, »Biblical Interpretation in Crisis: Foundations and Approaches of Biblical Exegesis,« *Origins. NC Documentary Service* 17: 35 (1988), p. 600, n. 30; reprinted in *This World: A Journal of Religion and Public Life* (1988), pp. 3–20.

[43] In this vein, Posthumus Meyjes in *Jean Gerson: Zijn Kerkpolitiek en Ecclesiologie,*

issue, however, Gerson points first to the *historical* context of the church, and above all to the early church (*ecclesia primitiva*) as the interpretive community. Gerson announced this judgment in a treatise written at the midpoint of his sojourn at Constance, the carefully argued response to the »utraquists« which he entitled *De necessaria communione laicorum sub utraque specie* (1417). He there concluded that »sacred scripture in its authentic reception and interpretation [*in sui receptione et expositione authentica*] is ultimately resolved by the authority, reception, and approbation of the universal church, and *above all by the early church* which received [these scriptures] *and its understanding* [of them] directly from Christ through the revelation by the Holy Spirit at the day of Pentecost and at many others.«[44] *Et ejus intellectum*: not only did the church — and he deliberately emphasizes the primary role of the *early* church in this regard,

---

pp. 259 ff., suggests that Gerson so emphasized the role of the spirit over the church and church over scripture that he countenanced a »two source« theory of revelation. Oberman in the same year published similar views on Gerson in his *Harvest*, pp. 385 ff., identifying Gerson as an advocate of what he called the »Tradition II« position: characterizing Gerson's exegesis as governed by »a spirit-guided church,« Oberman concludes that »through the ongoing definition of truth by the Church, the canonical boundaries are enlarged and Holy Scripture is materially extended« (*ibid.*, p. 389). And, finally, Samuel Preus in his *From Shadow to Promise. Old Testament Interpretation from Augustine to the Young Luther* (Cambridge, MA, 1969), pp. 79–82, goes even further to suggest that Gerson represents a »Tradition III« position, one which held that »the *fundamentum* rests in the church *alone*« because only the »spirit-governed Church« is able »to judge and declare what the *literal* sense of Scripture is.« Each of these studies has rightly identified Gerson's defense of the church's role in determining the proper »sense« of the biblical text, but he conceives of this role at least in his writings after the Council of Pisa (1409) not by pointing to an authority exercised by the present church — whether identified with the magisterium, the doctors, canon lawyers, etc. — but by pointing to the role played by the historical church. Gerson does, of course, point out — as Oberman reminds us — that the present church *does* maintain an authority to interpret scripture in an ongoing manner; in this sense he holds a view of tradition as developing within history, in part as a response to historical circumstances. But he sets this authority beneath that of the *ecclesia primitiva*, since the early witness has a normative role in this process; we shall explore this point more fully in the following discussion, reviewing there the textual basis for this historiographical correction.

[44] This assertion is the ninth of the »ten rules of theory« guiding biblical exegesis; G 10, p. 58 (my emphasis). This treatise, written in direct response to the Hussite demand for eucharistic communion »in both kinds« for the laity (the »utraquist« position), is of particular pertinence in considering Gerson's exegesis, a point which his inclusion in this treatise of a lengthy theoretical preface on biblical interpretation makes abundantly clear. His dispute with the Hussite faction was not merely over theological issues but was more deeply rooted in disagreements regarding the rationale — exegetical, above all — by which theological positions were established. This approach did not presume, however, that the present conception of the church was to be modelled on an ideal of the apostolic church; Gerson allowed for development within the church's order in the post-Constantinian age, while insisting that the task of exegesis favored the interpretation of the »primitive church.« This contrasts with Marsilius' view as expressed in *Defensor pacis*; for a penetrating discussion of the latter, see Leff, »The Apostolic Ideal,« esp. pp. 64–73.

emphasizing that their reception of revelation occurred not only at Pentecost but at other times as well — receive the scriptures *immediate a Christo* but it had received »its understanding of them« *a Christo*. This thesis echoes a claim he had made earlier in *De sensu litterali sacrae scripturae* (1414), in which he pointed to tradition, and above all the »primitive« tradition, as the recipient and bearer of revelation.[45] Here he had argued, in strikingly similar terms, that the church received the *sensus litteralis* as revealed *per Christum et apostolos*, an original revelation not only as a text but as a text together with an authentic recognition of its proper *sensus litteralis*; subsequently, the later tradition of the *sacri doctores ecclesiae* has merely »drawn forth« (*elicuerunt*) this sense through further reasoning — a development necessitated because of the need to oppose heretics and offer a clearer grasp of that revelation. Again, the emphasis falls not upon the present, spirit-guided church, and not upon additional revelation which would extend the scriptural canon. Rather, Gerson underscores the historical witness of the early church which received the revelation together with an »authentic interpretation« of it — that is, a knowledge of its proper literal sense and the implications of that sense.

In his treatise *De necessaria communione laicorum* written toward the close of the Council, Gerson resorts to an argument which he cites elsewhere in his writings, one which is something of a commonplace in the theological literature of this period: namely, Augustine's assertion that »I would not have believed the gospel if the authority of the church had not compelled me.«[46] Gerson had utilized this claim in various ways and under diverse circumstances to point out that the authority of scripture is inextricably related to the authority of the church which »conveys« it.[47] He apparently recognized the

---

[45] Note especially the sixth thesis in this short work, a passage which we have discussed in considerable detail already; see above, 4.A.3. What should now be clear is that Gerson distinguished the historical »tradition« in such a manner that he attributes to the church what Albert Lang has called — in reference to a general tendency of the later Middle Ages, and *not* to Gerson's work in specific — »eine entscheidende *und unentbehrliche Bedeutung* für die Vermittlung der Offenbarung« such that the church fulfills a »normative« rather than »constitutive« role in this mediation; see *Die theologische Prinzipienlehre*, pp. 217–20. Oberman approaches the same point by suggesting that scripture conveys the »matter« and the Spirit and the church represent the »form« in this process, a point which is only misleading in ignoring the persistent emphasis Gerson placed upon the *early* church in this process. Cf. *Harvest*, p. 387. The *ecclesia primitiva* renders the »sense« of the text, in other words, and does not add to it in any substantial manner; the biblical canon is not expanded, though it is clearly interpreted by later theologians and via the church's decretals.
[46] Cf. *Contra epistolam Manichaei quam vocant fundamenti liber unus*, in *CSEL* 25. 197, 22; G 10, p. 358. Oberman has noted that this particular passage receives wide circulation during the later Middle Ages, standing as »invariably the medieval authority in this context«; *Harvest*, p. 385.
[47] See also *De vita spirituali animae*, G 3, p. 139; *De sensu litterali sacrae scripturae*, G 3, p. 335; *Quae veritates sint de necessitate salutis credendae*, G 6, p. 82, etc. Oberman notes the variance already in d'Ailly, which recurs in Gerson, by which Augustine's *commovere* has

ambiguity of Augustine's reference to *ecclesia* in this frequently cited aphorism, adding in one of his early uses of it that *ecclesia* was a reference not to the *present* but to the *primitive* church which stood in direct proximity to Christ: »Ibidem enim ecclesiam sumit pro primitiva congregatione fidelium eorum qui Christum viderunt, audierunt et sui testes exstiterunt.«[48] In other words,

---

been replaced with *compellere*; he argues that this alters the meaning in a decisive fashion, since it »suggests more of a duality between Scripture and the Church than the phrasing of Augustine's text itself.« *Harvest.*, p. 385. But does this interpretation stand alongside Gerson's more detailed explication of how the relation of scripture and tradition was to be understood? In terms of the broad range of texts we have here studied, this conclusion does not accurately portray Gerson's position. To return to our earlier discussion (see above, 4.A.4), one must be quite precise in interpreting Gerson's »grades« of truth in *Quae veritates*, a text which has been utilized in defense of the thesis that Gerson's hermeneutics posits in »tradition« a second source of revelation (i. e., Oberman's »Tradition II«). On the basis of a critical reading of this text and of the varying degrees of emphasis which he, unlike Ockham in the *Dialogus*, places upon these grades, we now recognize that Gerson identifies only the first grade (i. e., the »entire canon of sacred scripture and every single thing which is asserted in the literal sense«) as necessary to be believed by all; the second grade (those truths »determined by the church« and carried through the apostolic succession) he places in a »mutual« relation to the first, such that »in diverse respects both authorities confirm each other mutually.« In this sense Gerson's inversion of the Augustinian maxim is extremely significant: he »would not have believed the church *if the authority of sacred scripture had not compelled*« him to do so. In other words, Gerson refuses to apply claims made by the church in a later period – i. e., the spirit-guided tradition – as »necessary« to be believed by the *whole* church, unless they can *also* be confirmed in scripture. With the third grade – viz., those truths »specially revealed to some« – we have to reckon with truths which are necessarily to be believed, but *only* »by those to whom this revelation has been made,« and so on. He did not oppose these extrascriptural revelations, but insisted that these were not to be binding upon the whole church. In both of these cases Gerson leaves no room for extrascriptural truths which must be believed by all the church, and even those of the »second grade« which are not contained explicitly in the scriptures Gerson limits in terms of a strictly »mutual« relationship to the biblical text in its literal sense. Hence, it is true to say, with Oberman, that Gerson allows for extrascriptural truths; this has never been disputed, and indeed he could not have imagined a *sola scriptura* principle which excluded additional revelations since this would have been tantamount to a blasphemous limitation of God's »absolute power.« As a devoted advocate of *theologia mystica*, which has been astutely characterized as »a science of the *potentia Dei absoluta*« (see Ozment, »Mysticism, Nominalism, and Dissent,« pp. 80 ff.), Gerson would not have tolerated placing such strictures upon God – an argument which stood as a flagrant assault upon piety, as he understood it. But it is not an accurate reading of these texts to conclude on this basis that these additional revelations would have had any binding authority on the whole church or that they extended the canon in a material sense. For the entire church scripture provided the »sufficient« authority for faith. To return, therefore, to the question of Gerson's peculiar use of *compellere* here, we must now doubt a reading of this variance which would conclude that this establishes a second source of truth, or what Oberman calls »a duality between Scripture and the Church«; it is merely Gerson's way of affirming the role which the church plays in moving *viatores* to *assent* to the truths found in scripture.

[48] See *De vita spirituali animae* (1402); G 3, p. 139. This is not, then, an affirmation of a duality of sources of revelation, but a matter of the *text* in *context*, and specifically in the

Gerson lodges the hermeneutic question within an ecclesiological framework, one defined not in terms of the present hierarchy or magisterium but in the quite different context of the earlier tradition: the historical church − and, above all, the »primitive« church − functions as the guide of a contextual interpretation because it had received both the revelation and an »authentic understanding« of it, both the text and the proper interpretation of what he simply calls its »proper sense.«

As a consequence of this not just any interpretation of the scriptures will disclose their truth,[49] but only one that discerns the authentic *sensus litteralis* of the text. He illustrates this point in another treatise, »Réponse à la consultation des maîtres,« written during the early stages of the Council of Constance (1415).[50] In this treatise Gerson discusses how the true *sensus litteralis* is to be discerned, particularly given the controversies of his day − above all the Petit affair and the Hussite challenge − in which varying interpretations of scripture provoked a debate about how one might ascertain the true literal sense of the text. Here he aligns his exegetical method with Augustine, Nicholas of Lyra, and Henry Totting of Oyta, to argue that one must follow three rules: first, one must interpret a given text in the broader literary and historical context; second, one must give heed to the *modus loquendi* through »figures, tropes, and rhetorical expressions«; and, third, one must follow the *usus loquendi* established by »the holy doctors and expositors of sacred scripture.«[51] This final argument is of critical important to our understanding of Gerson's use of tradition as the final arbiter in the exegetical task: as he goes on to argue here, scripture must not be explained »according to a power of logic or dialectic

---

context of the early church which had received the text not with an additional revelation but with what he calls »an authentic understanding« of it.

[49] Burger also recognizes this point, concluding that »es steht eben nicht jedem Christ frei, sich seine eigene Deutung zurechtzulegen!« *Aedificatio*, p. 145. He cites in defense of this interpretation Gerson's treatment in *De sensu litterali*: »Sensus scripturae litteralis iudicandus est prout ecclesia spiritu sancto inspirata et gubernata determinavit, *et non ad cuiuslibet arbitrium et interpretationem*.« G 3, p. 335. Burger rightly suggests that the obligation of identifying the literal sense falls to the church, without however suggesting that this duty moved beyond this normative function; he does not cite Oberman's thesis here regarding Gerson's supposed placement in »Tradition II« (i. e., scripture and tradition as two sources of revelation), but his position clearly rejects such a conclusion. What still needs to be added to Burger's generally correct reading, however, is that by church Gerson means above all *ecclesia primitiva*: the church as »normative« tradition points above all to the historical church of the pre-Constantinian period (i. e., *ecclesia primitiva*).

[50] See G 10, pp. 232−53. Gerson wrote this treatise in explanation and defense of the condemnation of heresy by the council gathered at Constance; he aligns himself in this argument with similar judgments rendered by Cardinal d'Ailly who had publicly declared that certain teachings were erroneous »in fide et moribus,« as well as the declamations rendered »... nedum Universitatis Parisiensis sed de aliis Universitatibus ac provinciis regni Franciae.« *Ibid.*, p. 233.

[51] *Ibid.*, p. 241.

applied in the speculative sciences . . .; sacred scripture has its own proper logic and grammar,« and this peculiar »logic« and »grammar« can be apprehended only insofar as we recognize the *usus loquendi* which has held in the church. Biblical interpretation depends, therefore, upon the commitment to »read with the church.« Gerson thus interprets the hermeneutical question in *perspectival* terms: the »original« meaning of scripture is discernible not by applying contemporary scientific methods of linguistic analysis common to other disciplines such as the »speculative« or »moral« sciences; rather, this meaning is to be discerned in the historical tradition, and above all that of the early church since it received both an »authentic reception and interpretation« of scripture. In other words, Gerson accepts Aquinas's claim that biblical interpretation demands that we consider not only the »words« themselves but the proper »sense« or meaning of the words. But he advances beyond Thomas, prompted in large measure by the doctrinal controversies he faced which involved diverging methods and principles of exegesis, to insist that the interpretive task required an ecclesial context.[52] And, as the treatises we have considered suggest, Gerson's emphasis of this ecclesial setting focused attention not primarily upon the present church, but upon the church of the apostles and early fathers.

We are now in a position to move directly to *De consolatione theologiae*, for it is here that we find a text by which Gerson again clarified his understanding of the historical church as the normative framework for faithful biblical exegesis. In an extended discussion of what it means to be a theologian, a passage in which he asserted that the theologian is »a good man learned in sacred scripture,« Gerson characterizes those who fail to gain this character: »such persons,« he concludes, »impudently force the holy scriptures to serve their own corrupt habits and desires, distorting the sense [of the text] passed down by the holy fathers [*sensum a sanctis patribus traditum distorquentes*], if they are not indeed ignorant of it.«[53] This is a key passage for our consideration of the interrelatedness of ecclesiological and hermeneutical issues in Gerson's thought, since he here locates »tradition« as the functional context for his exegetical method. The task of exegesis involves assuming the proper perspective, and he illustrates the character of such perspective on two levels. First, one cannot understand what a biblical text means outside the context of

---

[52] Froehlich has pointed to the development during the later Middle Ages of a refined approach to interpreting the literal sense as a movement away from »the older line of tying it to the human words and thus to the *surface meaning* of a text«; he also rightly suggests that Aquinas's »restatement of the theory« of the literal sense (cf. *Summa theologiae* Ia q. 1 a. 10), by identifying the authorial intention as the fulcrum of the matter, may well have been the stimulus or »turning point« which »fostered the change« in the following period. See »Fifteenth-Century Hermeneutics,« pp. 40 ff.

[53] G 9, p. 237.

the *usus loquendi* of the church's tradition, the »use« which he clarifies in this treatise as *sensus a sanctis patribus traditus*. In other words, Gerson describes the task of the exegete not within the present boundaries of the church's authority; had this been his intention, he simply would have noted that one must submit to the *superiores* within the spirit-guided church, those authorities within the hierarchical order who are the present safeguards of the authentic literal sense. This he does not say, but rather suggests in a manner consistent with earlier statements we have explored that one must interpret scripture within the context of tradition, above all the »holy doctors and expositors« of the »primitive church« who received the scriptures *and* an understanding of their proper meaning. Second, the perspective which one adopts vis-à-vis the biblical text has much to do with how one reads that text: the reader's perspective also enters into the interpretive process, a claim which has recently emerged in the modern discussion of hermeneutics.[54] Applying this theme to the exegetical task, he concludes of the *usus loquendi* — the »sense transmitted by the holy fathers« — is not the only barrier to proper exegesis, particularly if one »compels« the sacred scriptures not through the church's lead but through the distortion of one's own »corrupt habits and desires«;[55] perhaps this should be read as an application of his earlier insistence that »not ignorance but pride makes one a heretic,«[56] since pride gives birth to *singularitas* and thereby disrupts an obedient reception of the tradition. On this second level, Gerson argues that not only historical but also moral perspective determines through prejudice one's exegetical approach; as he here insists, the arduous work of discerning the authentic »literal sense« of the biblical text included alongside academic qualifications the »professional« tools of »a pious life and moral character.«[57] As he elsewhere notes in a similar vein, one of the characteristics

---

[54] This theme stands at the center of Gadamer's work, particularly in his provocative discussion of »Prejudices as Conditions of Understanding« in *Truth and Method* (New York, 1975), pp. 245 ff. He articulates this same point with the language of »horizons.« That is, each person already perceives reality out of a peculiar »horizon« of understanding: »Understanding of the past undoubtedly requires an historical horizon. But it is not the case that we acquire this horizon by placing ourselves within a historical situation. Rather, we must always already have a horizon in order to be able to place ourselves within a situation. For what do we mean by ›placing ourselves‹ in a situation? Certainly not just disregarding ourselves. This is necessary, of course, in that we must imagine the other situation. But into this other situation we must also bring ourselves.... A truly historical consciousness always sees its own present in such a way that it sees itself, as it sees the historically other, within the right circumstances. We are always affected, in hope and fear, by what is nearest to us, and hence approach, under its influence, the testimony of the past. Hence, it is constantly necessary to inhibit the overhasty assimilation of the past to our own expectations of meaning. Only then will we be able to listen to the past in a way that enables it to make its own meaning heard.« *Ibid.*, pp. 271–72.

[55] See above, nn. 47, 51.

[56] See *De sensu litterali sacrae scripturae*; G 3, p. 339.

[57] Froehlich, »Fifteenth-Century Hermeneutics,« p. 40. Gerson is here careful to

necessary for the exegete was an »immunity from the effects of vices,« or moral character.[58] The primary thrust of this passage in *De consolatione theologiae*, however, falls upon the first of these perspectival themes: one must work within the »sense handed down by the holy fathers,« and particularly that received and transmitted by the early church, if one would rightly interpret scripture in its proper literal sense.

Gerson thus delineates biblical exegesis in ecclesiological terms, defining the apostolic church as the historical community in which the authentic sense of the scriptural text is to be discerned. The locus of interpretive authority is not the present hierarchy, but the historical tradition — above all the primitive church which had received revelation and an understanding of its proper »sense« directly from Christ. This conceptualization of the hermeneutical method bears a remarkable similarity to one facet of Hans-Georg Gadamer's work, since both are interested in delineating the authoritative »horizon« in which one approaches textual traditions. Through an approach approximating Gadamer's notion of the »effective-historical consciousness,« Gerson projects the historical tradition — *sensus a sanctis patribus traditus* — as the vehicle for discerning the »legitimate prejudices« toward the past, such that an argument from this particular locus of authority establishes the proper horizon in which the biblical text is to be interpreted.[59] Although Gerson and Gadamer clearly differ in the constructive hermeneutical models they propose, their approaches

---

distinguish this issue from the Donatist problematic, insisting in *De consolatione theologiae* that a priest's moral worthiness had no affect upon the performance or efficacy of his sacramental duties. But he denies that a morally corrupt person might read the biblical text accurately, since the prejudice inherent in such a perspective would cause such a person to »distort« the sense of the text »as handed down by the holy fathers« for reasons of self-legitimation. Thus, a morally corrupt priest might continue to fulfill his pastoral duty regarding the sacraments, but he could carry out the pastoral duties of preaching only with grave difficulties, if at all, since these involved the biblical text in a fundamental way. This is for Gerson, therefore, a qualification of the pastoral task of interpreting scripture rather than a diminishment of a priest's sacramental responsibilities. Furthermore, it is intriguing to note that Gerson identifies the three duties of the priest in this treatise, all of which draw upon scripture as he understood and utilized it, as preaching, admonishing, and correcting — without mention of the sacramental office. Burger notes the centrality of preaching for Gerson and as a theme more generally during the early fifteenth century; see *Aedificatio*, pp. 152–53.

[58] See the fourth rule in *De necessaria communione laicorum*; G 10, p. 56. He lists this alongside talent, diligence, and humility of judgment.

[59] Cf. Gadamer, *Truth and Method*, pp. 247–48: he goes on here to insist that »what is necessary is a fundamental rehabilitation of the concept of prejudice and a recognition of the fact that there are legitimate prejudices if we want to do justice to man's finite, historical mode of being.... The distinction the enlightenment draws between faith in authority and the use of one's own reason is, in itself, legitimate. If the prestige of authority takes the place of one's own judgment, then authority is in fact a source of prejudices. But this does not exclude the possibility that [authority] can also be a source of truth, and this is what the enlightenment failed to see when it denigrated all authority.«

are in curious agreement in identifying the central hermeneutical question which the latter characterizes as »epistemologically its fundamental question«: namely, »Where is the ground of the legitimacy of prejudices?«[60] Gerson poses this question in more specific terms: From what vantage point must one read the biblical text to ascertain its proper (literal) sense?

Gerson answers this question with remarkable consistency in treatises written during the period of the Council of Constance, insisting again and again in these later writings that the church's *usus loquendi* − or what he calls in *De consolatione theologiae* the *sensus a sanctis patribus traditus* − functions as the normative guide for biblical interpretation.[61] According to his careful hermeneutical logic, *viatores* discern the meaning of the text within the context neither of the present hierarchy nor in some presumed restitution of the apostolic church.[62] Rather, he insists that one must read scripture within the horizon of the historical church − and this means for him *ecclesia primitiva* because it received the text along with what we might now call, to borrow Gadamer's language, »a legitimate prejudice« toward it. As he had earlier expressed it, this primitive community received scripture together with an understanding of it from Christ. Biblical hermeneutics for Gerson is ultimately a matter of the church's *historical* authority, tradition understood not in a »constitutive« sense which would add new revelation to the old nor solely with reference to a present magisterial authority, but as a »normative« factor[63] by

---

[60] *Ibid.*, p. 246.

[61] Here we might also suggest a further dimension of Gerson's approach, suggested to us by Hübener's careful analysis of Gerson's »conservatism«: Gerson »ermahnt die Theologen, bei ihren spekulativen Untersuchungen den *modi significandi* zu folgen, *quibus utitur communis schola doctorum,* und die *termini* nicht zu verachten oder zu verändern, *quos posuerunt patres nostri, qui in impositione terminorum fuerunt magni metaphysici.* Da die Stabilität der Wissenschaft wesentlich vom *quid nominis terminorum* abhänge, beschleunige nichts den Verfall der Wissenschaft mehr als die Veränderung der *termini a sanctis patribus usitati.*« See Hübener, »Der theologisch-philosophische Konservativismus des Jean Gerson,« pp. 172−73. This is an extremely important interpretive point, and one which corresponds quite closely to my analysis of the pertinent texts from *De consolatione theologiae.* Indeed, Hübener's point amplifies what it is that Gerson means in this specific passage when he speaks of the »sense« of the text. The tradition of biblical exegesis shares with other forms of science the necessity for a continuity of critical terminology, particularly when the *modi significandi* are *termini a sanctis patribus usitati.* Here one might add Gerson's later claim, when pressed to explain whether doctrine »conformed« to scripture: »Attendendum in examinatione doctrinarum, primo et principaliter, si doctrina sit conformis sacrae scripturae, tam in se quam in modi traditione.« G 9, p. 465.

[62] On this point, Gerson's argument might justifiably be read as an opposition to the Hussite ecclesiology, which, following Marsilius' view, sought to reinstitute the ideal of the apostolic church. For a discussion of this point, see Leff, »The Apostolic Ideal,« pp. 67 ff.

[63] This terminological distinction is to be found first in Karl Werner, *Die Scholastik des späten Mittelalters;* in the fourth volume of this work, *Die nachschotistische Scholastik* (Vienna, 1887), Werner argues that with Gerson the literal sense can only be rightly interpreted

which the church might discern with »the holy fathers« the *sensus litteralis*, or intended literal meaning, of the text. Gerson's concern is to deny that the scriptures convey an authoritative meaning which belongs in the public domain and could thus be grasped according to the logic utilized by the speculative or moral sciences or by strictly private interpretation. But he does this precisely in order to deflect the focus away from the *magisterial* authority, placing it rather within the matrix of the church's *historical* tradition.[64] And, as we have already suggested, Gerson thus advances his argument by addressing the fundamental problematic couched in the approach Aquinas had taken: the difficulty facing the exegete has to do with grasping the sense underlying the words themselves, a task complicated by controversies arising from the multivalence of the strictly grammatical meaning.

These controversies provoked Gerson to recognize that one might discern several levels of the literal sense, or interpret the text »literally« in various ways.[65] Given such ambiguities by which the text appears to be replete with a surplus of meaning, Gerson invokes *historical* tradition as the key to recovering the authentic sense: only by placing oneself within the horizon of the historical church can one discern the proper literal sense, avoiding the danger of private judgment leading to arbitrary interpretation (»et non ad cuiuslibet arbitrium

---

»durch treues Festhalten an den kirchlichen Normen der Schriftauslegung« (*ibid.*, p. 205 ff.). In a more recent study, Lang returns to the same conclusion, arguing that we must distinguish the approach pursued by Gerson and others following Ockham as one which saw the church's role not as bringing any »Zuwachs zum Glaubensinhalt,« but rather as exercising »eine normative, nicht konstitutive Aufgabe bei der Vermittlung der Offenbarung«; *Die theologische Prinzipienlehre*, p. 220.

[64] It is intriguing to note that Gerson's argument here is set against any attempt to enoble the *present* over this normative *past* in terms of biblical exegesis, but his argument also confronts an individualism which might prevail even within the *magisterium*. For this reason he wrote *De sensu litterali sacrae scripturae*, as Froehlich has convincingly argued, against the capricious interpretation of Jean Petit which he held to be a »monumental fraud« (cf. »Fifteenth-Century Hermeneutics,« p. 37); it was just such an individualistic interpretation, which avoided the traditional interpretation offered »by the holy fathers« and explicated later by the doctors and councils, which Gerson opposed.

[65] See e. g., G 10, pp. 239–40: »Sed pro responsione ad illud Apostoli: littera occidit, notandum quod in Sacra Scriptura, Spiritus Sanctus tripliciter loquitur: uno modo loquendo terminis impositis et assumendo terminos ultimate et principaliter pro expressione conceptuum suae locutionis in nobis; et isto modo loquitur in moralibus contentis in Sacra Scriptura et in historiis aliquibus. Secundo modo loquitur Spiritus Sanctus in Sacra Scriptura utendo terminis principaliter, sed assumendo res significatas per terminos ad significandum res alias tantummodo. ... Tertio modo loquitur Spiritus utroque modo, scilicet per terminos et per res significatas per terminos; et hujusmodi locutiones duplicem habent sensum litteralem; et sunt locutiones illae quae non solum erudiunt intellectum ad aliquod spirituale sed etiam excitativae vel exercitativae sunt effectus, ut circa sacramenta in Veteri et Nova Lege, circa ceremonialia in Veteri; similiter sunt plures historiae David ceterorumque regum quibus non solum figuratur Christus sed eorum gesta morum sunt exempla.«

vel interpretationem«). Between irresolvable ambiguity and irrepressible caprice, therefore, Gerson establishes the *sensus a sanctis patribus traditus* as the authoritative context of biblical exegesis. Viewing the text from the *author's* vantage point, Gerson readily accepts Aquinas's thesis that the *verba* were pregnant with meaning, but he insists that for all readers removed from *ecclesia primitiva* the problem did not lie in the positing of such a multivalent *sensus litteralis* but in its proper apprehension. In other words, Gerson's hermeneutic theory no longer countenanced Aquinas's premise that »holy scripture sets up no confusion, since all meanings are based on one, namely the literal sense«;[66] this was a true assertion perhaps, but not ultimately helpful as a practical rule for the controversy-ridden church, a point which was of more than theoretical concern for Gerson during the Council of Constance. He found himself immersed in theological debates in which diverging principles and conclusions of biblical interpretation meant that theological differences were often as much the consequence as the cause of exegetical arguments. The broadened meaning (*multiplicitas horum sensuum*) which Aquinas had identified in the literal sense may not have imposed an ambiguity (*aequivocatio*) or »other kind of mixture of meanings« (*aliam speciem multiplicitatis*) upon the text from within its inherent logic, but this premise would only complicate the exegetical debate within the later medieval church.

This is the arena in which Gerson makes his contribution to the medieval discussion of exegesis, for he identified the ambiguity not within the text but in its interpretation: it is with this intention that he invokes the church's historical authority (tradition), identifying it as the normative guide to interpretation precisely as a safeguard against such multiplicity of readings. But his position is not only a defensive one, set against an individualistic or unauthorized reading of the text; rather, he anchors it in a constructive argument, refusing to concede any presumption of immediacy to the biblical text by recognizing the necessity of a properly guided interpretation. *Viatores* must read the text not only in terms of its »original words« (revelation) but in terms of the authentic interpretation of those words (tradition), the »sense« which delineates the proper meaning of potentially ambiguous words.[67] The context of the

---

[66] *Summa theologiae* Ia q. 1 a. 10, ad 1.

[67] G 10, p. 57: »Scriptura sacra recipit interpretationem et expositionem nedum in suis verbis originalibus, sed etiam in suis expositoribus.« In this regard we must now call into question Oberman's suggestion that Gerson »does not oppose *littera sola* but *scriptura sola*, not the isolated and naked letter but the isolated and naked Scripture« (cf. *Forerunners*, p. 289). Our conclusions reach precisely the opposite point, such that we must invert this claim to understand Gerson's intention properly: Gerson does indeed affirm the »sufficiency« of scripture, an argument which viewed on its functional side is a close approximation to the later *scriptura sola* of the Protestant reformers; more importantly for our discussion here, he also opposed the »isolated and naked letter,« since this too demanded the proper understanding which could be ascertained only within the historical tradition.

historical tradition of exegesis provides for Gerson what Gadamer has called
the method of »effective-history,« the theoretical basis for a »fusion of
horizons« by which we are able »to listen to the past in a way that enables it to
make *its own meaning* heard. «[68]

---

[68] Gadamer, *Truth and Method*, pp. 272–73. With this interpretation before us we are
now in a position to offer in an excursus a critical revision of the prevailing historical
analysis of Gerson's exegesis, a cumulative view which has placed heavy emphasis upon the
present dimensions of the church's authority. Here we must first examine in this regard the
conclusions Posthumus Meyjes reached in the chapter devoted to »Kerk, Schrift en
Traditie« in his important study of Gerson's ecclesiology (*Jean Gerson: Zijn Kerkpolitiek en
Ecclesiologie* ['s-Gravenhage, 1963]). In this discussion Posthumus Meyjes considers the
relationship of ecclesiology and hermeneutical theory in Gerson's writings and delineates
what he understands to be the general structure of Gerson's hermeneutics. In discussing a
series of texts from Gerson's *De necessaria communione laicorum sub utraque specie*, several of
which we have also considered above (e. g., see n. 47), Posthumus Meyjes concludes that
Gerson had placed »the spirit over the church and the church over the scriptures, « and asks
the rhetorical question whether Gerson did not after all envision the spirit-led church as »a
second source of revelation« (*ibid.*, pp. 259–60). Posthumus Meyjes's analysis remains
unconvincing, however, in part because the narrow textual basis upon which he forms his
conclusions does not tell the whole story. But another part of the difficulty surrounding his
conclusion arises from our suggestion that such texts do not seem to bear his interpretation,
particularly if one considers the polemic context of such statements: Gerson appears to have
in mind not only those Posthumus Meyjes calls »the revolutionary grouping,« which
includes along with Hus both Wyclif and Marsilius of Padua (*ibid.*, p. 256), but also the
recent difficulties brought on by Jean Petit's exegetical defense of »tyrannicide.« On the
latter, Froehlich has convincingly argued that the polemic context in which Gerson debated
his theological position is vital to understanding his exegetical method. As he points out in
this regard, Gerson's fears were not simply set against a kind of autonomous »spiritualism,«
such as Posthumus Meyjes suggests to be the case vis-à-vis Hus, and thus resolved simply
by resorting to the church's magisterial authority; rather, Gerson was concerned with two
issues: first, to root exegesis within a *moral* context; and, second, to establish the authentic
interpretation within the *historical* context of the church. See Froehlich, »Fifteenth-Century
Hermeneutics,« pp. 39–40. The argument of context, therefore, is not merely opposed to
the spiritualists, and it does not root the matter in the church's present magisterial authority;
rather, this context is a matter of the moral and historical tradition of exegesis, the
apprehension of the »understanding« (*intellectus*) received together with the text by the early
church and passed on *a sanctis patribus*. Hence, even in his treatise *De necessaria communione
laicorum*, the text upon which Posthumus Meyjes depends for his thesis, Gerson opposed a
reading of the text *nude et in solidum*, not however in order to impose the magisterial
authority of the church as Posthumus Meyjes suggests, but in order to avoid showing
contempt for the broader tradition – or what he here calls »other human traditions« – and
thus he recommends that one might »frequently and with humility« utilize »human and
canon law and decretals as well as the glosses of the holy [fathers].« G 10, p. 57. For similar
reasons one must now question Preus's conclusions, since he too assumes that Gerson's
emphasis upon the »spirit-guided church« collapses into the present context
(=magisterium), such that »the Bible itself has no theologically authoritative literal
meaning« (*From Shadow to Promise*, p. 81). What Preus fails to recognize is Gerson's wary
attitude not only toward the »spiritualists« of his day, but also (and quite understandably)
toward an unbounded confidence in the *magisterium* itself; Gerson's insistence on the need

B. The church in the interim:
An ecclesiology of humility

One of the consistent emphases which we have discerned in *De consolatione theologiae* is the moderate nature of Gerson's perspectives, both theological and pastoral. As a reformer it is his patience and his adherence to the hierarchical order — in a word, his conservatism — which mark his character. One is hard-pressed to find traces of a revolutionary tendency in Gerson, even though his primary interest was decidedly progressive: viz., reforming the hierarchical church by restoring it according to the heavenly image of »the new city of Jerusalem.«[69] Yet his use of such imagery must be located within the mainstream of traditional patristic and medieval ecclesiology, for he consistently utilizes these images in a manner which avoided the extreme apocalyptic applications such as those provoked and apparently confirmed by the disordered circumstances of the papal schism.[70] Indeed, we must say even

---

for continuity with the *early* church's exegesis is crucial here, since this emphasis orients his hermeneutical method not toward the present but toward an authoritative *past* horizon as the key to discerning the true *sensus litteralis* of the text.

[69] In advocating reform Gerson often borrowed language like this from the book of Revelation, but he utilized these provocative images in cautious, conservative fashion. These become in his hands the metaphorical instruments by which he conveys his mystical view of the church, and thus stand in stark contrast to a more revolutionary use in the usage of apocalyptic preachers of his day. See for example, *De auferibilitate sponsi ab Ecclesia* (1409/1415), G 3, p. 294: »Rursus deducitur quod dictum est ex ipsa conditione matrimonialis vinculi Christum sponsum et Ecclesiam sponsam, sicut Joannes in Apocalypsi Ecclesiam sub typo civitatis novae Jerusalem vidit descendentem de coelo sicut sponsam ornatam viro suo. Nam ad exemplar coelestis Ecclesia terrena formata est.« Pascoe addresses this dimension of Gerson's ecclesiology in greater detail (see *Jean Gerson*, pp. 17–22); he also notes the dynamism of Gerson's view of ecclesiology, while also pointing to his conservatism in terms of matters involving church reform. *Ibid.*, pp. 207, 211 f.

[70] On this point Marjorie Reeves has argued that »the Great Schism brought into the sharpest possible focus all the various elements of the prophetic tradition . . .: the forces of the Antichrist creating schism and persecution in the church, the expectation of terrible tribulation and judgement, the prophetic summons of the Pope back to Rome to fulfill the full destiny of the *renovatio ecclesiae*. Above all, it was the fact of the Great Schism itself which set the seal of truth on the prophets from Joachim and St. Francis to Jean de Roquetaillade.« See *The Influence of Prophecy in the Later Middle Ages: A Study in Joachimism* (Oxford, 1969), p. 422. Bernard McGinn adds to this general observation the more specific conclusion that »the [papal] Schism bulks large in almost every apocalyptic text of the period after 1380,« and notes that even moderate conciliarists such as Pierre d'Ailly »dabbled in apocalypticism«; *Visions of the End: Apocalyptic Traditions in the Middle Ages* (New York, 1979), pp. 254 ff. This is certainly true of the young d'Ailly; his *Epistola Diaboli Leviathan* comes immediately to mind (cf. *Unity, Heresy, and Reform. 1378–1460. The Conciliar Response to the Great Schism*, ed. C. M. D. Crowder [New York, 1977], pp. 41–45). But it is less clear whether this theme remains in the mature d'Ailly's thought, and such expressions are altogether absent from Gerson's works.

more than this: not only does Gerson make guarded use of such imagery, but his ecclesiology in its general framework seems set squarely against any form of apocalypticism, particularly extreme manifestations which often enough devolved into hysteria.[71] But it was not primarily the manifestation of hysteria which Gerson opposed, though this mood seems singularly incompatible with his decidedly moderate temperament. His criticism was at once broader and more fundamental than this, settling upon the very rationale which this apocalypticism embraced: against such unbounded and typically impatient fervor Gerson insisted on envisioning life *in via* as structured in terms of hierarchical order, a decidedly more tempered view supported by cautious and even conservative ecclesiological convictions.

In this final section, we shall turn to consider the general theme of restraint through which Gerson articulates his approach to reform, an issue which illumines various critical aspects of his theology and ecclesiology. In this endeavor our attention will settle upon familiar Gersonian themes, including zeal, discretion, and edification, yet our perspective moves beyond earlier studies by setting these themes as he himself does in his later writings within the context of ecclesiology. In so doing the conservative bent of his mind will become more clearly evident: Gerson here presents himself as a patient reformer, largely because of his conviction that the church itself was *peregrinus*, a pilgrim »between the times« bound toward a goal which could never be realized in any full sense. As such his moderation as a reformer establishes the shape of what we might call a patient reform, one rooted squarely in the empirical realities and frustrations of the earthly church which is and remains only a shadow of the church to come, the *gloriosa ecclesia* which will be *sancta et immaculata* only at the end of time (cf. Eph. 5.27). Gerson is careful to dissociate this eschatological vision from his reform efforts, allowing in the process for a peculiar blend of toleration and reform, of conservatism and progressivism, as the church advanced *ad Deum*. This journey he interprets, eschatologically, as an »interim,« a communal movement ultimately leading *peregrini* toward God as *humanae peregrinationis refugium*; it is this dynamic conceptualization, finally, which establishes the broad arena within which Gerson understood his work as university chancellor and reform-minded churchman. Thus, it is fitting that we bring this study to a close by examining this parameter of his thought.

---

[71] On this theme see McGinn, *Visions of the End*, especially pp. 239–69. One articulate spokesman of this apocalyptic tradition who was an older contemporary of Gerson's, Henry of Langenstein (d. 1397), insisted that the desired »reformation of the church« could happen only after the coming of Antichrist, an eschatology later shared by Nicholas of Cusa. The most visible proponents of such a position would have been Hus and his circle, and this appears to be the view over against which Gerson developed his ecclesiology during the period of his residence in Constance. See further Pelikan, *Reformation*, pp. 109 ff.

1. *De moderamine zeli*: the patience of reform

Patience and zeal, character traits which might well be considered as conflicting in general usage, nonetheless coinhere in Gerson's approach to reform: zealous as a reformer, he insisted early and late that reform itself was a matter better moderated by reason than the irascible passions,[72] and ultimately was to be governed by the related virtues of patience and discretion. This *coincidentia oppositorum* finds its mediating bridge above all in his persistent use of the theme of *discretio*,[73] as we shall see in a moment. First, however, we must inquire about the more comprehensive if often diffuse teleological perspective he adopts toward life as *peregrinatio ad Deum*, a theme he explores in a curious passage in this treatise under the rubric *rerum conditio*. In an explanation of this general *conditio* which discloses the dynamic contours of his ecclesiology, Gerson adopts a view of the creative sphere redolent with neo-Platonic/Augustinian overtones, describing the »condition of all things« in life as tending of themselves toward their proper end:

The desire and weight of the human heart is to be carried to God, as toward its proper locus and center. This is the highest point, beyond which is left no other refuge for the human pilgrimage. Aside from this there is nothing either beneath or beyond toward which the human heart is able to turn itself or from which it might flee, since by its own weight it disposes itself to adhere to God [*adhaerere Deo*]. As things now are, in the meantime, it constitutes itself through faith, hope, and love, nor does its present status afford it any other way.[74]

---

[72] When Gerson introduces the *vis irascibilis* in this discussion, he locates his discussion within a well-developed medieval tradition. But here as elsewhere he proves the eclecticism of his mind and goes his own way. On this theme, it appears that Gerson's anthropology owes a significant debt once again to Aquinas, this time in terms of his discussion of the soul's structure with its various »irascible« and »concupiscible« powers; he agrees with Aquinas in conceiving reason — both »universal« and »particular« reason, as discussed in *Summa theologiae* Ia q. 81 a. 3 — as that higher part of the human person which is responsible for ordering the passions. But beyond this point his affinities are more decidedly with the *via moderna*, particularly as he follows the Franciscan emphasis on the will as the organizing center of the person. The will, rather than reason, must finally overcome the disruptive force of the *appetitus sensualis*, according to Gerson. For further discussion of his analysis of the »powers« of the soul, see Pascoe, *Jean Gerson*, pp. 111–14, 182–83.

[73] For Bernard of Clairvaux's contribution to this theme, which influenced the subsequent discussion — including, perhaps, Gerson — see *Sermones super Cantica Canticorum*, ed. J. Leclercq et al., 2:25–76 (49.2.5).

[74] G 9, p. 196. In the midst of an earlier academic sermon, delivered on the occasion of the university's granting of degrees to canon lawyers, Gerson expanded upon this theme from a different vantage point: »Omnia enim fecit in numero, pondere et mensura, et ita sub lege certa, ait Boetius, quippe sicut fecit omnia propter se et ad se, sic *omnibus dedit certam tendentiam ad se*, quae dicitur appetitus vel amor et pondus trahens rem ad suum dominativum et initiale principium, quod est ipse, ut sit ipse alpha et omega, principium et finis.« *Dominus his opus habet*; G 5, p. 221 (my emphasis).

What is striking about this passage is the deliberately provisional nature of the pilgrimage *ad Deum* which Gerson here emphasizes: *nunc interim* we are to live *per spem, fidem et amorem* — in a word, through the guidance of the theological virtues.[75] Absent is any suggestion of *unio Dei*, the mystical embrace of God by which one might gain the very object of the pilgrimage: namely, God himself. Also absent is any trace of apocalypticism, at least of the hysterical or revolutionary pedigree which prevailed in his day.[76] In the place of

---

[75] Gerson returns to this theme later in the treatise, though he offers it here in a curious form. In addressing the difficulty of attaining »moral certitude,« he concludes that »for this there are established, according to the biblical figure [*in figura*] (Joshua 21), three cities of refuge [*tres civitates refugii*]: faith, hope, and charity, containing the cleansing bath of penance and an asylum of immunity, such that the peace — which is disturbed through those things which one fears one has done — might be reformed.« G 9, p. 240. This is the single reference to penance to be found in this treatise, and it is probably not accidental that Gerson applies this theme not to the sacramental acts but to the (theological) virtues themselves. In this sense, *viatores* have direct access to the »cleansing bath« of penance as well as an »asylum of immunity« (presumably, *coram judice Deo*) through virtue itself. It is also worth noting that Gerson utilizes these theological virtues to contrast the »learned« but misguided theologians for whom a form of theology »not mixed with faith, hope and love« would simply »inflate and thwart« (*inflat et officit*), on one hand, with the *idiotae* on the other, in whom a »simple faith, certain hope, and sweet charity« instills the »spirit of catholic judgment.« Cf. G 9, p. 238. The overtones to 1 Cor. 13 are profound and probably deliberate, and his suggestion that the theological virtues might be »more fruitfully« possessed by the *idiotae* marks a decided change of perspective over his earlier university writings. For a concise review of this position see Burger, *Aedificatio*, pp. 191—93; the fact that Burger chooses to conclude his study with a discussion of »die Überlegenheit der Theologen über die einfachen Christen« suggests something of the centrality he accords this theme in Gerson's earlier writings. See also Pascoe, *Jean Gerson*, pp. 182—83.

[76] See above, nn. 69, 70. Our assessment of the broader perspective Gerson adopted toward apocalypticism can only be quite preliminary at this juncture, though it appears to be a theme conspicuous by its absence for the most part. Of course, Gerson's use of the *tau* in Ezekiel fits this general theme; this itself may, however, reflect polemic interests in the first instance, since the image emerges apparently for the first time in 1416 — i. e., during the Council of Constance, and immediately following the tragic events of Hus's death which only furthered the apocalyptic fervor of his circle. That is, he identified *himself* as marked by this *tau,* and thus one of those »set apart« by God to be spared from the slaughter awaiting Jerusalem. (It is worth noting that the iconographical portrait of Gerson which Albrecht Dürer prepared for a 1489 edition of his works should be consulted on this point; this woodcut shows Gerson as a pilgrim, carrying the shield he designed with Ezekiel's *tau* emblazoned upon it, as he departs from the city of Constance after the council.) This image emerges again in *De consolatione theologiae*, and here the context clarifies Gerson's intent: in the midst of an extended defense of the »solitary life,« he follows Ezekiel's prophecy in identifying with the sign of the *tau* those whose vocation it was to »lament frequently« (*crebro ingemuerit*) and intercede through prayer as the reformers able »to remove scandals from the church.« Cf. G 9, p. 224. This is an apocalyptic theme, if one might still call it that, of quite controlled proportions, since with it Gerson identifies those *solitarii* as »chosen« whose prayers brought quiet reform to the church. Once again, his quite traditional Augustinian view of time and eschatology provides the foundation for his reticent and

these themes we find him emphasizing the deliberately muted eschatological imagery of the later Paul, describing the kind of »supernatural certitude« by which *viatores* make their way as an »adherence solely in a mirror, and in darkness,«[77] even though this knowledge has a »supernatural certitude« by

---

apparently even anti-apocalyptic approach to reform. This might well be anything but an omission in general terms, particularly given the centrality afforded to apocalyptic themes among radical voices of his day, among which we must include above all preachers associated with the Hussite movement. Of these Ferdinand Seibt has observed that their criticism threatened »den Begriff der katholischen Kirche überhaupt an seiner Wurzel,« such that »man sieht, wie diese These [i. e., a view of the church as the invisible community of the elect] sich weiterbilden ließ von der Reform zu Ablehnung der sichtbaren Kirche.« See »Geistige Reformbewegungen zur Zeit des Konstanzer Konzils,« in *Das Konstanzer Konzil,* ed. Remigius Bäumer (Darmstadt, 1977), p. 328; and, for further discussion, McGinn, *Visions of the End,* pp. 259 ff., and Howard Kaminsky, »Chiliasm and the Hussite Revolution,« *Church History* 26 (1957), pp. 43–71. One is indeed hard-pressed to find any significant discussion of Gerson and apocalypticism in the recent and older secondary literature, perhaps another index of the paucity of explicitly pertinent texts; this is a theme worthy of further examination. Pascoe does address this issue, pointing out that Gerson conceived of the church in terms reminiscent of Dionysius' coordination of the celestial and ecclesiastical hierarchies, though he notes that Gerson's application of this theme lacked the »strict eschatological sense« to be found in the book of Revelation, and offered in its place »what might be called a realized eschatology.« *Jean Gerson,* p. 20.

[77] G 9, p. 231; this phrase reads *solius adhaerentiae in speculo et in aenigmate,* and is an obvious reference to 1 Cor. 13.12. The remarkable aspect of Gerson's use of this Pauline theme is the broader context in which he applies it. He is here describing three levels of supernatural certitude through »a distinction of doctrine,« by which the first has to do with the »direct« certitude (i. e., the »clear and intuitive evidence«) possessed by the saints, the second the revealed evidence had by the prophets through illumination, and the third the evidence »by divine authority« (*auctoritati divinae*). This last level is what interests us here, because Gerson insists that this »evidence« cannot deceive us – not even through the »absolute power of God,« because »otherwise God would be able to deny himself.« Here, then, we find another instance of the retreat by which nominalist theologians in general avoided any explicit application of the arguments *de potentia Dei absoluta;* in this case, Gerson explicitly affirms this reticence, apparently because he recognized in the biblical promises and covenants – i. e., those given *de potentia Dei ordinata* – the very basis of certitude, and thus the supporting structure for one of his most decisive pastoral arguments. On this theme more generally, and in particular on the growing hesitation to apply the argument regarding the »absolute« power of God, Ozment concludes that »nominalism reveals itself as a science of the *potentia Dei ordinata.«* Cf. »Mysticism, Nominalism, and Dissent,« p. 80. Courtenay also reaches similar conclusions about this broad trend, but adds the insightful interpretation that »the distinction [of the powers of God] is deceptive for the modern reader because it seems to be talking about possibilities and avenues for divine action when in fact it is making a statement about the non-necessity of the created order. Both parts of the dialectic, which must be taken together to be meaningful, face in the direction of creation, not God. Together they declare the contingent, non-necessary, covenantal character of our created world . . . . Even in the later ›nominalists‹ the distinction excludes the idea of a capricious, arbitrary God who might change his mind and reverse the established laws that obtain in the orders of nature and salvation.« See »Nominalism and Late Medieval Religion,« pp. 39, 43.

which *viatores* cannot be deceived. The parallel of these passages derives from Gerson's adoption of the eschatological horizon conveyed by the Pauline logic, emphasized above all by his similar use of the stylistic device found in 1 Cor. 13: namely, the *nunc . . . tunc* structure by which Paul contrasts the dim knowledge possessed *in via* with the direct vision of the beatified.

> Videmus *nunc* per speculum in aenigmate: *tunc* autem facie ad faciem.
> *Nunc* cognosco ex parte: *tunc* autem cognoscam sicut et cognitus sum.
> *Nunc* autem manent, fides spes charitas. . . . (1 Cor. 13.12−13)

This literary dependence also explains why for Gerson the theological virtues of faith, hope, and love function to guide *viatores* in life − i. e., during the pilgrimage *ad Deum*, and thus before we see God directly (*facie ad faciem*).

It may well be that Gerson's application of this Pauline theme reflects if it does not in fact arise from a conservative and in this case anti-apocalyptic posture. This in any event is the final scope of his decidedly moderate approach to the church and its reform in the »interim. «[78] The church, too, stands as *viator* in this world, and it cannot hurry its progress *ad Deum* nor expect any violent detour by which it might arrive at that final (eschatological) destination and thus claim its identity as *sponsa Christi*. Its concern, rather, must accentuate the provisionality of its life and underscore the edifying function of the theological virtues − i. e., faith, hope, and love − by which it lives and seeks to be reformed »in this present time. « This framework might also explain why Gerson ends the treatise as he does, with a curious digression upon the theme of the martyrs: here he takes over the language exalting »the defense of the catholic truth« (*defensio catholicae veritatis*), which may well have echoed the less moderate voices of reform heard in his day, but applies it in conservative posture to those »searching out vices« and »correcting errors« − »coram judice legitimo, nunc ordinario, nunc supremo, « in a manner which preserved the hierarchical order and essential dignity of the church.[79] Indeed, Gerson goes further to survey the tradition of the martyrs and thereby inverts the argument as expressed by anxious preachers of the apocalypse in his day: in decidedly conservative guise he aligns those established authorities defending the church rather than her zealous attackers as the true proponents of the *lex Dei*, the divine law which alone could lead *viatores* through the church to embrace *pax Dei*. Not the harbingers of the apocalypse, to whom Gerson attributes the *desolationum omnium causa*, but those exercising legitimate jurisdiction for reform served as the »faithful« belonging to the revered tradition of the martyrs.[80] But here we

---

[78] On this point see Pascoe, *Jean Gerson*, pp. 207−208.
[79] G 9, p. 243. It is not accidental that Gerson here identifies the »legitimate judge« by aligning the »ordinary« or earthly and »supreme« or heavenly forums. It also seems that he is not here referring to canon lawyers, but to the judicial authority invested in the church's *magisterium* and administered by her bishops and theologians duly gathered in council.
[80] G 9, pp. 242 ff.

must turn from this general framework to the more specific treatment he affords this theme, above all through his detailed consideration of *discretio* and *zelus*.

Much of the third book of *De consolatione theologiae* Gerson devotes to the theme of discretion, thereby fulfilling his intention to set forth how it is that theology brings forth consolation »through the moderation of zeal.«[81] This is not a new theme for Gerson, of course. As early as 1401 Gerson introduced *discretio* as the third test of »spiritual genuineness« regarding visions and private revelations; discretion, defined as »the willingness to accept counsel,« stood for him as »the daughter of humility.« And, because humility — the antithesis of arrogance or pride — stands as a hallmark of Gerson's theology, early and late, the sustained attention he devoted to the theme of »discretion« comes as no surprise.[82] In the following year (1402), he again turned to this theme, introducing *discretio* — one of the voices in this early »trilogue« — as »residing properly in the human reason«; its specific function provides the necessary and suitable counterbalance for zeal, since discretion as a tempering influence determines whether the means of reform are also suited to the desired end.[83] Already in his early works, therefore, he had occupied himself with this theme, specifically in the much discussed question of the proper approach to *ecclesiae reformatio*. In his later works he maintained a consistent interest in this theme, but approaches it with distinctive variations from this earlier use. Thus his analysis of *discretio* in *De consolatione theologiae*, while not moving beyond this earlier use of the word in terms of material content, nonetheless acquires a different context: Gerson here offers a sustained treatment of this theme within a carefully crafted exegetical argument not to be found in his early university writings. Furthermore, it appears to be the case, though he nowhere explicitly names his targeted opponent, that he intends this polemical argument as a

---

[81] G 9, p. 215: »Locuturus ergo de consolatione per patientiam recte mihi videor id agere si de moderatione zeli inchoavero.« At the outset of the treatise he had declared his intention in similar terms, alerting the reader to the theme of the third book as follows: »tertia, per patientiam in zeli moderatione«; *ibid.*, p. 185.

[82] See *De distinctione verarum visionum a falsis*; G 3, pp. 42 ff. This theme of *discretio*, of course, had already a well-established medieval tradition behind it. It stands near the center of the Victorine theology of the later twelfth century, reflecting the theological and pastoral interest in »intent« and »circumstance« for a properly nuanced evaluation of moral acts. The writings of Richard of St. Victor must be considered as representative of a broader interest in this theme; see his *On the Twelve Patriarchs*, Chs. 66—76; in *The Twelve Patriarchs, The Mystical Ark, Book Three of the Trinity*, trans. and ed. G. A. Zinn (New York, 1979), pp. 123—29; *Benjamin Minor*, PL 196: 47—55. In a later century Aquinas had also devoted considerable attention to the theme of discretion, addressing it to his analysis of »circumstances« in *Summa theologiae* IaIIae q. 7 aa. 1—7, and later in IaIIae q. 12 aa. 1—5. Gerson's general approach, therefore, stands within a well defined tradition, and reflects the general mood as well as specific emphases as found above all in Aquinas's writings.

[83] Cf. *Trilogus in materia schismatis*; G 6, especially pp. 69—70.

direct response to the Hussite circle. Such an interpretation, based upon a reconstruction of Hus's defense at his trial before the conciliar fathers, obliges us to consider this thesis more carefully.

»Zeal« as Gerson here defines it is a human trait of marked ambivalence: it is basically nothing other than »the vehement desire« (*desiderium vehemens*) by which one seeks to remove that which appears opposed to what one loves.[84] He illustrates this with the classic biblical reference often to be heard in the more radical and less patient apocalyptic rhetoric of his day: namely, the account of Jesus' cleansing of the temple (cf. Jn. 2.13–22). Yet Gerson here qualifies the »text within a text« found in this pericope — i. e., the Old Testament scripture which clarifies this incident for the early Christian community, »The zeal for your house has consumed me« (Ps. 68.10) — by adding his own gloss to this quite general reference to *zelus*. »This [understanding of zeal] is indeed true,« Gerson concedes, »as long as benevolence, discretion, and constancy accompany it. But if zeal abandons or despises these three attributes, you might more rightly compare it to a two-edged sword in the hands of a frenzied man [*in manu furiosi*], or again to fire and lightning spreading without any obstacle.«[85] In the following poem, he further expands upon this »gloss« of *zelus*:

> Zeal is like fire, flames which burn
> Within the heart, stimulating it with great force
> In those matters toward which it inclines.
> Subdue it! Make zeal hold to its due measure. . . .[86]

Once again we find the theme and tone of moderation at the center of Gerson's thought, this time as a general qualification of the otherwise valuable exercise of zeal.

In the following prose section (III pr. 2), Gerson amplifies this gloss in more specific terms, and with this argument we begin to discern more clearly the historical context out of which this argument apparently arose and within which it would have been heard with particular urgency. Here we find, again, the theme of means and ends,[87] as Monicus in the role of *advocatus diaboli* suggests that harm inflicted in the cause of attaining »a worthy goal« ought to be excused, particularly if one's intent — as an expression of *imitatio Christi* —

---

[84] For the discussion which follows here, see G 9, pp. 215 ff.

[85] *Ibid.*, pp. 215–16.

[86] Cf. G 4, p. 107: »Est igni similis zelus et aestuat,« etc. Prof. C. Lee Miller has suggested that Ps. 78.5 may stand behind this simile: »Accendetur velut ignis zelus tuus?« The final clause also echoes the classical theme of consolation, viz. *metriopatheia* or the moderation of the passions. For a full discussion of this theme in classical literature, see Robert Gregg, *Consolation Philosophy. Greek and Christian Paideia in Basil and the Two Gregories* (Philadelphia, 1975).

[87] See above, n. 30.

was »to remove scandals from God's house.« At this juncture Monicus adds to this rhetorical question another biblical text: this reference, read against the proceedings of Hus's trial at the recently concluded council, offers further support for interpreting the entire argument as a critical rejoinder to the Hussite position. Gerson cites »Christ's saying,« in glossed form, in support of the conciliar condemnation: » ›if your eye‹ which is your intention ›be sound, your whole body will be full of light‹« (Mt. 6.22). The gloss is traditional, deriving originally from Augustine's comment upon this text though he might have known it from Thomas Aquinas who later utilized the same gloss in his *Summa theologiae*: »The ›eye‹ therefore we ought to take as meaning in this place the intention by which we do whatever we do; if it is clean and upright and keeping in view what it ought to keep in view, all our works which we perform in accordance with it are necessarily good.«[88] But is this the only form in which Gerson had heard this gloss?

The specific application he makes of this glossed passage suggests a more immediate source: it appears likely that this text was familiar to Gerson, and probably in precisely this form, not from Augustine nor even from Aquinas but from Hus's defense during his trial at Constance. The broader context of this passage, along with a series of striking verbal and thematic parallels, confirms this suggestion. In one of the closing arguments of that trial Hus had offered this biblical text in his own behalf, citing it with specific reference to Augustine's gloss that »if a man is virtuous, whatever he does, he does virtuously; and if he is wicked, whatever he does, he does wickedly.«[89] Gerson fashions his quite exhaustive rebuttal to this assertion by countering with a string of biblical texts, including Rom. 10.2, »For I bear witness of them that they have zeal, but not according to knowledge [*non secundum scientiam*],« an allusion to a theme of central importance in Gerson's thought.[90] He adds to this

---

[88] See Augustine, *The Lord's Sermon on the Mount* II.13.45, *CCSL* 35: 136. This passage is also to be found again, not without critical comment, in Aquinas's systematic analysis of *intentio*; cf. *Summa theologiae* IaIIae q. 12 a. 1, obj. 1 and ad obj. 1. It may be that Gerson had this text before him, particularly given the evidence earlier cited regarding his explicit dependence upon Aquinas during the Council of Constance.

[89] Cf. Peter Mladoňovice's account of this segment of the trial, *Relatio de Mag. Joannis Hus causa*, reprinted in *Hus at the Council*, pp. 197 f.

[90] It would appear that we find here a distinct variation upon Gerson's favored argument against a flawed form of mystical knowledge, a posture which he attributed in a series of passionate attacks to mystics such as the Beguines and Beghards (or, Turlupins). These groups he recognized as *devoti*, but argued that their form of mystical experience was *non secundum scientiam*; cf. for example, *De mystica theologia speculative conscripta* cons. 8.20, ed. Combes, 20: »Deinde compertum est multos habere devotionem ›sed non secundum scientiam‹, quales procul dubio pronissimi sunt ad errores, ›etiam supra indevotos‹, si non regulaverint affectus suos ad normam legis Christi, si ›praeterea capiti proprio‹, propri ›scilicet‹ prudentie inheserint, spreto aliorum consolio.« Ozment has correctly identified

insistence a remark which locates his argument in the historical circumstances of his day, noting that »such zeal has deceived many in our own stormy time, a zeal for removing scandal from God's house through this or that way of preaching. «[91] Gerson no longer veils his reference to the Hussite attacks upon the institutional church, citing the arguments offered by »such heretics« in short order, including: the contention »against the primacy of the Roman Church,« that there is salvation outside her ranks; the argument that the church's endowment should be opposed (*contra dotationes universalis ecclesiae*); the claim that simony should not be tolerated under any circumstances, and that any public display of prelates' status and retinue »should be taken from them by the secular arm«; the insistence that the observance of religious orders opposed the freedom of Christ's law; the demand that all ruling over others, particularly when the rulers stood in mortal sin, was intolerable. In short, Gerson here clarifies the context of his insistent message *de moderamine zeli*, offering a concrete list of the salient themes heard in »this or that way of preaching« within the Hussite circle.[92] Moderation, therefore, is not merely a

---

this as a »characteristic« theme in Gerson's writings, citing it as »one of the strongest, clearest, most common sensical, and yet most overlooked motifs in Gerson's mystical theology. « Indeed, Ozment goes on to delineate this theme as Gerson's conviction regarding the »naturally correlative and reciprocal character and operation of the affective and intellective powers. Gerson is convinced that the only *devotio* worthy of the Christian is that which is *secundum scientiam*, and the only *scientia* worthy of the Christian is that which is *secundum devotionem.* « See *Homo Spiritualis*, pp. 53, 64 ff.; see also Connolly, *John Gerson*, p. 122, and Pascoe, *Jean Gerson*, pp. 121. Apparently, therefore, Gerson has taken this central theme, which he had normally applied with critical reference to aberrant mysticism, and here utilized it to criticize also the Hussite position which had *zelus . . . non secundum scientiam*.

[91] For a discussion of Gerson's advocacy of preaching as the vehicle of reform, see Pascoe, *Jean Gerson*, pp. 118 ff. As I suggest elsewhere in this study, Gerson's view of the efficacy of preaching as expressed after the council is markedly less optimistic; see above, 4.C.2 and below, 6.B.3.

[92] The parallels to Hus's arguments in particular are quite striking and extensive. Thus, for instance, Hus had opposed what he considered to be »the grave error« of Pope Sylvester and Constantine — i.e., the »Donation of Constantine,« called here simply *donatio . . . ecclesiae*, which he considered an error rather than a forgery, writing as he did before Lorenzo Valla had exposed the textual basis for it as spurious — here following Wyclif whom the council had also condemned on this point (cf. »Errores Iohannis Wyclif,« No. 33 in *DS* 1183). Hus's defense of the same position is recorded in Peter Mladoňovice's account; see *Hus at the Council*, pp. 172, 192—93, and C. M. D. Crowder, *Unity, Heresy, and Reform, 1378—1460: The Conciliar Response to the Great Schism* (New York, 1977), p. 91. Hus also repeatedly contested such other claims as the primacy of the Roman church (see *Hus at the Council*, pp. 188 ff.), again following Wyclif's lead (*DS* 1191), the outward »dignity« or »status« of clerics (see *Hus at the Council*, ed. Spinka, pp. 185—86), the validity of ruling over others (*ibid.*, pp. 195 ff.), and, of course, the matter of simony (cf. »On Simony,« in *Advocates of Reform*, trans. and ed. M. Spinka (Philadelphia, 1953). The theological faculty at Paris had, of course, condemned a list of Wyclifite theses, which they attributed to Hus; we find these included in the letter Gerson sent to the Archbishop of Prague, Conrad de

theme offering consolation and guidance to *viatores*, nor is it simply a consequence of Gerson's quite restrained eschatology. It is these, of course, but it is
at the same time the basis for his vigorous counter-attack against the more
radical measures of reform as well as the apocalyptic themes heard in the
preaching of Hus and his circle.

It is extremely significant that Gerson should offer this argument in the wake
of the Council at Constance, and that his defense of the conciliar decision —
which he considered a judgment rendered by the legitimately »ordained«
ecclesiastical authority[93] — should be grounded upon an exegetical argument,
since this is what Hus had demanded of the council fathers and apparently
found wanting in their official response. The records of the trial bear this out
again and again: Hus had demanded during the proceedings to be instructed
»by better and more relevant scripture than those that I have written and
taught,« a plea he later repeated with his demand to be »fairly, kindly, and
humbly instructed from the Holy Scriptures and the reasons derived from
them« regarding his alleged error. His requests were not entirely ignored;
Mladoňovice at least records several of Cardinal d'Ailly's responses which took
the form of biblical arguments offered in defense of the accusations levelled
against Hus.[94] But this did not satisfy Hus, apparently, and his repetition of this
demand finally »caused murmuring and tumult« among those authorities —
d'Ailly, of course, who presided over this trial, and presumably also Gerson[95]
— whom the conciliar fathers had charged with the responsibility of hearing his
case. Indeed, Hus apparently considered that the biblical arguments of those

---

Vechte, G 2, pp. 163—66. The reference earlier cited to the classic statement offered by
Cyprian (cf. »Ep. ab Iubaianum,« c. 21; *PL* 3: 1169a) — viz. *extra ecclesiam nulla salus* — had
become a commonplace in papal documents of the high Middle Ages (e. g., IV Lateran
Council, c. 1, »De fide catholica«; *DS* 802), occurring with peculiar emphasis in those
documents of the later Middle Ages which sought to establish an authority which had
become increasingly suspect. Thus, for example, Boniface VIII, *Unam sanctam* (*DS* 870):
»Unam sanctam ecclesiam catholicam et ipsam apostolicam . . . extra quam nec salus est nec
remissio peccatorum.« Consequently, it is anything but unusual to find this theme at the
heart of the Hussite attack upon the Roman church's authority and jurisdiction, nor should
Gerson's recital of this theme come as a surprise to us.

[93] G 9, p. 242.

[94] Cf. for example d'Ailly's argument, including several biblical citations from the New
Testament, against Hus's understanding of virtue, and his insistence — a theme leaning
apparently toward the »neo-Donatist« position — that virtuous acts were a necessary index
of one's identity among the elect; see *Hus at the Council*, ed. Spinka, p. 197.

[95] Pascoe notes that Gerson served as »close advisor« to d'Ailly who was in charge of the
judicial process leading to Hus's condemnation and eventual execution; see *Jean Gerson*,
p. 11. See also Paul de Vooght, *L'hérésie de Jean Huss* (Louvain, 1960), pp. 294 ff.; *idem*,
»Jean Huss et ses juges,« *Das Konzil von Konstanz. Festschrift für Hermann Schäufele*, ed. A.
Franzen, W. Müller (Freiburg i. B., 1964); and, finally, Matthew Spinka, *John Hus' Concept
of the Church* (Princeton, 1966), pp. 349 ff., and *idem, John Hus*, pp. 248—49.

who rendered judgment against him had not been adequate, since he reiterated this charge immediately after the sentence passed upon his writings had been publicly read.[96] Hence, Gerson may well have intended his argument, expressed in *De consolatione theologiae* through the magisterial voice of Volucer, as just such an exegetical rejoinder (albeit posthumous) to Hus's challenge. This at least would appear to be the case, particularly given the striking proximity of Monicus' argument with Hus's self-defense as recorded during his trial.

Thus, Gerson expands what had begun as an apparently straightforward »gloss« on *zelus* as found in Jn. 2.17, broadening his argument to fashion a sustained exegetical argument against the Hussite position. As it happens, Gerson offers — or, at least, intended to offer — the »better and more relevant« scriptural arguments which Hus had demanded, formulating in the process a cautious view of how zeal, moderated by *discretio* and proper *scientia*, ought to be utilized in advancing the cause of church reform. His is a decidedly conservative if also persistent reform, one shaped not by the hysteria of apocalyptic fervor nor by merely sentimental reverence for an idealized church but rather by a hierarchical ecclesiology and tempered by a subdued eschatology. It appears as we have here argued that his reticent and »conservative« approach to the question of zeal, shaped by his irenic spirit,[97] also carried a progressive message of reform, but he insists that progress is to be made only within the church's hierarchical structure. *De moderamine zeli*: this is Gerson's unnegotiable qualification of the momentum of reform. Zeal must be moderated as a means to a larger end: namely, the progress of a reform accomplished within the arena of a moderate eschatology and within the contours of a conservative ecclesiology of the »interim« church.

2. Toleration and the humility of restraint

It is now clear that moderation of zeal — or, following Paul, a zeal *secundum scientiam* (cf. Rom. 10.2) — stood as a central theme for Gerson's approach to church reform, not only in an abstract sense but as a deliberate and concrete response to the impatient voices of the extreme Hussite circle. We now see, moreover, that Gerson's theological and ecclesiological perspective reflects his

---

[96] *Hus at the Council*, ed. Spinka, p. 194. In the closing moments of the trial, again as reported by Peter Mladoňovice, Hus had apparently cried out, »Why do you condemn my books, when I have ever desired and demanded better scriptural proofs against what I said and set forth in them, and even today I so desire? But you have so far neither adduced any more relevant scripture in opposition, nor have shown one erroneous word in them.« *Ibid.*, p. 229.

[97] For further discussion of this aspect of Gerson's thought, see Pascoe, *Jean Gerson*, pp. 213–14.

skeptical disapproval of the zealous, critical preaching heard in his day, once again an only slightly veiled index of his anti-Hussite critique. Against such immoderate and impatient zeal, Gerson did not simply invoke the privilege and authority of ecclesiastical office: this is no argument simply from established and duly sanctioned law, even though it is also this through his allegiance to what he here calls the *lex divinitatis et ordo*.[98] As we have noted, he penetrates further and deeper than this in defense of his conservative vision of reform, qualifying the zeal to »remove scandal« from the church with an argument for *discretio* and *patientia*. To this caveat he adds the rejoinder apparently aimed at Hus's recent defense that those who removed themselves from the hierarchical authority of the church and »spurned the counsel of others« were no different from »an untamed mule which ran toward every precipice.«[99] Indeed, his caricature in this particular passage from *De consolatione theologiae* may have been intended, and heard, as a direct and deliberately polemical response to Hus who had characterized the »cardinals« at the council as »riding upon mules, but greedy and very contemptible.«[100] In other words, while the cardinals had been portrayed as riding upon mules, Gerson ridicules those he considered misguided zealots as the »untamed mules« themselves.

---

[98] We should also note, however, that he does occasionally fall back upon this argument from authority: at one point in the treatise he cites a theme he had earlier invoked, viz., the »common law« (*vulgata regula*) which held that »that which we are able to do, we are able to do on account of the law« (i. e., *de jure possumus*; G 9, p. 218); this is an argument he had earlier applied in similar manner in *De potestate ecclesiastica*, G 6, p. 214. In *De consolatione theologiae* he adds the insistence that »it makes an important difference whether the zealous person exercises judicial authority or lacks it; but in any event the law is to be observed which holds that ›you will exercise justly that which is just‹« (*juste quod justum est exequeris*). This is no small point, since here Gerson argues that acting »by judicial authority« (*auctoritate judiciaria*) determines the legitimacy of one's acts. And, of course, the emphasis of his final comment stands as his rejoinder to Monicus' exegetical claim (i. e., representing Hus's position) that a good intention made an act good, an argument that the end justifies the means; against this Gerson insists that the means, too, must be just if one is to act justly. With this »common rule« and its elaboration Gerson underscores the necessary role of »law and order« in establishing and governing our acts: *viatores* act under the rule of law (*de jure*) in every stratum of life — i. e., the »natural,« »civil,« and »ecclesiastical« spheres. On the centrality of »law« within Gerson's thought, see: Burger, *Aedificatio*, pp. 92—95; Pascoe, »Law and Evangelical Liberty in the Thought of Jean Gerson,« *Monumenta Iuris Canonici: Proceedings of the Sixth International Congress of Medieval Canon Law*, ed. S. Kuttner, K. Pennington (Vatican, 1985), pp. 354—55; *idem*, *Jean Gerson*, pp. 49—79; and, finally, Posthumus Meyjes, *L'Assemblée de Vincennes*, pp. 92—102.

[99] This is a metaphor he used in various contexts earlier in his writings. Thus, for example, he elsewhere described the human condition after the Fall with an image from the Psalms: »Et homo, cum in honore esset, non intellexit: comparatus est iumentis insipientibus, et similis factus est illis« (Ps. 48.13). The effect of sin, as he often argued, renders us like »mute beasts.« See *Poenitemini*; G 7, p. 797; for a broad discussion of this theme, see also Pascoe, *Jean Gerson*, pp. 194—97.

[100] For this reference, see *Hus at the Council*, ed. Spinka, p. 103.

As noted earlier in this study, Gerson's ecclesiology portrays the church itself as »pilgrim« *ad Deum*. He consequently focuses his concern less upon the immediate cleansing of all imperfections than upon progress *in via* toward the image of the »celestial Jerusalem.« Within this framework he interprets the lingering »spots« and »wrinkles« which detracted from this heavenly image not as signs of the end-time and hence as cause for fear or hysteria, but rather as incentive for undertaking concrete though also deliberately conservative measures of reform within the hierarchical church. Gerson's vision falls squarely upon *ecclesia visibilis*, the empirical church, which often enough stood in stark contrast to the Hussite ecclesiology, conveyed in an apocalyptic mood as »the invisible church« (*ecclesia invisibilis*) of the elect. Against such an approach to the church and as an implicate of his commitment to the church's progress *nunc interim* toward its celestial archetype, Gerson advocated toleration rather than revolt, particularly vis-à-vis what he by now considered to be the intractable *scandala* which plagued the church of his day. Indeed, this toleration which might be better described as resignation explains, perhaps, the puzzling fact that Gerson did not involve himself in any of the commissions established at Constance to implement reform measures in the church.[101]

Gerson defends this note of resignation in a further gloss of Jn. 2.17, which as we have noted stood at the center of Hus's attack upon the institutional church. Describing the desired posture of *viatores* as reformers, Gerson insists that »such scandals which are visible in the church he wishes to eradicate, if he is able; if not, he tolerates and bemoans them,« a further reference to Ezekiel's apocalyptic prophecy of the »tau.«[102] *Si non potest* [scandala tollere], tolerat et gemit: his clever play on the words *tolerare* and *tollere* would not have been lost on his readers, and might well have emerged in the heated rhetoric of this conflict. With this contrast he accentuates both the desire to reform the church

---

[101] On this point, see Pascoe, *Jean Gerson*, p. 210.

[102] G 9, pp. 217–18. See further n. 76 above; also, for a thorough discussion of the Franciscan use of this theme, and for the iconography of Francis as »the scribe of the tau,« see John Fleming, *From Bonaventure to Bellini. An Essay in Franciscan Exegesis* (Princeton, 1982), pp. 99–128. We find Gerson first articulating the theme of toleration, and in remarkably similar terms, in his correspondence to Conrad de Vechte. After listing the Wyclifite theses condemned by his colleagues at Paris, Gerson adds: »Asserentes notorie et pertinaciter articulos praefatos sunt haeretici et ut tales judicialiter condemnandi, et ne ceteros inficiant, sunt diligentissime cum doctrinis suis scandalosissimis expugnandi. Etsi enim videntur habere zelum contra vitia praelatorum et clericorum, nimis proh dolor abundantium, non tamen secundum scientiam; zelus itaque discretus ea peccata quae videt in domo Dei se non posse tollere, tolerat et gemit; non autem possunt per vitia et errores bene tolli quia non in Beelzebub ejiciuntur demonia sed in digito Dei; qui est Spiritus Sanctus, volens ut in corrigendo modus habeatur prudentiae, juxta illud: Quis, auid, ubi, cui, cur attendas, quomodo, quando.« G 2, pp. 165 f. This preference to accent the role of the Holy Spirit above strictly human initiatives in effecting reform is typical of Gerson's earlier work as well; see Ozment, »Patterns of Reform in Jean Gerson,« pp. 111 ff.

and the possibility that her ineradicable »scandals« might well represent the inevitable burdens (*tentationes*) facing *viatores*, the *adversitas* which he cites as the test of the genuineness of our love.[103] What is curious about this passage is its thematic proximity to the Hussite emphasis upon suffering as the justification of one's cause; Gerson corrects this with the rejoinder that all should expect suffering, since adversity tests our love of God. Disorder in the church, furthermore, should not be interpreted only as a sign of the end-time; it was also the natural condition of an institution which itself was *in via*. These were the conditions of life in the »pilgrim« church, the consequence of the only partial vision by which *viatores* see now *in speculo et in aenigmate*.

Thus Gerson's conservative advocacy of toleration is not to be interpreted as a call to resignation pure and simple, but as a recognition that the *defensio catholicae veritatis* will require acceptance of such »spots« and »wrinkles,« representing as they do the unavoidable signs that the church in the »interim« has not yet reached its eschatological destination.[104] As he had earlier conceded, God had not ejected *viatores* »from the garden of delights« (cf. Joel 2.3) in order that »we might build for ourselves a new one here, « a passage which appears to offer the rationale both for Gerson's toleration vis-à-vis the still imperfect pilgrim church and for his polemic directed toward those less patient voices who demanded her purity already in this »interim.«[105] Reform, Gerson insists, must be enacted within an eschatological parameter. This is the *theoria* which finally orients his approach to controversial matters of church *praxis*, bringing him to advocate efforts to remove (*tollere*) scandals if possible but to tolerate (*tolerare*) ineradicable blemishes in this »interim.« He adds in defense of this cautious position Jesus' parable of the end-time, concluding that such moderate zeal is preferable *in via* »lest in gathering weeds ... the wheat also might be uprooted.«[106] Such language demonstrates quite convincingly that Gerson's ecclesiology, embedded within the comprehensive structure of a traditional

---

[103] Cf. G 9, p. 225: »Porro quis nesciat veram dilectionem non in prosperis sed adversis inspici. Adversitas nempe sola probatrix est si quis in prosperitate verus amator sit.«

[104] In a similar vein Burger notes with regard to Gerson's earlier writings on the papal schism that »hier bündelt Gerson die Grundgedanken seiner konservativen Reform: Mißbräuche stellen keineswegs die hierarchische Struktur infrage«; *Aedificatio*, p. 148. Yet Gerson's insistent defense of the hierarchical church's inviolable structure in these earlier treatises was apparently, following Burger's conclusion, the direct result of the Dionysian influence (*ibid.*, p. 144). In *De consolatione theologiae*, in contrast, it is not this theoretical point of reference but rather his concrete opposition to (Hussite) apocalypticism which determines the shape of his argument, since he is here not as intent upon maintaining the hierarchical order against its critics as he is upon defending the imperfect form of the church *in via*. Thus, it is the specific context which, far from modulating the substance of his ecclesiological arguments, nonetheless alters the focus of characteristically Gersonian themes.

[105] See above, 5.A.2.

[106] G 9, p. 230; the biblical reference here is to Mt. 13.29.

Augustinian eschatology, establishes the very basis for his anti–Hussite
polemic. Heresy represents for him an assault upon the »divine law and order«;
the problem it presents is at the deepest level not doctrinal but
ecclesiological.[107] Within this eschatological context he advocates toleration
and counsels restraint, since if *discretio* is to moderate one's zeal for reform, so
also should *patientia* restrain an immoderate desire to remove *scandala* at any
cost from the pilgrim church. Once again we note the confluence of the
dynamic and conservative dimensions of his ecclesiology: his vision of reform
respects both the inherent structure of the church (i. e., as *ordo divinitatis*) as well
as her necessarily »unfinished« character in this interim.[108]

3. *Opus hoc solius Dei esse*: the solitary life and reform

Gerson articulates this critique on yet another level in *De consolatione theologiae*,
approaching the matter of restraint not only as a function of the requisite
humility vis-à-vis the divinely ordained hierarchical order but as a posture with
a more specific and extensive theological rationale. Raising the general question
of *reformatio ecclesiae* in this treatise, Gerson returns to a theme frequently found
in his earlier writings: the *pattern* of church reform which he envisioned
proceeded »from the highest downward through all its members.«[109] His
model of reform begins at the apex of the ecclesiastical hierarchy, which meant
that reform necessarily had to begin *a summo* before progressing »downward«
to address further difficulties.[110] In this treatise, however, his emphasis has
shifted quite dramatically, and this presumably for two reasons. In the first
case, and most obviously, Gerson wrote *De consolatione theologiae* in the wake of
the Council of Constance, and hence no longer faced the difficulties which the

---

[107] See also Pascoe, *Jean Gerson*, p. 40: »Heresy ... is ... seen in the context of order.
Heretics and heresy corrupt hierarchical order. ...«

[108] Pascoe points to this facet of Gerson's ecclesiology, concluding that the chancellor's
view of »the ecclesiastical hierarchy, finally, is dynamic.... The casual relationship
between hierarchy, reform, and the mystical body constitutes ... the most essential aspect
of Gerson's ideas on church reform.« *Jean Gerson*, pp. 45 ff., 205.

[109] That is, *a summo usque deorsum per omnem suorum membrorum*. See, for example,
Tractatus de unitate ecclesiae (1409), G 6, p. 141; see also *De sensu litterali sacrae scripturae*, G 3,
p. 340.

[110] The reference echoes the language of the conciliar document *Sacrosancta* (i. e., reform
»in head and members«), declared in the fifth session at Constance. Gerson is only here
interpreting the decree to the effect that the reform must begin *a summo*, or with the papal
see, and only then proceed downward in the hierarchy to effect a reform of »the members«
as well. Pascoe discusses how the papal schism influenced this assumption by shifting the
emphasis to the Holy Spirit who stands »above« the papacy, as it were, as the operative
cause of reform; see *Jean Gerson*, pp. 207 ff. On the same theme see also Ozment, »Patterns
of Reform in Jean Gerson.«

schism presented; it appeared that at this juncture the »head« at least had been re-formed (i. e., reinstated). The second circumstance, which we shall explore more fully here, is a matter of historical reconstruction based upon the mood of discouragement we find in this text. This is, as we have suggested, a sign apparently of the lingering frustration brought upon him by the Hussite attack upon the institutional church, an influence which triggered a decisive change of mind over against his earlier optimism regarding preaching as an effective instrument of reform.[111] It is this theme which we must explore more carefully, particularly since Gerson's approach to it after Constance departs from emphases familiar to us from his earlier writings and thereby suggests a distinct and unexpected modulation in his approach to church reform.

In an earlier chapter we considered the quite peculiar favor which Gerson, normally known for his stubborn advocacy of the *vita ambidextra*, bestowed in this treatise upon the *solitarii*, those who stood apart from the world in pursuit of prayer and contemplation.[112] *De consolatione theologiae* and specifically the allusions we here find to events which had transpired at the recently concluded council point to the concrete circumstances which seem to have influenced this change in his perspective. In the wake of the polemical confrontation with Hus and his circle at the council, Gerson had apparently begun to reconsider the functional basis of his ecclesiology, particularly with regard to the familiar theme in his writings of the *vita mixta ex utraque* — i. e., the union of the »active« and »contemplative« lives. Earlier in his writings, as we have suggested, Gerson had made himself known as a forceful advocate of the »mixed« life, defining the *vita contemplativa* not only in terms of prayer as one might expect in the medieval period but also as the domain of preaching and the administration of the sacraments. Indeed, he had quite transformed the traditional exegesis of the Mary/Martha pericope (Lk. 10.38–42), that biblical passage by which earlier theologians, often following the exegetical lead of Gregory the Great, had defended both forms of life but with a distinctive bias toward the *vita contemplativa* — as represented typologically by Mary — as the higher calling.[113] In this post-conciliar treatise, however, he has changed his

---

[111] For a thorough discussion of Gerson's earlier commitment to preaching as a vehicle for reform, see Pascoe, *Jean Gerson*, pp. 118–28, 171 f.

[112] See above, 4.C.2.

[113] See Gregory the Great, *On Morals in Job*, 5.6.9: » ›Thou shalt come to thy grave in fulness, like as a shock of corn cometh in his season.‹ For what is denoted by the name of the grave, saving a life of contemplation? which as it were buries us, dead to this world, in that it hides us in the interior world away from all earthly desires. For they, being dead to the exterior life, were also buried by contemplation, to whom Paul said, ›For you are dead, and your life is hid with Christ in God.‹ An active life is also a grave, in that it covers us, as dead, from evil works; but the contemplative life more perfectly buries us, in that it wholly severs us from all worldly courses. « This translation is taken from the text in the *Library of Fathers of the Catholic Church* (Oxford, 1844), p. 355; *Moralia in Iob*, CCSL 143: 224–25.

point of view dramatically: he here offers an extended and for him unprecedented defense of what he calls the »solitary« life, no longer defining this as *vita contemplativa* by which he had earlier included the »secular« tasks of preaching and administering sacraments, but now confining his attention to the task of prayer alone.[114] Yet his defense of prayer, set squarely within the scope of the solitary life, nonetheless acquires an ambitious and quite »worldly« dimension to it: prayer stands as the support for those engaged in the secular *cura animarum*, which he identifies here as »preaching, admonishing, and correcting,« and he insists in contrast to his earlier stance that prayer is finally a more effective antidote against vices than preaching itself.[115] We are now in a position to suggest that this altered approach, by which he emphasized prayer above all as the principal means of *reformatio ecclesiae*, is not only attributable to the social structure of his ecclesiology, as we earlier suggested: it appears to stand as the consequence of his disillusionment in the efficacy of preaching more generally, and perhaps as a measure of his frustration at the success enjoyed by what he considered the indiscreet preaching of the Hussite circle. This is certainly not yet a quietist position, though Gerson's resignation does suggest that he had reached a level of disappointment regarding the efficacy of concrete approaches to reform not found in his earlier writings.[116] This might also explain why Gerson did not involve himself in the work of the reform commissions instituted at Constance.[117]

---

[114] On this point Pascoe has observed that Gerson »does not consider the religious orders of his day as a dynamic force in the reform of the church .... For Gerson ..., hope for ecclesiastical reform lay not with the religious orders but with the hierarchical structures of the church.« *Jean Gerson*, p. 164. It would now appear that this thesis, which offers an adequate summary of the chancellor's earlier views, does not fully account for the more skeptical view Gerson embraced in *De consolatione theologiae* toward preaching as a vehicle of reform, and his corresponding emphasis of the constructive role of *solitarii* in effecting reform. See also above, 4.C.2.

[115] As earlier noted, Gerson's literary strategy adds a poignant irony to this argument, since it is the hermit Monicus who questions the legitimacy and »utility« — a key Gersonian theme — of the *solitarius*, while Volucer is left to defend this vocation within and for the broader church. Such an argument would have been inconceivable in Gerson's writings before this point, because he had earlier in his career devoted considerable and unwavering attention to defending the *active* life, and had broadened his interpretation of the contemplative life to endorse those ministries of the secular clergy devoted to the *cura animarum*; on this see Abramowski, »Johann Gerson,« pp. 63 ff. for an excellent discussion of Gerson's *De consiliis evangelicis et statu perfectionis*. For the details of Gerson's discussion in *De consolatione theologiae*, as here reported in general terms, see G 9, pp. 224 ff.

[116] Gerson had earlier opposed the Beguines and others because their position moved in the direction of an antinomian quietism, by which they held that the tranquility they had attained freed them from all laws; Gerson is clearly not moving in this direction, but rather offers a defense of the solitary life precisely in order to engage in the concrete work of church reform — if first of all by prayer. On the matter of Gerson's view of the Beguines, see Brown, *Pastor and Laity*, pp. 202–203; Pascoe, *Jean Gerson*, pp. 121–22.

[117] See Pascoe, *ibid.*, pp. 209–10.

Here we must also note one final argument Gerson offers on this point. In the midst of his extended defense of the solitary life, and his definition both of this particular status as the foundation for the church's »secular« ministries and of prayer as the most effective antidote against vice, the chancellor adds a theological qualification which returns the discussion to his concern for humility: as the capstone of his argument he cites the passage from Job, »If you have the arm of God, and if you thunder with a voice like [God's], disperse the proud in your fury, abasing every arrogant person whom you regard« (Job 40.4, 6). The rhetorical force of this passage and the ironic inference which this citation conveys seem clear enough, though Gerson leaves nothing to the reader's imagination. He goes on to clarify this passage himself, adding that »there [the scripture] openly teaches that this reforming work belongs to God alone«: *opus hoc solius Dei esse*. In other words, because we do not have the power of God at our disposal (i. e., *brachium sicut Deus*), ours is not the task of actively intervening to bring about what remains finally *opus Dei*; as the »work of God,« prayer becomes the vehicle by which *viatores* might finally effect reform, personal and institutional, through »conforming our wills to the first will most free.« Beyond this his modest, reticent advice in this post-conciliar treatise is to »live well yourself and pray for others; tolerate them, and bemoan them,« another reference to the by now familiar prophecy of Ezekiel that *viatores* should seek to bear the »tau« by »frequently lamenting« and intervening with »constant prayer.« Gerson thus draws upon a distinctive apocalyptic theme, but mutes it in terms of his hierarchical ecclesiology in order to serve his essentially conservative program of reform.

This emphasis upon the work of prayer and the corresponding retreat from the active functions of ministry suggest that Gerson had come to recognize at Constance the difficulty if not also futility of extreme visions of ecclesiastical reform. In the immediate context of Constance we hear Gerson answering the radical voices of his day, and above all those of the Hussite circle, by reminding *viatores* that reform must occur within the structure of the hierarchical church which as a »pilgrim« itself would be »spotless and without wrinkle« only at the end of time. Gerson's polemic against the Hussite preaching of his day, rooted in the logic of his hierarchical ecclesiology and in his traditional eschatology, thus offers the key to rightly interpreting the broader and deeper shifts in his theology at this juncture of his career: namely, his abandonment of the *facere quod in se est* doctrine with its confidence in the human contribution to salvation, and his preference for a Scotist approach to predestination *ante praevisa merita*. Let us consider this thesis now more carefully.

An examination of the documents preserved from Hus's trial at Constance and, above all, Peter Mladoňovice's *Relatio* which offers an extensive and detailed account of these proceedings,[118] suggests that these two themes – i. e.,

---

[118] That is, his *Relatio de Magistro Johannis Hus*; this work is included in *Hus at the Council*,

the anthropological theme regarding the potential of human virtue[119] and the related soteriological matter of predestination — also stood at the foundation of Hus's constructive theological argument. It was his view of predestination, above all, which supported his ecclesiology: he viewed the church as the »congregation of the predestined,« a model of an »invisible church« which emphasized not the external office or »position of dignity« one held within the institutional church but one's »unofficial« status as predestined through God's election alone.[120] Related to this ecclesiology of the *ecclesia invisibilis*, and functioning as its *modus operandi*, is Hus's view of predestination as the »hidden« election of God *ab aeterno*. In this respect Hus's soteriology grounds his ecclesiology; his ecclesiology stands as the inevitable consequence of the former. Furthermore, a soteriological implicate of this anthropology, and one which determined the extreme shape of Hus's ecclesiology, was his view of virtue: he held, apparently, that just as »virtue vivifies all acts of the virtuous,« so also did one »living in grace« as one of the predestinate »pray and deserve merit while sleeping or doing anything whatsoever,« adding here Augustine's gloss of Lk. 11.34 as earlier noted.[121] That is, the elect could not help but be virtuous and merit election simply because they had been chosen by God; Hus cites their ability to accomplish this »even in their sleep« as testimony of an extreme Augustinian flavor that grace is indeed »irresistible« for them and that it inevitably manifests itself in a virtuous life. For this reason he held the position, already earlier condemned by the theological faculty at Paris, that »only the church containing the predestined and morally upright is the universal church to which obedience is owed.«[122] This perspective, then, is the external side of his insistence that the *true* church of the predestined was already

---

ed. Spinka, pp. 89–236. In introducing Mladoňovice and this text, Spinka notes that »since he was an eyewitness of most of the events described by him, his work is generally regarded as the most complete and reliable record of all that is connected with Hus's trial and death.« *Ibid.*, p. 79. It is particularly instructive for our purposes since it offers a detailed account of Hus's public argument, noting the outline of the official condemnation along with Hus's specific responses to these accusations. For detailed discussion of Hus's trial, see also C. J. Héfélé, *Histoire des conciles d'après les documents originaux* (Paris, 1869–78), 10: 330–68, 445–76; and, more recently, de Vooght, *L'hérésie de Jean Huss*, Ch. 10.

[119] Hus defended the Aristotelian principle that »if a man is wicked, whatever he does, he does wickedly; and if he is virtuous, whatever he does, he does virtuously. ... Virtue vivifies all man's acts efficaciously.« See »Last Reply,« in *Hus at the Council*, ed. Spinka, p. 262, no. 16.

[120] Cf. for example, Mladoňovice, in *Hus at the Council*, ed. Spinka, pp. 182–88. Also, see Hus, *The Church*, in *Forerunners*, trans. and ed. Oberman, pp. 219 ff., and *idem, Tractatus de ecclesia*, ed. S. H. Thomson (Cambridge, 1956), pp. 11 ff., and Hus's »Last Reply to the Final Formulation of the Charges against Him,« in *Hus at the Council*, ed. Spinka, pp. 260–61, especially nos. 3–6.

[121] Cf. Mladoňovice, »Account,« in *Hus at the Council*, ed. Spinka, p. 197.

[122] See G 2, p. 164, art. 12.

»without spot and wrinkle« – and thus could be identified in terms of the morality of its members as a faithful remnant.[123]

On the basis of this summary of Hus's position we might now offer an explanation for the decisive and unprecedented shifts in Gerson's theology, particularly on these two foundational themes of his soteriology – i. e., predestination and the role of human merit. It now appears plausible, and indeed even probable given the confluence of specific arguments and occasional thematic references in *De consolatione theologiae*, that we interpret Gerson's change of perspective on these key points as a response to specific church-related controversies of the preceding years. On this basis we are now in a position to suggest that the shift in Gerson's theological position after Constance, and specifically in *De consolatione theologiae*, might well be his magisterial response to the challenges advanced by Hus and his circle. Indeed, this hypothesis would explain not only the specific arguments we have analyzed in this and preceding chapters, but a plump supplemental list as well: e. g., Gerson's careful exegetical defense of ecclesiastical benefices, including his direct attack upon Hus's argument regarding simony; his anti-Donatist argument for obedience as a necessary condition of life within the hierarchical church, regardless of the »worthiness« of the superior in question; his defense of ecclesiastical and civil law as well as the »ordained« judges without qualification as the hierarchical channel of divine law; his defense of *correctio judicaria*, and its distinction from *correctio fraterna*; his support of religious orders and his sustained defense of both the legitimacy and efficacy of the *solitarii* in the matter of church reform; his peculiar and unexpected reticence toward preaching as an effective vehicle for reform; his dismissal of the contention that the title to rule is radically founded in charity rather than the jurisdictional authority of the church itself.[124]

---

[123] See, for example, Hus, *The Church*: »For no one is a member of this Church unless he be predestined and in due time without spot or blemish. But no one without great caution or revelation could assert that he is predestined or holy without spot or blemish.« *Forerunners*, trans. and ed. Oberman, p. 226; *De ecclesia*, ed. Thomson, p. 86. The allusion to Eph. 5.16 is quite clear, establishing another striking contrast to Gerson's ecclesiology and his related soteriology. Pelikan rightly notes that this perspective, since it deliberately obscured the identity of the true church (cf. *The Church*, in *Forerunners*, trans. and ed. Oberman, p. 227; *De ecclesia*, ed. Thomson, p. 37) while also withholding any assurance that one was a member thereof, caused Gerson no small consternation; responding to such an ecclesiology the chancellor could only conclude that Hus left no certainty whatsoever about the identity and functional ministry of the church. Pelikan, *Reformation*, pp. 91 f.; see also Seibt, »Geistige Reformbewegungen,« pp. 324–31.

[124] Alone among Gerson studies, Schwab's detailed analysis (Ch. 13) of »die Schritte des Concils zu Constanz gegen Wycliffe und Hus zur Reinerhaltung der kirchlichen Lehre« points to the force of the Hussite threat upon Gerson's later writings; indeed, he cites a passage from *De consolatione theologiae* (III pr. 2; G 9, p. 216), already noted in this study, as a vital clue to this factor. See Schwab, *Johannes Gerson*, p. 597, n. 3.

But what is even more decisive in understanding the ecclesiological and soteriological developments we have observed in the later Gerson is the correlation of the Hussite background with the broad theological reorientation articulated in this treatise. Apparently, the events which had transpired at Constance only confirmed his suspicious and polemical attitude toward Hus, expressed already in his earlier correspondence of 1414 with Conrad de Vechte, the Archbishop of Prague.[125] As we have suggested, this specific conflict supplies the rationale for the groundshift in Gerson's theology that we have traced during and after the council, particularly in terms of two decisive points: first, his strident criticism of human pride and any trust in human works, against Hussite preaching; and, second, his appropriation of specific themes familiar to their preaching — above all the emphasis upon predestination — which Gerson reformulates within the bounds of his mediating soteriology and his hierarchical ecclesiology. These are not, of course, unrelated themes. Yet he refutes any pretense of human righteousness *coram judice Deo*, any pride in one's moral accomplishments as the outward measure of election, and thereby articulates a sharp opposition to the Hussite insistence that a direct and even verifiable correspondence existed between the two.[126] It is this historical context, in other words, that has provoked Gerson to reformulate his theology in quite thorough and far-reaching terms. For this reason, the effort we have undertaken to place Gerson within the complex horizon of late-scholastic theology in earlier chapters has now received a further clarification, specifically in terms of the immediate circumstances in which Gerson wrote *De consolatione theologiae*. The rationale prompting this dramatic theological shift apparently has to do in the first place with the troubled circumstances within the church of his day, a church disordered through papal schism and moral decay and threatened by increasingly strident voices calling for change. To recall the language of the conciliar decree, »Sacrosancta« (1415), it was a church in need of »reform in head and members.« In this troubled context Gerson found himself called upon to speak of reform on two fronts: first, that of preserving the »divine law« and hierarchical order which alone could preserve the fabric

---

[125] See G 2, pp. 157–66.

[126] Thus, for example, Peter Chelčický had argued, in his *The Holy Church*, that calling the church the congregation of the predestinate meant that »in the saints, the righteousness commanded by God and predestination go together, and if a predestinated person keeps the righteousness commanded by God, he is then a member of the holy church« (cited in Pelikan, *Reformation*, p. 85). This syllogistic reasoning would have allowed for a kind of moral verification of election, perhaps in both an introspective and public sense, which would have stimulated scrupulosity or — worse yet according to Gerson's perspective — pride. Hus's view articulates this theme with similar if less extreme formulations and consequences; see *The Church*, in *Forerunners*, trans. and ed. Oberman, pp. 226–27; and *idem, De ecclesia*, ed. Thomson, pp. 36–37. We have already pointed to Gerson's warning against such a position; see above, n. 120.

of society itself; and, second, that of offering *viatores* a »firm« and »solid« theological consolation under such chaotic and desolate conditions.

4. Social control or social order? Authority, obedience, and *conversio*

Throughout this chapter we have explored Gerson's insistence that the church was to be an ordered body, an institution in which the laws governing human acts as well as the relations among its members were not the accidents of history nor of human invention but were part of a divinely instituted order. We have also noted that Gerson understood these matters principally in terms of his hierarchical view of reality, and more particularly vis-à-vis the hierarchical structure governing life within the church. We have also suggested that this framework, while based at a deep level upon a Dionysian approach, reflects the profound and immediate influence of Thomas Aquinas as well: with the Angelic Doctor Gerson views the church's reality in the »interim« not with the giddy cosmological speculations of the Areopagite, but in the more mundane terms of a mediating locus leading *viatores* on pilgrimage toward the unseen world. Yet unlike Aquinas and indeed in a form uncharacteristic of his own broader oeuvre, Gerson here avoids all reference to the sacraments as this concrete point of access, choosing to speak in more general terms of *theologia* — in a manner, as we have argued, distinctly reminiscent of Boethius' *philosophia* — as the companion and guide in this journey *ad Deum*. But is this »order,« and this sustained and articulate defense of the mediating structure of the hierarchical church, anything other than a thinly veiled attempt at control, both ecclesiastical and social? Is Gerson's ecclesiology, in other words, fashioned as an attempt to maintain the church's privilege in turbulent times, suppressing by an argument which finally resorts to authority the revolutionary voices which did not accord with his moderate and even conservative vision of reform? These are questions which we must finally address, and we shall do so by looking at a cluster of themes from *De consolatione theologiae* which go to the heart of his ecclesiology.

It is clear enough from this and other earlier treatises written while at Constance (1415–1418) that Gerson was no advocate of passivity in times of crisis, apparently despite both his defense here of the *solitarii* and his decisive application of *epikeia* even in terms of the *correctio judicaria*. Particularly during the years of the council he demonstrated no reluctance in advising forceful intervention by the civil arm when this was necessary either to maintain the peace and guard the ecclesiastical *status quo*[127] or to defend the church's doctrinal

---

[127] On this point see his correspondence with Conrad de Vechte, frequently referred to elsewhere in this study; G 2, pp. 157–66. See also Schwab, *Johannes Gerson*, pp. 597–603,

and jurisdictional authority when it came under attack. Yet we must interpret his perspective not merely as the reactionary efforts of one threatened by popular uprising, as true as this certainly is on one level, but within the theoretical framework of his ecclesiology, particularly since this had been the matrix early and late in which he formulated pastoral, theological, and even political decisions. In other words, his advocacy of an often severe »law and order« position was an implicate of his ecclesiology, and not vice versa: he viewed the *ordo ecclesiasticus* as an order instituted by divine sanction, and for this reason inviolable. Thus, his defense of the social peace in *De consolatione theologiae* comes as no surprise, though he accomplishes this not as he later would do with reference to Augustine's view of *ordo* but rather in terms of the theological virtues and hence through the lens of what we have called his »moderate« eschatology.[128] Once again it appears that his view of the church in the »interim« shaped this particular perspective, since his thrust seems directed against those who expected such a peace immediately and in perfect form; against such a position, with its impatient defiance of the present (dis-)order, Gerson insisted that this order even at its best would bring but a dim sense of that longed for tranquility, the eschatological peace which *viatores* would receive in full form only when the celestial and ecclesiastical hierarchies would be one (i. e., *tunc autem facie ad faciem*).

Gerson's stand toward social order, however, penetrates even beyond the matrix of his ecclesiology: in the midst of a discussion of »moral certitude« here he admits in a provocative digression that he considered »the authority of ruling [*auctoritas regiminis*] to be the very basis of religion.«[129] This is no small point, not only in terms of the theoretical basis of his ecclesiology but for grasping the broader question of his functional view of religion: *religio* represented for Gerson, as in its classical sense, the structuring force for society in general terms. Obedience, therefore, was not a matter of one's reasoned conclusion that the structures or duties imposed by *superiores* were correct and

---

and Connolly, *John Gerson*, pp. 180 ff. Brown has also rightly noted that Gerson viewed the use of »coercive power« as a necessary condition of the Fall; *Pastor and Laity*, pp. 162–63.

[128] Cf. for instance his later *Ep. à Guillaume Minaudi* of 1402 (G 2, p. 233): »Quid autem magis processit a Deo quam religio christiana, quam Ecclesia Christi sponsa? Est igitur in ea ordo qui describitur esse parium dispariumque rerum sua unicuique tribuens dispositio seu collatio.« This reference, as noted by Pascoe (*Jean Gerson*, p. 23, n. 29), is to Augustine's definition of *ordo* in *De civitate Dei* 19.13 (*CCSL* 48: 679), and in *De ordine* (*CSEL* 63: 121). For one instance of his quite different discussion of *pax* in *De consolatione theologiae*, defined primarily in terms of the theological virtues and expressed under the biblical figure of the »three cities« of Josh. 20, see G 9, p. 240.

[129] G 9, p. 236. In broader context he interprets this to mean that an authority external to human reason, which is »dubious, weak, and uncertain in many things,« is necessary to bring us certitude; he amplifies this with a string of illustrations, including his admission that »authority has to prevail for younger people in relation to their teachers or parents because their own judgment is still lacking or imperfect.«

hence acceptable. Quite the contrary: authority itself served as the basis of religion, even if concrete instances of its exercise were somehow misguided:

The *correctio judicaria* ought to be attentive lest it surpass in any respect the hierarchical order, that order namely by which inferiors have to be led back to God via superiors, even where there appears to be either inertia or outright fault in those superiors. On this account let no one usurp public power: neither in preaching, nor in the administration of the sacraments, nor in the satirical reprimanding of superiors before those subject to them. This does not bring any moral edification, and only causes indignation and contempt.[130]

»Even where there appears to be . . . fault in those superiors«: this claim Gerson undoubtedly intended as a direct and polemic response to the Hussite position, the magisterial reaction to an intensely moral perspective representing what has been identified as the »rising tide« of »neo-Donatism« during this period.[131] Gerson apparently intends this caveat, as one might well expect, not in terms of doctrinal purity alone but as a necessary corrective within the concrete realm of pastoral affairs. Corresponding to his emphasis upon the visible or empirical church, this theme underscored the legitimacy of the church's hierarchical structure without qualification or further apology − »Let no one usurp public power. . . .« Just as *inferiores* were ordered beneath *superiores* in this hierarchy,[132] so also it was the »judicial authority«[133] rather than the priest's personal virtue which established the legitimate basis of office within the church.

But this was a theme which Gerson applied not only to his ecclesiology, though it appears first of all to exert its influence most directly upon this sphere. In a broader sense Gerson interprets this as a disclosure of the very nature of

---

[130] G 9, p. 222.

[131] Thus, Pelikan, *Reformation*, pp. 92−98. Oberman has noted that this »rising tide« is »part of a larger pan-European Donatist upsurge«; *Harvest*, pp. 220−21. For Hus's perspective on this issue, see *The Church*, in *Forerunners*, trans. and ed. Oberman, pp. 228 f., and *idem*, *De ecclesia*, ed. Thomson, pp. 36 ff., and Mladoňovice, in *Hus at the Council*, ed. Spinka, pp. 195 f.

[132] Not without cause did Gerson often refer to the laity variously as *simplices*, *inferiores*, and *subditos*, yet this was not meant to exclude them from the integrity of the church (contra Brown); it was merely a way of identifying their place within a hierarchical ecclesiology, a framework within which Gerson here and elsewhere affirmed the »mutual« obligations of higher and lower members. See above, 4.C.2; cf. also Brown, *Pastor and Laity*, pp. 38 f. Our study of the later Gerson also requires a qualification of the broad conclusions which Burger reached in this regard; cf. *Aedificatio*, pp. 191 ff., and particularly his conclusion that theologians occupy a higher position for Gerson than »the simple Christians.« As we have demonstrated on the basis of *De consolatione theologiae*, Gerson here offers a definition of *theologus* which goes beyond his earlier insistence that these be morally upstanding or pious persons; he here adds that true theologians are not the »professional« university masters, who are often filled with a kind of knowledge which »puffs up,« but rather the *idiotae* solicitous of their own salvation in whom one finds »a simple faith, certain hope, and sweet charity« (G 9, p. 238, and above, 4.C.1, 3).

[133] G 9, p. 218.

religion itself. Here following the course set forth by Dionysius and later modified by Aquinas, Gerson too conceived of the institutional church with its hierarchical lines of authority both as the actual or historical conduit of revelation and as the means by which *viatores* return *ad Deum*. In this sense his ecclesiology functions as a concrete instance of the neo-Platonic model of *processus* and *conversio*.[134] As such Gerson's conviction about the necessity of obedience and authority as an ecclesiological principle establishes at the same time the functional framework in which *theologia* guides wayfarers in their journey to God. In this specific sense the *ordo ecclesiasticus* holds broad pastoral implications for Gerson, many of which he explores in *De consolatione theologiae*. His ecclesiology derives, in other words, from a comprehensive, cosmological perspective by which he envisioned the disorder still prevailing in the church as but one consequence of the *processus*, and its ordered life as the essential means of *conversio*. This becomes clear in an unexpected digression Gerson offers late in the treatise, a passage in which he once again describes in neo-Platonic terms the »ordering« purpose of God's creation of humanity:

> Let them recognize the excellent state of the human condition which is created for this: that through reason [*per rationem*] they [i. e., *viatores*] might lead the entire sensible world, which enters through the doors of the senses [*per sensuum portas ingreditur*], back to the first principle, which is God . . .. For as the world proceeds from God [*procedens a Deo mundus*] it becomes continuously degraded [*vilior*] in its parts; but it is rendered more and more spiritual once again through the work of the agent intellect upon the corporeal phantasms. . . .[135]

This passage clarifies Gerson's application of the general neo-Platonic principles of *processus* and *regressus* or *conversio*, for it is this broader structure which tells us something of the coherence underlying Gerson's view of the *ordo*

---

[134] For further discussion of this general theme, cf. H. Dörrie, »Neuplatonismus,« *Religion in Geschichte und Gegenwart* (Tübingen, 1960 [3rd ed.]), 4: 1428 f.

[135] G 9, p. 238. It appears that Gerson, ever the eclectic thinker, has here combined Boethius' notion of *ratio* as the organizing principle and constitutive fabric of the universe (cf. *De consolatione philosophiae* III m. 9, *CCSL* 94: 51) together with Aquinas's identification of the created light in the human soul with the »agent intellect,« a concept that for Aristotle stood as a faculty of the soul itself. This would explain why Gerson (following Aquinas and, indirectly, Aristotle) interprets the principle of *ratio* in decidedly personal terms, yet at the same time maintaining the cosmic dimensions in which *ratio* operates (following Boethius and neo-Platonism generally); we must conclude that it is the overarching framework of the latter which finally dominates the urgency Gerson attributes to the right exercise of reason, and its necessary submission to *superiores* in order to be rightly ordered, since the latter is a concrete participation in the *conversio mundi* itself (see also above, n. 132). On Aquinas's view of human psychology, and his notion of the »agent intellect,« see *De veritate*, Q. 11; *Compendium theologiae*, 104; and, finally, *Disputationes de anima*, 15; Ralph McInerny treats this theme in *St. Thomas Aquinas* (Notre Dame and London, 1982), pp. 115–18.

ecclesiasticus.[136] Admittedly, this is a structure meant in a certain sense to order society and the church, but it functions as »control« in a teleological rather than merely punitive manner, guiding not only *viatores* but as we here see »the entire sensible world« in its pilgrimage of return to God (i. e., *in primum principium Deum*).

This comprehensive neo-Platonic imagery, therefore, rather than the more focused Dionysian view of the corresponding relation of the celestial and ecclesiastical hierarchies finally provides the overarching framework in which Gerson makes sense of authority and obedience. The submission of *inferiores* to *superiores*, in other words, acquires a remarkable significance within his ecclesiology as the functional mechanism of a broad cosmological schema: it is a vital means for the *conversio*, the return of all reality *in Deum*, and hence part of what might well be described as the universal pilgrimage or »regression« *in primum principium Deum*. The application of authority, therefore, is only part of

---

[136] This is no new theme for Gerson; we find a similar treatment of this idea in an early sermon, *A Deo exivit* (1402), in which he argues that »regredi autem nonnisi creaturae rationali proprie datum est, quamquam velit Boetius omnia in suum regredi principium, velut si flumina unde exeunt revertantur. Eccl. 1(.7). Et quando hoc? Quando ›repetunt proprios quaeque recursus redituque suo singula gaudent. Nec manet ulli traditus ordo nisi quod fini junxerit ortum stabilemque sui fecerit orbem.‹ *De consolatione philosophiae* III m. 2. Hoc fit dum motus inditos naturae suae custodiunt, dumque vices indulta peragunt, agendo, patiendo movendoque. . . . Ceterum anima humana praecipue illa est inter omnes rationales spiritus quae non solum regredi ad Deum sed omnia alia in eum referre debet. Propterea enim ipsa corpori conjuncta est et nervis certis ligata secundum Platonicos; propterea nexum duplicis mundi tam spiritualis quam corporalis operatur, quasi duas illas catenas causarum, auream et argenteam, nectens. Deinde in horizonte duplicis mundi statuitur facies sua, prout divini theologi et elevati metaphysici docuerunt, quatenus per ipsam ea omnia referrentur in Deum, cognoscendo et utendo quae ab eo egressa sunt in creando.« G 5, pp. 14–15. Ozment has rightly noted that already in this early sermon Gerson »appeals to the hierarchical nature of Aristotle's political theory and Platonic metaphysics to document his own peculiar position«; *Selections*, ed. and trans. Ozment, p. 81, n. 17. Combes had earlier arrived at a more nuanced conclusion, suggesting on the basis of a careful analysis of Gerson's mystical texts that it was improbable that Gerson had actually derived this teaching *secundum Platonicos*, as he himself argues: »Rien de tel ne se lit chez les philosophes où l'on aurait pu supposer que Gerson avait, immédiatement ou médiatement, puisé cette thèse. Ni Proclus, ni Némésius (le Grégoire de Nysse d'Albert le Grand), ni Platon, ni même Plotin n'enseignent que l'âme humaine soit unie à un corps afin de ramener l'univers à Dieu.« *Essai* 3: 242. This is a strange admission to hear from Combes, that most formidable and exhaustive of Gerson specialists, for he has apparently ignored or dismissed the possibility that Gerson simply perceived Boethius to be a Platonist, albeit one as Gerson himself suggests in *De consolatione theologiae* who was »established in the light of prophecy« and not natural reason alone. This thesis is not only tenable but convincing in light of texts earlier cited from *De consolatione theologiae*, where he borrows the very language – verbatim – from Boethius' famous hymn to the *sator terrarum caelique* (i. e., *De consolatione philosophiae* III m. 9), though applying it in quite eccentric manner; here, too, he perceived along with Boethius *ratio* as the governing order of the universe, and it might well be this same Boethian text which inspired the passage cited above from *A Deo exivit*.

a wider dynamic, since this order on the discrete level of the church participates in the converging rhythms of the universe itself, as Gerson understands them. As he clearly argues in this passage and elsewhere in his writings *ratio* above all is the mechanism of this return, the same *ratio* which must submit »with true humility and the reverence of a faithful and pious heart« by »bringing the entire intellect under the obedience of faith« (*cum captivatione omnis intellectus in obsequium fidei*).[137] The argument for authority is yet another instance of his resolute insistence upon humility, in this case apparently moving from an individual (psychological) dimension to the ecclesiological (institutional) plane: *ratio* governs life on both levels, and it is for this reason that Gerson applies an institutional check upon what he understands to be the capricious and wayward intellect of the individual *viator*. In this same vein Gerson addresses the theme of submission – by which *viatores* are to subject both the »affects of the will« and »the judgment of reason« to *superiores*[138] – once again as an individual instance of discipline which has ramifications within a comprehensive vision of reality.

Clearly, then, »order« within the mind and within the church is only one consequence of a more extensive story. Is this »control«? Certainly. But by setting his instructions for church discipline within the universal framework of a dynamic cosmology, we begin to understand just what »control« means for Gerson. The stakes are as high as they could possibly be, for he envisioned this concrete arena of submission to *superiores* not principally either as »church maintenance« or as a matter of jurisdictional authority: this was a matter rather of ultimate significance, since *viatores* were ultimately responsible to serve as instruments to effect the cosmic *regressus ad Deum*. Judged from this vantage point, therefore, Gerson's view of »control« within the church loses something of its punitive sting, at least in terms of the expectation he placed upon this order. Everything for him depended upon the »legitimacy« of law and order (*lex divinitatis et ordo*) because the ordained structures of authority within the church – and this, in such a neo-Platonic schema, had nothing to do with the virtue of individual *superiores*[139] – functioned as the dynamic cause of the *conversio mundi* itself.

---

[137] G 9, p. 191. The language suggests that Gerson is here alluding to 2 Cor. 10.5: »et in captivitatem redigentes omnem intellectum in obsequium Christi.« In this sense his use of »faith« in the place of »Christ« is intriguing, another index perhaps to the striking soteriological argument in which he places *per fidem* and *per Christum* in direct and parallel relation (cf. G 9, p. 196). See also above, 5.C.1., 5.D.1.

[138] In a passage describing the legitimacy of »the power of ruling« (*potestas regitiva*), Gerson concludes in a general sense that »it is fitting (*convenit*) to submit to the superior (*superiori subjicere convenit*) not only the affects of one's will but also the judgments of the intellect.« Both the intellect and the will were to be submitted to the authority of a superior, an admonition which takes on a peculiar urgency given Gerson's high estimate (apparently following Boethius) of the role *ratio* plays in the *conversio mundi*.

[139] That is, contra Hus; cf. *The Church*, in *Forerunners*, ed. and trans. Oberman, pp. 228–29, and *idem*, *De ecclesia*, ed. Thomson, pp. 36 ff. See also above, nn. 94, 131.

In the final analysis, Gerson's ecclesiology finds its shaping logic in a broader cosmology, in this case by borrowing the neo-Platonist notion of the cosmic »return« to God. This is the ultimate panorama in which Gerson envisions his ecclesiology functioning, and in this sense his vision of »order« is anything but pedestrian in scope. It is for this reason, too, that obedience and humility – the personal dynamics without which his hierarchical model would be unintelligible – must finally overcome any vestiges of individualism: society itself can tolerate (*tolerare*) the lingering presence of *scandala* which cannot be removed (*tollere*), but as a social »body« cannot endure an autonomous or »self-governed« behavior which ignored the »divine law and order.« »Public power,« as he calls it, was not to be usurped under any circumstances, nor was the divine law to be violated even for what might appear to be justifiable proximate ends. On the contrary, human acts of obedience within the hierarchical church serve for Gerson as the very fabric of a dynamic process of *conversio*, an overarching structure which grants both momentum and order to his view of the »interim« church en route *ad Deum*. Within this ordered framework Gerson would have us understand the confluence of what we have called the »conservative« and »progressive« dimensions of his thought and work – viz. not only vis-à-vis his ecclesiology but in terms of *theologia* properly speaking. Order is thus not only the unnegotiable norm of life within the church: order is life itself, and theology serves this end as an ordering force within an otherwise disordered world. Or, at least, this is the case *nunc interim*; *theologia* itself will become unnecessary and indeed obsolete when the journey ends, the denouement of this *regressus* when the church will be united with her bridegroom and *viatores* see God *facie ad faciem*. This finally is the eschatological point toward which all reality tends, the divine order of God's peace which as Gerson reminds us at the close of this enchiridion »surpasses all understanding«: *pax Dei quae exuperat omnem sensum.*[140]

---

[140] G 9, p. 245; the reference here is to Phil. 4.7.

Chapter VII

Conclusion:
A Reorientation of Gerson Studies

The contribution of this study devoted to Gerson's *De consolatione theologiae*, set within the context of his later writings and interpreted against the backdrop of his sojourn in Constance (1415–1418), alters the view which has prevailed in modern studies of his thought. It no longer seems tenable to assume that his later post-conciliar writings are thematically consistent with his earlier university treatises. On the basis of the fundamental theological shifts which emerge in this treatise – explicable to a great extent as pastoral »remedies,« to return to Gilson's description with which we began, for the crises which dominated the Council of Constance – we must now accentuate not only or even primarily the eclecticism of Gerson, but the distinctive change in his thought which emerges at this juncture.[1] The structure of his »Vermittlungstheologie,«[2] in other words, has taken a new and unexpected shape under the pressure of the controversies he faced, several of which came into sharp focus at Constance. Hence, the portrait of Gerson's theology, and with it the implications this holds for our appreciation of the age in which he lived, must now take into account the deliberate and decisive theological development which we find in his thought. More broadly speaking, we must also consider what this shift means for our grasp of the theological pressures and ecclesiastical problems of this period, an era described with only slightly exaggerated chauvinism as the »siècle de Gerson.«[3]

---

[1] Again, Combes has argued that such a shift toward a more severe Augustinian position on the doctrine of grace is detectable in Gerson's writings after 1425. On this point, see *La théologie mystique,* 2:465 ff., and 557–68; see also above, Ch. 1, nn. 56, 57. This shift approaches, as I have earlier suggested, a Scotist view of predestination (see 5.B.1), though it is worth noting that Gerson's attempt to delineate providence as a »cooperation« of human and divine agency (see above, 5.D.3) more closely parallels Bradwardine's formulation of a »coefficiency« of the divine and human wills; on this point, see above, Ch. 5, nn. 3, 161.

[2] Lang characterized Oyta, a theologian whom Gerson held in high esteem, as expounding an »eklektisch-nominalistische Vermittlungstheologie.« See his *Heinrich Totting von Oyta,* pp. 161, 177; see also above, Ch. 5, n. 8. Oberman applied the same description to Gerson in his »Some Notes,« p. 55.

[3] This is Delaruelle's phrase in *L'Eglise,* p. 837; see above, Ch. 1, n. 9.

Our analysis of *De consolatione theologiae*, therefore, calls for a revision of the prevailing assessment of Gerson in recent studies of late-medieval scholasticism in general and Gerson studies in specific, as a nominalist standing within the Ockhamist tradition. The striking developments found in this comprehensive treatise, which go to the very heart of his theological method and concerns, should warn us against speaking too confidently of Gerson's oeuvre without addressing the question of his own theological pilgrimage within the broad and complex tradition of the *via moderna*. If only to serve as a stark warning to the assumption of a homogeneity of thought, our efforts will not have been in vain. But this study has advanced beyond this rather cautious corrective, as necessary as such a caveat must be at the first stage in a historiographical revision of such proportions. Beneath the surface of this warning our analysis of the exiled chancellor's thought, set within the broader theological horizon in which he wrote, has added a needed chapter to a comprehensive portrait of Gerson. And, by examining the evidently shifting contours of his thought against the broader framework of his writings during the conciliar period (1409–1418), we have moved beyond earlier and for the most part uncontested characterizations of his theology as simply »eclectic« or »syncretistic.«

It is this, of course, but much more as well: the complexity which has become evident to those who have advanced more deeply into Gerson's thought is not without deliberate design, and in this case we must contend with a significant revision of fundamental proportions to the structure of his »mediating theology.« As we have suggested, the shift now evident in his post-conciliar thought must be measured not as a strictly academic issue, but as an index of his pastoral style, the contextual manner in which he sought to interrelate thought and life, theology and experience, *theoria* and *praxis*. This study, by examining this particular treatise within the context of his later writings and in terms of the controversial circumstances that had faced this exiled *viator* during the years of the Council of Constance, attempts to overcome the temptation to systematize and hence categorize his thought. By focusing upon this late treatise in some detail we must now expose the limitations of earlier studies, even those which treated the younger Gerson's texts with empathy and insight, largely as the consequence of the misguided assumption that Gerson's thought is uniform from beginning to end – scholarly sins of omission, as it were.

The result of this analysis of *De consolatione theologiae* thus yields a fresh appreciation of the later theological perspective of *doctor christianissimus*, and this in several dimensions of his thought. First, this study suggests (Ch. 3) that this treatise, which functions as a pastoral handbook of comprehensive scope, affords an insight into the confluence of pedagogical and theological method in Gerson's thought, a convergence which we have referred to as a »paideutic« approach to theology. He here interprets theology primarily as a pastoral discipline – specifically by identifying, through graphic metaphors in prose and poetry, its consolatory function for *viatores*, both trained theologians and the *idiotae*. In short, he here »reforms« the method and style of theological argument, emphasizing above all the obligation facing all theologians, both the trained and the »simple,« to bring consolation to those overwhelmed with desperation and thereby lead *viatores* forward in their journey »home« to God.

Second, we have explored the foundations he here provides for the theological task (Ch. 4). Theology for Gerson is a pastoral discipline grounded in scripture (*theologia biblica*), and as such becomes the horizon in which he interprets the problems facing viatores and the solutions promised by God (i.e., *de potentia Dei ordinata*). As a biblical reformer who has been aptly characterized as a »sophisticated fundamentalist,«[4] Gerson's exegetically-grounded approach to doing theology aims to link the world of biblical narrative and metaphor with the experiences facing *viatores* in his own day. His is a voice for the fusion not only of piety (*devotio*) and knowledge (*scientia*), but of scripture and experience, and thus his vision of re-form – personal, ecclesiastical, and social – demanded a »de-professionalization« of theology. He views *theologia* as a guide for life and not for learning only, a voice of consolation offering patience and hope in the midst of confusion and despair, an advocate of *stabilitas* leading toward the *pax Dei* in the face of social and ecclesiastical disorder. Personal and professional categories coalesce in his writings, a trait which is particularly vivid in this enchiridion for *viatores*: he never loses sight of the concrete human context in which theology must be articulated, the pastoral obligations he held as *ecclesiae theologus* – if not also *ecclesiae doctor*, as he would later be portrayed.[5] Theology thus understood must not be »made« practical, nor must it justify the practical context in which to implement its mission. And, beyond all else, *theologia* did not stand in need of reform as a strictly intellectual endeavor, even though the use made of it by theologians might well subject it to abuses: theology is itself primarily about the task of »re-formation,« of reconstituting the human person and community in the pilgrimage *ad Deum*.

Third, it now appears that we should no longer locate Gerson – at least not on the basis of his later writings – within the Ockhamist tradition of the fifteenth century (Ch. 5). Our appreciation of his theological shift to the »right,« as it were, suggests that the force of events at Constance caused him to

---

[4] See Froehlich, »Fifteenth-Century Hermeneutics,« p. 44.
[5] I am indebted to Karlfried Froehlich for reminding me of the sculpted pulpit in the church at Urach which portrays Gerson as the fifth »doctor« of the western church – i.e., alongside Cyprian, Ambrose, Augustine, and Gregory the Great. Burger also notes that this iconography also is to be found in the church at Weilheim an der Teck; both churches were built in the later fifteenth century by Peter of Koblenz as houses for the Brethren of the Common Life; see *Aedificatio*, p. 146, n. 9; Oberman, *Werden und Wertung*, p. 68; and Hamm, *Frömmigkeitstheologie*, p. 136, n. 29.

reconsider and finally reformulate his soteriology after the manner of a more severe Augustinianism than he had earlier held. As we have noted, this theological shift appears to be prompted not by academic arguments heard in university lecture halls, but by the public controversies facing the church in his day – and, more specifically, the pastoral foundations and implications of such crises. Against Hus's vision of the church as the »congregation of the predestined« and the prevailing climate in such circles which has been characterized as a »neo-Donatist« revival, Gerson addressed himself to the ancient dilemma of divine and human freedom by positing a »covenant of seeking« as the model of salvation conceived *sola gratia*. In this regard it is his Christology, together with his reliance upon the role of faith in salvation, which establishes what we have called his »mystical« doctrine of justification as a *via media et regia* – a mediating approach which blended what have recently been characterized as »pastoral« and »confessional« concerns.

Finally, we have seen that ecclesiology functions as the comprehensive and ultimately determinative horizon of his theology, and that ecclesiological concerns guide the shift we have noted in his soteriology (Ch. 6). The task facing *viatores*, as he here interprets it, is not only to »seek« God with humility, but to progress on this journey by remaining obediently within the hierarchical *ecclesia visibilis* – a theme which reminds us of Gerson's unswerving con- servatism. Over against Hus, whose early allegiance to the »instruction« of the council finally gave way to a higher obedience to *lex Christi* and to Christ »the most just judge,«[6] Gerson insists in this treatise that the law of the visible church is not to be abrogated; it is itself coterminous with the *lex divinitatis et ordo*. As a consequence of this identification of *lex divina* and lex *ecclesiastica*, he viewed the church as the arena in which »those of lower status are to be led back to God by those of higher rank,« to recall the Dionysian formulation within which he justified the hierarchical obligations binding clerics and lay persons within the church.[7] Against the apocalypticism of Hus, which increasingly identified the visible church with Antichrist and interpreted his own plight as that of the faithful witness to Christ »... for whose law I desire to die,«[8] Gerson held forth an hierarchical ecclesiology grounded in a moderate eschatology.

---

[6] Thus, Hus wrote to John of Chlum in early January, 1415, that he had verbally agreed during the proceedings of his trial to »abide by the decision of the Council« and to submit to the council's »instructions«; see his »Letters,« in *Hus at the Council*, ed. Spinka, pp. 247–48, 253. By early June, 1415, he began to include in his letters explicit doubts as to the legitimacy of the council's judgment; thus, he wrote that »not everything the Council does, says, or defines is approved by the most true judge, Christ Jesus. Blessed are those, therefore, who, observing the law of Christ, recognize, abandon, and repudiate the pomp, avarice, hypocrisy, and deceit of Antichrist and his ministers, while they patiently await the advent of the most just Judge.« See »Letters,« in *ibid.*, p. 273.

[7] See above, 6.A.1, and G 9, p. 222.

[8] See his final letter addressed to »the entire Christian world« dated July 5, 1415, the day before his execution, in *Hus at the Council*, ed. Spinka, p. 293.

On the basis of this conservative approach he viewed the church as a place of reluctant but progressive reform and himself rather than Hus as a martyr or witness to Christ's law, even to the point of marking himself with the *tau* of Ezekiel's prophecy.[9] The church, as Gerson perceived it in stark contrast to Hus's
apocalyptic vision as a bride »spotless and without wrinkle,« approximated in
the »interim« a »mixed body,« a clear echo to Augustine's image of the church
as *corpus permixtum*. It is the church itself which provides the voice of consolation for a disordered world, functioning as the context in which that world
might find itself »re-formed« in its *regressus ad Deum*, its pilgrimage back to
God. The ecclesiastical order, in other words, is not the object of reform, but
the context for reform.

This detailed analysis of *De consolatione theologiae* has offered a sharp impression of the correct but vague characterization of Gerson's thought as »a mirror
of his age,« and by analyzing the images we have found in the broader *speculum*
of his later works written during and after Constance, our perception of Gerson
and of this controversy-ridden period has become more critically nuanced. It
still remains for us, of course, to consider whether the Gerson of *De consolatione
theologiae* is the source of his widespread recognition during the fifteenth and
sixteenth centuries as *doctor consolatorius*. This inquiry must be the subject of another study, one which would explore the *Wirkungsgeschichte* of this treatise and
of Gerson's later writings more generally.

The questions we have raised and the explanations we have advanced concerning this transitional text do suggest that Gerson studies cannot remain content with previously held assumptions regarding the consistency of the broad
theological contours of his thought. Nor should historical studies of this period
ignore the peculiar contribution which Gerson makes with this treatise, particularly since this work has much to say about perceptions of order — psychological, social, ecclesiastical, political, theological and even cosmological — articulated from a magisterial point of view. In the mirror of these writings we find
reflected, paradoxically, a constellation of images both conservative and progressive — theological themes some of which were remarkably progressive in
his own day but all of which he articulated in the context of a conservative
ecclesiology that functioned as the »shaping matrix« of his pastoral theory and
practice.

We must thus read *De consolatione theologiae* in terms of this paradox,
interpreting it as a text which illumines an otherwise largely unnoticed facet of

---

[9] See G 9, pp. 243–44, in which Gerson has »Lady Theology« interrupt for the first time
the dialogue between Monicus and Volucer to articulate a martyrology of peculiar
character, one which identified the defense of *lex divina* as a stubborn obedience to the
church and her law (*lex ecclesiastica*, which he identified with *lex divinitatis et ordo*). For
further discussion of this point, see above, pp. 46–47, and 6.A.1. On the matter of the *tau*,
see above, Ch. 6, nn. 76, 102.

Gerson's intellectual and pastoral »remedy« for the controversies and problems facing the church during the disordered age in which he lived. This was, after all, an era of struggle and tragedy which did not, he contended, allow for a simple retreat to »the garden,« but which prompted him in a manner unprecedented in his earlier career to sing the praises of the *solitarii* as the most effective practical reformers. Is this, then, a conservatism which finally points toward quietism? This seems too ambitious a conclusion to draw on the basis of a single text, though Gerson's subsequent life confirms this treatise as the announcement of his retirement from public life. It is also a noteworthy index of the significant shifts present in his later thought, offering a clue to what he intends when he closes *De consolatione theologiae* with a call for the »peace of God.« This is no desire for a sudden apocalyptic revolution nor an unreasoned endorsement of its silencing, but rather a patient call for the inbreaking of what Augustine conceived as the »full and perfect« peace to be found only at the end of history.[10] Such a vision, he might remind us, is the true conservatism of life, the inspired desire to reach the »end« which is also our true beginning, the home which all *viatores* ultimately seek.

---

[10] G 9, p. 238; for Augustine's formulation of this concept, see *Enchiridion*, *CCSL* 46:113; cf. also above, Ch. 4, n. 61.

Bibliography

I. Primary Sources

Ailly, Pierre d'. Epistola Diaboli Leviathan. In Unity, Heresy, and Reform, 1378–1460. The Conciliar Response to the Great Schism. Edited by C. M. D. Crowder. New York: St. Martin's Press, 1977.
– Quaestiones super libros Scntentiarum. N.p., 1500. Frankfurt am Main: Minerva GmbH., 1970.
– Tractatus et sermones. Strassburg, 1490. Frankfurt am Main: Minerva GmbH., 1971.
– Tractatus utilis supra Boetium ›de consolatione philosophiae.‹ Bibliothèque Nationale, ms. paris. lat., 3122, F. 110–69v.
Altenstaig, Johannes. Vocabularius theologie. Hagenau, 1517.
Aquinas, Thomas. Opera omnia. Edited by S. E Fretté, P. Maré, et al. Paris: Vivès, 1861–1880.
– Summa contra gentiles. Turin: Marietti, 1961 ff.
– Summa theologiae. Blackfriars Edition. London: Eyre and Spottiswoode, 1964.
– Theological Texts. Edited and translated by Thomas Gilby. Oxford: Oxford University Press, 1955.
Augustine, Aurelius. De doctrina christiana. PL 34; CCSL 32.
– Opera omnia. PL 32–47; CCSL 28–50 a.
Bernard of Clairvaux. Sermones super Cantica Canticorum. Edited by J. Leclercq, C. H. Talbot, H. M. Rochais, et al. Rome: Editiones Cisterciensis, 1957–1966.
Biblia Sacra, iuxta vulgatam versionem. 2 vols. Edited by Robert Weber, O.S.B. et al. Stuttgart: Deutsche Bibelgesellschaft, 1969.
Biel, Gabriel. Collectorium circa quattuor libros Sententiarum Guillelmi Occam. 4 vols. Edited by Wilfrid Werbeck and Udo Hofmann with Volker Sievers and Renata Steiger. Tübingen: J. C. B. Mohr (Paul Siebeck), 1973–1984.
Boethius, Anicius Manlius Severinus. The Consolation of Philosophy. Translated by Richard Green. Indianapolis: Bobbs-Merrill, 1962.
– De consolatione philosophiae. PL 63; CCSL 94.
– Tractates. De consolatione philosophiae. Translated by H. F. Stewart, E. K. Rand and S. J. Tester. Loeb Classical Library, vol. 74. Cambridge, MA: Harvard University Press, 1928.
Boethius of Dacia. On the Supreme Good. On the Eternity of the World. On Dreams. Translated and introduced by John Wippel. Toronto: Pontifical Institute of Medieval Studies, 1987.
Bradwardine, Thomas. De causa Dei contra Pelagium, et de virtute causarum. Edited by Henrici Savilii. London, 1618.
Duns Scotus, John. Opera omnia. Paris: Vivès, 1891–1895.
– De Primo Principio. Edited and translated by Allan B. Wolter, O. F. M. Chicago: Franciscan Herald Press, 1966.

Enchiridion Symbolorum. Definitionum et Declarationum de rebus fidei et morum. Edited by Heinrich Denzinger, Adolf Schönmetzer. Freiburg i. B., Rome: Herder, 1976.

Gerson, Jean. De consolatione theologiae. Köln: Arnold Therhoernen, 1471.

– De mystica theologia. Edited by André Combes. Lugano: Thesaurus mundi, 1958.

– Œuvres complètes. Edited by Palémon Glorieux. Ten vols. Paris: Desclée et Cie, 1960–1973.

– Opera omnia. Edited by Ellies du Pin. Four vols. Antwerp: Petrus de Hondt, 1706.

– Selections from ›A Deo exivit,‹ ›Contra curiositatem,‹ and ›De mystica theologia speculativa.‹ Introduced, edited, translated, and annotated by Steven E. Ozment. Leiden: E. J. Brill, 1969.

Gregory I. Expositiones in Canticum Canticorum. CCSL 144.

– Homiliae in Hiezechihelem prophetam. PL 76; CCSL 142.

– Moralia in Job. PL 75; CCSL 143–143b.

– Opera omnia. PL 75–79; CCSL 142 ff.

– Regula pastoralis. PL 77.

Holcot, Robert. Super libros sapientiae. Hagenau, 1494.

Hus, John. The Letters of John Hus. Translated by Matthew Spinka. Manchester: Manchester University Press, 1972.

– Opera omnia. Prague: Akademia, 1959 ff.

– Polemica. Vol. 22, Opera omnia, edited by Jaroslav Eršil. Prague: Academia, 1966.

– Quodlibet; Disputationis de Quolibet Pragae in Facultate artium mense Januario anni 1411 habitae enchiridion. Edited by Bohumil Ryba. Prague: Orbis, 1948.

– Sermones de tempore qui Collecta dicuntur. Vol. 7, Opera omnia, edited by Anezka Schmidtova. Prag: Ceskoslovenska Akademie Ved, 1959.

– On Simony. In Advocates of Reform, edited and translated by Matthew Spinka. Philadelphia: Westminster Press, 1953.

– Tractatus de ecclesia. Edited by S. Harrison Thomson. Cambridge: Cambridge University Press, 1956.

– Tractatus responsivus. Edited by S. Harrison Thomson. Princeton: Princeton University Press, 1927.

Lombard, Peter. Libri quattuor sententiarum. 2 vols. Rome: St. Bonaventure College, 1916; PL 192.

– Opera omnia. PL 191–92.

Luther, Martin. D. Martin Luthers Werke. Kritische Gesamtausgabe. Weimar: Hermann Böhlau und Hermann Böhlaus Nachfolger, 1883 ff.

Lyra, Nicolas de. Postilla super totam Bibliam. Rome: Sweynheym, 1471–1472.

Mansi, Giovanni Domenico et al., editor. Sacrorum Conciliorum nova et amplissima collectio. Paris: H. Walter, 1900–1927.

Mladoňovice, Peter. Relatio de Magistro Joannis Hus causa. In John Hus at the Council of Constance, translated and edited by Matthew Spinka. New York and London: Columbia University Press, 1965.

Ockham, William of. Dialogus. Frankfurt am Main, 1668.

– Opera philosophica et theologica. Edited by G. Gál et al. St. Bonaventure, NY: St. Bonaventure University, 1964–1985.

– De praedestinatione et de praescientia Dei respectu futurorum contingentium. In Opera philosophica et theologica, ad fidem codicum manuscriptorum edita, edited by Philotheus Boehner et al. St. Bonaventure: St. Bonaventure University, 1978.

– Quodlibeta septem. In Opera philosophica et theologica, ad fidem codicum manuscriptorum edita, edited by Joseph Wey et al. St. Bonaventure, NY: St. Bonaventure University, 1980.

- De sacramento altaris. Edited by T. Bruce Birch. Burlington, Iowa: The Lutheran Literary Board, 1930.
- Super quattuor libros sententiarum. Vols. 2—4, Opera plurima. Lyon, 1494. London: The Gregg Press Ltd., 1962.

Oyta, Heinrich Totting of. Quaestio de sacra scriptura et de veritatibus catholicis. In Opuscula et Textus, edited by Albert Lang. Münster i. W.: Aschendorffsche Verlagsbuchhandlung, 1953.

Pseudo-Dionysius, the Areopagite. The Complete Works. Edited and translated by Colm Luibheid. New York: Paulist Press, 1987.

- Opera omnia. PG 3—4.

II. Secondary Sources

Abramowski, Luise. »Johann Gerson, De consiliis evangelicis et statu perfectionis.« In Studien zur Geschichte und Theologie der Reformation. Festschrift für Ernst Bizer, ed. Luise Abramowski, J. F. G. Goeters. Neukirchen: Neukirchener Verlag, 1969.

Adams, Marilyn McCord. William Ockham. 2 vols. Publications in Medieval Studies, edited by Ralph McInerny, vol. 26. Notre Dame, IN: University of Notre Dame Press, 1987.

Appel, Helmut. Anfechtung und Trost im Spätmittelalter und bei Luther. Leipzig: M. Heinsius, 1938.

Arendt, P. Die Predigten des Konstanzer Konzils. Freiburg i. B.: Herder, 1933.

Artz, Frederick B. Renaissance Humanism: 1300—1550. Oberlin, OH: Kent State University Press, 1966.

Aulén, Gustav. Christus Victor. An Historical Study of the Three Main Types of the Idea of Atonement. Translated by A. G. Hebert. New York: Macmillan, 1969.

Auer, Johann. Die Entwicklung der Gnadenlehre in der Hochscholastik. Vol. 2, Das Wirken der Gnade. Freiburg i. B.: Herder, 1951.

Auer, P. Albert. Johannes von Dambach und die Trostbücher vom 11. bis zum 16. Jahrhundert. Münster i. W.: Aschendorffsche Verlagsbuchhandlung, 1928.

Bäumer, Remigius, editor. Das Konstanzer Konzil. Darmstadt: Wissenschaftliche Buchgesellschaft, 1977.

—, editor. Die Entwicklung des Konziliarismus. Werden und Nachwirken der konziliaren Idee. Darmstadt: Wissenschaftliche Buchgesellschaft, 1976.

Barrett, Helen. Boethius. Some Aspects of His Times and Work. Cambridge: Cambridge University Press, 1940.

Bauer, Martin. Die Erkenntnislehre und der ›Conceptus entis‹ nach vier Spätschriften des Johannes Gerson. Meisenheim: Verlag Anton Hain, 1973.

Baylor, M. G. Action and Person: Conscience in Late Scholasticism and the Young Luther. Leiden: E. J. Brill, 1977.

Beintker, Horst. »Neues Material über die Beziehungen Luthers zum mittelalterlichen Augustinismus.« Zeitschrift für Kirchengeschichte 76 (1957): 144—48.

Bernstein, Alan E. Pierre d'Ailly and the Blanchard Affair: University and Chancellor of Paris at the Beginning of the Great Schism. Leiden: E. J. Brill, 1978.

Berschin, Walter. Greek Letters and the Latin Middle Ages. From Jerome to Nicholas of Cusa. Translated by Jerold C. Frakes. Washington, DC: Catholic University of America Press, 1988.

Bess, Bernhard. Frankreichs Kirchenpolitik und der Prozess des Jean Petit über die Lehre vom Tyrannenmord bis zur Reise König Sigismunds. Zur Geschichte des Konstanzer Konzils, vol. 1. Marburg: O. Ehrhardt, 1891.

Bizer, Ernst. Fides ex auditu. Neukirchen: Buchhandlung des Erziehungsvereins, 1958.

Bloch, Ernst. Christliche Philosophie des Mittelalters. Philosophie der Renaissance. Leipziger Vorlesungen zur Geschichte der Philosophie. Frankfurt am Main: Suhrkamp Verlag, 1985.

Boehner, Philotheus. Collected Articles on Ockham. Edited by E. M. Buytaert. St. Bonaventure, NY: University Press, 1958.

Boissier, Gaston. »Le christianisme de Boèce.« Journal des Savants (1889): 449−62.

Boland, Paschal. The Concept of »Discretio Spirituum« in John Gerson's »De Probatione Spirituum« and »De Distinctione Verarum Visionum a Falsis.« Studies in Sacred Theology, vol. 112. Washington, DC: Catholic University of America Press, 1959.

Bonnaud, R. »L'éducation scientifique de Boèce.« Speculum 4 (1929): 198−206.

Bonnechose, Emile de. The Reformers before the Reformation. The Fifteenth Century: John Huss and the Council of Constance. Translated by Campbell Mackenzie. New York: Harper and Brothers, 1844.

Bouwsma, William J. »The Two Faces of Humanism. Stoicism and Augustinianism in Renaissance Thought.« In Itinerarium Italicum: The Profile of the Italian Renaissance in the Mirror of Its European Transformations, edited by Heiko Oberman and Thomas A. Brady, Jr. Leiden: E. J. Brill, 1975.

Boyle, Leonard E. Pastoral Care, Clerical Education and Canon Law, 1200−1400. London: Variorum Reprints, 1981.

− »The Summa for Confessors as a Genre and Its Religious Intent.« In The Pursuit of Holiness in Late Medieval and Renaissance Religion, edited by Heiko Oberman and Charles Trinkaus. Leiden: E. J. Brill, 1974.

Brehier, Emile. The History of Philosophy. Vol. 3, The Middle Ages and Renaissance. Translated by Wade Baskin. Chicago: University of Chicago Press, 1965.

Brémond, Henri. A Literary History of Religious Thought in France: From the Wars of Religion Down to Our Own Times. Translated by K. L. Montgomery. London: Society for Promoting Christian Knowledge, 1930.

Brown, D. Catherine. Pastor and Laity in the Theology of Jean Gerson. Cambridge: Cambridge University Press, 1986.

Bruder, Konrad. Die philosophische Elemente in den Opuscula sacra der Boethius. Ein Beitrag zur Quellengeschichte der Philosophie der Scholastik. Leipzig: Felix Meiner Verlag, 1928.

Burger, Christoph. Aedificatio, Fructus, Utilitas. Johannes Gerson als Professor der Theologie und Kanzler der Universität Paris. Tübingen: J. C. B. Mohr (Paul Siebeck), 1986.

− »Die Augustinschüler gegen die modernen Pelagianer. Das ›auxilium speciale dei‹ in der Gnadenlehre Gregors von Rimini.« In Gregor von Rimini. Werk und Wirkung bis zur Reformation, edited by Heiko Oberman. Berlin: De Gruyter, 1981.

− »Gerson, Johannes (1363−1429).« In Theologische Realenzyklopädie, vol. 12, pp. 532−38.

− »Nominalismus.« In Evangelisches Kirchenlexikon. Göttingen: Verlag von Vandenhoeck und Ruprecht, forthcoming.

Burrows, Mark S. »Another Look at the Sources of ›De consolatione philosophiae‹: Boethius' Echo of Augustine's Doctrine of ›Providentia.‹« In Proceedings of the Eleventh International Conference on Patristic, Medieval, and Renaissance Studies, Villanova University (1986): 27−41.

− »Christianity in the Roman Forum: Tertullian and the Apologetic Use of History.« In The Christian and Judaic Invention of History, edited by J. Neusner et al. Atlanta, GA: Scholars Press, forthcoming. (First published in Vigiliae Christianae 42 [1988]: 209−35.)

- »Christus intra nos vivens: The Peculiar Shape of Bullinger's Doctrine of Sanctification.« Zeitschrift für Kirchengeschichte 98 (1987): 48–69.
- »Devotio Moderna: Reforming Faith in the Fifteenth Century.« In Spiritual Traditions for the Contemporary Church, edited by Robin Maas, Gabriel O'Donnell. Nashville, TN: Abingdon Press, 1990.
- »Gerson after Constance: Via Media et Regia as a Revision of the Ockhamist Covenant.« Church History 59 (1990): 467–81.
- »Hierarchy, Authority, and Exegesis: Gerson against the Hussites.« Paper read at the Fourteenth International Conference on Patristic, Medieval, and Renaissance Studies at Villanova University, Villanova, PA, September, 1989.
- »Jean Gerson on the ›Traditioned Sense‹ of Scripture as an Argument for an Ecclesial Hermeneutic.« In Viva Vox Scripturae: Biblical Hermeneutics in Historical Perspective. Essays in Honor of Prof. Karlfried Froehlich on the Occasion of His Sixtieth Birthday. Grand Rapids, MI: Eerdmans, forthcoming.
- »Reimaging Boethius in the Fifteenth Century: Jean Gerson's ›De Consolatione Theologiae‹ at the End of a Tradition.« Paper read at the Thirteenth International Conference on Patristic, Medieval, and Renaissance Studies at Villanova University, Villanova, PA, September, 1988.
- »Revising a Medieval Obituary: The Medieval Quest for the Historical Boethius.« Paper read as the Alumni/ae Lecture in Honor of Prof. E. Graham Waring at Lawrence University, Appleton, WI, May, 1987.
- »›Via media et regia‹: A Reappraisal of Gerson and Late Medieval Nominalism.« Paper read at the winter meeting of the American Society of Church History, Cincinnati, December, 1988.
- »On the Visibility of God in the Holy Man: A Reappraisal of the Role of the ›Apa‹ in the Pachomian ›Vitae‹.« Vigiliae Christianae 41 (1987): 11–33.
- Bynum, Caroline Walker. Jesus as Mother. Studies in the Spirituality of the High Middle Ages. Berkeley: University of California Press, 1982.
- Caiger, B. J. »Doctrine and Discipline in the Church of Jean Gerson.« Journal of Ecclesiastical History 41 (1990): 389–407.
- Carnahan, D. H. The ›Ad Deum Vadit‹ of Jean Gerson. Urbana: University of Illinois Press, 1917.
- Carton, Raoul. »Le christianisme et l'augustinisme de Boèce.« Revue de Philosophie, n.s. 30 (1930): 573–659.
- Chadwick, Henry. Boethius: The Consolations of Music, Logic, Theology, and Philosophy. Oxford: Clarendon Press, 1981.
- Chenu, Marie Dominique. La théologie au XIIe siècle. Paris: J. Vrin, 1957.
- Nature, Man, and Society in the Twelfth Century. Essays on New Theological Perspectives in the Latin West. Edited and translated by Jerome Taylor and Lester Little. Chicago: University of Chicago Press, 1968.
- Clark, Francis, S. J. »A New Appraisal of Late-Medieval Theology.« Gregorianum 46 (1965): 733–65.
- Clebsch, William A. and Charles R. Jaekle. Pastoral Care in Historical Perspective: An Essay with Exhibits. Englewood Cliffs, NJ: Prentice Hall, Inc., 1964.
- Combes, André. »La Consolation de la Théologie d'après Gerson.« Pensée catholique 14 (1960): 8–26.
- »Denys l'Aréopagite. 5. Influence du Pseudo-Denys en occident. 4. Gerson.« In Dictionnaire de spiritualité, ascétique et mystique, vol. 3, pp. 365–75.
- »Les deux ›Lectiones contra vanam curiositatem in negotio fidei‹ de Gerson.« Divinitas 4 (1960): 299–316.

- Essai sur la critique de Ruysbroeck par Gerson. Vol. 1, Introduction critique et dossier documentaire. Paris: J. Vrin, 1945.
- Essai sur la critique de Ruysbroeck par Gerson. Vol. 2, La première critique gersonienne du ›De ornatu spiritualium nuptiarum.‹ Paris: J. Vrin, 1948.
- Essai sur la critique de Ruysbroeck par Gerson. Vol. 3/1– 2, L'évolution spontanée de la critique gersonienne. Paris: J. Vrin, 1959, 1972.
- »Etudes gersoniennes, I: L'authenticité gersonienne de l'Annotatio doctorum aliquorum qui de contemplatione locuti sunt.« Archives d'histoire doctrinale et littéraire du moyen-âge 14 (1939): 291–364.
- »Facteurs dissolvants et principe unificateur au concile de Constance.« Divinitas 5 (1961): 299–310.
- «Gerson a-t-il loué l'humilité de Duns Scotus.« Revue du moyen-âge latin 2 (1946): 277–84.
- «Gerson et la naissance de l'humanisme: Notes sur les rapports de l'histoire doctrinale et de l'histoire littéraire.« Revue du moyen-âge latin 1 (1945): 259–84.
- Jean Gerson, commentateur dionysien: Les ›Notulae super quaedam verba Dionysii de Caelesti Hierarchia‹. Texte inédit, demonstration de son authenticité. Appendices historiques pour l'histoire des courants doctrinaux à l'Université Paris à la fin du XIVe siècle. Paris: J. Vrin, 1940.
- Jean du Montreuil et le chancelier Gerson. Contribution à l'histoire des rapports de l'humanisme et de la théologie en France au debut du XVe siècle. Paris: J. Vrin, 1942.
- »Sur les ›Lettres de consolation‹ de Nicolas de Clamanges à Pierre d'Ailly.« Archives d'histoire doctrinale et littéraire du moyen-âge 41 (1940): 359–89.
- La théologie mystique de Gerson. Profil de son évolution. 2 vols. Rome: Libraria Editrix Pontificiae Universitatis Lateranensis, 1963–1964.
Congar, Yves M.-J., O.P. »Un témoignage des désaccords entre canonistes et théologiens.« In Etudes d'histoire du droit canonique. Paris: Sirey, 1965.
- Tradition and Traditions: An Historical and a Theological Essay. Translated by Michael Naseby and Thomas Rainborough. New York: Macmillan Company, 1967.
Connolly, James. John Gerson. Reformer and Mystic. Louvain: Librairie Universitaire, 1928.
Constable, Giles. »The Popularity of Twelfth-Century Spiritual Writers in the Late Middle Ages.« In Renaissance Studies in Honor of Hans Baron, edited by A. Molno and J. A. Tedeschi. Dekalb, IL: Northern Illinois University Press, 1971.
- »Twelfth-Century Spirituality and the Late Middle Ages.« In Medieval and Renaissance Studies: Proceedings of the Southeastern Institute of Medieval and Renaissance Studies, edited by O. B. Hardison, Jr. Chapel Hill: University of North Carolina Press, 1971.
Courcelle, Pierre. La Consolation de Philosophie dans la tradition littéraire. Antécédents et posterité de Boèce. Paris: Etudes augustiniennes, 1967.
- »Etude critique sur les commentaires de la Consolation de Boèce (IXe-XVe siècles).« Archives d'histoire doctrinale et littéraire du moyen-âge 40 (1939): 5–140.
- »Neuplatonismus in der Consolatio philosophiae der Boethius.« In Platonismus in der Philosophie des Mittelalters, edited by Werner Beierwaltes. Darmstadt: Wissenschaftliche Buchgesellschaft, 1969.
Courtenay, William J. Covenant and Causality in Medieval Thought. London: Variorum Reprints, 1984.
- »Late Medieval Nominalism Revisited: 1972–1982.« In Covenant and Causality in Medieval Thought. London: Variorum Reprints, 1984.
- »Nominalism and Late Medieval Religion.« In The Pursuit of Holiness in Late Medieval and Renaissance Religion, edited by Charles Trinkaus and Heiko A. Oberman. Leiden: E. J. Brill, 1974.

- »Nominalism and Late Medieval Thought: A Bibliographical Essay.« In Covenant and Causality in Medieval Thought. London: Variorum Reprints, 1984.
- »The Reception of Ockham's Thought at the University of Paris.« Preuve et raisons à l'université au XIVe siècle. Ontologie et théologie au XIVe siècle, edited by Zénan Kaluza, Paul Vignaux. Paris: J. Vrin, 1984.
- Schools and Scholars in Fourteenth Century England. Princeton: Princeton University Press, 1987.

Crowder, C. M. D., editor. Unity, Heresy, and Reform, 1378– 1460. The Conciliar Response to the Great Schism. New York: St. Martin's Press, 1977.

Cullmann, Oscar. »Scripture and Tradition.« Scottish Journal of Theology 6 (1953): 113–35.

Curtius, Ernst Robert. European Literature and the Latin Middle Ages. Translated by Willard R. Trask. Bollingen Series, vol. 36. Princeton: Princeton University Press, 1973.

Dachsel, Joachim. Jan Hus. Ein Bild seines Lebens und Wirkens. Seine Briefe vom Herbst 1414 bis zum Juli 1415, ins Deutsche übersetzt in Zusammenarbeit mit Frantisek Potmesil. Berlin: Evangelische Verlagsanstalt, 1964.

Daniel-Rops, Henri. L'Eglise de la Renaissance et de la Réforme, vol. 1. Paris: Librairie Antheme Fayard, 1955.

Davis, Charles. »Ockham and the Zeitgeist.« In The Pursuit of Holiness in Late Medieval and Renaissance Religion, edited by Charles Trinkaus and Heiko A. Oberman. Leiden: E. J. Brill, 1974.

Delaruelle, Etienne, et al. L'Eglise au temps du Grand Schisme et de la crise conciliaire (1378–1449). Histoire de l'église depuis les origines jusqu'à nos jours, vol. 14. Brussels: Bloud and Gay, 1964.

de Lubac, Henri. Exégèsè médiévale. Les quatre sens de l'écriture. 2 vols. Paris: Aubier, 1959–1964.

Denifle, Heinrich, with Emile Chatelain, editors. Chartularium Universitatis Parisiensis. Paris: Delalain, 1889– 1897.

Dettloff, Werner. Die Entwicklung der Akzeptations- und Verdienstlehre von Duns Scotus bis Luther mit besonderer Berücksichtigung der Franziskanertheologen. Münster i. W.: Aschendorff, 1963.

- Die Lehre von der ›acceptatio divina‹ bei Johannes Duns Scotus mit besonderer Berücksichtigung der Rechtfertigungslehre. Werl: Dietrich Coelde Verlag, 1954.

Dictionnaire de spiritualité, ascétique, et mystique. Edited by M. Viller, et al. Paris: Beauchesne, 1937 ff.

Douglass, E. Jane Dempsey. Justification in Late Medieval Preaching. A Study of John Geiler of Keisersberg. Leiden: E. J. Brill, 1966.

Dresden, Sem. »The Profile of the Reception of the Italian Renaissance in France.« In Itinerarium Italicum: The Profile of the Italian Renaissance in the Mirror of Its European Transformations, edited by Heiko A. Oberman and Thomas Brady. Leiden: E. J. Brill, 1975.

Dress, Walter. »Gerson und Luther.« Zeitschrift für Kirchengeschichte 52 (1933): 122–61.

- Die Theologie Gersons: Eine Untersuchung zur Verbindung von Nominalismus und Mystik im Spätmittelalter. Gütersloh: Bertelsmann, 1931.

Ebeling, Gerhard. Disputatio de homine. Vol. 1, Text und Traditionshintergrund. Tübingen: J. C. B. Mohr (Paul Siebeck), 1977.

Ehler, Sidney, and John B. Morrall, editors. Church and State through the Centuries. Westminster, MD: Newman Press, 1954.

Ernst, Wilhelm. Gott und Mensch am Vorabend der Reformation. Eine Untersuchung zur Moralphilosophie und -theologie bei Gabriel Biel. Leipzig: St. Benno-Verlag, 1972.

Evans, G. R. The Language and Logic of the Bible. Vol. 1, The Earlier Middle Ages. Cambridge: Cambridge University Press, 1984.

– The Language and Logic of the Bible. Vol. 2, The Road to Reformation. Cambridge: Cambridge University Press, 1985.

Feckes, Carl. Die Rechtfertigungslehre des Gabriel Biel und ihre Stellung innerhalb der nominalistischen Schule. Münster: Verlag der Aschendorffschen Verlagsbuchhandlung, 1925.

– »Die religionsphilosophischen Bestrebungen des spätmittelalterlichen Nominalismus.« Römische Quartalschrift 35 (1927): 183–208.

– »Die Stellung der nominalistischen Schule zur aktuellen Gnade.« Römische Quartalschrift 32 (1924): 157–65.

Feret, Pierre. La faculté de théologie de Paris et ses docteurs les plus célèbres. Vol. 4, Moyen-âge. Paris: Alphonse Picard et Fils, 1897.

Figgis, J. H. »Politics at the Council of Constance.« Transactions of the Royal Historical Society n.s. 13 (1899): 103–15.

– Studies of Political Thought from Gerson to Grotius. Cambridge: Cambridge University Press, 1950.

Fischer, E. H. »Bussgewalt, Pfarrzwang, und Beichtvaterwahl nach dem Dekret Gratiens.« Studia Gratiana 4 (1956): 187–230.

Fleming, John V. An Introduction to the Franciscan Literature of the Middle Ages. Chicago: Franciscan Herald Press, 1977.

– From Bonaventure to Bellini. An Essay in Franciscan Exegesis. Princeton: Princeton University Press, 1982.

Fliche, Augustin, and Victor Martin, editors. Histoire de l'église depuis les origines jusqu'à nos jours, vol. 14. Brussels: Bloud and Gay, 1964.

Frei, Hans. »The ›Literal Reading‹ of Biblical Narrative in the Christian Tradition: Does It Stretch or Will It Break?« In The Bible and the Narrative Traditione, edited by F. McConnell. Oxford: Oxford University Press, 1986.

Froehlich, Karlfried. »›Always to Keep the Literal Sense in Holy Scripture Means to Kill One's Soul‹: The State of Biblical Hermeneutics at the Beginning of the Fifteenth Century.« In Literary Uses of Typology from the Late Middle Ages to the Present, edited by Earl Miner. Princeton: Princeton University Press, 1977.

– »Justification Language and Grace: The Charge of Pelagianism in the Middle Ages.« In Probing the Reformed Tradition. Historical Studies in Honor of Edward A. Dowey, Jr., edited by Elsie McKee, Brian Armstrong. Louisville, KY: Westminster/John Knox Press, 1989.

– »Justification Language in the Middle Ages.« In Justification by Faith: Lutherans and Catholics in Dialogue, vol. 7, edited by H. George Anderson, T. Austin Murphy and Joseph A. Burgess. Minneapolis: Augsburg Publishing House, 1985.

– «Pseudo-Dionysius and the Reformation of the Sixteenth Century.« In Pseudo-Dionysius: The Complete Works. Translated and edited by Colm Luibheid. New York and Mahwah, NJ: Paulist Press, 1987.

Gabriel, Astrik L. »The Conflict between the Chancellor and the University of Masters and Students at Paris during the Middle Ages.« Miscellanea mediaevalia 10 (1976): 106–54.

– »›Via antiqua‹ and ›Via moderna‹ and the Migration of Paris Students and Masters to the German Universities in the Fifteenth Century.« Miscellanea mediaevalia 9 (1974): 439–83.

Gadamer, Hans-Georg. Truth and Method. New York: Crossroad, 1986.

Geiselmann, Joseph. »Das Missverständnis über das Verhältnis von Schrift und Tradition und seine Überwindung in der katholischen Theologie.« Una sancta 11 (1956): 131–50.

Gerwing, Manfred, and Godehard Ruppert, editors. Renovatio et Reformatio. Wider das Bild vom ›finsteren‹ Mittelalter. Festschrift für Ludwig Hoedl zum 60. Geburtstag, überreicht von Freunden sowie Kollegen und Schülern. Münster i. W.: Aschendorff, 1985.

Ghellinck, J. de. »›Pagina‹ et ›Pagina sacra‹: Histoire d'un mot et transformation de l'objet primitivement désigné.« Mélanges Auguste Pelzer. Louvain: Louvain University Press, 1947.

Gibson, Margaret, editor. Boethius. His Life, Thought and Influence. Oxford: Basil Blackwell, 1981.

Gill, Joseph. Konstanz und Basel-Florenz. Geschichte der ökumenischen Konzilien, edited by Gervais Dumeige, Heinrich Bacht, vol. 9. Mainz: Matthias-Grünewald Verlag, 1965.

Gillett, E. H. The Life and Times of John Huss, or the Bohemian Reformation of the Fifteenth Century. 2 vols. New York: Sheldon and Co., 1863.

Gilmore, Myron P. Humanists and Jurists: Six Studies in the Renaissance. Cambridge, MA: Belknap Press, 1963.

Gilson, Etienne. La philosophie au moyen-âge. Des origines patristiques à la fin du 14. siècle. Paris: Payot, 1947.

– History of Christian Philosophy in the Middle Ages. New York: Random House, 1955.

Glorieux, Palémon. »L'activité littéraire de Gerson à Lyon. Correspondance inédite avec la Grande Chartreuse.« Recherches de théologie ancienne et médiévale 18 (1951): 238–307.

– »Le Chancelier Gerson et la réforme de l'enseignement.« In Mélanges offerts à Etienne Gilson. Paris: J. Vrin, 1959.

– Le Concile de Constance au jour le jour. Tournai: Desclée, 1964.

– »L'enseignement au moyen-âge: Techniques et methodes en usage à la faculté de théologie de Paris au XIIIe siècle.« Archives d'histoire doctrinale et littéraire du moyen-âge 43 (1968): 65–186.

– »Gerson, Jean, théologien et auteur spirituel.« In Dictionairre de spiritualité, ascétique et mystique, vol. 6, pp. 314–31.

– »La vie et les oeuvres de Gerson. Essai chronologique.« Archives d'histoire doctrinale et littéraire du moyen-âge 25/26 (1950/51): 149–92.

Grabmann, Martin. Die theologische Erkenntnis- und Einleitungslehre des heiligen Thomas von Aquin auf Grund seiner Schrift ›In Boethium de Trinitate.‹ Freiburg in der Schweiz: Paulusverlag, 1948.

– Die Geschichte der scholastischen Methode. Vol. 1, Die scholastischen Methode von ihren Anfängen in der Väterliteratur bis zum Beginn des 12. Jahrhunderts. Freiburg i. B.: Herdersche Verlagsbuchhandlung, 1909.

Grafton, Anthony. »Epilogue: Boethius in the Renaissance.« In Boethius. His Life, Thought and Influence, edited by Margaret Gibson. Oxford: Basil Blackwell, 1981.

Grane, Leif. Contra Gabrielem. Luthers Auseinandersetzung mit Gabriel Biel in der Disputatio Contra Scholasticum Theologiam 1517. Translated by Elfriede Pump. Gyldendal: Aarhuus Stiftsbogtrykkerie, 1962.

Grant, Edward. »The Condemnation of 1277, God's Absolute Power, and Physical Thought in the Late Middle Ages.« Viator 10 (1979): 211–44.

Gray, Hanna. »Valla's Encomium of St. Thomas Aquinas and the Humanist Conception of Christian Antiquity.« In Essays in History and Literature presented to Stanley Pargellis. Chicago: University of Chicago Press, 1965.

Gregg, Robert. Consolation Philosophy. Greek and Christian Paideia in Basil and the Two Gregories. Philadelphia: Philadelphia Patristic Foundation, 1975.

Grendler, Paul F. Schooling in Renaissance Italy. Literacy and Learning, 1300–1600. Baltimore: Johns Hopkins University Press, 1989.

Greschat, Martin. »Die Bundesgedanke in der Theologie des späten Mittelalters.« Zeitschrift für Kirchengeschichte 81 (1970): 44–63.

Gruber, Joachim. Kommentar zu Boethius ›De Consolatione Philosophiae.‹ Texte und Kommentare, vol. 9. Berlin: De Gruyter, 1978.

Guelluy, Robert. »La place des théologiens dans l'église et la societé médiévale.« In Miscellanea historica in honorem Alberti de Meyer. Louvain: Bibliothèque de l'Université, 1946.

Hägglund, Bengt. The Background of Luther's Doctrine of Justification in Late-Medieval Theology. Philadelphia: Westminster Press, 1971.

– Theologie und Philosophie bei Luther und in der occamistischen Tradition. Luthers Stellung zu der Theorie der doppelten Wahrheit. Lund: C.W.K. Gleerup, 1955.

Hahn, Fritz. »Zur Hermeneutik Gersons.« Zeitschrift für Theologie und Kirche 51 (1954): 34–50.

Hamm, Berndt. »Frömmigkeit als Gegenstand theologiegeschichtlicher Forschung. Methodisch-historische Überlegungen am Beispiel von Spätmittelalter und Reformation.« Zeitschrift für Theologie und Kirche 74 (1977): 464–97.

– Frömmigkeitstheologie am Anfang des 16. Jahrhunderts. Studien zu Johannes von Paltz und seinem Umkreis. Tübingen: J. C. B. Mohr (Paul Siebeck), 1982.

– Promissio, Pactum, Ordinatio. Freiheit und Selbstbindung Gottes in der scholastischen Gnadenlehre. Tübingen: J. C. B. Mohr (Paul Siebeck), 1977.

Hardeland, August. Geschichte der speziellen Seelsorge in der vorreformatorischen Kirche und in der Kirche der Reformation. Berlin: Reuther und Reichard, 1898.

Héfélé, Charles-Joseph. Histoire des conciles d'après les documents originaux. 12 vols. Paris: Librairie Adrien le Cleve, 1869–1878.

Hildebrand, A. Boethius und seine Stellung zum Christentume. Regensburg: Reuther und Reichard, 1885.

Hochstetter, Erich. »Nominalismus?« Franciscan Studies 9 (1949): 370–403.

– »Viator mundi: Einige Bemerkungen zur Situation des Menschen bei Wilhelm von Ockham.« Franziskanische Studien 32 (1950): 1– 20.

Hoffmann, Fritz. »Einige Bemerkungen zum Problem der Unmittelbaren und der Vermittelten Erkenntnis in der Scholastik.« In Renovatio et Reformatio. Wider das Bild vom ›finsteren‹ Mittelalter. Festschrift für Ludwig Hoedl zum 60. Geburtstag. Münster: Aschendorff, 1985.

Hübener, Wolfgang. »Der theologisch-philosophische Konservativismus des Jean Gerson.« Miscellanea Mediaevalia 9 (1974): 171–200.

Huizinga, Johan. Men and Ideas, History, the Middle Ages, the Renaissance. Princeton: Princeton University Press, 1984.

– The Waning of the Middle Ages: A Study of the Forms of Life, Thought, and Art in France and the Netherlands in the Fourteenth and Fifteenth Centuries. Garden City, NY: Doubleday, 1954.

Hurley, Michael. »›Scriptura sola‹: Wyclif and his Critics.« Traditio 16 (1960): 275–352.

Ilsewijn, J. and J. Paquet, editors. The Universities in the Late Middle Ages. Louvain: Louvain University Press, 1978.

Izbicki, Thomas M. »Ecclesiological Texts of Jean Gerson and Pierre d'Ailly in Vatican Manuscript Collections Other than the Codices Vaticani Latini.« Manuscripta 33 (1989): 205–209.

Jaeger, Werner. Early Christianity and Greek Paideia. Cambridge, MA: Belknap Press, 1961.

Janz, Denis R. Luther and Late Medieval Thomism. A Study in Theological Anthropology. Waterloo, ON: Wilfrid Laurier University Press, 1983.

Jefferson, B. Chaucer and the Consolation of Philosophy of Boethius. Princeton: Princeton University Press, 1917.

Jörgenson, L. »Was verstand man in der Reformationszeit unter Pelagianismus?« Theologische Studien und Kritiken 82 (1909): 65–82.

Kadlec, Jaroslav. »Das Hussitentum und die Prager Theologieprofessoren.« In Renovatio et Reformatio. Wider das Bild vom ›finsteren‹ Mittelalter. Festschrift für Ludwig Hoedl zum 60. Geburtstag. Münster: Aschendorff, 1985.

Kaluza, Zénan. Les querelles doctrinales à Paris: Nominalistes et realistes aux confins du XIVe et du XVe siècles. Bergamo: Pierluigi Lubrina Editore, 1988.

Kaminsky, Howard. »Chiliasm and the Hussite Revolution.« Church History 26 (1957): 43–71.

– A History of the Hussite Revolution. Berkeley and Los Angeles: University of California Press, 1967.

Klinkenberg, Hans Martin. »Die Devotio Moderna unter dem Thema ›Antiqui-Moderni‹ Betrachtet.« Miscellanea Mediaevalia 9 (1974): 394–419.

Köhler, Walther. Luther und die Kirchengeschichte nach seinen Schriften, zunächst bis 1521. Erlangen: Verlag von Fr. Junge, 1900.

Kraume, Herbert. Die Gerson-Übersetzungen Geilers von Kaysersberg. Studien zur deutschsprachigen Gerson-Rezeption. Zürich and München: Artemis Verlag, 1980.

Kristeller, Paul Oskar. Medieval Aspects of Renaissance Learning: Three Essays, Edited by Edward Mahoney. Durham: Duke University Press, 1974.

– Renaissance Concepts of Man and Other Essays. New York: Harper and Row, 1972.

– Renaissance Philosophy and the Medieval Tradition. Latrobe, PA: Archabbey Press, 1966.

– Renaissance Thought. The Classic, Scholastic, and Humanist Strains. New York: Harper and Row, 1955.

Ladner, Gerhart. »Die mittelalterliche Reform-Idee und ihr Verhältnis zur Idee der Renaissance.« Mitteilungen des Instituts für österreichische Geschichtsforschung 60 (1952): 31–59.

– The Idea of Reform: Its Impact on Christian Thought and Action in the Age of the Fathers. Cambridge: Harvard University Press, 1959.

– »Reformatio.« In Ecumenical Dialogue at Harvard: The Roman Catholic and Protestant Colloquium, edited by Samuel Miller and G. Ernest Wright. Cambridge: Harvard University Press, 1964.

Lagarde, Georges de. La naissance de l'ésprit laique au déclin du moyen-âge. 5 vols. Paris: Editions Béatrice, 1942–1946.

Lampe, G. W. H., editor. The Cambridge History of the Bible. Vol. 2, The West: From the Fathers to the Reformation. Cambridge: Cambridge University Press, 1969.

Landeen, W. M. »Gabriel Biel and the Brethren of the Common Life.« Church History 20 (1951): 23–36.

Landgraf, Artur Michael. Dogmengeschichte der Frühscholastik. Vol. 1/1, Die Gnadenlehre. Regensburg: Verlag Friedrich Pustet, 1952.

– Dogmengeschichte der Frühscholastik. Vol. 3/1–2, Die Lehre von den Sakramenten. Regensburg: Verlag Friedrich Pustet, 1954.

Lang, Albert. Heinrich Totting von Oyta: Ein Beitrag zur Entstehungsgeschichte der ersten deutschen Universitäten und zur Problemgeschichte der Spätscholastik. Beiträge zur Geschichte der Philosophie und Theologie des Mittelalters, vol. 33/4–5. Münster i. W., Aschendorffsche Buchverhandlung, 1937.

– Die theologische Prinzipienlehre der mittelalterlichen Scholastik. Freiburg i. B.: Herder, 1964.

– »Das Verhältnis von Schrift, Tradition und kirchlichem Lehramt nach Heinrich Totting von Oyta.« Scholastik 40 (1965): 214–34.

– Die Wege der Glaubensbegründung bei den Scholastikern des 14. Jahrhunderts. Beiträge zur Geschichte der Philosophie und Theologie des Mittelalters, edited by Clemens Bäumker, vol. 30/1–2. Münster i. W.: Aschendorffsche Buchverhandlung, 1930.

Lea, H. Charles. A History of Auricular Confession and Indulgences in the Latin Church. 3 vols. Philadelphia: Lea Brothers, 1896.

Leclerq, Jean, Francois Vandenbroucke and Louis Bouyer. A History of Christian Spirituality. Vol. 2, The Spirituality of the Middle Ages. New York: Seabury Press, 1982.

– »L'idée du loyauté de Christ pendant le grand schisme et le crise conciliaire.« Archives d'histoire doctrinale et littéraire du moyen-âge 17 (1949): 249–65.

Leff, Gordon. »The Apostolic Ideal in Later Medieval Ecclesiology.« Journal of Theological Studies, n.s. 18 (1967): 58–82.

– Bradwardine and the Pelagians. A Study of his ›De causa Dei‹ and its Opponents. Cambridge: Cambridge University Press, 1957.

– The Dissolution of the Medieval Outlook. An Essay on Intellectual and Spiritual Change in the Fourteenth Century. New York: New York University Press, 1976.

– Gregory of Rimini. Tradition and Innovation in Fourteenth Century Thought. Manchester: Manchester University Press, 1961.

– Heresy in the Later Middle Ages. The Relation of Heterodoxy to Dissent, c. 1250–1450. 2 vols. Manchester: Manchester University Press, 1967.

– »The Making of the Myth of a True Church in the Later Middle Ages.« Journal of Medieval and Renaissance Studies 1 (1971): 1– 15.

– Paris and Oxford Universities in the Thirteenth and Fourteenth Centuries: An Institutional and Intellectual History. New York: John Wiley and Sons, Inc., 1968.

LeGoff, Jacques. »Métier et profession d'après les manuels de confesseurs au moyen-âge.« In Beiträge zum Berufsbewusstsein des mittelalterlichen Menschen, edited by Paul Wilpert, with Paul Eckert. Berlin: De Gruyter, 1964.

Lewis, C. S. The Discarded Image. An Introduction to Medieval and Renaissance Literature. Cambridge: Cambridge University Press, 1964.

– Studies in Medieval and Renaissance Literature. Cambridge: Cambridge University Press, 1966.

Lindbeck, George. »Nominalism and the Problem of Meaning as Illustrated by Pierre d'Ailly on Predestination and Justification.« Harvard Theological Review 52 (1959): 43–60.

Loomis, Louise. »Nationality at the Council of Constance: An Anglo-French Dispute.« American Historical Review 64 (1939): 508–27.

Lourdaux, W. and D. Verhelst, editors. The Bible and Medieval Culture. Louvain: Louvain University Press, 1979.

McDonnell, E. W. »The ›Vita apostolica‹: Diversity or Dissent?« Church History 24 (1955): 15–31.

Macek, Josef. Jean Hus et les traditions hussites: XVe - XIXe siècles. Paris: Plon, 1973.

McGinn, Bernard, editor. Visions of the End. Apocalyptic Traditions in the Middle Ages. New York: Columbia University Press, 1979.

McGrath, Alister E. »The Anti-Pelagian Structure of ›Nominalist‹ Doctrines of Justification.« Ephemerides Theologicae Lovanienses 57 (1981): 107–19.

– »Augustinianism? A Critical Assessment of the so-called ›Medieval Augustinian Tradition‹ on Justification.« Augustiniana 31 (1981): 247–67.

– Iustitia Dei: A History of the Christian Doctrine of Justification. Vol. 1, Beginnings to 1500. Cambridge: Cambridge University Press, 1986.

– »Justification – ›Making Just‹ or ›Declaring Just‹? A Neglected Aspect of the Ecumenical Discussion on Justification.« Churchman 46 (1982): 44–52.

McInerny, Ralph. St. Thomas Aquinas. Notre Dame, IN, and London: University of Notre Dame Press, 1982.

McKeon, Peter R. »The Status of the University of Paris as ›parens scientiarum.‹« Speculum 39 (1964): 651–75.

McNally, Robert E., S. J. The Bible in the Early Middle Ages. Westminster, MD: The Newman Press, 1959.

McNeill, John T. A History of the Cure of Souls. London: SCM Press, 1952.

Mallard, William. »John Wyclif and the Tradition of Biblical Authority.« Church History 30 (1961): 50–60.

Marenbon, John. Later Medieval Philosophy, 1150–1350: An Introduction. London and New York: Routledge and Kegan Paul, 1987.

Martin, Dennis. »The Via Moderna, Humanism, and the Hermeneutics of Late Medieval Monastic Life.« Journal of the History of Ideas 51 (1990): 179–97.

Mathon, G. »La tradition de la consolation de Boèce.« Revue des études augustiniennes 14 (1955): 213–57.

Meijering, E. P. Calvin wider die Neugierde. Ein Beitrag zum Vergleich zwischen reformatorischem und patristischem Denken. Nieuwkoop: B. de Graaf, 1980.

Meller, Bernhard. Studien zur Erkenntnislehre des Peter von Ailly. Freiburger theologische Studien, vol. 67. Freiburg i. B.: Herder, 1954.

Miller, Clyde Lee. »Where Is the Consolation in Gerson's ›De Consolatione Theologiae‹?« Paper read at the Thirteenth International Conference on Patristic, Medieval, and Renaissance Studies at Villanova University, Villanova, PA, September, 1986.

Minnis, A. J. Medieval Theory of Authorship. Scholastic Literary Attitudes in the Later Middle Ages. Philadelphia: University of Pennsylvania Press, 1988.

Moeller, Bernd. »Frömmigkeit in Deutschland um 1500.« Archiv für Reformationsgeschichte 56 (1965): 5–31.

Moos, Peter von. Consolatio. Studien zur mittellateinischen Trostliteratur über den Tod und zum Problem der christlichen Trauer. 3 vols. München: Wilhelm Fink Verlag, 1971.

Moran, Gabriel. Scripture and Tradition. A Survey of the Controversy. New York: Herder and Herder, 1963.

Moran, Jo Ann Hoeppner. The Growth of English Schooling, 1340–1548. Learning, Literacy, and Laicization in Pre-Reformation York. Princeton: Princeton University Press, 1984.

Morrall, John B. Gerson and the Great Schism. Manchester: Manchester University Press, 1960.

Mourin, Louis. Jean Gerson, prédicateur francais. Brügge, 1952.

– Six sermons inédits de Jean Gerson. Etudes doctrinale et littéraire suivie de l'édition critique et de rémarques linguistiques. Paris: J. Vrin, 1946.

Murphy, James J. Rhetoric in the Middle Ages. A History of Rhetorical Theory from St. Augustine to the Renaissance. Berkeley: University of California Press, 1974.

Oakley, Francis. »Medieval Theories of Natural Law. William of Ockham and the Significance of the Voluntarist Tradition.« Natural Law Forum 6 (1961): 67–68.

– Omnipotence, Covenant, and Order: An Excursion in the History of Ideas from Abelard to Leibniz. Ithaca and London: Cornell University Press, 1984.

– »Pierre d'Ailly and the Absolute Power of God: Another Note on the Theology of Nominalism.« Harvard Theological Review 56 (1963): 59–73.

– The Political Thought of Pierre d'Ailly: The Voluntarist Tradition. New Haven: Yale University Press, 1964.

– »The ›Propositiones Utiles‹ of Pierre d'Ailly: An Epitome of Conciliar Theory.« Church History 29 (1960): 398–403.

– The Western Church in the Later Middle Ages. Ithaca and London: Cornell University Press, 1979.

Oakley, T. P. »The Penitentials as Sources of Medieval History.« Speculum 15 (1940): 210–23.

Oberman, Heiko A. Archbishop Thomas Bradwardine: A Fourteenth Century Augustinian. A Study of His Theology in Its Historical Context. Utrecht: Drukkerij en Uitgevers-Maatschoppij, 1957.

– ›Contra vanam curiositatem.‹ Ein Kapitel der Theologie zwischen Seelenwinkel und Weltall. Zürich: Theologischer Verlag, 1974.

– The Dawn of the Reformation. Essays in Late Medieval and Early Reformation Thought. Edinburgh: T. and T. Clark, 1986.

– «Duns Scotus, Nominalism, and the Council of Trent.« In John Duns Scotus, 1265–1965, edited by J. K. Ryan, B. M. Bonansea. Washington, DC: The Catholic University of America Press, 1965.

– »›Facientibus quod in se est Deus non denegat gratiam‹: Robert Holcot, O. P. and the Beginnings of Luther's Theology.« Harvard Theological Review 55 (1962): 317–42.

– , editor. Forerunners of the Reformation: The Shape of Late Medieval Thought Illustrated by Key Documents. Philadelphia: Fortress Press, 1966.

– »Fourteenth-Century Religious Thought: A Premature Profile.« Speculum 53 (1978): 80–93.

– »From Occam to Luther: A Survey of Recent Historical Studies on the Religious Thought of the Fourteenth and Fifteenth Centuries.« Concilium 17 (1966): 126–30.

– »Gabriel Biel and Late Medieval Mysticism.« Church History 30 (1961): 259–87.

– The Harvest of Medieval Theology. Gabriel Biel and Late Medieval Nominalism. Cambridge: Harvard University Press, 1963.

– , editor. Itinerarium Italicum. The Profile of the Italian Renaissance in the Mirror of Its European Transformations. Leiden: E. J. Brill, 1975.

– »Iustitia Christi and Iustitia Dei: Luther and the Scholastic Doctrine of Justification.« Harvard Theological Review 59 (1966): 1–26.

– Masters of the Reformation. The Emergence of a New Intellectual Climate in Europe. Translated by Dennis Martin. Cambridge: Cambridge University Press, 1981.

– »Reformation — Epoche oder Episode?« Archiv für Reformationsgeschichte 68 (1977): 56–111.

– »Some Notes on the Theology of Nominalism with Attention to its Relation to the Renaissance.« Harvard Theological Review 53 (1960): 47–76.

– »›Wir sein pettler. Hoc est verum.‹ Bund und Gnade in der Theologie des Mittelalters und Reformation.« Zeitschrift für Kirchengeschichte 78 (1967): 232–52.

Obertello, L., editor. Congresso Internazionale di Studi Boeziani. Rome: Editrice Herder, 1981.

Oediger, Friedrich Wilhelm. Über die Bildung der Geistlichen im späten Mittelalter. Studien und Texte zur Geistesgeschichte des Mittelalters, edited by Josef Koch, vol. 2. Leiden: E. J. Brill, 1953.

O'Kelly, Bernard, editor. The Renaissance Image of Man and the World. Ohio: Ohio State University Press, 1966.

Ozment, Steven. The Age of Reform, 1250–1550. An Intellectual and Religious History of Late Medieval and Reformation Europe. New Haven: Yale University Press, 1980.

– Homo spiritualis: A Comparative Study of the Anthropology of Johannes Tauler, Jean Gerson, and Martin Luther (1509–1516) in the Context of Their Theological Thought. Leiden: E. J. Brill, 1969.

– »›Homo viator‹: Luther and Late Medieval Theology.« Harvard Theological Review 62 (1969): 275–87.

- »Humanism, Scholasticism, and the Intellectual Origins of the Reformation.« In Continuity and Discontinuity in Church History. Studies in the History of the Church, edited by F. F. Church and T. George, vol. 19. Leiden: E. J. Brill, 1979.
- »Mysticism, Nominalism and Dissent.« In The Pursuit of Holiness in Late Medieval and Renaissance Religion, edited by Charles Trinkaus and Heiko A. Oberman. Leiden: E. J. Brill, 1974.
- »The University and the Church: Patterns of Reform in Jean Gerson.« Mediaevalia et humanistica n.s. 1 (1970): 111–26.

Pannenberg, Wolfhart. Die Prädestinationslehre des Duns Scotus im Zusammenhang der scholastischen Lehrentwicklung. Forschung zur Kirchen und Dogmengeschichte, vol. 4. Göttingen: Vandenhoeck und Ruprecht, 1954.

Pascoe, Louis. »Gerson and the Donation of Constantine: Growth and Development within the Church.« Viator 5 (1974): 469–85.
- »Jean Gerson: The ›Ecclesia Primitiva‹ and Reform.« Traditio 30 (1974): 379–409.
- »Jean Gerson: Mysticism, Conciliarism, and Reform.« Annuarium historiae conciliorum 6 (1974): 135–53.
- Jean Gerson: Principles of Church Reform. Leiden: E. J. Brill, 1973.
- »Law and Evangelical Liberty in the Thought of Jean Gerson.« In Monumenta Iuris Canonici: Proceedings of the Sixth International Congress of Medieval Canon Law, edited by Stephan Kuttner and Kenneth Pennington. Vatican: S. Congregatio de Seminariis et Studiorum Universitatibus, 1985.

Patch, H. R. The Tradition of Boethius. A Study in His Importance in Medieval Culture. New York: Oxford University Press, 1935.

Pelikan, Jaroslav. The Christian Tradition: A History of the Development of Doctrine. Vol. 3, The Growth of Medieval Theology (600–1300). Chicago: University of Chicago Press, 1978.
- The Christian Tradition: A History of the Development of Doctrine. Vol. 4, Reformation of Church and Dogma (1300–1700). Chicago: University of Chicago Press, 1984.

Persson, Per Erik. »Sacra Doctrina«: Reason and Revelation in Aquinas. Translated by Ross Mackenzie. Philadelphia: Fortress Press, 1970.

Pesch, Otto Hermann, and Albrecht Peters. Einführung in die Lehre von Gnade und Rechtfertigung. Darmstadt: Wissenschaftliche Buchgesellschaft, 1981.

Peters, Edward, editor. Heresy and Authority in Medieval Europe: Documents in Translation. Philadelphia: University of Pennsylvania Press, 1980.

Petry, Ray. Late Medieval Mysticism. Philadelphia: Westminster Press, 1957.
- »Social Responsibility and the Late Medieval Mystics.« Church History 21 (1952): 3–19.
- »Unitive Reform Principles of the Late Medieval Conciliarists.« Church History 31 (1962): 164–81.

Plitt, Gustav. Gabriel Biel als Prediger. Erlangen: Verlag von Andreas Deichert, 1879.

Poschmann, Bernhard. Die abendländische Kirchenbusse im frühen Mittelalter. Breslau: Müller und Seiffert, 1930.
- Sakramente und Eschatologie. Busse und letzte Ölung. Handbuch der Dogmengeschichte, vol. 4/3. Freiburg i. B.: Herder Verlag, 1956.

Post, R. R. The Modern Devotion. Confrontation with Reformation and Humanism. Leiden: E. J. Brill, 1968.

Posthumus Meyjes, G. H. M. Jean Gerson et l'Assemblée de Vincennes (1329). Ses conceptions de la juridiction temporelle de l'église. Leiden: E. J. Brill, 1978.
- »Jean Gerson.« In Mittelalter II, edited by Martin Greschat. Stuttgart, 1983.
- Jean Gerson. Zijn Kerkpolitiek en Ecclesiologie. S'Gravenhage: Martinus Nijhoff, 1963.

Preller, Victor. Divine Science and the Science of God. A Reformulation of Thomas Aquinas. Princeton: Princeton University Press, 1967.

Preus, James Samuel. From Shadow to Promise. Old Testament Interpretation from Augustine to the Young Luther. Cambridge: Harvard University Press, 1969.

Rahner, Karl. Theological Investigations. Vol. 15, Penance in the Early Church, translated by Lionel Swain. New York: Crossroad, 1990.

Rand, E. K. «On the Composition of Boethius' ›Consolatio philosophiae.‹« Harvard Studies in Classical Philology 15 (1904): 1–28.

– Founders of the Middle Ages. Cambridge: Harvard University Press, 1928.

Rashdall, Hastings. The Universities of Europe in the Middle Ages. Revised edition, edited by F. M. Powicke, A. B. Emden. Vol. 1, Salerno, Bologna, Paris, Oxford. Oxford: Clarendon Press, 1936.

Ratzinger, Joseph Cardinal. »Biblical Interpretation in Crisis: Foundations and Approaches of Biblical Exegesis.« Origins: National Catholic Documentary Service 17/35 (1988): 594–602.

Reeves, Marjorie. The Influence of Prophecy in the Later Middle Ages: A Study of Joachimism. Oxford: Oxford University Press, 1969.

Rénaudet, Augustin. Préréform et humanisme à Paris pendant les premières guerres d'Italie 1494–1517. 2 vols. Paris: E. Champion, 1953.

Ritter, Gerhard. Studien zur Spätscholastik. Vol. 2, Via antiqua und via moderna auf den deutschen Universitäten des XV. Jahrhunderts. Heidelberg: Carl Winters Universitätsbuchhandlung, 1922.

Robertson, D. W., Jr. A Preface to Chaucer: Studies in Medieval Perspectives. Princeton: Princeton University Press, 1962.

Rorem, Paul. Biblical and Liturgical Symbols Within the Pseudo-Dionysian Synthesis. Studies and Texts, vol. 71. Toronto: Pontifical Institute of Mediaeval Studies, 1984.

Saccaro, Alexander Peter. Französischer Humanismus des 14. und 15. Jahrhunderts. Studien und Berichte. Freiburger Schriften zur romanischen Philologie, edited by Hugo Friedrich, vol. 27. München: Wilhelm Fink Verlag, 1975.

Saenger, Paul. »Silent Reading: Its Impact on Late Medieval Script and Society.« Viator 17 (1982): 367–441.

Salembier, Louis. »Jean le Charlier de Gerson.« In Dictionnaire de théologie catholique, vol. 6, pp. 1313–332.

– The Great Schism. New York and Cincinnati: Benzinger Brothers, 1907.

Scheible, Heinz. Die Gedichte in der ›Consolatio philosophiae‹ des Boethius. Heidelberg, 1972.

Schmid, W. »Boethius and the Claims of Philosophy.« Texte und Untersuchungen 64 (1957): 368–75.

Schüler, Martin. Prädestination, Sünde, und Freiheit bei Gregor von Rimini. Forschungen zur Kirchen- und Geistesgeschichte, vol. 3. Stuttgart: W. Kohlhammer, 1934.

Schwab, Johann Baptist. Johannes Gerson. Professor der Theologie und Kanzler der Universität Paris. Eine Monographie. Würzburg: Verlag der Stahel'schen Buchhandlung, 1858.

Schwarz, Reinhard. Vorgeschichte der reformatorischen Busstheologie. Arbeiten zur Kirchengeschichte, vol. 41. Berlin: Walter de Gruyter, 1968.

Seibt, Ferdinand. »Geistige Reformbewegungen zur Zeit des Konstanzer Konzils.« In Das Konstanzer Konzil, edited by Remigius Bäumer. Darmstadt: Wissenschaftliche Buchgesellschaft, 1977.

Shank, Michael. ›Unless You Believe, You Will Not Understand.‹ Logic, University, and Society in Late Medieval Vienna. Princeton: Princeton University Press, 1988.

Silk, E. T. »The Study of Boethius' ›Consolatio philosophiae‹ in the Middle Ages.« Transactions and Proceedings of the American Philological Association 62 (1931): 37–38.

– »Boethius' ›Consolation of Philosophy‹ as a Sequel to Augustine's Dialogues and Soliloquies.« Harvard Theological Review 32 (1939): 19–39.

Smalley, Beryl. «The Bible in the Middle Ages.« In The Church's Use of the Bible: Past and Present, edited by Dennis E. Nineham. London: SPCK, 1963.

– The Study of the Bible in the Middle Ages. Notre Dame: University of Notre Dame Press, 1964.

Smith, John Holland. The Great Schism. New York: Weybright and Talley, 1970.

Smolinsky, Heribert. «Johannes Gerson (1363–1429), Kanzler der Universität Paris, und seine Vorschläge zur Reform der theologischen Studien.« Historisches Jahrbuch 96 (1976): 270–95.

Southern, R. W. Medieval Humanism and Other Studies. Oxford: Basil Blackwell, 1970.

Spinka, Matthew. John Hus. A Biography. Princeton: Princeton University Press, 1968.

– John Hus and the Czech Reform. Chicago: University of Chicago Press, 1941.

– , editor and translator. John Hus at the Council. New York and London: Columbia University Press, 1965.

– John Hus' Concept of the Church. Princeton: Princeton University Press, 1966.

Spitz, Lewis. The Renaissance and Reformation Movements. Vol. 1, The Renaissance. St. Louis: Concordia Publishing House, 1971.

Steiner, George. Language and Silence. Essays on Language, Literature and the Inhuman. New York: Atheneum, 1982.

Steinmetz, David C. Luther and Staupitz: An Essay in the Intellectual Origins of the Protestant Reformation. Durham, NC: Duke University Press, 1980.

– »Luther and the Late Medieval Augustinians: Another Look.« Concordia Theological Monthly 44 (1973): 245–60.

– Luther in Context. Bloomington: Indiana University Press, 1986.

– ›Misericordia Dei‹. The Theology of Johannes von Staupitz in Its Late Medieval Setting. Leiden: E. J. Brill, 1968.

Stelzenberger, Johannes. Die Mystik des Johannes Gerson. Breslauer Studien zur historischen Theologie, edited by Franz Seppelt et al., vol. 10. Breslau: Verlag Müller und Seiffert, 1928.

Swanson, R. N. Universities, Academics and the Great Schism. Cambridge: Cambridge University Press, 1979.

Tatnall, Edith C. »The Condemnation of John Wyclif at the Council of Constance.« In Councils and Assemblies, edited by G. J. Cuming and D. Baker. Studies in Church History, vol. 7. Cambridge: Cambridge University Press, 1971.

Tavard, George H. Holy Writ or Holy Church: The Crisis of the Protestant Reformation. New York: Harper and Row, 1959.

Tentler, Thomas N. Sin and Confession on the Eve of the Reformation. Princeton: Princeton University Press, 1972.

– »The Summa for Confessors as an Instrument of Social Control.« In The Pursuit of Holiness in Late Medieval and Renaissance Religion, edited by Charles Trinkaus and Heiko Oberman. Leiden: E. J. Brill, 1974.

Thorndike, Lynn. University Records and Life in the Middle Ages. New York: Columbia University Press, 1944.

Tierney, Brian. Foundations of the Conciliar Theory. The Contribution of the Medieval Canonists from Gratian to the Great Schism. Cambridge: Cambridge University Press, 1955.

Secondary Sources 293

– »Ockham, the Conciliar Theory, and the Canonists.« Journal of the History of Ideas 15 (1954): 40–70.

Trinkaus, Charles. In Our Image and Likeness. Humanity and Divinity in Italian Humanist Thought. 2 vols. London: Constable and Co., 1970.

– and Heiko A. Oberman, editors. The Pursuit of Holiness in Late Medieval and Renaissance Religion. Leiden: E. J. Brill, 1974.

Tschackert, Paul. Peter von Ailli: Zur Geschichte des grossen abendländischen Schisma und der Reformconcilien von Pisa und Constanz. Amsterdam: Editions Rodopi, 1968.

Ullmann, Walter. The Individual and Society in the Middle Ages. Baltimore: Johns Hopkins Press, 1966.

– Medieval Foundations of Renaissance Humanism. London: Paul Elek, 1977.

– The Origins of the Great Schism. A Study in Fourteenth-Century Ecclesiastical History. London: Burns, Oates, and Washburn, 1938.

Underhill, Evelyn. Mysticism. A Study in the Nature and Development of Man's Spiritual Consciousness. New York: E. P. Dutton, 1961.

Van Engen, John, editor and translator. Devotio Moderna. Basic Writings. New York and Mahwah, NJ: Paulist Press, 1988.

Varvis, Stephen L. The Consolation of Boethius. Ph.D. dissertation, Claremont Graduate School, 1985.

Verbeke, G. and J. Ijsewijn. The Late Middle Ages and the Dawn of Humanism Outside Italy. Mediaevalia Lovaniensia, vol. 1. Louvain: University Press, 1972.

Vignaux, Paul. Luther. Commentateur des Sentences (Livre I, Distinction XVII). Paris: J. Vrin, 1935.

– Nominalisme au XIVe siècle. Paris: J. Vrin, 1948.

– Philosophy in the Middle Ages. An Introduction. Translated by E. C. Hall. New York: Meridian Books, Inc., 1959.

Vooght, Paul de. »Gerson et le conciliarisme.« Revue d'histoire ecclésiastique 63 (1968): 857–67.

– L'hérésie de Jean Huss. Louvain: Bibliothèque de l'Université, 1960.

– »Jean Huss et ses juges.« Das Konzil von Konstanz. Festschrift für Hermann Schäufele, edited by A. Franzen, W. Müller. Freiburg i. B.: Herder, 1964.

Wayman, Dorothy G. »The Chancellor and Jeanne d'Arc: February–July, A.D. 1429.« Franciscan Studies n.s. 17 (1957): 273–305.

Werbeck, Wilfrid. »Voraussetzungen und Wesen der scrupulositas im Spätmittelalter.« Zeitschrift für Theologie und Kirche 68 (1971): 327–50.

Werner, Karl. Der Augustinismus in der Scholastik des späteren Mittelalters. Wien: Wilhelm Braumüller, 1883.

– Die nominalisirende Psychologie der Scholastik des späteren Mittelalters. Wien: Carl Gerold's Sohn, 1882.

– Die Scholastik des späteren Mittelalters. Vol. 4, Der Endausgang der mittelalterlichen Scholastik. Wien: Wilhelm Braumüller, 1887.

Wilks, Michael. »›Reformatio regni‹: Wyclif and Hus as Leaders of Religious Protest Movements.« In Schism, Heresy and Religious Protest, edited by D. Baker. Studies in Church History, vol. 9. Cambridge: Cambridge University Press, 1972.

Zumkeller, Adolar. »Das Ungenügen der menschlichen Werke bei den deutschen Predigern des Spätmittelalters.« Zeitschrift für katholische Theologie 81 (1959): 265–305.

Index of Biblical References

Index of Persons and Places

Index of Subjects

- argument for *sensus a sanctis patribus traditus*, 226–40
- and ecclesiology, 116, 120ff; *see* also ecclesiology: as hermeneutical context
- hermeneutical circle, 90
- late medieval, 55
- of tradition, 124, 229
- and revelation, 117

history. *See* also law: three-fold succession of
- Augustine's conception of, 127, 127 n61

Holy Spirit
- as means of reform, 254 n102, 256 n110
- as uncreated grace, 169 n47

homo viator. *See viator*; anthropology; pilgrimage

hope. *See* also desperation: and hope; humility
- and consolation, 43, 46
- theology of, 53

humanism
- and Gerson, 25 n52, 132 n78
- relation to Stoicism, 32 n8

humility. *See* also ecclesiology
- and discretion, 247–56
  - in Aquinas, 247 n82
- and hope, 185–89
- and metaphysical speculation, 120
- mystical accent on, 194
- relation to pride, 65, 188
- theology of, 188–89, 189 n110

Hundred Years' War, VII

Hus, John
- anthropology of, 162
- on Antichrist, 8 n5
- attack upon simony, 106, 106 n11, 223, 261; *see* also benefices
- biblicism of, 123 n53
  - demand for scriptural correction, 251, 252 n96
- call for church reform, 54
- and canon law, 123 n53
- challenge of church authority, 39 n21
- on church as congregation of the predestined, 260, 261 n123
- condemnation of
  - by Paris faculty, 106 n9, 106 n11, 260
  - at Constance, 251 n95
- death as martyrdom, 224

- defense of communion »in both kinds« (*utraquism*), 229
  - Gerson's argument against, 230
- denial of sinful priests' hierarchical authority, 78 n58, 261
- on the »elect,« 162, 162 n31; *see* also Hus: on virtue
- Gerson's polemic against, 10 n19, 26 n53, 69 n29, 106, 122 n50, 162, 190, 219, 245 n76, 250
- and the Hussite circle, 6, 39 n20, 45 n33
- Hussite controversy, X, 27 n57; *see* also neo-Donatism: and Hussitism
- philosophical realism of, 19 n35
- trial at Constance, 52, 251 n95
- on virtue and the elect, 162 n31, 190, 260

Hussite controversy. *See* neo-Donatism: and Hussitism

idiotae. *See* also laity
- and *fides simplex*, 78
- and the theological life, 13 n23, 78, 89, 95, 265 n132

image of God, and human formation, 110
imitatio Christi
- and the *conformitas voluntatis*, 49 n43, 51 n46, 201
- psychological discussion of, 50

imitation, as literary technique; *see aemulatio*

initium fidei, in Aquinas, 179 n76

intention. *See* also benefices
- in Aquinas, 249, 249 n88; *see* also circumstances

irony, and narrative voice, 37, 141, 144
itinerarium in Deum. *See* pilgrimage
iustitia Dei, 48, 55, 192–93
- and Christology, 169 n47
- as *damnans iustitia*, 186 n97
- and *misericordia Dei*, 186, 186 n97
- as theme of treatise, 194
iustitia fidei, 56

Jacob's ladder, 54 n53, 84, 126
Jerusalem
- as celestial city, 241, 254
- desolation of, 30
Jesus. *See* Christ
judgment, order of
- and eschatology, 84
- and fear, 182–83
- forensic context of, 49

- *ordo judiciorum supremi judicis Dei*, 48, 56, 84, 185, 186
- as three-fold tribunal, 93

justification
- anti-Pelagian understanding of, 4, 152 n7, 176–77 n70
  - in Scotus, 169 n49
- Biel's understanding of, 170 n51, 183 n86
- and Christology, 169 n47, 180
- and doctrine of *acceptatio Dei,* 202 n146
- forensic model of, 188
- and humility, 190
- mystical doctrine of, IX, 189–95, 203
- and non-imputation of sin, 190, 190 n114
- Ockhamist approach to, 8
- *per fidem*, 177–82, 185; *see also* faith
- Pauline language of, 164–68
- predestination and, 8 n16
- and the sacraments; *see* faith: and sacraments
- *simul iustus et peccator*, 188

knowledge, of God. *See cognitio Dei*

Lady Theology, as lover, 47

laity
- and *eruditio sacrae scripturae*, 110, 124; *see also* scripture
- as *ecclesia audiens*, 220
- explicit faith of, 112; *see also* faith
  - Aquinas's approach to, 113
  - use of creed and scripture, 112, 113
- defense of, IX, 11, 12, 12 n23, 29 n2, 30 n3, 219 n20
- and democratization of theology, 109; *see also* theology: deprofessionalizing of
- in *devotio moderna*, 189 n110, 219 n20
- and spirit of catholic judgment, IX, 56, 89, 112 n27, 136, 219 n20, 220

law, 57, 79, 117
- divine law and order, 54, 54 n53, 54 n54, 57, 79, 79 n61, 126, 253, 263–69
  - as implicate of ecclesiology, 264
- and *doctrina christianae religionis*, 226
- and theology in pre-Constantinian church, 128–29 n67
- as God's self-disclosure, 126
- historical continuity of, 79 n61, 126

- progressive dispensations of, 79 n61, 126–27, 196 n132
- single eternal law of God, 201
- three-fold succession of, 79 n61
- and the three-fold will, 200
- *vulgata regula*, 253

lethargy
- as form of tribulation, 66
- and philosophy, 75

lex antiqua. See lex vetus
lex Dei. See law
lex divina. See law
lex divinitatis et ordo. See law
lex evangelica, 79, 127. *See also* canon law
lex naturae, 57, 127
- and the *ratiocinatio naturalis*, 127, 132
- and *theologia supernaturaliter infusa*, 127
lex nova, 79, 127
- Jesus' elevation of the Ten Commandments, 127 n64
lex vetus, 57, 79, 127
literal sense. *See* scripture: literal sense of
liturgy. *See* drama

Maccabaean brothers, 57
martyrdom
- and defenders of the church's order, 246
- and desolation, 57
- discussion of, 26 n53, 57, 246
- as journey to God, 26; *see also* pilgrimage: *ad Deum*
Mary, and the »Magnificat,« 30
Mary and Martha
- Aquinas's interpretation of, 139 n103, 147 n119
- biblical account of, 87 n87
- as defense of *vita contemplativa*, 87 n88
- exegesis of, 140 n107, 142
- Gregory's exegesis of, 142 n111, 147, 257; *see also vita ambidextra*
mass, Luther's criticism of, 113 n32
massa peccati, 96, 157; *see also* Fall.
melancholy, in late-medieval culture, 63–64, 155 n12, 184
merits
- *de congruo*, or »natural,« 154, 158–63, 165, 173 n62
- and justification, 172
- retreat from language of, 186; *see also* grace: habit of
metaphor, and theological method, 92–96

Beiträge zur historischen Theologie

Alphabetisches Verzeichnis

Axt-Piscalar, Christine: Der Grund des Glaubens. 1990. *Band 79*

Bauer, Walter: Rechtgläubigkeit und Ketzerei im ältesten Christentum. 1934, ²1964. *Band 10.*

Bayer, Oswald / Knudsen, Christian: Kreuz und Kritik. 1983. *Band 66.*

Betz, Hans Dieter: Nachfolge und Nachahmung Jesu Christi im Neuen Testament. 1967. *Band 37.*

–: Der Apostel Paulus und die sokratische Tradition. 1972. *Band 45.*

Beyschlag, Karlmann: Clemens Romanus und der Frühkatholizismus. 1966. *Band 35.*

Bonhoeffer, Thomas: Die Gotteslehre des Thomas von Aquin als Sprachproblem. 1961. *Band 32.*

Brecht, Martin: Die frühe Theologie des Johannes Brenz. 1966. *Band 36.*

Brennecke, Hanns Christof: Studien zur Geschichte der Homöer. 1988. *Band 73.*

Burger, Christoph: Aedificatio, Fructus, Utilitas. 1986. *Band 70.*

Burrows, Mark S.: Jean Gerson and »De Consolatione Theologiae« (1418). 1991. *Band 78.*

Campenhausen, Hans von: Kirchliches Amt und geistliche Vollmacht in den ersten drei Jahrhunderten. 1953, ²1963. *Band 14.*

–: Die Entstehung der christlichen Bibel. 1968. *Band 39.*

Conzelmann, Hans: Die Mitte der Zeit. 1954, ⁶1977. *Band 17.*

–: Heiden - Juden - Christen. 1981. *Band 62.*

Elliger, Karl: Studien zum Habakuk-Kommentar vom Toten Meer. 1953. *Band 15.*

Evang, Martin: Rudolf Bultmann in seiner Frühzeit. 1988. *Band 74.*

Friedrich, Martin: Zwischen Abwehr und Bekehrung. 1988. *Band 72.*

Gese, Hartmut: Der Verfassungsentwurf des Ezechiel (Kapitel 40-48) traditionsgeschichtlich untersucht. 1957. *Band 23.*

Gestrich, Christof: Neuzeitliches Denken und die Spaltung der dialektischen Theologie. 1977. *Band 52.*

Gräßer, Erich: Albert Schweitzer als Theologe. 1979. *Band 60.*

Gülzow, Henneke: Cyprian und Novatian. 1975. *Band 48.*

Hamm, Berndt: Promissio, Pactum, Ordinatio. 1977. *Band 54.*

–: Frömmigkeitstheologie am Anfang des 16. Jahrhunderts. 1982. *Band 65.*

Hoffmann, Manfred: Erkenntnis und Verwirklichung der wahren Theologie nach Erasmus von Rotterdam. 1972. *Band 44.*

Holfelder, Hans H.: Solus Christus. 1981. *Band 63.*

Hübner, Jürgen: Die Theologie Johannes Keplers zwischen Orthodoxie und Naturwissenschaft. 1975. *Band 50.*

Hyperius, Andreas G.: Briefe 1530-1563. Hrsg., Übers. und Komment. von G. Krause. 1981. *Band 64.*

Jetter, Werner: Die Taufe beim jungen Luther. 1954. *Band 18.*

Jorgensen, Theodor H.: Das religionsphilosophische Offenbarungsverständnis des späteren Schleiermacher. 1977. *Band 53.*

Kasch, Wilhelm F.: Die Sozialphilosophie von Ernst Troeltsch. 1963. *Band 34.*

Knudsen, Christian: siehe *Bayer, Oswald*

Koch, Dietrich-Alex: Die Schrift als Zeuge des Evangeliums. 1986. *Band 69.*

Koch, Gerhard: Die Auferstehung Jesu Christi. 1959, ²1965. *Band 27.*

Köpf, Ulrich: Die Anfänge der theologischen Wissenschaftstheorie im 13. Jahrhundert. 1974. *Band 49.*

–: Religiöse Erfahrung in der Theologie Bernhards von Clairvaux. 1980. *Band 61.*

Korsch, Dietrich: Glaubensgewißheit und Selbstbewußtsein. 1989. *Band 76.*

Kraft, Heinrich: Kaiser Konstantins religiöse Entwicklung. 1955. *Band 20.*

Krause, Gerhard: Studien zu Luthers Auslegung der Kleinen Propheten. 1962. *Band 33.*

–: Andreas Gerhard Hyperius. 1977. *Band 56.*

Krause, G.: siehe *Hyperius, Andreas G.*

Krüger, Friedhelm: Humanistische Evanglienauslegung. 1986. *Band 68.*

Lerch, David: Isaaks Opferung, christlich gedeutet. 1950. *Band 12.*

Lindemann, Andreas: Paulus im ältesten Christentum. 1979. *Band 58.*

Mauser, Ulrich: Gottesbild und Menschwerdung. 1971. *Band 43.*

Mostert, Walter: Menschwerdung. 1971. *Band 57.*

Ohst, Martin: Schleiermacher und die Bekenntnisschriften. 1989. *Band 77.*

Osborn, Eric F.: Justin Martyr. 1973. *Band 47.*

Raeder, Siegfried: Das Hebräische bei Luther, untersucht bis zum Ende der ersten Psalmenvorlesung. 1961. *Band 31.*

–: Die Benutzung des masoretischen Textes bei Luther in der Zeit zwischen der ersten und zweiten Psalmenvorlesung (1515-1518). 1967. *Band 38.*

–: Grammatica Theologica. 1977. *Band 51.*

Schäfer, Rolf: Christologie und Sittlichkeit in Melanchthons frühen Loci. 1961. *Band 29.*

–: Ritschl. 1968. *Band 41.*

Schröder, Richard: Johann Gerhards lutherische Christologie und die aristotelische Metaphysik. 1983. *Band 67.*

Schwarz, Reinhard: Die apokalyptische Theologie Thomas Müntzers und der Taboriten. 1977. *Band 55.*

Senft, Christoph: Wahrhaftigkeit und Wahrheit. 1956. *Band 22.*

Sträter, Udo: Sonthom, Bayly, Dyke und Hall. 1987. *Band 71.*

Wallmann, Johannes: Der Theologiebegriff bei Johann Gerhard und Georg Calixt. 1961. *Band 30.*

–: Philipp Jakob Spener und die Anfänge des Pietismus. 1970, ²1986. *Band 42.*

Werbeck, Wilfrid: Jakobus Perez von Valencia. 1959. *Band 28.*

Zschoch, Hellmut: Klosterreform und monastische Spiritualität im 15. Jahrhundert. 1988. *Band 75.*

ZurMühlen, Karl H.: Nos extra nos. 1972. *Band 46.*

–: Reformatorische Vernunftkritik und neuzeitliches Denken. 1980. *Band 59.*

Den Gesamtkatalog »Theologie« schickt Ihnen der Verlag
J. C. B. Mohr (Paul Siebeck), Postfach 2040, D-7400 Tübingen.